The Writer's Tutor

The Writer's *Tutor*

One Hundred Self-correcting Lessons

J. N. Hook
William H. Evans

Purdue University

Harcourt Brace Jovanovich, Publishers

San Diego   New York   Chicago   Austin   Washington, D.C.

London   Sydney   Tokyo   Toronto

ISBN: 0-15-597670-2

Library of Congress Catalog Card Number: 87-81093

Printed in the United States of America

To the Instructor

The Writer's Tutor is intended to help students overcome many of their individual problems in sentence structure, usage, diction and style, and such mechanical matters as punctuation and capitalization.

Through a unique self-instructional procedure, the *Tutor* leads students to understand and apply the principles involved, for instance, in placement of apostrophes, agreement of subject and verb, parallel structure, and strong sentence endings.

A college writing course has so much important content that only as much class time as is absolutely necessary should ordinarily be given to such topics as commas, the avoidance of dangling or misplaced modifiers, *lie* vs. *lay*, *he* vs. *him*, and scores of similar items. Yet students must somehow master commas, placement of modifiers, and the rest. The *Tutor*'s instructional formula helps them to move more rapidly toward such mastery.

Students Who May Profit

The *Tutor* is intended for students in freshman writing courses. Nearly all students who are not in the bottom five percent or the top five percent *do* need assistance of the kind that the *Tutor* can provide. A tool of many uses, the book can guide both the student who is uncertain about *did* and *done* and the student who never has such elementary difficulties but is not sure about when to use the subjunctive mood.

The Formula

The authors some years ago developed the formula that each *Tutor* lesson follows. Material based on that same formula has been used successfully with thousands of students in hundreds of high school and college classrooms. The authors have refined the formula for the *Tutor* and have applied it specifically to those writing problems that plague many beginning college students.

The formula has four parts, presented—with occasional slight variations—in the same order in every lesson:
1. Inductive learning of a principle
2. Summary of the principle
3. Application of the principle
4. Review of the principle

1. Inductive Learning

Each lesson begins with a simple example relevant to the principle. Students answer an easy question about it—sometimes absurdly easy so that every student can respond correctly. Then, through additional examples and increasingly challenging questions, students build inductively toward an understanding of the principle.

Instructors who are not familiar with inductive procedures may want to glance at the first few frames of any lesson in this book and then follow that lesson through the three remaining steps.

For instance, Lesson 52 is entitled "Unnecessary Passive Voice: Is It Better to Do or to Be Done Unto?" The first frame uses this example:

Wheat was harvested by threshing crews as farm after farm was moved to by them.

After reading a couple of sentences of comment, students write in the space provided the answer to this question:

> Did the wheat and the farms do anything?

They then look in the left-hand column to check the correctness of their response.

Frames 2–6 provide additional examples to develop the point that despite an occasional need for a passive verb, the active voice is ordinarily "shorter, stronger, and more emphatic."

Throughout each lesson in the *Tutor*, the left-hand column provides the correct answer or, where varied answers are likely or inevitable, a "model answer" that each student's response should resemble.

In addition, most of the answer frames contain material for added practice. This reinforces the points explained in the right-hand column. Students may write their answers to these questions at once, or they may ignore the questions unless at a later time they find that they are repeating the same kind of mistake.

2. Summary of the Principle

An inductive process should lead to a conclusion. On the basis of a number of observations, scientists, literary scholars, and even small children arrive at whatever generalization the observations afford. Two-year-olds with surprising speed draw the conclusion that such-and-such actions lead to such-and-such results. Most human learning appears to be based on induction.

The *Tutor* usually devotes a single frame to a summary or generalization of the basic principle. Students complete one or more statements that focus the points they have just seen illustrated.

For example, in Lesson 52, Frame 7 reads as follows:

A. In the first six frames, we have seen that the _____ voice is ordinarily more emphatic than the _____ voice.

B. However, the _____ voice is necessary or at least preferable when the person or thing performing the action is unknown or relatively unimportant.

3. Application

Application, obviously, involves practicing. In several frames following the summary, students answer questions, write sentences, or perform other tasks designed to help them remember what they have just learned and to apply it to their own writing.

In Lesson 52, Frames 8 and 9 require students to read pairs of sentences and to state which sentence (the one in the active voice, of course) is stronger.

The next few frames provide the initial payoff of the lesson. Students write their own examples, often with the approximate content suggested in order to minimize time-consuming head-scratching. Frame 10 of Lesson 52 asks the students to write a sentence about John's mowing the lawn and then to specify whether they have used active or passive voice. Frame 11 calls for a recasting of their Frame 10 sentence in the other voice and for a decision as to which of the two versions is stronger. Frame 12, somewhat more challenging, necessitates their writing still another sentence, and Answer Frames 10 and 11 make suggestions for additional practice.

4. Review

A looking back and a restatement assist in fixing a general principle in mind and in remembering its application.

The final frame in the *Tutor* is exactly the same in all one hundred lessons:

> Finish honestly: One thing I hope to remember from this lesson is that . . .

The authors of the *Tutor* tell students, "In this [final] frame, any answer that you consider honest and accurate is acceptable." College tryouts of the book have shown that most students pause to look back over the lesson before writing their responses. A small percentage of responses are flippant, but the others all offer a restatement of the generalization or else comment on a specific point that seems of special importance to the individual.

Assigning Lessons in *The Writer's Tutor*: The Diagnostic and Mastery Tests

Some instructors may want to discuss in class certain lessons that concern problems common to many of their students, perhaps using those lessons to supplement assignments in a basic textbook. Such discussion may clarify points still obscure to some students.

Chiefly, however, the *Tutor* is useful for work by individual students on their own specific problems in sentence structure, usage, diction and style, and mechanics. Perhaps no student needs *every* lesson.

In evaluating students' writing, instructors ordinarily write comments and also make marginal notes, often using symbols such as those inside the front and back covers of this book. The authors of the *Tutor* offer this suggestion: Beside two or three marginal notations (such as *s s* or 7 for "too many short sentences"), write *Tutor*. That tells the student that he or she should independently do the indicated two or three lessons. Not more than two or three should normally be assigned at one time, because a large number will discourage the attentive study that is desirable.

A systematic way to assign lessons is to ask all students to take the diagnostic test preceding each of the four sections of the *Tutor*. As a glance at those tests will reveal, the item numbers correspond to lesson numbers. Each test item has three parts to be judged by students as "acceptable" or "unacceptable" in appropriately formal college writing. If a student misses any one of the three parts, he or she should complete independently the corresponding lesson. Obviously some students will need to complete more lessons than others.

At the end of each of the four sections of the *Tutor* is a mastery test. Its format and degree of difficulty are similar to those of the diagnostic test. After a student completes all of the required lessons in a section of the book, he or she should take the corresponding mastery test and then repeat study of those lessons for which test scores were not perfect.

We thank Professor Muriel Harris, Professor Irwin Weiser, and Ms. Carole Cole, all of Purdue University, for their careful reviews of the manuscript of this book.

J. N. Hook
William H. Evans

To the Student

The Writer's Tutor is a trouble-shooter.

Do you sometimes wonder whether to use *was* or *were*, *better* or *best*, *I* or *me* in a sentence? How assured are you about *who* and *which* and *that*?

Do some parts of your sentences sometimes fall into odd places? Does an instructor sometimes criticize your sentence structure? Does anyone ever say to you, "I don't understand what you mean"?

Are you ever uncertain about the use of a comma, or about where quotation marks belong when another mark is demanding the same space?

If such questions ever occur to you, and if you are serious about trying to improve your writing, you can take aim at your troubles with the *Tutor* to advise you.

This book is designed for you to study independently. You are responsible for your own learning. The *Tutor* can provide information and helpful hints, but only you can convert them into actual improvement of your writing.

Here's how to get the most for the money you paid for your *Tutor*.
The book is divided into four sections:

Part I: Sentence Structure
Part II: Usage
Part III: Diction and Style
Part IV: Punctuation and Mechanics

At the beginning of each part is a diagnostic test. It will show you which of the lessons in that section you need to study. (Studying the others won't hurt you any, but you apparently need them less.)

All one hundred lessons are similar in organization. The first few frames, proceeding from extremely simple to more challenging, lead toward your understanding of a basic principle. In a middle frame, you will complete a statement of what that basic principle is. The several frames that follow will ask you to apply the principle, sometimes by composing sentences of your own.

The final frame is the same in all the lessons. It says: "Finish honestly: One thing I hope to remember from this lesson is that . . ." In responding to that, look back through the lesson and pick out some one item that promises to be especially useful to you. Or you may want to restate the basic principle in your own words.

Take your time on each lesson. You are unlikely to remember very much if you hurry. Try to understand each frame before going on to the next. In the space provided, actually *write* the answer to every question, attempting to follow the instructions exactly.

Opposite the next frame down, you'll find the answer. If you responded incorrectly, find out where you went wrong and do the added practice question that you'll find in most answer frames. You'll find the answers to added practice questions at the end of each lesson.

Some instructors may indicate in the margins of your compositions that you should do certain lessons in the *Tutor*. They may write, for instance, *57* or *Trite*. Inside the front or back cover of this book you will see that you should study Lesson 57, which is entitled "Trite Expressions: Almost as Old as the Hills." If you have already done that lesson, obviously you need to study it again, perhaps this time writing your answers on a separate sheet of paper and doing *all* the questions for added practice.

At the end of each of the four sections is a mastery test, intended to show you what you have completed with apparent success and which lessons you should study some more.

As the year goes on, your conscientious use of your *Tutor* should considerably reduce the problems you may be having in sentence structure, usage, diction and style, and punctuation and other mechanics.

Two Tutors

CONTENTS

x

Part III Diction and Style

Diagnostic Test   233

Part IV Punctuation and Mechanics

Diagnostic Test   335

I

Sentence Structure

Diagnostic Test
Sentence Structure

Directions

Because each test item consists of three parts, a, b, and c, you will have three chances to test your knowledge of each principle. In some items each part will contain only one sentence or word group; in others it will include two or more sentences. In this test, you are to decide quickly whether or not the sentence or sentences in a, b, and c seem satisfactory as formal written English. As a guideline, ask yourself whether the sentence structure would be acceptable in a college essay. If you believe that everything written after 1.a, for example, is acceptable, circle the letter A. If the sentence structure is unacceptable, circle the letter U.

Sample Item

1. a. Coming out of the exhaust pipe, we saw a cloud of black smoke.   A (U)

   b. After traveling six blocks, we heard a loud explosion.   (A) U

   c. While coasting to a stop, the muffler fell down.   A (U)

Note: *The writing in part a was marked U for* unacceptable *because the phrase* coming out of the exhaust pipe *is closer to* we *than to* smoke. *Certainly* we *are not coming out of the pipe. The writing in part c is marked U because it is unlikely that the muffler was coasting to a stop. Beginning the sentence with the words* While we were *would give the word* coasting *something sensible to modify.*

How to Use the Test

Like the lessons in this book, this diagnostic test is self-instructional. When you have finished it, score it with the key provided on page 511. The test will measure your awareness of the sentence structure generally expected in college essays. Each test item will give you three *chances to recognize acceptable sentence structure.*

If you miss one or more of the three chances, you should plan to do the corresponding lesson in the pages that follow. For example, making one or more errors in test item 12 means that you should do Lesson 12.

At the end of this group of lessons, on page 95, is a matching Mastery Test. Take that test after you have completed the needed lessons. It will show you the items in which you have improved and those in which you need further work. Study once more the lessons corresponding to the missed items.

1. a. Living in a small, crowded college dormitory room for two semesters.   A U

   b. With a roommate who plays the stereo constantly.   A U

   c. Just thinking about the spacious room I had at home depresses me.   A U

2. a. People who have been drinking should not drive. Because they could kill themselves and others.   A   U

 b. Whenever people go out as a group to drink, someone in the group should be a designated driver.   A   U

 c. Who can stay sober and drive the others home safely.   A   U

3. a. Last week a friend of mine borrowed two books from the library that had been damaged.   A   U

 b. My friend tried to renew the books that a roommate had given him with his own ID card.   A   U

 c. Needless to say, my friend, who had never been in trouble, was detained by the librarian.   A   U

4. a. After the dean of students canceled the concert, Susan and Lynn talked to him and then wrote a letter to the editor of the student newspaper.   A   U

 b. Before their letter appeared, the dean reversed his decision.   A   U

 c. Unfortunately, the newspaper published their letter after they tried to stop it following the dean's latest announcement.   A   U

5. a. I was confident on Friday I would write my essay.   A   U

 b. I should have realized eventually I would have to start writing.   A   U

 c. At last, on Saturday afternoon, for a single hour I felt like writing.   A   U

6. a. While not paying attention, the lab assistant gave us our instructions.   A   U

 b. In trying to finish before the end of the period, the experiment was done too quickly.   A   U

 c. Boiling and splattering out of the test tube, we saw a thick, purple substance.   A   U

7. a. In the interest of reducing the crime rate, the city council voted to hold a public meeting on handgun control.   A   U

 b. During the two weeks before the meeting, council members told news reporters they wanted only police officers to have handguns.   A   U

 c. At least fifty handgun owners attended the meeting. All of them seemed angry. Some claimed to be just gun collectors. All said they had a right to own handguns. They used the Constitution to support their arguments.   A   U

8. a. This time we thought we would win because we were playing on our home court a team we had beaten five seasons in a row.   A   U

 b. When we got the ball at the beginning and made the first basket quickly, even Coach Ricco looked confident.   A   U

 c. We got off to a fast start, and we had some success getting the ball inside, but we missed almost every jumpshot, and we missed most of our free throws, and so we lost.   A   U

9. a. I usually try to register as early as possible, but because I fell behind in my classes I didn't have time to see my advisor.   A   U

b. I had three papers due and two tests, and my roommate registered last week.   A U

c. Two days before the spring semester, I tried to register, but by that time three classes I wanted were full.   A U

10. a. Six of my former high school classmates are also attending this university, four of them have even shown up in two of my classes.   A U

    b. John Peters, our class valedictorian, is in my math class, he has already agreed to study with me.   A U

    c. I am glad to have these friends from my hometown; seeing them will help me to get over my homesickness.   A U

11. a. My instructor for my freshman course in English composition pointed out that because I had met with exceptional success in the areas of computer science and physics, I should consider the desirability of taking courses in technical writing to apply my interests in preparing for a writing career in the modern world of today.   A U

    b. He challenged me to rewrite several crowded and overly complicated sentences found in computer manuals.   A U

    c. After struggling all night long with this huge, monumental, and awesome task of coping with redundancy and circumlocution, I was rendered inoperative as far as writing was concerned and felt strongly inclined to accept the premise that I needed more experience in the area of writing.   A U

12. a. When I was waiting in the airport, a tall man with a black mustache left quickly without his briefcase.   A U

    b. I was standing in the terminal with his briefcase when I saw three heavily armed police officers near my seat.   A U

    c. Before I could tell them what had happened, they grabbed me and took me to a small room behind the baggage area.   A U

13. a. Recitation Hall, the first classroom building on campus, is now a museum strongly supported by older alumni.   A U

    b. I am glad to know that it is true that this old structure that has stood for over a hundred years will remain, and that it will be restored.   A U

    c. In this building, Professor Puremind taught philosophy to my great grandfather, who was a friend of Jeremy Fuller, who taught Latin here to my grandfather, who endowed the Puremind Distinguished Professorship.   A U

14. a. I have wondered why students who complain about their heavy course loads spend hours watching TV soap operas in the Student Center.   A U

    b. It seems to me that in many cases students have a tendency to engage in this kind of activity in spite of the fact that they know that it is of a wasteful and time-consuming nature.   A U

    c. This habit of theirs is so fascinating that day after day and hour after hour I find myself watching and observ-

ing these students who can't
seem to budget their time.

15. a. I tried to in every imagin-   A   U
    able way explain my reasons
    for missing five lectures,
    three labs, and two tests.

    b. At the beginning of the se-   A   U
    mester, my professor made
    it a point clearly to state that
    he would allow only two
    unexcused absences.

    c. To be entirely honest about   A   U
    my absences would be too
    embarrassing.

16. a. Harry Jones, my friend's   A   U
    roommate, is taller than the
    height of the door to their
    room.

    b. In his spare time, Harry   A   U
    likes to play chess, read nov-
    els, or he writes programs
    for his computer.

    c. Most people are surprised to   A   U
    learn that Harry prefers to
    challenge his mind but not
    playing any sports.

17. a. My friends and I tried to de-   A   U
    cide whether to eat in the
    cafeteria or to get a carry-
    out pizza.

    b. We agreed to get a large   A   U
    pizza with four ingredients
    and that would have extra
    cheese.

    c. Sometimes buying one pizza   A   U
    is more expensive than to
    buy three meals in the cafe-
    teria.

18. a. Music videos are usually   A   U
    filled with violent scenes, but
    which often have nothing to
    do with the music or the
    lyrics.

    b. Dr. James Clark, a psychol-   A   U
    ogist, and who studied rea-
    sons for violent behavior,

concluded that music videos
can cause people to commit
violent acts.

    c. It is interesting that music   A   U
    videos which are poorly or-
    ganized and which motivate
    people to commit violent
    acts are so popular.

19. a. This time I was in good   A   U
    shape for the test because I
    almost studied all night.

    b. When I took the test, I   A   U
    nearly knew every answer.

    c. I am almost completing   A   U
    twenty hours of coursework
    this semester, so I need to
    keep up the good work.

20. a. We worked for three weeks   A   U
    to organize the party. We
    cleaned the house for three
    days. We thought the noise
    ordinance didn't apply to
    fraternity houses. We were
    told that the city police
    wouldn't bother us.

    b. Just ten minutes after mid-   A   U
    night, two city police officers
    came to the door and told us
    they had received a com-
    plaint about loud music.
    As if this weren't enough
    trouble for us, six of our
    members started playing
    trumpets and drums in the
    back yard.

    c. Although the noise ordi-   A   U
    nance protects the rights of
    residents to peace and quiet,
    it is enforced too strictly
    near campus. Surely the
    city's leaders don't expect
    students to be quiet all week-
    end.

Answers to this test can be found on page 511.

Fragments of Sentences: Phrases

After writing your answer(s) in the right-hand column, check this column to see whether you have responded correctly. If you have made a mistake, or if you need more practice, do whatever is asked below the dotted line in each answer frame.

Answers to questions for added practice can be found at the end of each lesson.

Understanding and Applying the Principles

1

> **along the beach   in the evening**
> **speaking only a few words**
> **happy to be together again   hand in hand**

Groups of words like those above are called *phrases*. How many phrases are printed above? _____

Answers and Added Practice

1

Five

....

seeing a sunset in technicolor with red dominating

How many phrases are printed above? _____

2

Phrases are useful. Almost every sentence contains one or more, and often as many as a half dozen. The five phrases in Frame 1 provide *some* information but leave out other information essential to understanding the whole.

A. Do you know for sure how many people are being discussed? _____

B. Do you know for sure whether they are walking, jogging, or moving in some other way? _____

2

A. No   B. No

....

When you read the phrase *watching the sandpipers*, do you know who is (are) watching and what else the watcher(s) may be doing? _____

3

Let's see how we may put the phrases in Frame 1 into a sentence that answers the questions in Frame 2:

> **In the evening the lanky cowhand and the ballerina strolled along the beach hand in hand, speaking only a few words, happy to be together again.**

Does that sentence tell more or less than the phrases in Frame 1? _____ [*More* or *Less*?]

3

More

· ·

Use the phrase *watching the sand-pipers* in a complete sentence. Use *They* as the subject, and add any other needed word(s).

4

In conversation, or in making a list, we often use phrases instead of complete sentences. For instance, when someone asks "Where were they?" we may answer with the phrase "On the beach."

Write a phrase that might answer the question "When did they come back?"

_____

4

Model Answer

"At nine o'clock."
(Your answers should be similar to model answers but need not be identical.)

· ·

Write a simple, short question starting with *When, Where,* or *What*, and then write its answer in a phrase.

5

Most phrases begin with prepositions (words like *to, of, in, along, between,* or *over*) or else with participles (*-ing*-words, such as *speaking*). Is each of the following groups of words a phrase?

  A. in the department store _____ [*Yes* or *No?*]

  B. buying some clothing and kitchen utensils _____
     [*Yes* or *No?*]

5

  A. Yes B. Yes

· ·

  a. Add a preposition to make each of these into a phrase:
    _____ her eyes, _____
    his face, _____ the door.

  b. Add a participle to make each of these into a phrase:
    _____ an old song,
    _____ loudly, _____
    _____ the piano
    vigorously but not well.

6

Another way to recognize a phrase is to note that it does not have both a subject (s) and a verb (v).

          s   v

Pelicans glide.

(This is a sentence, for it has both a subject and a verb.)

With surprising grace.

(This is not a sentence, for it _____ [*does* or *does not?*] have a subject and a verb.)

6

does not

. . . .

Tell whether each is a sentence (S) or a phrase (P).

_____ Gulls call raucously.

_____ On the posts and buoys.

_____ Swooping down to snatch bits of food.

_____ Then returning to their perches.

7

Experienced writers sometimes use phrases or other sentence fragments for stylistic reasons, but inexperienced writers ordinarily should write complete sentences except in reporting conversations.

A common mistake is the separation of a phrase from the sentence to which it belongs:

The cowboy tilted his head back and inhaled deeply. Smelling the tangy salt air.

The last five words are a phrase, a fragment of a sentence. The period after *deeply* should be changed to a _____ [What mark?] and *Smelling* should start with a _____ [*small* or *capital*?] letter.

7

comma, small

. . . .

Change as necessary:

The ballerina gazed at the first star to appear. Perhaps silently repeating the old "Starlight, star bright" rhyme.

8

Which two of the following groups of words are phrases rather than complete sentences?

    A. Living in earthen lodges in winter and in flimsy wooden structures in summer.

    B. The early Navahos moved often from place to place.

    C. Through much of the area now known as Arizona, New Mexico, and Utah.

_____ [A and B, A and C, or B and C?]

8

A and C

. . . .

Copy and combine A, B, and C from Frame 8, making necessary changes in punctuation and capitalization.

9

Proceed as in Frame 8.

    A. With the addition of millions of women to the working population of the United States.

    B. The percentage of the total population who were employed outside the home increased steadily.

    C. Rising to a higher level than most business forecasters had ever dreamed.

_____ [A and B, A and C, or B and C?]

9

A and C

· ·

Copy and combine A, B, and C from Frame 9, making necessary changes in punctuation and capitalization.

10

Make up a sentence, opening it with a fairly long phrase starting with the word *Looking*. Complete the following pattern:

Looking _____

_____

_____ , Stan _____

_____ .

10

Model Answer

Looking carefully at his new set of wrenches, Stan noticed that they were all metric.

· ·

In the model answer above, you could add in any of three places the words *for the first time*:

   A. After _____
      [What word?]
   B. After _____
      [What word?]
   C. After _____
      [What word?]

11

Make up another sentence. End it with the phrases *near the end of the line closest to the door.*

11

Model Answer

My sister was standing near the end of the line closest to the door.

· ·

Now end a sentence with these phrases: . . . *from the office to his home.*

12

Finish honestly: One thing I hope to remember from this exercise is that . . .

(Any answer that you consider honest and accurate is acceptable.)

Lesson 1: Answers to Questions for Added Practice

1. Three **2.** No. **3.** MODEL: They were watching the sandpipers darting along the wet edges of the sand. **4.** MODEL: Where is the alarm clock? In the bedroom. **5.** MODELS: A. in her eyes, across his face, near the door B. humming an old song, singing loudly, playing the piano vigorously but not well **6.** S P P P **7.** . . . appear, perhaps . . . **8.** Living in earthen lodges in winter and in flimsy wooden structures in summer, the early Navahos moved often from place to place through much of the area now known as Arizona, New Mexico, and Utah. **9.** With the addition of millions of women to the working population of the United States, the percentage of the total population who were employed outside the home increased steadily, rising to a higher level than most business forecasters had ever dreamed. **10.** A. carefully B. wrenches C. noticed **11.** MODEL: He had to drive two miles from the office to his home.

2

Fragments of Sentences: Dependent Clauses

After writing your answer(s) in the right-hand column, check this column to see whether you have responded correctly. If you have made a mistake, or if you need more practice, do whatever is asked below the dotted line in each answer frame.

Answers to questions for added practice can be found at the end of each lesson.

Answers and Added Practice

1

No

· ·

Do the groups of words below leave you wondering about something? [Answer *Yes* or *No* to each.]

   A. Because inferior cement had been used. _____

   B. Although a break had been predicted for years. _____

_____

Understanding and Applying the Principles

1

         s   v

When the dam broke.

The group of words above looks somewhat like a sentence. It has a subject (s) and a verb (v). Yet it leaves you wondering, "When the dam broke, what happened?"

   Does the group of words answer that question? _____

2

      s   v   s   v

When the dam broke. Water poured down into

the valley.

By adding the sentence *Water poured down into the valley*, we have told what happened. But the first four words still stand lonely and unsupported.

   Is it possible to fasten those four words to the sentence? _____

_____

2

Yes

....

Can these two groups of words be combined as a complete sentence?

Houses were swept off their foundations. Because the force of the water was so great.

_____ [*Yes* or *No?*]

3

$$\overset{s}{\frown}\overset{v}{\frown}\quad\overset{s}{\frown}\overset{v}{\frown}$$

When the dam broke, water poured down into the valley.

In the sentence above we have fastened a group of words that cannot stand alone to another group that can stand alone. A group of words that has a subject and a verb but that cannot stand alone, like *when the dam* (s) *broke* (v), is called a dependent clause. It depends on something else to add strength and meaning.

A dependent clause _____ [*should* or *should not?*] be punctuated as a complete sentence.

3

should not

....

From Answer Frame 2, copy and combine the two groups of words as one complete sentence. Do not capitalize *Because*.

4

Dependent clauses often start with such words as *after, although, because, so that, until, when, whenever, wherever,* or *while,* and sometimes with *that, which, who, whom,* or *whose.* They have subjects and verbs, as complete sentences do, but they _____ [*can* or *cannot?*] stand alone as a sentence.

4

cannot

....

Two of these groups of words should be considered dependent clauses. Write *Dependent* after each of the two.

A. while the dam was washing out _____

B. the dam washed out _____
   _____

C. so that lives would not be endangered again _____
   _____

5

In Frame 3 we noted that *when the dam broke* is a dependent clause. *Water poured down into the valley,* on the other hand, can stand on its own and is therefore an independent clause. Something is independent if it can stand without help.

Although the damage was great, no lives were lost.

A. Copy the dependent clause from the sentence above.

_____

_____

B. Copy the independent clause. _____

_____

5

A. Although the damage was great

B. no lives were lost

....

Add an appropriate independent clause before or after this dependent clause:

before the dam washed out

6

Many independent clauses have one, two, or more dependent clauses attached:

Although the damage was great, no lives were lost, because an efficient warning system was in operation.

How many dependent clauses are in that sentence? _____
_____

6

Two

....

Write a dependent clause in the blank at each end of this sentence:

Because _____
_____
_____
_____
_____ ,

dams should be inspected yearly so that _____
_____
_____ .

7

To recapitulate (that's a fancy synonym of *summarize*):

A. A dependent clause _____ [*is* or *is not*?] a sentence.

B. A dependent clause needs to be attached to an _____
_____ [What kind of?] clause.

7

A: is not   B: independent

....

Underline the two dependent clauses in this sentence:

Whenever I hear the term "Pennsylvania Dutch," which is widely used but inaccurate, I am tempted to say "German."

8

Which one of the following groups of words is a dependent clause?

A. Several thousand English words come from Greek.

B. Which has contributed heavily to the Romance languages as well.

C. English grammar, however, is basically Germanic rather than Greek or Latin.

_____ [A, B, or C?]

8

B

·····························

Copy and combine A and B in Frame 8.

9

Compose a sentence in which you tell about a concert or a play. End the sentence with a dependent clause starting with *while*.

9

Model Answer

The clarinets carried the melody while the other instruments supplied various decorations.

·····························

Reverse your own answer, putting the *while*-clause first, followed by a comma and the independent clause. End the sentence with a period.

10

Compose a sentence starting with *I like* and ending with a dependent clause starting with *because*.

10

Model Answer

I like basketball because the action is so fast.

·····························

Reverse your own answer, putting the *because*-clause first. Place a comma after the dependent clause.

11

Compose a sentence ending with *which is a colorful kind of bird*.

11

Model Answer

My neighbor owns a macaw, which is a colorful kind of bird.

. . . .

Complete this sentence:
I like to visit my neighbor, whose
. . .

12

Compose one more sentence. Tell about starting toward a nearby city. At the end, attach a dependent clause beginning with *although*.

12

Model Answer

Dad and I started toward Beloit, although the weather forecasters were predicting snow.

. . . .

Rewrite your sentence, this time beginning the dependent clause with *because*.

13

Finish honestly: One thing I hope to remember from this exercise is that . . .

(Any answer that you consider honest and accurate is acceptable.)

Lesson 2: Answers to Questions for Added Practice

1. A. Yes B. Yes **2.** Yes. **3.** Houses were swept off their foundations because the force of the water was so great. **4.** A. Dependent C. Dependent **5.** MODEL: Before the dam washed out, only a few people had predicted such a disaster. **6.** MODEL: Because early danger signs can sometimes be found, dams should be inspected yearly so that repairs can be made. **7.** Whenever I hear the term "Pennsylvania Dutch," which is widely used but inaccurate, **8.** Several thousand English words come from Greek, which has contributed widely to the Romance languages as well. **9.** MODEL: While the other instruments supplied various decorations, the clarinets carried the melody. **10.** MODEL: Because the action is so fast, I like basketball. **11.** MODEL: I like to visit my neighbor, whose hobby is exotic birds. **12.** MODEL: Dad and I started toward Beloit because we had some business there.

═3═ *Phrases and Clauses: Everything in Place*

After writing your answer(s) in the right-hand column, check this column to see whether you have responded correctly. If you have made a mistake, or if you need more practice, do whatever is asked below the dotted line in each answer frame.

Answers to questions for added practice can be found at the end of each lesson.

Understanding and Applying the Principles

1

> **Jack could see the magician sawing the woman in half with his own eyes.**

The sentence above is confusing because it sounds as though the magician used _____ _____ _____ [What three words?] to saw the woman in half.

Answers and Added Practice

1

his own eyes

....

Here is a similar sentence:

> **Bonnie heard the noise that the clarinetist made with her own ears.**

In that sentence, someone's _____ _____ apparently made the noise.

2

The problem in Frame 1 is that the phrase *with his own eyes* is in the wrong place. It should be at the beginning of the sentence, or after the word _____ , or after the word _____ .

2

see, Jack

....

In Answer Frame 1 the phrase *with her own ears* could be placed

    A. at the _____ of the sentence

    B. ·or after the word _____
    _____

    C. or after the word _____
    _____

3

> **A German shepherd was standing in the back seat of my car, which was growling a warning.**

    A. Was my car growling? _____
    B. What was growling? _____
    C. Should *which was growling* be placed close to *shepherd* or close to *car*? _____

3

A. No
B. (a German) shepherd
C. *shepherd*

....

Here is a similar sentence:

She bought some cheese in the delicatessen that looked moldy.

The best way to correct that sentence is to move *in the delicatessen* to the _____ . [*beginning* or *end?*]

4

Dan accidentally dropped some paint on his sister's hair, which was bright green.

The clause *which was bright green* could be better placed after _____ . [What word?]

4

paint

....

The cities in *A Tale of Two Cities* are London and Paris, which I read last week.

The clause at the end should be placed after _____ . [What word?]

5

Dan accidentally dropped some paint, which was bright green, on his sister's hair.

A. That sentence is better than the one in Frame 4. It could be improved further by deletion of *which was* and by placing _____ _____ [What two words?] before *paint*.
B. Making those changes, copy the sentence.

5

A. *bright green*
B. Dan accidentally dropped some bright green paint on his sister's hair.

....

As that example shows, if you make one change in a sentence, others also may be desirable.

6

A suspect was arrested in the house before any damage was done by two off-duty police officers.

A. Is the probable meaning that damage would have been done by (1) the suspect or (2) the officers? _____ [1 or 2?]
B. The best placement of *by two off-duty police officers* is after the word _____ .

6

A. 1   B. *house*

· ·

Alex found a golf ball that was almost new in a gopher hole.

A better place for the phrase *in a gopher hole* would be immediately before the word _____ or _____ but not immediately before the word _____ .

7

If each phrase or clause is not carefully placed, a sentence may be

   A. unclear _____
   B. funny _____
   C. silly _____
   D. ridiculous _____

Check all that seem true.

7

(All four answers should be checked.)

· ·

Look again at the sentences in Frames 1, 3, 4, and 6. Do all of them seem unclear, funny, silly, and ridiculous? _____

8

Which sentence is better?

   A. She took a pitcher in which a spider had left its web from the dusty cupboard.
   B. She took from the dusty cupboard a pitcher in which a spider had left its web.

_____ [A or B?]

8

B

· ·

Rearrange for clarity:

Flo asked me to call her in thirty minutes three times before I went home.

9

Which sentence is best?

   A. She caught the ball in her bare hand that the batter had hit.
   B. She caught in her bare hand the ball that the batter had hit.
   C. She caught the ball that the batter had hit in her bare hand.

_____ [A, B, or C?]

9

B

· ·

Rearrange for clarity:

A dog followed her to her apartment, which was white with a black tail.

10

Which sentence is best?

   A. Joe had a pair of shoes on his sore feet that had holes in both soles.
   B. Joe had a pair of shoes that had holes in both soles on his sore feet.
   C. On his sore feet Joe had a pair of shoes that had holes in both soles.

_____ [A, B, or C?]

10

C

· ·

Rearrange for clarity:

The plane is taken for a checkup after every flight into the hangar.

11

of a friend of mine   in the house
that can play a toy piano
there is a monkey

Copy the groups of words above as a sentence, arranging them in the best order.

11

In the house of a friend of mine there is a monkey that can play a toy piano.

· ·

Arrange in the best order:

who lived next door
after a year   but
with Penny
he lost interest
he had wanted a date

12

when you were a child   as a pet
the turtle you had   of six
do you remember

Follow the instruction for Frame 11.

12

Do you remember the turtle you had as a pet when you were a child of six?

· ·

Arrange in the best order:

of parts   in meaning
of a sentence
can sometimes suggest
the arrangement
a considerable difference

13

Finish honestly: One thing I hope to remember from this exercise is that . . .

(Any answer that you consider honest and accurate is acceptable.)

Lesson 3: Answers to Questions for Added Practice

1. ears **2.** A. beginning B. *Bonnie* C. *heard* **3.** beginning **4.** *Cities* **6.** *Alex, a, that* **7.** Yes **8.** Three times before I went home Flo asked me to call her in thirty minutes. **9.** A dog, which was white with a black tail, followed her to her apartment. **10.** After every flight the plane is taken into the hangar for a checkup. **11.** He had wanted a date with Penny, who lived next door, but after a year he lost interest. **12.** The arrangement of parts of a sentence can sometimes suggest a considerable difference in meaning.

4

Arrangement of Details: If It Happened First, Tell It First

After writing your answer(s) in the right-hand column, check this column to see whether you have responded correctly. If you have made a mistake, or if you need more practice, do whatever is asked below the dotted line in each answer frame.

Answers to questions for added practice can be found at the end of each lesson.

Understanding and Applying the Principles

1

Beowulf slew a dragon after he had killed the monstrous mother of Grendel following the slaying of Grendel himself.

Three events are described: (A) killing the dragon, (B) killing Grendel's mother, (C) killing Grendel. A careful reading of the sentence will show you the order in which these events took place. Put events A, B, and C in the correct order: _____, _____, _____.

Answers and Added Practice

1

   C, B, A

. . . .

   (A) **Lillian walked boldly up to the skunk** (B) **after she learned it had been descented.**

In that sentence _____ [A or B?] happened first.

2

If writers do their job properly, readers _____ [*will* or *will not*?] need to untangle the time sequence in a sentence.

2

will not

....

Rewrite the sentence about Lillian in Answer Frame 1, showing what happened first. Start with *After Lillian learned*.

3

Rewrite the sentence about Beowulf in Frame 1, putting the events in the order in which they happened. Start your sentence with *After*.

3

Model Answer

    After killing Grendel, Beowulf slew Grendel's monstrous mother and then a dragon.

....

Note that this revision is much more clear than the original.

4

    (A) **The boys swam across the river** (B) **after eating their lunch of cold fried chicken and baked beans,** (C) **which was followed by a short hike to the stream.**

The order of events in that sentence is _____, _____, _____. [Put A, B, C in the order in which they happened.]

4

    B, C, A

....

Rewrite this sentence, putting the earlier event first:

    Roses were now in bloom, and the spring flowers had already vanished.

Rewrite the sentence in Frame 4. Start with *The boys ate. . . .* Put the events in order, and make any other changes that will add smoothness.

5

Model Answer

    The boys ate a lunch of cold fried chicken and baked beans, hiked a short distance to the river, and swam across it.

....

Note that this revision happens to be a little shorter than the original, as well as more clear.

6

    (A) **Fafner killed Fasolt to obtain the Rheingold** (B) **that Wotan had given to the two of them** (C) **after he had taken it from Alberich** (D) **who had stolen it from the Rhein Maidens.**

The order of events in Wagner's opera was _____, _____, _____, _____. [Put A, B, C, D in chronological order.]

6

D, C, B, A

....

Note that this sentence contains so much information that it may best be divided into two sentences.

7

Rewrite the sentence in Frame 6 as two sentences. In the first, tell of Alberich's theft and Wotan's seizure of the gold. In the second, tell of Wotan's gift and the murder that resulted.

7

Model Answer

Alberich stole the Rheingold from the Rhein Maidens, but Wotan took it from him. Wotan then gave it to Fafner and Fasolt, and Fafner killed Fasolt to get it all for himself.

....

(Blame Richard Wagner if the story still seems complicated.)

8

Sometimes, especially when we use a word such as *before*, a sentence is satisfactory even though events are not placed in the right order. For instance:

Before I made my decision, I talked with my parents.

Does that sentence seem completely clear? _____

8

Yes

....

The sentence in Frame 8 may be arranged in two ways; either is satisfactory. Write the one that starts with *I talked*.

9

Generally, however, it is best to tell about events in the order in which they occurred.

So, if you are writing about beginning to eat, washing your hands, and sitting down at the table, the one you mention first is _____.

9

washing your hands

. . . .

Write a sentence relating the events described in Frame 9.

10

Compose a sentence about three things that you did this morning. Put them into the right order. Start with a word such as *After*.

10

Model Answer

After the alarm clock awakened me, I went back to sleep and missed my eight o'clock class.

. . . .

Write a sentence about three things that you need to do tomorrow morning, afternoon, and evening.

11

Finish honestly: One thing I hope to remember from this exercise is that . . .

(Any answer that you consider honest and accurate is acceptable.)

Lesson 4: Answers to Questions for Added Practice

1. B **2.** After Lillian learned that the skunk had been descented, she walked boldly up to it. **4.** The spring flowers had already vanished, and roses were now in bloom. **8.** I talked with my parents before I made my decision. **9.** I washed my hands, sat down at the table, and began to eat. **10.** MODEL: Tomorrow morning I must study some more, in the afternoon I have to take that dreaded test, and in the evening I ought to get some needed sleep.

Squinting Modifiers: Looking Toward Both Sides

After writing your answer(s) in the right-hand column, check this column to see whether you have responded correctly. If you have made a mistake, or if you need more practice, do whatever is asked below the dotted line in each answer frame.

Answers to questions for added practice can be found at the end of each lesson.

Answers and Added Practice

1

    A. in the haunted house
    B. eerie lights began to glow

. . . .

Read twice the sentence in Frame 1, aloud if possible. On the first reading, pause slightly after *house.* On the second, pause after *midnight.* Note the slight difference in meaning.

2

    careless

. . . .

The teacher said when we went out we should start the next lab project.

In that sentence, which words are the squinting modifier?

Understanding and Applying the Principles

1

    When the clock chimed midnight in the haunted house eerie lights began to glow.

The sentence above has two possible but slightly different meanings:

    A. Perhaps the writer means that the clock chimed _____ _____ . [Where?]

    B. Or perhaps he means that in the haunted house _____ _____ . [What happened?]

2

In the example in Frame 1, the phrase *in the haunted house* is called a squinting modifier. One meaning of *squint* is "to look or glance to the side." The squinting modifier seems to look toward both sides, but we cannot be sure which one the writer intended.

Although squinting modifiers may not affect meaning greatly, they suggest that the writer is _____ . [*careful* or *careless*?]

3

    Practicing frequently improves coordination.

In some sentences a squinting modifier confuses meaning more than in others.

    A. One meaning of the example above is that in order to improve coordination, practicing should be done _____ _____ . [When?]

    B. The second meaning is that with practice, coordination improves _____ . [When?]

3

A. frequently   B. frequently

. . . .

Helen said during her trip she might stop in New Orleans.

Maybe Helen made the statement

_____

_____ , [When?] or maybe she will stop in New Orleans

_____ .

[When?]

4

Sometimes a squinting modifier may be corrected by inserting a comma, which can show where a pause is intended. In the boldface sentence in Frame 1 a comma should be placed after _____ [What word?] for meaning A and after _____ [What word?] for meaning B.

4

midnight   house

. . . .

While we were shopping with the help of a conscientious clerk we found a vase we liked.

A comma after _____ [What word?] will show one meaning, and a comma after _____ will show another.

5

Rewrite twice the boldface sentence in Frame 1. Start the first version with *In*. End the second with *house*. Observe that in both versions the changed position of the squinting modifier has improved the sentence.

5

In the haunted house when the clock chimed midnight, eerie lights began to glow.

When the clock chimed midnight, eerie lights began to glow in the haunted house.

. . . .

Note how the commas also contribute to the clarity.

6

Sometimes a correction may require a slight rewording. One way to correct *Practicing frequently improves coordination* is this:

A. Frequent _____

_____ . [Finish the sentence.]

Now finish this one and note the difference in meaning:

B. _____ is often likely to _____

_____ .

6

    A. . . . practice improves coordination.

    B. Practicing . . . improve coordination.

. . . .

Rewrite to get rid of the squinter:

A man who had been yelling impatiently tried to break down the door.

7

Squinting modifiers should be avoided because they make a sentence ambiguous. That is, they make it so that a sentence can be interpreted in either of _____ [How many?] ways.

7

    two

. . . .

The foreigner to whom I was speaking slowly began to understand.

In that sentence my speaking may have been _____ [What?] or the foreigner's understanding may have come _____ . [How?]

8

She agreed on Friday to write the letter.

Write one version of that sentence showing an agreement on Friday, and a second version showing the writing to take place on Friday.

8

    On Friday she agreed to write the letter.

    She agreed to write the letter on Friday.

. . . .

The blind student to whom she was reading softly began to cry.

To show that the crying was soft, *softly* should be placed after _____ . [What word?]

9

The last contest to be started promptly began at nine o'clock.

Rewrite that sentence to show that the beginning occurred promptly.

9

. . . began promptly at nine o'clock (*or*) . . . began at nine o'clock promptly

. . . .

Max asked Sally in a little while to call his mother for him.

For one meaning, *in a little while* should be placed before _____ _____ . For another, it should be placed after _____ .

10

> **whom Maude   held out his hand**
> **the old man   shyly   approached**

Combine those words and groups of words in such a way that *shyly* does not squint.

10

The old man whom Maude approached held out his hand shyly.

(*or*) The old man whom Maude shyly approached held out his hand.

(*but not*) The old man whom Maude approached shyly held out his hand.

. . . .

What's wrong with the third answer?

11

Solve this puzzle:

> **in a logical order   of a sentence**
> **the parts   given here   put together**

11

In a logical order, put together the parts of a sentence given here. (*or*) Put together in a logical order . . . (*but not*) Put together the parts of a sentence given here in a logical order.

. . . .

Combine these groups of words in two different ways, each with a different meaning:

> **At eight o'clock   I said**
> **I would go to work**

12

Finish honestly: One thing I hope to remember from this exercise is that . . .

(Any answer that you consider honest and accurate is acceptable.)

Lesson 5: Answers to Questions for Added Practice

2. *when we went out* **3.** MODEL: while she was taking her trip, during her trip **4.** *shopping, clerk* **6.** A man who had been impatiently yelling tried to break down the door. (*Or*) A man who had been yelling tried impatiently to break down the door. **7.** slow, slowly **8.** *cry* **9.** *Max, him* **10.** MODEL: The third answer is ambiguous, meaning either that Maude approached shyly or that the old man held out his hand shyly. **11.** I said I would go to work at eight o'clock. At eight o'clock I said I would go to work.

=6=

Dangling Modifiers: Unintended Laugh-getters

After writing your answer(s) in the right-hand column, check this column to see whether you have responded correctly. If you have made a mistake, or if you need more practice, do whatever is asked below the dotted line in each answer frame.

Answers to questions for added practice can be found at the end of each lesson.

Understanding and Applying the Principles

1

Reaching the top after running up the hill, my heart was pounding fast.

The sentence above sounds as though my _____ [What?] ran up the hill and reached the top.

Answers and Added Practice

1

   heart

. . . .

After howling all night long, Dad decided that I could not keep the hound.

That sentence sounds as though _____ [Who?] howled all night long.

2

In Frame 1, the intended meaning is that _____ [Who?] reached the top of the hill.

2

    I

. . . .

In the sentence about Dad's decision (above), the intended meaning is that the _____ [What?] howled all night long.

3

One way to correct the sentence in Frame 1 is to write:

Reaching the top after running up the hill, _____ [Who?] felt my heart pounding fast.

3

    I

. . . .

While going up the stairs toward her apartment, a piano started to play.

Draw a picture of what that sentence seems to say.

4

A second way to correct the sentence in Frame 1 is to write:

When _____ [Who?] reached the top after running up the hill, my heart was pounding fast.

4

    I

. . . .

The sentence about the piano (above) could be rewritten to identify the _____ [*person* or *piano*?] that was really going up the stairs.

5

Modifiers such as *reaching the top, after howling all night long,* or *while on the fire escape* need to be placed so that the reader will know immediately who or what reached the top, howled, or was on the fire escape. A modifier that seems to modify the wrong thing is called "misplaced." If it does not clearly modify anything at all, it is "dangling."

Grinning drunkenly, Jake's fist wobbled toward my nose.

In that sentence, the dangling modifier is _____

_____ .

5

Grinning drunkenly

....

Being a former secretary, the office procedures were easy for Alice to learn.

In that sentence, the dangling modifier is _____

_____ .

6

Which is the best correction of the sentence in Frame 5?

    A. Grinning drunkenly, I could see Jake's fist wobbling toward my nose.

    B. Grinning drunkenly, Jake wobbled his fist toward my nose.

    C. Grinning drunkenly, my nose was the target of Jake's fist.

_____ [A, B, or C?] is best.

6

B

....

A good way to correct the sentence about office procedures (above) is to write:

Being a former secretary, _____
_____ [Who?] found the office procedures easy to learn.

7

Which sentences contain dangling modifiers?

    A. Hitting the ball sharply toward left center, the left fielder made a superb leaping catch.

    B. The garden is still muddy, caused by yesterday's rain.

    C. Caused by yesterday's rain, the garden is still muddy.

_____ [A and B, A and C, B and C, or A, B, and C?]

7

A, B, and C

....

To correct sentence A in Frame 7, we need to make clear who _____
_____ . [Did what?]

8

The trouble with B and C in Frame 7 is that neither really seems to tell what was caused by yesterday's rain. Certainly the g ____
_____ [Fill in the missing letters] was not caused by rain, and it does not make sense to say that m _____ [Fill in] was caused by rain.

8

garden, muddy

....

Sizzling in the frying pan, Janice could hear the bacon.

Draw a picture of what that sentence seems to say.

9

One way to improve sentence B or C in Frame 7 is to write:

The garden is still muddy because _____
_____ [What did what?] yesterday.

9

rain fell (*or*) it rained

. . . .

Rewrite the sentence about Janice (*above*) to make clear what sizzled.

10

When opening the door, an alarm sounds in the back room.

Correct that sentence by inserting needed words in each version:

A. Whenever anyone _____ , an alarm sounds in the back room.

B. When opening the door, _____ causes an alarm to sound in the back room.

C. Opening _____ causes an alarm to sound in the back room.

10

A. opens the door
B. an intruder (*or*) a person (*or something similar*)
C. the door

. . . .

Rewrite for greater clarity:

In falling from the second-floor window, her left leg was broken.

11

Complete the sentence below. The first word(s) you write should show who the singer is.

Being a singer, _____

_____ .

11

Model Answer

Being a singer, Dave thought he should be temperamental.

. . . .

Now try completing this one:

Being an only child, _____

_____

_____

_____ .

12

Complete this sentence:

After making an A in biology, _____

_____ .

Check to make sure that you showed who made the A.

12

Model Answer

After making an A in biology, Belle decided to change her major.

· ·

Now complete this:

While shopping, _____

_____

_____

_____ .

13

Complete this sentence:

Kicking and yelling, _____

_____ .

Check to make sure that you showed who kicked and yelled.

13

Model Answer

Kicking and yelling, the little boy tried to gain attention.

· ·

Complete this:

By using leftovers, _____

_____

_____

_____ .

14

Finish honestly: One thing I hope to remember from this exercise is that . . .

(Any answer that you consider honest and accurate is acceptable.)

Lesson 6: Answers to Questions for Added Practice

1. Dad **2.** hound **3.** (A picture of a piano climbing a stairway) **4.** person **5.** *Being a former secretary* **6.** Alice **7.** hit the ball **8.** (A picture of Janice sizzling in a frying pan) **9.** Janice could hear the bacon sizzling in the frying pan. **10.** MODEL: When Georgette fell from the second-floor window, her left leg was broken. **11.** MODEL: Being an only child, Lois might have become badly spoiled. **12.** MODEL: While shopping, she always finds unbelievable bargains. **13.** By using leftovers, the Madisons save thirty dollars a month.

═══7═══

Too Many Short Sentences: How to Combine Them

After writing your answer(s) in the right-hand column, check this column to see whether you have responded correctly. If you have made a mistake, or if you need more practice, do whatever is asked below the dotted line in each answer frame.

Answers to questions for added practice can be found at the end of each lesson.

Understanding and Applying the Principles

1

A wall surrounded the construction site. It was made of wood. Several peepholes had been cut in it. People were looking through the holes. They were watching the workmen.

The _____ [How many?] sentences above contain _____ _____ [How many?] words, an average of fewer than _____ [How many?] words per sentence.

Answers and Added Practice

1

   five, twenty-nine, six

. . . .

The sentences in Frame 1 seem unusually _____. [*short* or *long*?]

2

Although short sentences are often useful, good writers ordinarily mix them with longer ones. In most modern American prose, sentences average about eighteen or twenty words, with a likely range of two or three words up to fifty or more.

   A. The sentences in Frame 1 _____ [*conform* or *do not conform*?] to the average.
   B. They seem _____. [*mature* or *childish*?]

2

   A. do not conform
   B. childish

. . . .

In a passage of about two hundred words in a recent magazine or book, find the average number of words per sentence. _____

3

Let's try to put together some of the short sentences of Frame 1. (We could use several *and*'s, but that wouldn't improve the writing, as we will see in Exercise 8. A good way to combine the first two sentences is to reduce the second sentence to one word:

   A _____ [What kind of?] wall surrounded the construction site.

3

wooden

....

A clamshell digger was lifting scoops of dirt into large trucks. It was huge.

We may combine those sentences by putting the word _____ before the word _____ .

4

We can combine the third sentence of Frame 1 with the first two by reducing it to a few words:

A wooden wall with _____ [What?] cut in it surrounded the construction site.

(We probably could dispense with *cut in it*, but keeping that phrase shows that the holes were made intentionally.)

4

peepholes

....

Several men were building wooden frames. This was in another area. The frames would be used for the concrete foundation.

Combine those three sentences, starting with *In another area.*

5

We can combine the fourth and fifth sentences of Frame 1 in several ways. One way is this:

Through those holes people _____ _____ . [Finish the sentence in four words.]

5

were watching the workmen

....

Combine the fourth and fifth sentences of Frame 1 in another, different way.

6

A wooden wall with peepholes cut in it surrounded the construction site. Through these holes people were watching the workmen.

Our revised sentences are still not long: they average only ten words. However, they seem _____ [*more* or *less*?] mature than the passage in Frame 1.

6

more
....

Rewrite as a single sentence:

Surveyors were there. Some were peering through instruments. Some were making notes. Some were driving stakes.

7

As we have seen, we should often _____ [Do what with?] babyish sentences. Instead of using *and*'s to make such a combination, we may also omit unnecessary words, reduce a sentence to a single _____ [What?] as we did in Frame 3, or reduce it to a _____ as we did in Frames 4 and 5.

7

combine
word
phrase (*or*) few words
....

Rewrite as a single sentence:

We put on some old clothes. Then we went to a grocery store. We needed some picnic supplies.

(Hint: Use *to buy* near the end.)

8

Hippocrates was a Greek. He lived from c. 460 to c. 367 B.C. He has been called the father of medicine.

Combine those three sentences. Hint: Use parentheses around the dates.

8

Model Answer

The Greek Hippocrates (c.470–c.367 B.C.) has been called the father of medicine.

. . . .

Combine these in a similar way:

Geoffrey Chaucer was an English poet. He was born about A.D. 1340 and died in 1400. He is most famous for his *Canterbury Tales*.

9

Model Answer

Jan's uncle lived in Utah as a boy but later moved to Colorado.

. . . .

Combine the following sentence with your answer to Frame 9:

Still later he moved to Vermont.

9

Jan's uncle lived in Utah. That was when he was a boy. He later moved to Colorado.

Combine those three sentences in thirteen words.

10

I watched part of a TV program. It was dull. It was boring. I turned it off.

Combine those four sentences. Use *so . . . that . . .* in the combination.

10

Model Answer

I watched part of a TV program, but it was so dull that I turned it off.

. . . .

Combine with your answer:

It was called "Skeletons I Have Known."

11

We enjoyed an opera last night. It was by Wagner. It was *The Flying Dutchman*. It concerns a Dutch sea captain's attempt to overcome a curse.

Hint: In combining these sentences, start with *Last night,* and use *which* near the middle.

11

Model Answer

Last night we enjoyed Wagner's opera *The Flying Dutchman,* which concerns a Dutch sea captain's attempt to overcome a curse.

12

Finish honestly: One thing I hope to remember from this exercise is that . . .

(Any answer that you consider honest and accurate is acceptable.)

Lesson 7: Answers to Questions for Added Practice

1. short **2.** (Although numbers may vary considerably, the average is likely to be between 15 and 20.) **3.** *huge, clamshell* **4.** MODEL: In another area several men were building wooden frames to be used for the concrete foundation. **5.** MODEL: People were looking through those holes to watch the workmen. **6.** MODEL: Surveyors were peering through instruments, making notes, and driving stakes. **7.** MODEL: We put on some old clothes and went to a grocery store to buy some picnic supplies. **8.** MODEL: Geoffrey Chaucer (A.D. c. 1340–1400) was an English poet, most famous for his *Canterbury Tales*. **9.** . . . but later moved to Colorado and still later to Vermont. **10.** . . . a TV program called "Skeletons I Have Known" . . .

≡≡8≡

Failure to Subordinate: The and . . . and . . . *Sentence*

After writing your answer(s) in the right-hand column, check this column to see whether you have responded correctly. If you have made a mistake, or if you need more practice, do whatever is asked below the dotted line in each answer frame.

Answers to questions for added practice can be found at the end of each lesson.

Understanding and Applying the Principles

1

> **And I speeded up to about forty-five, and it was only a thirty-mile zone, but I thought it was safe because of light traffic, and a red Camaro popped out from a side street, but it should have stopped, and I couldn't brake soon enough, so I broadsided it.**

Out of breath? Well, some people talk and write like that, tying most of their sentences together with *and, but, for, or, nor, yet,* or *so.*

In the boldface sentence, how many times is *and* used? _____ *but?* _____ *so?* _____

Answers and Added Practice

1

four, two, one

. . . .

Do you know anyone who talks like the example in Frame 1? _____
Do you yourself talk that way? _____

_____

2

A sentence like that in Frame 1 is often called an *and . . . and* sentence. It not only leaves the reader rather breathless, but it also fails to show which parts are most important.

Probably the two most important facts in the example are that the narrator was _____ [Doing what?] and that as a result he _____ .
[Did what?]

2

Model Answers

    speeding, hit another car

. . . .

If you disagree with the model answers, explain why.

3

Often an *and . . . and* sentence can best be corrected by dividing it into two or three sentences. We may decide which facts or ideas are most important and then arrange the rest around them.

    For instance, we may combine the parts of Frame 1 related to speeding in this way:

    Although I was in a _____ [What kind of?] zone, I speeded up to about forty-five, which seemed safe because _____ .

3

    thirty-mile, of light traffic

. . . .

Note that the main idea is expressed in the main clause (the independent clause).

4

One way to combine the parts of Frame 1 describing the accident is this:

    When a red Camaro popped out from _____ _____ [Where?] without stopping, I couldn't _____ [Do what?] soon enough to avoid _____ . [Doing what?]

4

    a side street, brake, broadsiding it

. . . .

In this combination, *I couldn't brake soon enough* is the main clause. In another version the main clause could be *I broadsided it.*

5

Observe that the corrections made in Frames 3 and 4 divide the long, breathless Frame 1 sentence into _____ [How many?] sentences.

    Observe also that some unimportant words have been omitted. Are any important facts omitted? _____

5

    A. two B. No

. . . .

Sometimes, of course, an *and . . . and* sentence can be improved without dividing it. At other times, in contrast, more than two sentences are needed.

6

Let's review the steps in improving an *and . . . and* sentence:

    A. First, we decide which are the most _____ facts or ideas.

    B. Second, we decide how we can best change the form of the less important statements to attach them to the more _____ ones.

6

    A. important B. important

. . . .

Look back at Frames 3 and 4 to see just how the forms of the less important statements were changed.

7

    Our drive to Miami was long, and nothing much happened, and my little brother and sister were bored, and they kept fussing with each other.

The two most important facts in that *and . . . and* sentence concern:

    A. the tiresomeness of _____ . [What?]
    B. the behavior of _____ . [Whom?]

7

Model Answers
    A. the drive
    B. the children

. . . .

They quarreled about their seats, and they played a game, and they argued about that, and one wanted to stop for ice cream, and one didn't want to stop.

    The children disagreed about

(a) _____ , (b) _____

_____ , and (c)

_____ .

8

One way to improve the sentence in Frame 7 is this:

    The drive to Miami was long and unev _____ . My

    b _____ little brother and sister kept _____

_____ . [Doing what?]

8

    uneventful, bored, fussing with each other

. . . .

Rewrite the sentence in the answer to Frame 7. Use no more than fourteen words, starting with *They argued.*

9

It is also possible to combine the two sentences in Frame 8, perhaps like this:

    During the _____ , _____ drive to Miami,
    my bored _____

_____ .

9

long, uneventful, little brother and sister kept fussing with each other

. . . .

The original sentence (in Frame 7) had no central focus. This revision focuses on the actions of _____ _____ _____ .

10

I enjoy life in a college dormitory, and I have gained several friends, and I especially enjoy being with them.

Rewrite that sentence in whatever way seems best to you.

10

Model Answer

In my college dormitory I especially enjoy being with several new friends.

. . . .

Add to your rewritten sentence the fact that you share with those friends an interest in sports.

11

High school life was different, for all of us lived at home, and we were not often together at night, and on weekends we usually went our own ways.

Again, rewrite in the way that seems best.

11

Model Answer

High school life was different because we all lived at home and were seldom together at night or on weekends.

. . . .

Note that the improved version often is more compact. The model answer above (twenty words) is _____ _____ [How many?] words shorter than the original sentence.

12

Finish honestly: One thing I hope to remember from this exercise is that . . .

(Any answer that you consider honest and accurate is acceptable.)

Lesson 8: Answers to Questions for Added Practice

1. (Either *Yes* or *No* is acceptable.) **2.** (Some people may want to emphasize the reckless driver of the Camaro.) **7.** MODEL: their seats, a game, and making a stop for ice cream. **8.** MODEL: They argued about their seats, a game, and making a stop for ice cream. **9.** MODEL: the quarrelsome children **10.** MODEL: In my college dormitory I especially enjoy sharing with several new friends my interest in sports. **11.** nine

═══9═══
The Compound Sentence: The Parts Should Be Clearly Related

After writing your answer(s) in the right-hand column, check this column to see whether you have responded correctly. If you have made a mistake, or if you need more practice, do whatever is asked below the dotted line in each answer frame.

Answers to questions for added practice can be found at the end of each lesson.

Understanding and Applying the Principles

1

> **The quarterback successfully sneaked across the goal line, but because of a penalty he scored no touchdown.**

A satisfactory compound sentence, such as the one above, has two or more related and equally important parts. Each part is called an *independent clause*, because it can stand alone, or independently, as a sentence.

In the example above, the first independent clause ends with the word _____ .

Answers and Added Practice

1

line

. . . .

If a clause is independent, it can be written correctly with a capital letter and a period. Test the two clauses in Frame 1 (*The . . . line*, and *because . . . touchdown*) to see that they are independent.

2

In the example in Frame 1, both independent clauses describe the same event. Write a complete sentence to tell what event both describe.

2

Model Answer

Both describe a play in a football game.

. . . .

Is it *likely* that a compound sentence would have one clause about football and another about the Sargasso Sea? _____

3

Sometimes a compound sentence is poor because the two (or more) independent clauses are not sufficiently alike, or because the similarity is not clearly shown. When two thoughts are expressed in the same sentence, they should be closely and clearly related.

In other words, the clauses of a compound sentence should be about _____ [*connected* or *unconnected*?] events, things, or ideas.

3

connected

. . . .

Is it likely that a compound sentence might have one clause concerning alligators, and a second clause starting with *but* and concerning crocodiles? _____

4

The hillsides have only a few trees, and skiing is a delightful and rather safe sport.

Those two clauses seem to be _____ . [*related* or *unrelated*?]

4

unrelated

. . . .

Alligators have short, flat heads, but crocodiles have long, narrow heads.

Is that a good compound sentence?

_____

5

The student who wrote the sentence in Frame 4 had a relationship in mind, but he did not show what it was. He intended to say that because the hillsides are not heavily wooded, skiing in that area is delightful and relatively safe. He might have written:

The hillsides have only a few trees, and for that reason skiing down them _____

_____ .

---

5 ·

is delightful and rather safe.

. . . .

Here is another good version, although not a compound sentence:

Skiing is delightful and rather safe on those almost treeless hillsides.

6

Martha Malone has a keen mind, and she is almost eighty years old.

Both clauses in that sentence concern Martha Malone, but their relationship is otherwise not completely clear. A good way to clarify relationships is to make one of the clauses dependent (which results in a complex rather than a compound sentence).

The sentence above could thus be written:

Although Martha Malone is almost 80 years old, she still _____ . [Finish the sentence.]

6

has a keen mind

· ·

Heavy rains came, and the farmer's corn was not picked.

Clarify the relationship by starting with *When* and putting *yet* in the second clause.

7

Another way to improve the sentence in Frame 6 is to change one of the independent clauses into two or three words:

Though almost eighty, _____
_____ . [Finish
the sentence.]

7

Martha Malone still has a keen mind.

· ·

Keen-minded Martha Malone is
_____

_____ .

[Finish the sentence.]

8

We have been seeing that the parts of a compound sentence should be closely related and that the relationship must be made clear. We also have observed that sometimes it is wise to
_____ [Do what?] the sentence to show the relationship.

8

rewrite (*or*) revise

· ·

Sometimes the revised sentence is complex or simple, not compound. (See also Exercise 12.)

9

In which compound sentence are the two clauses more closely related?

    A. The word processor has a black case, and I use it regularly in my writing.

    B. The lost word processor has a black case, and its serial number is 846–2491K.

_____ [A or B?]

9

B

· ·

    A. **Louise Long is an artist, and she gave me some used brushes.**

    B. **Louise Long, an artist, gave me some used brushes to help me in learning basic techniques.**

_____ [A or B?] is the better sentence.

10

Again, in which of the following sentences is the relationship more clearly shown?

    A. I saw a chipmunk hurry into its burrow, and a shadow passed across the ground.

    B. I saw a chipmunk hurry into its burrow, and the swift shadow of a hawk told me why.

_____ [A or B?]

10

B

. . . .

Add a closely related clause to this one:

I was happy to be admitted to this college

11

Rewrite to show a clear relationship between the clauses:

Traffic was heavy that day, and Christmas was only a week off.

11

Model Answer

Traffic was heavy that day, for Christmas shoppers knew they had only a week left.

. . . .

Rewrite to clarify the relationship:

Her car wouldn't start, and batteries are expensive.

12

Write a sentence in which you combine these three sentences and show some sort of relationship:

Phoenix is the largest city in Arizona.

Mesa is a suburb.

The Cubs hold spring training in Mesa.

12

Model Answer

The Cubs hold spring practice in Mesa, a suburb of Phoenix, Arizona's largest city.

. . . .

Improve:

Our high school band won the state championship, and my brother played a tuba.

13

Finish honestly: One thing I hope to remember from this exercise is that . . .

(Any answer that you consider honest and accurate is acceptable.)

Lesson 9: Answers to Questions for Added Practice

1. The quarterback successfully sneaked across the goal line. Because of a penalty he scored no touchdown. **2.** No **3.** Yes **4.** Yes **6.** When heavy rains came, the farmer's corn was not yet picked. **7.** MODEL: almost eighty years old. **9.** B **10.** MODEL: I was happy to be admitted to this college, for it has excellent professors in my field. **11.** Her car wouldn't start, and she hoped she would not have to buy an expensive new battery. **12.** MODEL: My brother played a tuba in the state champion high school band.

══10══

The Run-together Sentence: The Comma Splice

After writing your answer(s) in the right-hand column, check this column to see whether you have responded correctly. If you have made a mistake, or if you need more practice, do whatever is asked below the dotted line in each answer frame.

Answers to questions for added practice can be found at the end of each lesson.

Understanding and Applying the Principles

1

> **One of the pioneers of glider flight was a German named Otto Lilienthal he was followed by the French-born American Octave Chanute and by the Wright brothers.**

Read carefully the passage above. It could be divided by a period and a capital letter after _____ . [What word?]

Answers and Added Practice

1

Lilienthal

. . . .

Lilienthal studied buoyancy and air resistance he also tried to find ways to stabilize aircraft.

That passage could be divided after the word _____ .

2

In Frame 1 the first thirteen words are an independent clause. That is, they can be written and punctuated as a separate sentence. Read those words, aloud if possible, to decide whether or not they sound complete.

Read the rest of the passage, aloud if possible.

A. Does it also sound complete? _____

B. Is it an independent clause? _____

2

A. Yes   B. Yes

....

In 1891 Lilienthal began testing his gliders the first ones sailed only very short distances.

That passage could be divided after the word _____ .

Does it contain two independent clauses? _____

3

The reason for punctuation marks is that they help readers to understand each sentence quickly and easily.

A. Would the passage in Frame 1 be easier to understand if a punctuation mark followed *Lilienthal*? _____

B. In Answer Frames 1 and 2, would the boldface passages be easier to read if they were punctuated properly? ____

_____

3

A. Yes   B. Yes

....

Lilienthal constructed a hill that had the slope he wanted he took off by running downhill into the wind with his glider.

That sentence needs punctuation after the word _____ .

4

One of the pioneers of glider flight was the German Otto Lilienthal. He was followed by the French-born American Octave Chanute and by the Wright brothers.

Often the best way to prevent run-together independent clauses like those in Frame 1 is that illustrated above.

To avoid running the independent clauses together, we have added a _____ [What mark?] after *Lilienthal* and have _____ [Done what to?] *he.*

4

period, capitalized

....

Copy the boldface sentence in Answer Frame 3, adding a period and a capital letter in the appropriate places.

5

One of the pioneers of glider flight was the German Otto Lilienthal; he was followed by the French-born American Octave Chanute and by the Wright brothers.

When two independent clauses are closely related in meaning, they may be separated by a semicolon rather than a period. (For more information about semicolons, see Lesson 77.)

A. In the passage above, does the semicolon go in the same place a period would? _____

B. Is the letter capitalized after the semicolon? _____

5

     A. Yes B. No

. . . .

Copy your sentence from Answer Frame 4, but use a semicolon.

6

One of the pioneers of glider flight was the German Otto Lilienthal, and he was followed by the French-born American Octave Chanute and by the Wright brothers.

A third way to avoid a run-together sentence is to separate the independent clauses with a comma and a coordinating conjunction: *and, but, for, or, nor,* and possibly *yet* or *so.*

    A. In the passage above, a _____ [What mark?] is used in the place where a semicolon appeared in Frame 5.

    B. The comma is aided by the coordinating conjunction _____ . [What word?]

6

     A. comma   B. *and*

. . . .

Copy the boldface sentence from Answer Frame 2. Use a comma and *but* between the two independent clauses.

7

One of the pioneers of glider flight was the German Otto Lilienthal, who was followed by the French-born American Octave Chanute and by the Wright brothers.

A final way to avoid the run-together sentence is illustrated above. One independent clause has been changed to a dependent clause.

    A. A _____ [What mark?] has been used.

    B. The first word of the dependent clause is _____ .

7

     A. comma   B. *who*

. . . .

Copy the boldface sentence from Answer Frame 3. However, start the sentence with *After,* and put a comma after *wanted.*

8

WRONG: One of the pioneers of glider flight was the German Otto Lilienthal, he was followed by the French-born American Octave Chanute and by the Wright brothers.

Note that in this incorrect passage only a comma separates the independent clauses. Most writers, editors, and teachers do not consider a comma strong enough to perform that job. A sentence punctuated in that way is still considered run together. The error is also sometimes called a "fused sentence," a "run-on sentence," or a "comma splice." Many teachers penalize it.

    Obviously it is _____ [*wise* or *unwise*?] to use only a comma to separate independent clauses.

8

unwise

....

Which one of these remedies for a run-together sentence is generally considered wrong?

period and capital

semicolon alone

comma plus a coordinating conjunction

comma with a dependent clause

comma alone

9

Let's summarize four correct ways to avoid a run-together sentence:

   A. Use a _____ [What mark?] and a _____ [What kind of?] letter.

   B. Use a _____ [What mark?] alone.

   C. Use a _____ [What mark?] and *and, but, for, or, nor,* or possibly *yet* or *so.*

   D. Change one of the independent clauses into a _____ _____ [What kind of?] clause.

9

   A. period, capital

   B. semicolon

   C. comma

   D. dependent

....

Look again at the boldface sentence in Answer Frame 1. Note that any of the first three methods of correction could easily be used there.

10

Octave Chanute first built railroads and railroad bridges his interest during his sixties turned to gliding.

   A. That run-together sentence needs to be divided after _____ . [What word?]

   B. As a divider we can use a _____ [What mark?] and a _____ [What kind of?] letter, or a _____ [What mark?] alone.

10

   A. *bridges*

   B. period, capital, semicolon

....

In the boldface sentence in Answer Frame 2, what dividers obviously can be used?

11

To avoid the run-together sentence in Frame 10 we could also:

   A. Use a _____ [What mark?] and the coordinating conjunction _____ [What word?] after *bridges.*

   B. Start the sentence with *Although,* and put a comma after _____ . [What word?]

11

    A. comma, *but*

    B. *bridges*

. . . .

Rewrite the boldface sentence in Answer Frame 2, using *when* or *although* to correct the run-together problem.

12

In 1896 Lilienthal was killed in a glider crash Chanute made over two thousand flights without accident.

A. That run-together sentence should be divided after _____ . [What word?]

B. A period and a capital, or else a semicolon would be an easy way to mark the division, but neither would show how the two parts are related. A comma and the coordinating conjunction _____ would be more appropriate.

C. An additional kind of change would be to put *although* at the _____ of the sentence and a _____ _____ [What mark?] after *crash*.

D. Using a comma alone as the divider between the independent clauses would be _____ . [*correct* or *incorrect*?]

12

    A. *crash* B. *but*

    C. beginning, comma

    D. incorrect

. . . .

In what ways may this run-together sentence be corrected?

Chanute knew the Wright brothers well he helped them by providing data and by visiting Kitty Hawk frequently.

13

Finish honestly: One thing I hope to remember from this exercise is that . . .

(Any answer that you consider honest and accurate is acceptable.)

Lesson 10: Answers to Questions for Added Practice

1. *resistance* **2.** *gliders* Yes **3.** *wanted* **4.** Lilienthal constructed a hill that had the slope he wanted. He took off by running downhill into the wind with his glider. **5.** . . . wanted; he . . . **6.** In 1891 Lilienthal began testing his gliders, but the first one sailed only short distances. **7.** After Lilienthal constructed a hill that had the slope he wanted, he took off by running downhill with his glider. **8.** comma alone **10.** period and capital, semicolon alone, comma plus a coordinating conjunction, comma with a dependent clause **11.** When in 1891 Lilienthal began testing his gliders, the first ones sailed only very short distances. **12.** period and capital, semicolon alone, comma plus a coordinating conjunction (probably *and*), dependent clause (perhaps starting with *Because*, and with a comma after *well*)

11

The Stuffed Sentence: Too Fully Packed

After writing your answer(s) in the right-hand column, check this column to see whether you have responded correctly. If you have made a mistake, or if you need more practice, do whatever is asked below the dotted line in each answer frame.

Answers to questions for added practice can be found at the end of each lesson.

Understanding and Applying the Principles

1

> The national parks of the United States, according to the National Parks Act of 1916, which established the National Park Service and has not been basically altered since that time, are priceless possessions of the American public and should be carefully preserved and maintained, it is generally agreed.

That sentence seems almost as crowded as a subway car in rush hour. Why wouldn't you like to read several pages of sentences like that?

_____

_____

Answers and Added Practice

1

Model Answer
> The writer squeezes too much information into a single sentence. (*or*) Such sentences are tiring to read.

. . . .

Name one specific change you would now recommend to improve the sentence in Frame 1.

2

If you suspect that one of your own sentences is too fully packed, the first step in correcting it is to see whether any part(s) of it may be completely eliminated.

In the Frame 1 sentence, are the last four words needed?

_____

2

　　　No

. . . .

In addition to being unnecessary in this sentence, *it is generally agreed* ends the sentence _____ .
[*strongly* or *weakly*?]

3

Look at the words *and should be carefully preserved and maintained* in Frame 1.

A. Isn't it true that all "priceless possessions" should be carefully preserved and maintained? _____
B. If so, can we eliminate those seven words? _____

3

     A. Yes B. Yes

. . . .

Another example: A newspaper article referred to "the modern world of today." Which word or words should be left out? _____

_____ (See also Exercise 48.)

4

After those deletions the original sentence has been reduced to this:

> The national parks of the United States, according to the National Park Act of 1916, which established the National Park Service and has not been basically altered since that time, are priceless possessions of the American public.

    A. Is that sentence better than the original? _____
    B. Does it still seem a little too fully packed? _____

4

     A. Yes B. Yes

. . . .

Obviously we should avoid both overlong sentences and a large number of short sentences. Aristotle said, "Nothing too much!"

5

Let's try dividing the sentence in Frame 4. One possibility:

    A. The national parks of the United States are _____

    _____ .

    [Finish the sentence.]

    B. So says the National Park Act, which established the National Park Service in 1916 and _____

    _____ .

    [Finish the sentence.]

5

    A. priceless possessions of the American public.
    B. has not been basically altered since that time.

. . . .

Possibly in Answer B three more words can be cut: _____

_____ _____ .

6

We have seen two possible ways to improve an excessively crowded sentence:

    A. We can remove _____ [What kind of?] words, phrases, or clauses.
    B. We can _____ [Do what?] the sentence into two or more shorter sentences.

6

    A. unnecessary (*or*) redundant
    B. divide (*or*) separate, etc.

. . . .

Look back at Frames 2, 3, and 5 to review the ways these things were done in the example.

7

> The National Park Act said that the parks should "conserve the scenery and the natural and historic objects and the wildlife therein and provide for the enjoyment of the same in such manner and by such means as will leave them unimpaired for the enjoyment of future generations," but some unthinking or selfish people, as they always are likely to do, have attempted to undermine that purpose.

Name one way in which that sentence is like the example in Frame 1.

7

Model Answer

It includes unnecessary information. (*or*) It should be divided.

....

In a few words, what do you dislike most about the sentence in Frame 7?

8

Perhaps in the Frame 7 sentence we should not try to simplify or shorten the quotation from the Act. If we do choose to summarize it, we can save a few words, maybe in this way:

The National Park Act says that the parks should conserve

_____

_____ [What four things?] for the enjoyment of people today and _____ .
[When?]

8

Model Answer

scenery, natural and historic objects, and wildlife . . . for the future

....

Do you prefer to keep the legal language of the Act or to summarize it?

9

Some unthinking or selfish people, as they always are likely to do, have attempted to undermine that purpose.

That is the end of the sentence in Frame 7. What words are not really necessary?

_____

9

as they always are likely to do

....

Explain briefly why those words are unnecessary.

10

The second sentence in Frame 7 will look like this:

Some unthinking or selfish people, however, _____
_____ . [Finish the sentence.]

10

have attempted to undermine
that purpose

. . . .

Read to yourself the complete revision of the sentence in Frame 7.

11

They have, for instance, asked to build in
parks miniature golf courses, which certainly
are not "natural and historic," sell helicopter
rides, which would disturb wildlife, build
railroads for sightseeing, which would drive
most wildlife out of sight, develop mines, build
summer theaters or gambling casinos or
gunnery ranges or full-sized golf courses,
which would require roads and parking lots
and perhaps teaching animals to flee when
they hear "Fore!" and run a cable car into the
Grand Canyon.

That sentence is richly packed with interesting details, most of
which should no doubt be kept, although better arranged. The
sentence might be improved if it were divided. The first new
sentence might mention the less extreme suggestions for park
use, and the second could tell about the wilder ideas. It could
start with an expression such as *Among the most ridiculous requests
are . . .*

Suggest a different possible beginning:

_____

_____

11

Model Answer

Some developers even wanted
to . . .

. . . .

Think about which of the listed
proposals seem most ridiculous to
you. Then write about them, starting your sentences with the words
you wrote in Frame 11.

12

Finish honestly: One thing I hope to remember from this lesson
is that . . .

(Any answer that you consider honest and accurate is acceptable.)

Lesson 11: Answers to Questions for Added Practice

1. MODEL: I would divide it into two sentences. (*Or*) I would omit some parts of it. **2.** weakly **3.** Either *modern* or *of today* **5.** *Since that time* **7.** (Answers will vary. Take credit for whatever you wrote.) **8.** Either answer is satisfactory. **9.** MODEL: The statement is too obvious. **11.** MODEL: Some developers even wanted to build gambling casinos, gunnery ranges, or full-sized golf courses.

══12══

In a Complex Sentence: Stress the Main Idea

After writing your answer(s) in the right-hand column, check this column to see whether you have responded correctly. If you have made a mistake, or if you need more practice, do whatever is asked below the dotted line in each answer frame.

Answers to questions for added practice can be found at the end of each lesson.

Understanding and Applying the Principles

1

Karen was walking past the Blake house.

She saw smoke pouring from a window.

Which drawing shows the more important event? _____
[First or Second?]

Answers and Added Practice

1

Second

. . . .

Why is the second more important?

2

If we talk about the two events in Frame 1, we are likely to emphasize the _____ . [*first* or *second*?]

2

second

. . . .

Why?

3

When we combine the two sentences in Frame 1, we have at least three choices. The first is a compound sentence:

> **Karen was walking past the Blake house, and she saw smoke pouring from a window.**

In a good compound sentence, the content of the two clauses should be about equally important. Is that true in our sentence?

3

No

. . . .

How do you know?

4

Unsatisfied with our first attempt, we try this complex sentence:

> **Karen was walking past the Blake house when she saw smoke pouring from a window.**

Here we have put the more important fact (the smoke) into the less important clause of the sentence (the dependent clause, starting with *when*). A dependent clause should depend on—be attached to—the stronger, independent clause.

Is our sentence a good one? _____

4

No

. . . .

A complex sentence has at least one independent clause with one or more dependent clauses attached to it. A dependent clause most often provides useful but incidental information.

5

Still unsatisfied, we revise our complex sentence:

> **When Karen was walking past the Blake house, she saw smoke pouring from a window.**

This time the less important information (walking past the house) has been placed in the _____ [*more* or *less*?] important clause.

5

less

....

Sometimes the independent clause in a complex sentence is called the main clause. Why?

6

Our example in Frame 4 is upside down. That is, it has the less important fact in the more important clause.

Our example in Frame 5, however, is right side up. It has the less important fact in the less important clause.

Obviously the sentence in Frame _____ [What number?] is better.

6

5

....

In Frame 5, the more important idea is in the _____ [*independent* or *dependent*?] clause.

7

Which statement is true?

   A. The "big information" belongs in the independent clause, and the "little information" in the dependent clause.

   B. The "big information" belongs in the dependent clause, and the "little information" in the independent clause.

_____ [A or B?]

7

A

....

While Karen was wondering whether to turn in an alarm, she heard the siren of an approaching fire engine.

In that sentence, is the "big information" in the independent clause?

_____

8

In writing about Glenn's appearance, should we probably emphasize his good looks or the small scar on his cheek? _____

8

His good looks

....

Using *although*, combine these two facts in a good complex sentence:

The skies were cloudy.
It did not snow.

9

Which is the better way to write about Glenn's appearance?

   A. Although Glenn is handsome, he has a tiny scar on one cheek.

   B. Although Glenn has a tiny scar on one cheek, that does not really hurt his appearance.

_____ [A or B?]

9

B

....

Using *when*, and perhaps changing the order of the clauses, combine these two facts in a good complex sentence.

The probable victor still could not be predicted.
The war was eight months old.

10

Combine in a good complex sentence:

Ken was riding his bicycle down Tremont Street.

He almost was hit by a car fleeing from a police car in fast pursuit.

10

When (or While) Ken was riding his bicycle down Tremont Street, he was almost hit by a car fleeing from a pursuing police car.

. . . .

That sentence is good because it emphasizes that Ken was _____ _____. [*riding* or *almost hit?*]

11

Compose a good complex sentence based on those two drawings. The swimmer's name is Ralph.

11

Model Answer

While Ralph was swimming in the Gulf, he suddenly saw a shark only a few feet away.

. . . .

Explain why your answer is better than one that emphasizes the swimming.

12

Finish honestly: One thing I hope to remember from this lesson is that . . .

(In this frame, any answer you consider honest and accurate is acceptable.)

Lesson 12: Answers to Questions for Added Practice

1. MODEL: A house on fire is usually more important than a stroll. **2.** See 1. **3.** See 1. **5.** It supposedly carries more important information. **6.** independent **7.** Yes **8.** MODEL: Although the skies were cloudy, it did not snow. **9.** MODEL: When the war was eight months old, the probable victor still could not be predicted. **10.** almost hit **11.** MODEL: Ralph's danger is more important than his taking a swim.

≡13≡

The House That Jack Built: Too Many that's, who's, because's

After writing your answer(s) in the right-hand column, check this column to see whether you have responded correctly. If you have made a mistake, or if you need more practice, do whatever is asked below the dotted line in each answer frame.

Answers to questions for added practice can be found at the end of each lesson.

Understanding and Applying the Principles

1

> **This is the cat**
> **That killed the rat**
> **That ate the malt**
> **That lay in the house**
> **That Jack built.**

How many *that*'s are in the part of the old rhyme quoted here?

Answers and Added Practice

1

   Four

. . . .

What is the title of the old rhyme?

_____

(If you don't know, look at the title of this lesson.)

2

Sentences that have several clauses starting with *that, who, which, because,* or possibly some other connecting word, are sometimes called "house-that-Jack-built" sentences.

   A. The reason, obviously, is that such sentences are similar to _____ .

   B. Those sentences may be unintentionally amusing, and they _____ [*are* or *are not*?] likely to seem awkward.

2

    A. "The House That Jack Built"

    B. are

. . . .

Note this example from a news story:

> **"Mr. Collins is the officer who arrested the suspect who is charged with attacking Samuel Rice, who is a prominent local pharmacist."**

3

Let's play with rewriting the cat sentence. We'll chop out a few words and make other changes.

    This _____ [What?] killed the _____ [What?] that ate the malt _____ [In three words, where was the malt?] that _____. [Who did what?]

3

    This cat killed the rat that ate the malt in the house that Jack built.

. . . .

Or we could end it like this: the house constructed by _____.

4

> **Thad Wiggins, who is a Democrat, is one man who surely will vote for Marston, who is the Democrat who has the best chance to beat Kruger, who has strong Republican support.**

The writer of that sentence may be over-friendly with an _____ _____. [What three-letter bird?].

4

    owl (of course)

. . . .

Rewrite the boldface sentence in Answer Frame 2. Reduce the *who*'s to one or none.

5

After one has written a sentence like that in Frame 4, it's obviously time to commit *who*icide.

    Thad Wiggins, a _____, will surely vote for Marston, the Democrat _____ [Substitute one word for *who has*.] the best chance to beat Kruger, who has strong Republican support.

5

Democrat, with

. . . .

Note that the changes also make the sentence more compact. By eliminating _____ [How many?] words, we've saved some paper and ink.

6

The covered bridge, which spans a stream which powers a grist mill which my great-grandfather built and which is still in operation, is over a hundred years old.

A. A *which*-hunt reveals _____ [How many?] in that sentence.

B. Rewrite the sentence, keeping only the first *which* or none at all.

6

A. four

B. **Model Answer**
The covered bridge, which spans the stream that powers a grist mill built by my great-grandfather and still in operation, is over a hundred years old.

. . . .

Rest for a moment.

7

Laura is afraid that she will unintentionally say something that will offend the others that ride to work with her.

Rewrite to eliminate all three *that*'s.

7

Model Answer

Laura is afraid she will unintentionally say something to offend the others who ride to work with her.

. . . .

Either *who* or *that* may refer to people. Some inexperienced writers avoid *who* because they are afraid it should be *whom*.

8

As a high school junior and senior I studied hard because I wanted to be admitted to State University because State is strong in civil engineering because of a faculty with much theoretical and practical knowledge because I want to become a civil engineer.

That sentence needs much work and not only because of *because's*. Try to rewrite it as two good sentences.

8

Model Answer

As a high school junior and senior I studied hard because I wanted to be admitted into civil engineering at State University. State's faculty members, who have had much practical experience, make its civil engineering program strong.

9

Finish honestly: One thing I hope to remember from this lesson is that . . .

(Any answer that you consider honest and accurate is acceptable.)

Lesson 13: Answers to Questions for Added Practice

1. "The House That Jack Built" **3.** Jack **4.** MODEL: Mr. Collins is the officer who arrested the suspect charged with attacking Samuel Rice, a prominent local pharmacist. **5.** nine

═══14═══

More about Clauses: A Slenderizing Diet

After writing your answer(s) in the right-hand column, check this column to see whether you have responded correctly. If you have made a mistake, or if you need more practice, do whatever is asked below the dotted line in each answer frame.

Answers to questions for added practice can be found at the end of each lesson.

Understanding and Applying the Principles

1

> **That which one does in a manner that is unnecessarily hasty is likely to bring about a result that is wasteful.**

The sentence above is wordy. It consists of one independent clause embedding three dependent clauses.

It contains _____ [How many?] words.

Answers and Added Practice

1

twenty-one

· ·

If a man goes to bed early, and if he gets up early, it is probable that he will have good health, that he will amass a fortune, and that he will possess wisdom.

How many words are in that disguised old saying? _____

2

The sentence in Frame 1 is a disguised old saying. Over four hundred years ago, when John Heywood first wrote it down, he said it all in a three-word independent clause.

If you recognize the old saying, write it. _____

_____ _____

2

"Haste makes waste."
Give yourself credit whether or not you knew the answer. Heywood actually wrote, "Haste maketh waste."

. . . .

What old saying is this?

A feathered creature that is actually in one's grasp is preferable to two other such feathered ones that are only sitting in some bush.

3

Of course, clauses are necessary. Almost every good sentence has at least one. But, like other good things, clauses may be overused.

Which is better, A or B?
A. The four-clause sentence in Frame 1
B. "Haste makes waste."

_____

3

B

. . . .

Look again at the disguised old sayings in Answer Frames 1 and 2. Which are better, the short original versions or the inflated versions?

4

Here is another example of a sentence with clauses that need slenderizing (s = subject, v = verb).

$$\overset{s}{\text{Billy's toy}}\ \overset{s}{\text{car,}}\ \overset{s}{\text{which}}\ \overset{v}{\text{was made of plastic,}}$$

$$\overset{v}{\text{was broken}}\ \text{by Mike,}\ \overset{s}{\text{who}}\ \overset{v}{\text{was a little neigh-}}$$

$$\text{bor boy}\ \overset{s}{\text{who}}\ \overset{v}{\text{was visiting at our house.}}$$

The basic parts of the independent clause are *car was broken*. In addition, the sentence contains _____ [How many?] dependent clauses.

4

three

. . . .

The length of the sentence in Frame 4 seems _____.
[*about right* or *excessive?*]

5

In the example in Frame 4, instead of the first ten words, we could write:

Billy's _____ [What kind of?] car was broken.

5

plastic

....

Shorten:

Dave bumped into a wall that was made of concrete.

6

Now we'll slenderize the other two dependent clauses in Frame 4.

    A. Would the sentence be clear if we left out the first *who was?* _____

    B. *Who was visiting at our house* is _____
_____. [*probably essential* or *probably not needed at all?*]

6

    A. Yes

    B. probably not needed at all

....

Rewrite in twelve words the boldface sentence in Frame 4.

7

Label each statement *True* or *False*.

_____ 1. We should use no more clauses than necessary.

_____ 2. Some clauses can be reduced to a single word.

_____ 3. Some clauses can be reduced to a few words.

_____ 4. Some clauses can be omitted.

_____ 5. Every clause should be shortened or omitted.

7

    1–4. True

    5. False

....

Explain why statement 5 in Frame 7 is false.

8

                  s   s   v   v

A large cat that was yellow was stalking a

         s   v

robin that was too young to fly.

    A. The word _____ can replace the clause *that was yellow.*

    B. The two words _____ _____ can be omitted from *that was too young to fly.*

    C. Write the slenderized sentence.

8

    A. *yellow*

    B. *that was*

    C. A large, yellow cat was stalking a robin too young to fly.

. . . .

Your revision of the sentence in Frame 8 saved _____ [How many?] words.

9

A good vocabulary can be of considerable value. There's a single word that means that a bird does not yet have its flight feathers and so is obviously unable to fly.

    A. If you know that word, write it. _____

    B. If you don't, look at the answer to A.

    C. Rewrite the sentence in Frame 8, using the word.

9

    A. unfledged

    C. A large yellow cat was stalking an unfledged robin.

. . . .

Unfeathered or *naked* might be all right, but *unfledged* refers specifically to having no feathers suitable for flying.

10

    People who think for themselves prefer newspapers that present details of important events.

    A. The clause *who think for themselves* can be shortened to the word _____ (and placed before *people*).

    B. Can *that present details of important events* be reduced to one or two words? _____

10

    A. thinking (*or*) thoughtful

    B. No

. . . .

Shorten to about ten words:

    Children who are active usually have fewer physical problems than those do who sit around most of the time.

(Hint: Do you know the word *sedentary*?)

11

    Because they planned to arrive early, they would have enough time that they could ride donkeys down into the canyon.

Rewrite, starting your sentence with *By*. Try for fourteen words in all.

11

Model Answer

By arriving early, they would have enough time to ride donkeys into the canyon.

. . . .

What three changes were made in the revision of the sentence?

12

Write a sentence about a child who was intelligent and who was something else and something else. Use at least three clauses in all.

12

Model Answer

Clara was a little girl who was intelligent, and she was also unusually athletic.

. . . .

Including the independent clauses, that sentence contains _____ [How many?] clauses.

13

Now slenderize the sentence you wrote in Frame 12.

13

Model Answer

Clara was an intelligent and unusually athletic little girl.

. . . .

Is a good sentence *compact* or *spread out?* _____

14

Finish honestly: One thing I hope to remember from this lesson is . . .

(In this frame, any answer that you consider honest and accurate is acceptable.)

Lesson 14: Answers to Questions for Added Practice

1. Thirty-four **2.** A bird in the hand is worth two in the bush. **3.** The short versions are better. **4.** excessive **5.** Dave bumped into a concrete wall. **6.** MODEL: Billy's plastic toy car was broken by Mike, a little visiting neighbor. **7.** Some clauses are necessary and are not too long. **8.** four **10.** MODEL: Active children usually have fewer physical problems than sedentary children do. **11.** Two clauses were reduced to phrases, and *down* was eliminated. **12.** Three **13.** Compact

═══15═══

Infinitives: May They Ever Be Split?

After writing your answer(s) in the right-hand column, check this column to see whether you have responded correctly. If you have made a mistake, or if you need more practice, do whatever is asked below the dotted line in each answer frame.

Answers to questions for added practice can be found at the end of each lesson.

Understanding and Applying the Principles

1

An infinitive is a verb form that usually appears after *to*. Copy the five verb forms below that are infinitives.

to complain	**to laugh**	**having been lost**
departing	**to be told**	**were recalled**
to detect	**collapsing**	**to have been sold**

Answers and Added Practice

1

to complain, to laugh, to be told, to detect, to have been sold

. . . .

Note: A few infinitives appear without *to*, as in "Dad made me *try* again" or "Let me *help* you," but these cause no problems.

2

In Latin an infinitive, such as *videre*, "to see," is a single word and so cannot be separated. Eighteenth-century grammarians of English, influenced by Latin, argued that because a Latin infinitive is not split by inserting a word or words, an English infinitive should not be.

Does that seem to be a convincing argument? _____

2

(Probably not)

. . . .

Although the English language has borrowed thousands of *words* from Latin, its grammar is basically Germanic (also called Teutonic).

3

In the near-darkness it was difficult *to quickly see* whether a man was friend or foe.

Most eighteenth-century grammarians would have said that *to quickly see* is _____.
[*unquestionably wrong* or *possibly acceptable*?]

3

unquestionably wrong

· ·

Would those grammarians have liked this: "To hurriedly decide would be a mistake"? _____

4

Today's writers on usage are more flexible, more likely to sometimes say, "It depends." They may look at the example in Frame 3 and comment, "It's not bad, but *to see quickly* seems a little more smooth and natural. Usually, but not always, a split infinitive appears a little awkward."

In the first sentence of this frame, the authors have split an infinitive.

    A. Did you notice it when you first read the sentence? _____ _____

    B. Does it seem "wrong" to you? _____

    C. Would you prefer *likely to say sometimes*? _____

    D. Why is *likely sometimes to say* not good? _____

4

    A. Yes (*or*) No

    B. Yes (*or*) No

    C. Yes (*or*) No

    D. It's not clear. It's a squinting modifier. (See Lesson 5.)

· ·

She tried to immediately refute the accusation.

    A. The split infinitive is _____
_____
_____ .
[What three words?]

    B. Do you believe a different arrangement of those words would be better? ___
_____

5

Modern writers on usage would agree on one point that eighteenth-century grammarians would not accept: sometimes splitting an infinitive is necessary for clarity. A favorite example is this quotation from Theodore Roosevelt:

> "His fortune having been jeopardized, he hoped *to more than retrieve* it by going into speculations in the Western Lands."

Can you think of any way (other than restructuring the whole sentence) to avoid that split? _____

5

(Probably not)

· ·

The coach hopes to more than double last year's victories.

Is the meaning as clear if *more than* is placed after *hopes* or before *last*?

_____

6

It is impossible accurately to compute all costs.

It is impossible to compute all costs accurately.

It is impossible to accurately compute all costs.

    A. The _____ [*first, second,* or *third*?] sentence has a split infinitive.

    B. Most modern writers on usage _____ [*would* or *would not*?] be likely to condemn it.

6

    A. third   B. would not

. . . .

They would condemn it if it seemed unclear or awkward. Does it seem so to you? _____

7

In some sentences a split infinitive seems definitely awkward. Awkwardness is especially probable when several words appear between *to* and the rest of the verb form:

> A. **I hoped to without any substantial delay meet with the committee.**
>
> B. **I hoped to meet with the committee without any substantial delay.**

Does A or B seem more smooth and easy to read? _____

7

    B

. . . .

   A. **Try during the next hour to call the chief engineer.**
   B. **Try to during the next hour call the chief engineer.**

Which is better, A or B? _____

8

> A. In summary, the modern view is that an infinitive _____ _____ [*should* or *should not?*] be split if awkwardness or lack of clarity results.
>
> B. In other cases, the form that seems smoother, more natural, or easier to read _____ [*should* or *should not?*] be chosen.

8

    A. should not
    B. should (obviously!)

. . . .

   I want to clearly express my opposition.

Do you prefer this version or one of the three other possibilities?

9

   A. **Her goal was to strongly urge a yes-vote.**
   B. **To regardless of the consequences move ahead would be foolhardy.**

Which sentence contains an awkwardly split infinitive? _____

9

    B

. . . .

Rewrite sentence B in Frame 9 to make it smoother.

10

Write a sentence in which you use the split infinitive *to easily pay* in a way you consider justified.

10

Model Answer

It will be possible to easily pay off the mortgage in ten years.

. . . .

Now try one with *to be readily sold.*

11

Write a sentence in which you discover how to avoid the split infinitive in *to in every imaginable way find.*

11

Model Answer

In every imaginable way Glenn tried to find the misplaced or stolen heirlooms.

. . . .

Now make a change in this:

Mr. Tolan attempted to almost invariably remain calm.

12

Finish honestly: One thing I hope to remember from this lesson is . . .

(In this frame, any answer that you consider honest and accurate is acceptable.)

Lesson 15: Answers to Questions for Added Practice

3. No **4.** *to immediately refute* B. Yes (place *immediately* at the end). **5.** No ("hopes more than to double" is unclear, and "to double more than last year's victories" is nonsense.) **6.** (Either *Yes* or *No* is acceptable.) **7.** A **8.** (Personal opinion) **9.** To move ahead regardless of the consequences would be foolhardy. **10.** MODEL: The house is too costly to be readily sold. (Obviously that also could be "to be sold readily.") **11.** Mr. Tolan almost invariably attempted to remain calm. (*Or*) . . . to remain calm almost invariably.

16

Parallel Structure: Useful in Comparisons and Series

After writing your answer(s) in the right-hand column, check this column to see whether you have responded correctly. If you have made a mistake, or if you need more practice, do whatever is asked below the dotted line in each answer frame.

Answers to questions for added practice can be found at the end of each lesson.

Answers and Added Practice

1

    C, B

. . . .

    a useful tool

    stainless

Are those two items in the same grammatical form? _____

2

    No

. . . .

    I like hot chocolate better than drinking coffee.

Parallel or not? _____

Understanding and Applying the Principles

1

A. **to fish**	B. **to fish**	C. **fishing**
to hunt	**hunting**	**hunting**

The two items in Group A are in the same grammatical form. (Both are infinitives.)

The two items in Group _____ are also in the same grammatical form, but those in Group _____ are not.

2

Items that are in the same grammatical form, such as *to fish* and *to hunt*, or *fishing* and *hunting*, or *short* and *peppy*, or *in the daytime* and *at night*, are said to be "parallel."

The lines in each of these sets are parallel:

but these are not:

Grammatical items are not parallel if one "goes off in a different direction."

In *I like to fish but not hunting*, are the two items being compared parallel in form? _____

3

In comparisons, parallel structure helps the reader to understand quickly what things are being compared.

A. I like fishing better than hunting.
B. I like fishing better than to hunt.
C. I like to fish better than hunting.
D. I like to fish better than to hunt.

Which two comparisons have parallel structure? _____ _____

3

A, D

....

Finish in three ways, using parallel structure each time. Do not use people's names.

I enjoy _____
more than _____,
_____ more than
_____, and
_____ more than
_____.

4

The Eiffel Tower is taller than the height of the RCA Building.

To make the structure parallel in that comparison, the words _____ should be deleted.

4

the height of

....

Rewrite the boldface sentence in Frame 4 so that the structure is parallel.

5

In lists or series, also, the items should be stated in parallel form.

  A. Greg is short, bald, and overweight.

  B. Greg is short, bald, and weighs 195 pounds.

_____ [A or B?] has parallel structure.

5

A

....

Melvin has huge legs, a massive chest, and is strong in the arms.

Parallel or not? _____
If not, what change would you make? _____
_____
_____

6

Even when only two items are used in the same way in a sentence, they should be parallel in form.

  A. Coaches drilled us on shooting free throws and against fast breaks.

  B. Coaches drilled us on shooting free throws and defending against fast breaks.

  C. Coaches drilled us on free throws and defenses against fast breaks.

_____ [A and B, A and C, B and C, or A, B, and C?] have parallel structure.

6

B and C

. . . .

Coaches drilled us on shooting free throws, executing fast breaks, and playing zone defense.

Parallel or not? _____
Rewrite, starting with *Coaches taught us to.*

7

We have seen that the same grammatical form (parallel structure) should be used in these two kinds of sentences:

    A. those that name things that are being _____, and

    B. those that list two or more items in a _____.

7

    A. compared
    B. series

. . . .

Complete with parallel items:

    I'd rather _____ than _____, _____, or _____.

8

In Frames 8–15, fill in the blanks with anything that makes sense and is parallel in form.

    I like _____ less than _____.

8

Model Answer
    playing games
    watching television

. . . .

Complete with parallel items:

    At some time after _____ _____ but before _____, someone broke into Joan's apartment.

9

What we think is not always the same as _____.

9

Model Answer
    what we say

. . . .

Complete with a parallel item:

    What they did was no worse than _____ _____.

10

Ideally, politicians should be _____, _____, and _____.

10

Model Answer

intelligent, well-informed, un-
selfish

. . . .

Complete with parallel items:

Unfortunately, some of them
are _____,
_____, and
_____.

11

Model Answer

eat, drink, sleep

. . . .

Complete with parallel items:

The salesman stressed the
word processor's _____
_____, _____,
and _____.

12

Model Answer

reading history, scrubbing
floors

. . . .

Complete with parallel items:

I'd rather work in _____
_____ than
_____.

13

Model Answer

finding one's way through a
forest on a dark night

. . . .

Complete with a parallel item:

To work one's way through college is no more difficult than

_____

_____.

11

All that extremely lazy people like to do is _____,
_____, and _____.

12

She would rather spend her time in _____
than in _____.

13

Solving that intricate problem is as difficult as _____
_____.

14

Louise found that country life was _____ and
_____, but also _____.

14

Model Answer

    quiet, unexciting, not unpleasant

. . . .

Complete with parallel items:

    The student manager of an athletic team must look after equipment, _____, and _____ .

15

These three steps often come early in the writing process: choosing a general topic, _____ ,

and _____ .

15

Model Answer

    recalling and gathering information, narrowing the topic

. . . .

Complete with a parallel item:

    Using parallel structures often makes comparisons more understandable than _____ .

16

Finish honestly: One thing I hope to remember from this lesson is that . . .

(In this frame, any answer that you consider honest and accurate is acceptable.)

Lesson 16: Answers to Questions for Added Practice

1. No **2.** No **3.** MODELS: beef more than mutton, going to plays more than watching ballets, sleeping more than playing cards. **4.** The Eiffel Tower is taller than the RCA Building. **5.** No. Replace *is strong in the arms* with *strong arms*. **6.** Yes. Coaches taught us to shoot free throws, execute fast breaks, and play zone defense. **7.** MODEL: I'd rather swim than ski, hike, or bowl. **8.** MODEL: At some time after midnight but before daybreak . . . **9.** MODEL: What they did was no worse than what the other gang did. **10.** MODEL: Unfortunately, some of them are unpleasant, unkind, and intolerant. **11.** MODEL: The salesman stressed the word processor's speed, versatility, and sophistication. **12.** MODEL: I'd rather work in chemistry than in physics. (*Or*) . . . in Montreal than in Detroit. **13.** MODEL: To work one's way through college is no more difficult than to work hard at any other two jobs. **14.** MODEL: The student manager of an athletic team must look after equipment, uniforms, and locker rooms. **15.** MODEL: Using parallel structures often makes comparisons more understandable than using dissimilar grammatical forms.

17

Parallel Structure: With Words Like is *or* both . . . and

After writing your answer(s) in the right-hand column, check this column to see whether you have responded correctly. If you have made a mistake, or if you need more practice, do whatever is asked below the dotted line in each answer frame.

Answers to questions for added practice can be found at the end of each lesson.

Answers and Added Practice

1

    First

....

Explain why *First* is the correct answer.

2

Model Answer
    the part before *is* is an infinitive, but the part after it isn't. (It is a gerund.)

....

    Succeeding is opening the way to the next success.

Does that sentence have parallel structure? _____

Understanding and Applying the Principles

1

    To succeed is to open a new opportunity.
    To succeed is opening a new opportunity.

A linking verb (usually *am, is, are, was, were,* or a verb followed by *be* or *been*) is somewhat like an equal-sign. What is on the right of it should ordinarily be equal in form and meaning to what is on the left. For instance, an infinitive on the left generally requires an infinitive on the right.

    Which one of the boldface examples is correct?
    _____ [*First* or *Second?*]

2

Infinitives, as we have just noted, may be parallel with other infinitives. Adjectives may be parallel with adjectives, phrases with phrases, clauses with clauses, and so on.

    In Frame 1 the second example does not have parallel structure because _____

_____

_____ .

3

    A few tips can make sharpening an axe both simpler and with greater safety.
    A few tips can make sharpening an axe both simpler and safer.

After words used in pairs, as *both . . . and* often are, the parts following each word should be parallel.

    A. In the first example above, *simpler* and *with greater safety* _____ [*are* or *are not?*] parallel.

    B. In the second example, *simpler* and *safer* _____ [*are* or *are not?*] parallel.

3

    A. are not

    B. are

....

Grammatically, *simpler* and *safer* are both adjectives, and so are parallel. But the adjective *simpler* and the phrase *with greater safety* are not parallel.

4

Words used in pairs, such as *both . . . and*, are called correlative conjunctions or, more simply, correlatives. They relate one thing or quality to another, similar one.

    Other correlatives are *either . . . or, neither . . . nor, not only . . . but also, whether . . . or.*

        PARALLEL: **Rosalind wondered whether to stay in the cabin or to hide in the forest.**

    A. In that sentence the correlatives are _____ and _____ .

    B. After *whether* comes the infinitive phrase *to stay in the cabin,* and after *or* comes the infinitive phrase _____ .

4

    A. whether, or

    B. to hide in the forest

....

Bonnie prefers either chocolate cake or lemon pie.

In that sentence the correlatives are _____ and _____ .

5

    NOT PARALLEL: **Rosalind wondered whether to stay in the cabin or maybe the forest would be safer.**

    A. After *whether* comes the infinitive phrase *to stay in the cabin.* Is what follows *or* parallel in form? _____

    B. Is the sentence written correctly? _____

5.

    A. No

    B. No

....

Bonnie prefers either chocolate cake or to fulfill her longing for lemon pie.

Are the parts following *either* and *or* parallel? _____

6

    A. **Clara not only wants money but also fame.**

    B. **Clara wants not only money but also fame.**

A. Sentence _____ [A or B?] shows parallel structure.

B. The other is not parallel because _____ _____ .

6

A. B

B. **Model Answer**

    wants money and *fame* are not alike in structure

....

Not only does Clara want money but also fame.

Is that parallel and correct? _____

7

We saw in Frame 1 that linking verbs call for parallel structure. Especially awkward is pairing an infinitive (with *to*) and an *-ing* form of a verb.

    A. **Seeing is believing.**

    B. **To see is believing.**

    C. **To see is to believe.**

Sentence _____ is awkward because of its lack of parallelism, but sentences _____ and _____ have parallel structure.

7

    B, A, C

....

Complete this sentence by adding a parallel item:

    Marty enjoyed both visiting friends and _____

_____ .

8

In Frames 8–10, fill in the blank parts of sentences with anything that makes sense and is parallel in form.

    Franklin said that both death and _____ are certain.

    (Would *paying taxes* be satisfactory in that blank? _____)

8

    taxes   No

....

Complete this sentence by adding parallel items:

    Jeb wants neither _____

_____ nor

_____ .

9

The band marched not only in the late afternoons but also

_____ .

9

Model Answer

    on Tuesday and Thursday evenings

....

Complete this sentence by adding parallel items:

    This hash should have either

    more _____

    or _____ .

10

Jim took the job both because _____

_____ and _____

_____ .

10

Model Answer

    Jim took the job because he needed money and because the experience would be valuable.

....

Explain why *because* is used twice in the answer above.

11

Finish honestly: One thing I hope to remember from this lesson is that . . .

(In this frame, any answer that you consider honest and accurate is acceptable.)

Lesson 17: Answers to Questions for Added Practice

1. MODEL: *To succeed* and *to open* are alike in form, but *To succeed* and *opening* are not. **2.** Yes **4.** *either, or* **5.** No **6.** No **7.** MODEL: meeting girls **8.** MODEL: Jeb wants neither a large house nor a luxurious car. **9.** MODEL: This hash should have either more onions or more garlic. **10.** A second *because*-clause is needed to parallel the first.

===18===

Parallel Structure:
And who *or* and which *Needs a Mate*

After writing your answer(s) in the right-hand column, check this column to see whether you have responded correctly. If you have made a mistake, or if you need more practice, do whatever is asked below the dotted line in each answer frame.

Answers to questions for added practice can be found at the end of each lesson.

Understanding and Applying the Principles

1

AWKWARD:	**An opossum is an ugly animal, but which is one of the most interesting in the Americas.**
PARALLEL BUT WORDY:	**An opossum is an animal which is ugly but which is one of the most interesting in the Americas.**
BETTER:	**An opossum, although ugly, is one of the most interesting animals in the Americas.**

The words *but which* suggest that an earlier *which*-clause has been used.

   A. In the first example, *but which* _____ [*has* or *does not have?*] another *which*-clause as a parallel.

   B. Are there parallel *which*-clauses in the second example?

   _____

Answers and Added Practice

1

   A. does not have

   B. Yes

....

Improve this sentence:

An opossum is a sluggish animal, but which is less stupid than it appears.

2

NOT PARALLEL: Dr. William T. James, a Georgia psychologist, and who conducted experiments on animal intelligence, proved that an opossum can learn to open several latches to get at food.

If we want to keep *and who*, we need to have an earlier clause starting with _____ . [What word?]

2

   who

....

Improve this sentence:

Dr. James disagreed with Dr. Carl Hartman, an expert on opossums, and who asserted that an opossum is one of the dullest vertebrates.

3

PARALLEL: **The latch system, which was rather complex and which puzzled even rats of known intelligence, included a lower latch that had to be released before the two upper ones could be opened.**

In that sentence, is there a parallel *which*-clause before *and which*? _____

3

   Yes

....

Improve this sentence:

Baby opossums emerge while still in an underdeveloped stage, and which weigh in at fourteen babies to the ounce.

4

PARALLEL: **A zoologist whom I know and whom other zoologists respect has carefully studied the birth and infancy of opossum broods.**

Does the clause with *and whom* have an earlier parallel clause? _____

4

Yes

....

Improve this sentence:

Opossums are marsupials and which means they carry their young in a pouch and similar to kangaroos in that way.

5

The *and who(m)* or *and which* sentence is sometimes useful, but unfortunately it is usually wordy and unattractive. Use it if necessary, but not when a more compact or more graceful version is possible.

Look again at the examples in Frame 1.

    A. In the sentence labeled BETTER, does either *which*-clause survive? _____

    B. Is that sentence shorter or longer than the one that precedes it? _____

5

A. No   B. Shorter

....

Look back at Answer Frame 1. If your rewritten sentence contains one or two *which*'s, try rewriting it to eliminate them.

6

Write *True* before each correct statement.

  _____ A. A clause should not be written with *and who(m)*, *and which*, *but who(m)*, or *but which* unless there is a parallel clause containing *who(m)* or *which*.

  _____ B. When an *and which* or *and who(m)* clause has a parallel and is used correctly, it may still be wordy and may profit from revision.

6

A. True   B. True

....

Improve this sentence:

He has a tent which he hauls along with him and puts it up each night in a different camp.

7

In Frames 7–9, improve each sentence by rewriting it. You may use clauses with *who(m)* or *which*, or you may find an even better way.

Irma bought a used car, but which had only twenty thousand miles on the odometer.

7

Model Answer
    Irma bought a car which was used but which had only twenty thousand miles on the odometer.

. . . .

Try to write a better sentence than the "model."

8

Mark was an average student when he was in high school and who had spent two years in college.

8

Model Answer
    Mark, an average student when he was in high school, had spent two years in college.

. . . .

Would *who*-clauses improve that sentence? _____

9

For this position the company insists on proficiency in word processing and who has worked as a receptionist.

9

Model Answer
    For this position the company insists on proficiency in word processing, and experience as a receptionist.

. . . .

Complete this possible version:

    For this position the company must employ a person who has proficiency in word processing and _____

_____

_____ .

10

Write a sentence of your own about someone who is well informed and who reads widely. Use correctly a *who*-clause followed by an *and who*-clause.

10

Model Answer

　　Frances is a young woman who is well informed and who reads widely.

. . . .

Rewrite the model above, getting rid of both *who*'s and using *because*.

11

Finish honestly: One thing I hope to remember from this lesson is that . . .

(In this frame, any answer than you consider honest and accurate is acceptable.)

Lesson 18: Answers to Questions for Added Practice

1. An opossum is a sluggish animal which is less stupid than it appears. (*Or*) . . . sluggish animal, but is less stupid . . . (*Or*) . . . sluggish animal that is less stupid . . . **2.** (Delete *who* or *and*.) **3.** (Delete *which*.) **4.** MODEL: Opossums are marsupials; that means they carry their young in a pouch, as kangaroos do. **5.** (See the answer to 1.) **6.** (Delete *it*.) (*Or*) He has a tent which he hauls along with him and which he puts up every night in a different camp. **7.** MODEL: Irma bought a used car that had only twenty thousand miles on the odometer. **8.** No **9.** . . . experience as a receptionist. **10.** Frances is a well-informed young woman because she reads widely.

═══19═══

Words Such as only *and* almost: *Logical, Formal Placement*

After writing your answer(s) in the right-hand column, check this column to see whether you have responded correctly. If you have made a mistake, or if you need more practice, do whatever is asked below the dotted line in each answer frame.

Answers to questions for added practice can be found at the end of each lesson.

Understanding and Applying the Principles

1

　1. Only Lana would pay sixty dollars for that dress.
　2. Lana would only pay sixty dollars for that dress.
　3. Lana would pay only sixty dollars for that dress.
　4. Lana would pay sixty dollars only for that dress.
　5. Lana would pay sixty dollars for only that dress.
　6. Lana would pay sixty dollars for that dress only.

Do all the sentences above mean the same thing? _____

Answers and Added Practice

1

No

·····························

A. **Lana nearly paid sixty dollars for that dress.**

B. **Lana paid nearly sixty dollars for that dress.**

In which sentence did Lana probably not buy the dress?

_____ [A or B?]

2

sixty dollars

·····························

Lana would nearly pay sixty dollars for that dress.

Think about that sentence for a moment. Are you sure what it means? _____

3

the same thing

·····························

A. **Lana would only pay sixty dollars for that dress.**

B. **Lana would pay only sixty dollars for that dress.**

Americans prefer _____ [A or B?] for formal writing.

2

In Frame 1 the first sentence means that no one else—only Lana—would make that purchase. Sentence 2 is an informal American—or both informal and formal British—way of saying sentence 3.

A few American experts on usage assert that *only*, as in sentence 2, is an early and useful warning that some kind of limitation is coming. Most say that sentence 3 is more logical because it is a clear way of saying that the amount Lana paid was only _____ . [How much?]

3

Sentence 4 in Frame 1 is poor. The reader cannot be certain whether *only* goes along with *sixty dollars* (sixty dollars only) or with *that dress* (only for that dress). In that sentence, *only* is a squinting modifier (discussed in Lesson 5).

Now look at sentences 5 and 6 in Frame 1. Do they mean *the same thing* or *different* things? _____

4

When Americans try to be especially formal or logical in something they are writing or saying, they are likely to put *only* after the verb in sentences like those in Frame 4. So they would write:

This plane _____ [*only flies* or *flies only*] eight hundred miles an hour.

But in informal circumstances most Americans would say and write:

This plane _____ eight hundred miles an hour.

(Most British people would use *only flies* on both formal and informal occasions.)

4

    A. flies only

    B. only flies

....

Is *We only want one part* more or less formal than *We want only one part*?

_____

5

    No

....

    A. **Bob almost made A's in all his subjects.**

    B. **Bob made A's in almost all his subjects.**

In sentence A, Bob's average was _____ , but in B it was _____ .

6

    B

....

Explain the answer to Frame 6. (If you are puzzled, remember that if you nearly buy a car, you don't buy it.)

7

    Mr. Gray said that merely to be polite.

....

In formal English do Republicans *merely expect* or *expect merely* a slight margin in a Congressional vote?

_____

5

A few other words present somewhat the same problem as *only.* Among them are *almost, barely, even, ever, hardly, merely, mostly, nearly,* and *scarcely.* For instance:

    A. **Mr. Parke almost said nothing.**

    B. **Mr. Parke said almost nothing.**

Do those two sentences mean the same thing? _____

6

    A. **Marie nearly bought the whole bolt of cloth.**

    B. **Marie bought nearly the whole bolt of cloth.**

In which sentence did Marie spend some money? _____

7

    Mr. Gray merely said that to be polite.

That sentence is informal and illogical, but it is the way most people would express the point in casual speaking or writing.

    Rewrite it to make it formal and logical.

8

In formal usage, which is preferred in each sentence?

    A. Mr. Blair _____ [*almost tallied* or *tallied almost*?] all the ballots himself.

    B. He _____ [*only left* or *left only*?] a few hundred for Mr. Porter.

    C. He _____ [*merely said* or *said merely*?] that he had some spare time.

8

    A. tallied almost
    B. left only
    C. said merely

. . . .

Opening a window is usually an informal act. Are you more likely to say (A) "I barely opened the window two inches" or (B) "I opened the window barely two inches?"

_____

9

For a formal piece of writing, compose a sentence that contains *only*. The sentence should concern what a new military tank cost the government.

9

Model Answer

    Pentagon spokesmen said that the new tank cost only a billion dollars to develop.

. . . .

Now compose an informal sentence about the cost of a new pair of shoes. Again, use *only*.

10

       They are nearly certain to sell five gallons of syrup.

Rewrite by changing the position of *nearly*. With that change, make your sentence show that the amount of syrup sold will be about four and a half gallons.

10

Model Answer

    They are certain to sell nearly five gallons of syrup.

. . . .

    I ran four miles.

Insert *nearly* in two versions of that sentence. First, show that I walked very fast. Second, show a distance of three-plus miles.

11

Finish honestly: One of the things I hope to remember from this lesson is that . . .

(In this frame, any answer that you consider honest and accurate is acceptable.)

Lesson 19: Answers to Questions for Added Practice

1. A **2.** No **3.** B **4.** Less formal **5.** B, A− **6.** In sentence A, Marie did not buy the cloth, but in B she bought almost a whole bolt of it. **7.** Expect merely **8.** A **9.** MODEL: These new shoes only cost thirty dollars. **10.** I nearly ran four miles. I ran nearly four miles.

=20=

Variety in Sentence Structure: One Way to Avoid Monotony

After writing your answer(s) in the right-hand column, check this column to see whether you have responded correctly. If you have made a mistake, or if you need more practice, do whatever is asked below the dotted line in each answer frame.

Answers to questions for added practice can be found at the end of each lesson.

Understanding and Applying the Principles

1

The opposing linemen (s) took (v) their crouching positions, and (conj) the quarterback (s) bent (v) over behind the center. The center (s) snapped (v) the ball back, and (conj) the quarterback (s) dropped (v) it. Players from both sides (s) scrambled (v) after the ball, and (conj) the defense (s) recovered (v) the fumble.

(s = subject, v = verb, conj = conjunction)

Do all three sentences in the passage above follow the same general pattern? _____

Answers and Added Practice

1

Yes

....

Note that all three sentences are compound: independent clause—conjunction—independent clause. No statement seems more important or more vivid than any other.

2

Suppose that the example in Frame 1 continued in the same way:

$$\text{New teams came in, and the Pelicans went on}$$
$$\text{offense. The two lines crouched as before,}$$
$$\text{and the center snapped the ball back.}$$

Do the five sentences of Frames 1 and 2 seem (A) varied and interesting, or (B) dull and monotonous? _____

2

dull and monotonous

....

Write a sixth sentence, using the same pattern, which might follow the first five. Tell what the quarterback did and who did what after that.

3

In Lesson 7 we observed that one short sentence after another soon gets tiresome. Then Lesson 8 demonstrated that long *and . . . and* sentences leave the reader breathless, as well as uncertain about the relative importance of the parts.

Here the first two frames have shown that several consecutive compound sentences are _____ . [*desirable* or *undesirable*?]

3

undesirable

....

A dictionary defines *monotonous*: ". . . repetitiously dull . . . See synonyms at **boring**."

Does that definition describe sentences such as we are considering? _____

4

Complex sentences, especially when they repeat the same pattern, also may be monotonous. For instance:

[DC] After the ball changed hands once more, [IC] the comedy of errors persisted. [DC] If the quarterback didn't drop the ball, [IC] somebody else missed the handoff. [DC] When the quarterback passed, [IC] the receiver misjudged the path of the ball.

See what we have: a dependent clause followed by an independent clause

a dependent clause followed by an independent clause

a dependent clause followed by an independent clause

Each sentence is satisfactory by itself, but the three sentences together _____ .
[Finish the sentence.]

4

Model Answer

    are so similar that they are dull.

· ·

Add another sentence of the same pattern. Perhaps this time the quarterback tries to pass but is thrown behind the line of scrimmage.

5

We have seen that steady repetition of the same sentence pattern results in monotony.

    Often monotony can be prevented by starting sentences in different ways. We'll look at some of the possible variations of the first sentence in Frame 1.

    One possibility is to start with a dependent clause:

After _____

_____

[What happened?], the quarterback bent over behind the center.

5

    the opposing linemen took their crouching positions,

· ·

Among the conjunctions used to begin dependent clauses: *after, although, as, as if, because, before, if, since, so that, that, unless, until, when, whenever, where, while, why.*

6

Another way to vary the sentence opening is to use a prepositional phrase:

With the linemen in their customary crouching positions,

_____

_____ . [What happened?]

6

    the quarterback bent over behind the center

· ·

The players wore the usual helmets, face masks, and slick uniforms, and they looked like strangely shaped beings from outer space.

Rewrite the first part of that sentence, starting with *With their* or *In their.*

7

Sentence openers may sometimes be constructions with participles:

A. Bending over _____
[Where?], the quarterback looked across his own line and the crouching defensive linemen.

Or, less likely:

B. The two lines crouching before him, the quarterback
_____ . [Did what?]

7

    A. behind the center
    B. bent over behind the center

. . . .

The quarterback held his hands down to receive the ball, and he shouted some numbers.

Rewrite the first part, starting with *Holding*.

8

Often an adverb is a good sentence opener:

Quickly the linemen _____
_____ [Did what?], and the quarterback bent over behind the center.

8

    took their crouching positions

. . . .

One backfield man started toward the right, and another moved left.

What adverb might be used to open that sentence? _____
_____

9

Other sentence openings are possible, but we have seen illustrations of some of the most frequent and useful (in addition to the most frequent of all, the subject of the sentence). Other parts of the sentence also may be changed to prevent monotony.

    The point is that variety in sentence structure leads to _____ [*more* or *less*?] interesting reading.

9

    more

. . . .

In a good book or a high-quality magazine, note the openings of fifteen or twenty consecutive sentences. How many grammatically different kinds of opening do you find?

_____

10

We drove to Plymouth, Massachusetts. We found the famous Plymouth rock. We knew that the Pilgrims supposedly landed near it in 1620. We thought it would be bigger. We were told that years ago sightseers chipped off about eighty percent of it.

Those sentences are monotonous partly because they are short and partly because _____
_____
_____ .

10

Model Answer

    all start with the same subject and are similar in structure

. . . .

Is it also possible that a series of unusually long sentences can be dull? _____

11

Combine the first three sentences in Frame 10. Start with *In Plymouth*.

11

Model Answer

    In Plymouth we found the famous Plymouth rock, near which the Pilgrims supposedly landed in 1620.

· ·

Rewrite the three sentences, starting with *From Boston.*

12

Which of these openings would also be suitable for the combination of the three sentences?

    A. When we arrived at

    B. Reaching

    C. Finally coming to

_____ [A and B, A and C, B and C, or A, B, and C?]

12

    A, B, and C

· ·

Try to think of at least one unmentioned way to start the combination of the three sentences.

13

Revise the final two boldface sentences of Frame 10. Start with *We,* and use *but* in making the combination.

13

Model Answer

    We thought it would be bigger, but were told that years ago sightseers chipped off about eighty percent of it.

· ·

Rewrite the same sentences in a different way. One possibility: Start with *Perhaps the reason the rock is now small is that . . .*

14

Finish honestly: One thing I hope to remember from this lesson is that . . .

(In this frame, any answer that you consider honest and accurate is acceptable.)

Lesson 20: Answers to Questions for Added Practice

2. MODEL: The quarterback handed off to the fullback, and he found a small hole. **3.** Yes **4.** MODEL: When the quarterback moved back for another pass, an opposing lineman knocked him down. **6.** With their usual helmets, face masks, and slick uniforms, the players looked . . . **7.** Holding his hands down to receive the ball . . . **8.** Suddenly (*or*) Immediately, etc. **9.** (Answers will vary. Subjects are the most common openers.) **10.** Yes **11.** MODEL: From Boston we drove to Plymouth, where the Pilgrims supposedly landed at the famous rock in 1620. **12.** After driving . . . (*or*) Near Plymouth . . . **13.** MODEL: Instead of a majestic rock we found only a small one, chipped away years ago by stupid sightseers.

Mastery Test
Sentence Structure

For directions, see page 228.

1. a. Near the top of the arena holding my breath. A U
    b. Watching the clock with one minute to go. A U
    c. Seeing the ball roll around the rim and bounce away. A U

2. a. Although many drama students do not have successful careers in acting. A U
    b. After considering several fields of study, Phil chose to be a drama major. A U
    c. Because acting is the only career that interests him. A U

3. a. Larry bought a car through an ad in the newspaper that started squealing. A U
    b. The car, which had been standing out in the weather for two years, had a bad water pump. A U
    c. Larry had a new water pump installed before any serious damage was done to the car's cooling system by an auto mechanic. A U

4. a. Melissa, Brenda, and I dressed as quickly as possible, waited nervously for the physics building to open, and then rushed inside to see if our grades had been posted. A U
    b. After finding my grade in a list on Professor Erg's door, I saw Melissa sitting on a bench. A U
    c. Melissa and I finally found Brenda in the parking lot after we decided to leave the building after we had walked through every hallway. A U

5. a. The realization that I should stop my car immediately came to me. A U
    b. A campus police officer asked me when I reached the intersection whether I had looked both ways. A U
    c. I usually stop and look both ways before driving through an intersection. A U

6. a. Entering the museum, several shrunken heads caught my attention. A U
    b. After I read the explanation of headshrinking, I wasn't sure I wanted to see anything else in the museum. A U
    c. After reading about the shrunken heads, my stomach became upset. A U

7. a. Several fraternity men created an ice sculpture. It looked like Frankenstein's monster. It stood at least ten feet tall. The men worked on it the entire weekend. A U
    b. The fraternity men put a loudspeaker in its mouth. This was only a joke. They did it to frighten anyone walking by at night. A U

c. Two campus police officers parked next to the statue last week. One student shouted, "Freeze!" The officers didn't find any humor in the incident. The dean of students didn't think it was funny, either.   A   U

8. a. We wanted everyone to vote for Oscar, so we made signs, and we attached the signs to wire clothes hangers, and we stuck the signs along sidewalks all over campus.   A   U

b. Signs for other candidates said, "Vote for John" or "Vote for Jill," but we wanted to be different. Our signs said, "Oscar Has an Overbite" and "Oscar, What Big Teeth You Have."   A   U

c. When Oscar won a seat on the student senate, we had to tell everyone that he was our pet piranha.   A   U

9. a. We couldn't reach Chicago by telephone, and the sun was shining.   A   U

b. The weather report said that it was raining in the Windy City, and the operator asked us to call later.   A   U

c. A severe storm had hit, and lightning had damaged the telephone wires.   A   U

10. a. Some professors take attendance daily, and a few even lower the semester grade for more than two unexcused absences.   A   U

b. This practice has caused controversy on our campus, some students think that attendance is their own business.   A   U

c. Students who have been absent can occasionally borrow lecture notes, they cannot borrow skills and the experience of sharing points of view with other students.

11. a. According to the Student Handbook, with regard to obtaining a refund in the case of a request subsequent to registration but prior to the beginning of classes, a student will, in the event the registrar approves it, receive a refund in the amount of all fees and tuition.   A   U

b. I am of the opinion that in large measure the language as stated in some student handbooks with respect to rules and regulations makes it difficult for students to be truly cognizant of what the said rules and regulations really mean.   A   U

c. Pursuant to its purpose, a student handbook should be clear and concise for the reason that many students are truly desirous of accurate information.   A   U

12. a. I heard a warning about a bomb threat, and I was sitting in the library.   A   U

b. Before I could find an exit, all the lights went out.   A   U

c. While I was groping around in the dark, two police officers rushed into the hallway and knocked me flat.   A   U

13. a. The ghost told Hamlet that it was only a rumor that it was a serpent that had killed Hamlet's father, and that Claudius had done it.   A   U

b. Thinking that he was killing Claudius, Hamlet stabbed Polonius, who was hiding behind a curtain.   A   U

c. With his sword Hamlet pricked Laertes, who had   A   U

conspired with Claudius, who was killed by Hamlet, who died from the poison on Laertes' sword.

14. a. Gary is a lazy person who is forgetful, and he is also extremely messy. A U

b. Rose is highly motivated, organized, and very tidy. A U

c. It amazes me that a person who has Gary's habits and a person who has Rose's habits have a relationship that is serious and that they are planning to be married. A U

15. a. Roger tried to for at least two hours refrain from eating. A U

b. He found it impossible patiently to wait until his afternoon classes were over. A U

c. In fact, he found it extremely difficult to exist without eating something every hour. A U

16. a. My grandfather goes to the park by subway, takes a bus, or he walks. A U

b. He likes feeding the birds better than to stay in his room. A U

c. During the evening, he would rather read a novel than watch television. A U

17. a. We couldn't decide whether to go to the movie or maybe the party would be more fun. A U

b. Not only would the party be fun but also free. A U

c. The best formula for any weekend is having fun and saving money. A U

18. a. Mr. Swift is my biology instructor, and who thought A U

he could safely lock his bicycle in the rack in front of the building.

b. The bike rack, which was in public view and which was on a route patrolled by security officers, did nothing to protect Mr. Swift's bicycle from thieves. A U

c. Mr. Swift's new technique, which is certainly inconvenient, is to take his bicycle up in the elevator every day and store it in his office. A U

19. a. My roommate almost drank a quart of milk this morning. A U

b. I had bought only six doughnuts and a quart of milk for us to share. A U

c. My roommate is careful to pay only half of the grocery bill, but he almost eats all of the food. A U

20. a. Nickel is a silvery-white metallic element, and it is often used in alloys. It takes a high polish, and it will not rust. Nickel can be hammered into thin sheets, and it can be drawn into wires. A U

b. Highly resistant to impact, nickel is often used with steel in making machine parts. Because nickel will withstand hard use, printing plates are often electroplated with it. A U

c. In the United States and Canada, the word *nickel* is used for five-cent pieces. Being nickel alloys, these coins do not tarnish easily. A U

Answers to this test can be found on page 511.

Usage

Diagnostic Test
Usage

Directions

Because each test item consists of three parts, a, b, and c, you will have three chances to test your knowledge of each principle. You must decide quickly whether or not each sentence is satisfactory as edited written English. As a guideline, ask yourself whether or not all the words in each sentence would be acceptable in a college essay. If you believe that all the words in sentence 1. a, for example, are acceptable, circle the letter A. If even one word is unacceptable, circle the letter U.

Sample Item

1. a. This morning I arrived at my Economics 201 class early.   (A)   U

   b. While I was waiting for class to begin, the professor asked me some questions about the assigned reading.   (A)   U

   c. I sure ain't coming early no more.   A   (U)

Note: *The writing in part c was marked U for* unacceptable *because the words* sure, ain't, *and* no more *are not acceptable as edited written English.*

How to Use the Test

Like the lessons in this book, this diagnostic test is self-instructional. When you have finished it, score it with the key provided on page 511. The test will measure your awareness of the usage generally expected in college essays. Each test item will give you three chances to recognize acceptable usage.

If you miss one or more of the three chances, you should plan to do the corresponding lesson in the pages that follow. For example, making one or more errors in test item 44 means that you should do Lesson 44.

At the end of this group of lessons, on page 228, is a matching Mastery Test. Take that test after you have completed the needed lessons. It will show you the items in which you have improved and those in which you need further work. Study once more the lessons corresponding to the missed items.

21. a. While Paula, Robin, and I was driving on Interstate 95, the highway started feeling bumpy.   A   U

    b. Both Paula and Robin were convinced that the car was causing the trouble.   A   U

    c. In Melbourne, a mechanic discovered that one of my new tires was defective.   A   U

22. a. Last week almost everybody in my classes were sniffling and sneezing.   A   U

b. Nearly everyone gets a cold during exam week.   A   U

c. Because all of us are tired and nervous during exams, we catch colds easily.   A   U

23. a. A jazz festival and two dances are scheduled for the weekend.   A   U

b. Neither the dances nor the jazz festival is expensive.   A   U

c. Either the festival or the dances are a good remedy for my classroom fatigue.   A   U

24. a. Jill, along with several friends, was determined to try out for the spring musical.   A   U

b. Twelve students, including Jill, were given parts.   A   U

c. No other girl from this house except Fran and Betsy have been chosen for the spring musical.   A   U

25. a. Where have all the students gone?   A   U

b. There is hardly any cars on the campus.   A   U

c. When does the next flights leave for Florida?   A   U

26. a. The entire student body is concerned about recent attacks on women students at night.   A   U

b. This year one fraternity has conducted a free escort service.   A   U

c. So far, members of the fraternity have escorted three hundred women to their residence halls and sororities.   A   U

27. a. Last month a freshman drunk a pitcher of beer and tried to swim across the lake.   A   U

b. No one has ever swum across the lake after consuming that much beer.   A   U

c. His obituary was written more as a warning than as a public notice.   A   U

28. a. Even after getting several parking tickets, some students have never went to the police station.   A   U

b. Their stack of tickets has just grew taller during the semester.   A   U

c. Surely what they have done must make them nervous.   A   U

29. a. I found my wallet still lying where I laid it.   A   U

b. I had just set down for a few minutes to rest.   A   U

c. When I rose from the chair, I forgot that my wallet was on the table.   A   U

30. a. Senator Smedley will introduce me to Ambassador Jennings.   A   U

b. Together they will escort me to the White House.   A   U

c. I shall never forget their kindness.   A   U

31. a. The professor handed us a syllabus and tells us we have the wrong text.   A   U

b. I was furious about the change, because I had borrowed answers to questions in the book he used last semester.   A   U

c. I was angry because such a great disappointment had never been felt by me in any class before.   A   U

32. a. I wish my car was a 1956 Corvette.   A   U

b. If this old heap were a 1957 Thunderbird, I'd be satisfied.   A   U

c. If it were a 1965 Mustang convertible or a 1967 Camaro, I wouldn't complain.   A   U

33. a. Two weeks after classes had   A   U
started, Coach Bush walked
up to Kathy and I in the
gym.
   b. She asked Kathy and me a   A   U
question. "Have you
thought of trying out for the
women's basketball team?"
   c. Since Kathy and I didn't   A   U
know much about playing
basketball, we told her we
would do it if she wouldn't
laugh at us.

34. a. We Shanes are Boilermaker   A   U
Boosters.
   b. Our family, my parents and   A   U
I, are descended from a
long line of Boilermaker
Boosters.
   c. It is we who keep the spirit   A   U
alive in our small Indiana
town.

35. a. I chose a lab partner who I   A   U
thought knew more than I
did.
   b. She was a bright-looking   A   U
student in whom I placed
great hope.
   c. Unfortunately, she turned   A   U
out to be a freeloader whom
I had to help through every
experiment.

36. a. Louise has some notes for   A   U
you and me.
   b. You, she, and I could study   A   U
in the library tonight.
   c. You, I, and Louise will make   A   U
a good study group.

37. a. Mike's practicing his trom-   A   U
bone solos in our tiny room
really disturbs me.
   b. His watching TV, listening   A   U
to his compact disc player,
and singing also drive me
crazy.
   c. Everyone else on the floor   A   U
has heard him creating loud
noises.

38. a. Lisa often tells Mary that she   A   U
has left books or clothes in
her car.
   b. Whenever Lisa goes out   A   U
with her, Mary knows she
will forget something.
   c. Paula never has to remind   A   U
Ruth that she might forget
something.

39. a. In this library, they examine   A   U
all books at the exits.
   b. Last week I accidentally   A   U
walked up to an exit with a
research report, which
showed me that the security
system was working.
   c. This year the head librarian   A   U
is really reducing book
losses, which were heavy a
year ago.

40. a. I'll have to work harder, be-   A   U
cause if a person falls behind
in this course, they never
can pass.
   b. If a professor sees a student   A   U
falling behind, you create a
bad impression.
   c. When a student has trouble   A   U
in a course, he or she should
first study harder and then
see the professor for help.

41. a. Each of the band members   A   U
is conducting his own door-
to-door solicitation.
   b. Each of the sorority sisters is   A   U
selling tickets in her classes.
   c. Somebody in the Alumni   A   U
Association is volunteering
his time as a professional
fund-raiser.

42. a. My roommate, who was not   A   U
sure whether to take Miner-
alogy or Petrology, asked me
which sounded toughest.
   b. Being the greater joker of   A   U
the two roommates in room
415, I suggested that he con-

sider something more down to earth.

c. Of all the answers I have given him this semester, that one had to be the most ridiculous.   A   U

43. a. Something in the room smelled badly.   A   U

b. I looked carefully through my closet and under my bed.   A   U

c. Later I felt bad about leaving my sweaty socks in my closet during the spring break.   A   U

44. a. This old car looks good and runs good, but I have decided to sell it.   A   U

b. Only one person has called, so my advertisement in the newspaper hasn't worked very good.   A   U

c. My advertising on bulletin boards hasn't worked well either.   A   U

45. a. I don't have hardly any time for a party tonight.   A   U

b. I haven't done scarcely anything on my research paper.   A   U

c. I can't scarcely even think about going anywhere.   A   U

46. a. As my interest in the topic increased, I finally decided to give that research paper my best effort.   A   U

b. Once I became interested, neither parties or ballgames kept me from working.   A   U

c. While the professor said the paper was late, I left it with her anyway.   A   U

47. a. A prerequisite is when you are required to take a certain course before you are allowed to take one that is more advanced.   A   U

b. The reason college departments require prerequisites is because professors expect students to be prepared for advanced courses.   A   U

c. In other words, I first would have to take General Chemistry 115, because it would give me the necessary background to do well in General Chemistry 116.   A   U

Answers to this test can be found on page 511.

Verb Agreement: Basic Principles

After writing your answer(s) in the right-hand column, check this column to see whether you have responded correctly. If you have made a mistake, or if you need more practice, do whatever is asked below the dotted line in each answer frame.

Answers to questions for added practice can be found at the end of each lesson.

Understanding and Applying the Principles

1

The world's languages are very different. In some, for instance, a verb used with the subject *cow* or anything large may not be used with *mouse* or anything small. In other languages, words representing different genders, such as *boy*, *girl*, and *tree*, may require different verbs.

In English we frequently must use a different form of a verb to go with a plural subject, such as *girls*, than we use with a _____ subject, such as *girl*.

Answers and Added Practice

1

singular

. . . .

Write *S* for *Singular*, *P* for *Plural*:

cow _____	cows _____
mouse _____	mice _____
plums _____	plum _____
men _____	man _____
crisis _____	crises _____

2

       s   v

Her pen is lost.

       s   v

Her pens are lost.

(s = subject, v = verb)

A. In the first sentence, standard English requires the singular verb _____ [What word?] to agree with the singular subject _____. [What word?]

B. In the second, standard English requires the _____ _____ [*singular* or *plural*?] verb _____ [What word?] to agree with the _____ [*singular* or *plural*?] subject _____. [What word?]

2

A. *is, pen*
B. plural, *are*, plural, *pens*

. . . .

The children were in the yard.

In that sentence the _____ [*singular* or *plural*?] verb _____ [What word?] agrees with the _____ _____ [*Singular* or *plural*?] subject _____ . [What word?]

3

In many cases, we use the same form of a verb regardless of whether the subject is singular or plural (most often when we show past or future time). For instance:

Subjects	Verbs
He or *You* or	*bought* a clock.
They or *Sam*	*had* a headstart.
or *The girls*	*must decide.*
	will recover.

Write three other short sentences in which the same form of a verb can be used with all five of the subjects listed above.

3

(Reread your sentences to make sure that you have followed the instruction.)

. . . .

Which two of these verbs *cannot* be used properly with both *He* and *They*?

called	went	likes
have	found	will go

_____ _____

4

However, some English verbs require one form with a singular subject, a different form with a plural subject.

Singular	Plural
She *is, was* . . .	They *are, were* . . .
She *has* . . .	They *have* . . .
She *talks* . . .	They *talk* . . .
The girl *talks* . . .	The girls *talk* . . .

With *talks*, note that the singular ends in _____ [What letter?], but note also that there _____ [*is* or *is not*?] an s ending on the plural verb.

4

s, is not

. . . .

Nouns and verbs do not act alike. A plural noun, such as *girls*, generally has an s ending. But in a verb of the present tense, such as *talks*, it is the singular that requires the s:

The boy *talks* too much.

5

College students are unlikely to say or write *she are* or *they talks*, because they have learned to use most singular and plural verbs correctly even without thinking. But sometimes they do not realize instantly whether a subject is singular or plural.

One of the penguins _____ hurt.

Thoughtlessly, some writers or speakers may use *were* because the plural word *penguins* is so close. Actually, the subject is *one*: only one bird was hurt. The verb should be _____ . [*was* or *were*?]

5

was (or possibly *has been*)

. . . .

Is singular *was* or plural *were* needed in each of the following sentences?

One of the pearls _____ missing.

All of the pearls _____ missing.

_____ one of the pearls missing?

_____ both of the pearls missing?

6

One of the suggestions was accepted.
Both of the suggestions were accepted.

A. In the first sentence, the subject is _____ [What word?], and the verb is therefore the singular _____ .

B. In the second, the subject is _____ [*singular* or *plural*?], and the verb is therefore the _____ [*singular* or *plural*?] verb _____ .

6

A. *one, was* (accepted)
B. plural, plural, *were* (accepted)

. . . .

When used as a subject, should the words in each group below be considered *singular* or *plural*?

One child among the forty ___ _____

Several children from this city _____

Only Sandra, of all these children, _____

7

A pearl and a ruby were stolen.
A pearl or a ruby was stolen.

A. In the first sentence, how many gems were stolen? _____ . Because the subject is _____ [*singular* or *plural*?], a _____ [*singular* or *plural*?] verb is required.

B. In the second, only one gem was stolen, either a pearl or a ruby. So the subject is _____ [*singular* or *plural*?] and a _____ [*singular* or *plural*?] verb is required.

7

A. two, plural, plural
B. singular, singular

. . . .

When used as a subject, should the words in each group below be considered *singular* or *plural*?

A titmouse or a chickadee _____ _____

A titmouse and a chickadee ___ _____

Either a titmouse or a chickadee _____

A titmouse, a chickadee, or a nuthatch _____

8

We have seen that with those verbs that have different forms for singular and plural, we should use the singular form when the subject refers to _____ [How many?] person(s) or thing(s), and the plural form when the subject refers to _____ _____ [How many?] person(s) or thing(s).

(The choices are most often between *is* and *are*, *was* and *were*, *has* and *have*, and the *s* or *s*-less form of many verbs, such as *talks* or *talk*.)

8

one, more than one (*or*) two or more

······································

Some nouns ending in *-ics* may be either singular or plural. For instance, in *Acoustics is a science*, acoustics is being thought of as a single thing. But in *The acoustics in this concert hall are excellent*, the term means the structural features that determine how well sounds may be heard. So *is* is correct in the first, *are* in the second.

9

In each of these sentences, decide first whether the subject is singular or plural, and then choose the proper verb.

   A. One of the cars _____ [*is* or *are?*] not damaged.
   B. Not a building or a tree _____ [*was* or *were?*] left standing.

9

   A. is   B. was

······································

Choose as in Frame 9:

   A. A fawn or a doe _____ [*has* or *have?*] no antlers.
   B. A fawn and a doe _____ [*was* or *were?*] in the orchard.

10

Follow the instructions for Frame 9.

   A. Each of Sally's entries _____ [*has* or *have?*] won a blue ribbon.
   B. Both of Sally's entries _____ [*has* or *have?*] won blue ribbons.
   C. Sally and Roseann _____ [*differs* or *differ?*] in skill.

10

   A. has   B. have   C. differ

······································

Choose as in Frame 9:

   A. Either of her entries _____ _____ [*seems* or *seem?*] good enough to win.
   B. Both of her entries _____ _____ [*seems* or *seem?*] good enough to win.

11

Follow the instructions for Frame 9.

   A. A visit to a museum or a library _____ [*is* or *are?*] enjoyable.
   B. Visits to a museum or a library _____ [*is* or *are?*] often enjoyable.
   C. A museum or a library _____ [*is* or *are?*] often enjoyable to visit.

11

A. is   B. are   C. is

. . . .

Choose as in Frame 9:

A. This color or that one _____
   _____ [*looks* or *look?*]
   best for you.

B. This color and that one _____
   _____ [*is* or *are?*] equally
   good.

12

Make up three short sentences of your own, using the words
given.

A. *One, of, houses* + *is* or *are*
B. *Three, of, houses* + *was* or *were*
C. *Some, of, houses* + *has* or *have*

12

Model Answers

A. One of these houses is for
   sale.
B. Three of those houses were
   sold last week.
C. Some of these houses have
   been renovated.

. . . .

Follow the instructions in Frame
12.

A. *Each, of, sheep* + *is* or *are*
B. *Several, of, sheep* + *has* or
   have

13

Follow the instructions in Frame 12.

A. *A hawk and a vulture* + *soars* or *soar*
B. *A hawk or a vulture* + *is* or *are*
C. *Two hawks and a vulture* + *was* or *were*

13

Model Answers

   A. A hawk and a vulture soar effortlessly high above us.

   B. A hawk or a vulture is gracefully riding the air currents.

   C. Two hawks and a vulture were shot illegally.

....

Follow the instructions in Frame 12.

   A. *A raccoon or a fox + slides* or *slide*

   B. *A young raccoon and a young fox + has* or *have*

14

Finish honestly: One thing that I hope to remember from this lesson is that . . .

(In this frame, any answer that you consider honest and accurate is acceptable.)

Lesson 21: Answers to Questions for Added Practice

1. S—cow, mouse, plum, man, crisis P—cows, mice, plums, men, crises **2.** plural, *were*, plural, *children* **3.** likes, have **5.** was, were, Was, Were **6.** singular, plural, singular **7.** singular, plural, singular, singular **9.** A. has B. were **10.** A. seems B. seem **11.** A. looks B. are **12.** MODELS: A. Each of these sheep is a ewe. B. Several of these sheep have been sheared. **13.** MODELS: A. A raccoon or a fox slides past in the semidarkness. B. A young raccoon and a young fox have much in common.

═══ 22 ═══

Verb Agreement: To each Its Own Verb

After writing your answer(s) in the right-hand column, check this column to see whether you have responded correctly. If you have made a mistake, or if you need more practice, do whatever is asked below the dotted line in each answer frame.

Answers to questions for added practice can be found at the end of each lesson.

Understanding and Applying the Principles

1

Was anyone at home?

       (s = subject, v = verb)

Anyone refers to _____ [*one* or *more than one?*] person.

   For that reason, we use a singular verb, such as *is, was, has,* or *laughs,* to agree with the singular subject.

Answers and Added Practice

1

one

....

Fill each blank properly:

  A. If anyone _____ [*has* or *have*?] a question, raise your hand.

  B. If anyone _____ [*knows* or *know*?] the answer, raise your hand.

2

<u>Was anybody at home?</u>

Anybody refers to _____ [*one* or *more than one*?] person.

  For that reason we use a singular verb, such as *was*, to agree with the singular subject.

2

one

....

Fill each blank properly:

  A. Anybody who comes to the door _____ [*is* or *are*?] welcome.

  B. Anybody who knocks on our door _____ [*is* or *are*?] welcome.

3

<u>Was everybody at home?</u>

Everybody confuses some people, because it seems to refer to more than one person. However, it really means, "every single body" or "every person." For that reason *everybody* is properly considered singular, and we use with it a singular verb, such as _____ [*is* or *are*?], _____ [*was* or *were*?], and _____ [*laughs* or *laugh*?].

  (For *everybody* with other pronouns, see Lesson 40.)

3

is, was, laughs

....

Write a sentence beginning with *Nearly everybody in Detroit and Ann Arbor*

4

Either one is pleasing to the eye.

Either is pleasing to the eye.

These sentences illustrate the fact that *either* usually means the same as *either one*. For that reason, *either* normally takes a _____ [*singular* or *plural*?] verb, such as *is, was, has,* or *suggests*.

  The same statement is true of *neither*, as in **Neither is pleasing to the eye.**

4

singular

. . . .

In a rare situation *either* or *neither* may be plural. For instance, "The Swedes and the Finns were quarreling, and neither *were* willing to make concessions." Observe that in that sentence, *neither* refers to two plural words, *Swedes* and *Finns*.

Another example:

Either the books or the films *are* good sources for this topic.

5

s   v

Each of the children was playing alone.

That sentence shows that *each* is also a _____ [*singular* or *plural*?] word and takes a singular verb such as *is, was,* or *predetermines.*

IMPORTANT: Notice that the addition of a phrase such as *of the children* does not make any difference in the verb. Even if a dozen children were present, *each was playing alone,* the sentence tells us. Most verb agreement errors with subjects such as *each, either,* and so forth are caused by such distracting phrases as *of the children.* CONCENTRATE ON THE SUBJECT AND THE VERB.

5

singular

. . . .

Write a sentence beginning with *Each of the nine schools.*

6

s   v

Both of the children were in tears.

s   v

All of them were in tears.

These sentences show that these two subjects, _____ and _____, are _____ [*singular* or *plural*?] and require a _____ [*singular* or *plural*?] verb.

Note: Although *all* is most often plural, it is singular when followed by a singular, as in **All of the soup was eaten.**

6

both, all,
plural, plural

. . . .

Some and *most* may be either singular or plural, depending on what follows:

Some of the soup *was* eaten.

Some of the apples *were* eaten.

When countable things, such as apples, are involved, *some* and *most* require plural verbs.

7

To summarize:

  A. The words *anyone, anybody, everyone, everybody, either, neither,* and *each* are singular. When used as subjects, they require a _____ [*singular* or *plural*?] verb.

(For a note on *either* and *neither,* see Answer Frame 4.)

  B. The word *both* is plural. As a subject it takes a _____ _____ [*singular* or *plural*?] verb. (For notes on *all, some, most,* and *none,* see Frame 6 and Answer Frames 6 and 7.)

7

    A. singular

    B. plural

. . . .

None may mean either "not one" or "not any." Most writers treat it as they do *some* and *most*, using the plural verb with countable things: *None of the soup* was *eaten. None of the apples* were *eaten.* A few persons, however, insist that *none* is always singular, as in *None of the passengers* was *lost.*

8

In each sentence in Frames 8–10, choose the verb that agrees with the subject.

    A. Anybody _____ [*is* or *are?*] allowed two selections.

    B. All _____ [*is* or *are?*] welcome to attend.

    C. Both of the men in our office _____ [*is* or *are?*] un-married.

8

    A. is B. are C. are

. . . .

Choose the proper verb:

    A. In our home, each of the children _____ [*was* or *were?*] given certain tasks.

    B. Everybody running in these races _____ [*has* or *have?*] signed the agreement.

9

    A. Each _____ [*was* or *were?*] given two small presents.

    B. Each of the children _____ [*was* or *were?*] given two small presents.

    C. Everybody in the three buildings _____ [*was* or *were?*] evacuated.

9

    A. was B. was C. was

. . . .

Choose the proper verb:

    A. Both of the winners in the contest _____ [*was* or *were?*] from the East.

    B. Neither of the winners in the contest _____ [*was* or *were?*] from the West.

10

    A. Each of the two pianists _____ [*plays* or *play?*] well.

    B. Neither of the pianists _____ [*has* or *have?*] much chance in this competition.

    C. Nobody in these organizations _____ [*is* or *are?*] likely to disagree.

10

        A. plays   B. has   C. is

. . . .

Choose the proper verb:

   A. Most of the young people in this room _____ [*has* or *have*?] overcome drug addiction.

   B. Each of them _____ [*deserves* or *deserve*?] our praise.

11

Write a sentence beginning with *Each of* and using *is, was, has, are, were,* or *have* (any one that is correct) as the verb.

11

Model Answer

     Each of the boat owners has been charged with smuggling.

. . . .

Write a sentence beginning with *Everybody in these sororities* and using *is* or *are*, whichever is correct.

12

Write a sentence beginning with *If either of* and using *runs* or *run* (whichever is correct) in the opening clause.

12

Model Answer

     If either of these women runs, she will get my vote.

. . . .

Write a sentence beginning with *Although neither of* and using a correct verb.

13

Finish honestly: One thing I hope to remember from this lesson is that . . .

(In this frame, any answer that you consider honest and accurate is acceptable.)

Lesson 22: Answers to Questions for Added Practice

1. A. has B. knows **2.** A. is B. is **3.** MODEL: Nearly everybody in Detroit and Ann Arbor is rooting for the Michigan football team. **5.** MODEL: Each of the nine schools has sent a protest to the NCAA. **8.** A. was B. has **9.** A. were B. was **10.** A. have B. deserves **11.** MODEL: Everybody in these sororities is doing work for charity. **12.** MODEL: Although neither of my two answers was correct, I received partial credit.

═23═

Verb Agreement: Two Subjects and One Verb

After writing your answer(s) in the right-hand column, check this column to see whether you have responded correctly. If you have made a mistake, or if you need more practice, do whatever is asked below the dotted line in each answer frame.

Answers to questions for added practice can be found at the end of each lesson.

Understanding and Applying the Principles

1

Snoopy and Garfield are comic-strip characters.

(s = subject, v = verb)

In the sentence above, both *Snoopy* and *Garfield* are subjects. Two or more words used together in that way are called a *compound subject*.

For many years dogs and cats have been featured in comic strips.

In that sentence the compound subject is _____ and _____.

Answers and Added Practice

1

dogs, cats

. . . .

Add a word to complete the compound subject:

Children and _____ both seem to like the animal characters.

2

A compound subject may have three parts or even more. What are the three parts of the compound subject in this sentence?

Horses, dogs, and even pigs have been featured in movies and on television programs.

_____, _____, and _____

2

      horses, dogs, pigs

. . . .

Add a word to complete the three-part compound subject:

      Bears, wolves, and _____ are among the wild animals seen in movies.

3

      are

. . . .

The three-word plural verb in the second boldface sentence in Frame 1 is _____ _____ _____ .

4

      A. were   B. were

. . . .

Which verb is needed?

  A. The creek and the river _____ [*was* or *were*?] flooding.

  B. Jack and Gretchen _____ [*has* or *have*?] never seen so much water.

5

      A. pony

      B. singular, *is*

. . . .

Choose the correct verb and tell why it is correct:

      Either my cousin or my uncle _____ [*is* or *are*?] mistaken.

3

When the parts of a compound subject are joined by *and*, they obviously refer to more than one person or thing. That is, the subject is plural, and so requires a plural verb.

    In the first boldface sentence in Frame 1, the plural verb is _____ . [What word?]

4

Which verb is needed in each sentence?

  A. Lola and I _____ [*was* or *were*?] watching a movie last night.

  B. The hero and his sweetheart _____ [*was* or *were*?] endangered by a tigress defending her cubs.

5

In some sentences the parts of a compound subject are joined by *or* or *nor* rather than by *and*. For instance:

    A dog or a pony is a good pet for a child.

When *or* or *nor* is the connecting word, the verb agrees with the nearer part of the compound subject.

  A. Is *dog* or *pony* closer to the verb in the example above?

     _____

  B. Because the word *pony* is _____ [*singular* or *plural*?], the verb used in the example is the singular _____ . [What word?]

6

    Either the doctor or the two lawyers . . .

  A. The verb that follows that sentence-beginning should be _____ . [*singular* or *plural*?]

  B. Write the whole sentence, using *was* or *were* (whichever is correct) as the next word, and adding an appropriate conclusion.

6

A. plural

B. **Model Answer**
   Either the doctor or the two lawyers were the first to reach the accident.

....

Now finish this:

Either the two lawyers or the doctor _____

_____ .

7

A. Obviously, when both parts of a compound subject are plural the verb must be _____. [*singular* or *plural?*]

B. So we write:
   Neither my friends nor my enemies _____ [*is* or *are?*] likely to say that about me.

7

A. plural   B. are

....

Choose the correct verb and tell why it is correct:

The switches or the batteries _____ [*was* or *were?*] at fault.

8

To summarize:

A. When the parts of a compound subject are joined by *and*, the verb is _____. [*singular* or *plural?*]

B. When they are connected by *or* or *nor*, the verb agrees with the part of the subject that is _____. [Finish with one word.]

8

A. plural

B. closer (or a word similar in meaning)

....

The doctor or the nurses
The nurses or the doctor

When used as compound subjects, these two groups of words _____

_____ [*always* or *do not?*] require the same verb forms.

9

In Frames 9–11 choose the correct word for each sentence.

A. The planets and their sun _____ [*is* or *are?*] traveling through space at high speed.

B. The planets or their sun _____ [*seems* or *seem?*] unlikely ever to collide with another large celestial object.

9

    A. are   B. seems

. . . .

Choose the correct verb:

    Pluto or an undiscovered Planet X _____ [*is* or *are?*] the outermost planet in our solar system.

10

    A. _____ [*Is* or *Are?*] Jupiter or Saturn the largest of the planets?

    B. Neither the sun nor the moon _____ [*was* or *were?*] visible for a week.

10

    A. Is   B. was

. . . .

Choose the correct verb:

    Neither the planets nor the moon _____ [*is* or *are?*] large in comparison to the sun.

11

    A. I forget whether Mars, Venus, or Mercury _____ [*is* or *are?*] to be seen tonight.

    B. Delta Canis Majoris and Epsilon Canis Majoris _____ [*is* or *are?*] in the constellation Canis Major, obviously.

11

    A. is   B. are

. . . .

Choose the correct verb:

    The light areas and the dark areas of the moon _____ [*has* or *have?*] different physical features.

12

Make up a sentence using this skeleton:

                  s   s

_____ and _____

       v

_____ [*was* or *were?*] _____

_____ .

12

Model Answer

    Clyde and Oscar were driving out of the city.

. . . .

Make up another sentence with the same grammatical structure.

13

Now this one:

                 s   s

A _____ or several _____

       v

_____ [*is* or *are?*] _____

_____ .

13

Model Answer

A clove of garlic or several small onions are needed to add flavor.

. . . .

Make up another sentence with the same grammatical structure.

14

Now turn around the parts of the compound subject that you used in Frame 13.

s   s

Several _____ or a _____

v

_____ [*is* or *are?*] _____

_____ .

14

Model Answer

Several small onions or a clove of garlic is needed to add flavor.

. . . .

Make up another sentence with the same grammatical structure.

15

Finish honestly: One thing I hope to remember from this lesson is that . . .

(In this frame, any answer that you consider honest and accurate is acceptable.)

Lesson 23: Answers to Questions for Added Practice

1. MODEL: adults **2.** MODEL: tigers **3.** *have been featured* **4.** A. were B. have **5.** is MODEL: Only one is mistaken. **6.** MODEL: Either the two lawyers or the doctor is culpable. **7.** were MODEL: Both subjects are plural. **8.** do not **9.** is **10.** is **11.** have **12.** MODEL: Ray and Carol were excellent hosts. **13.** MODEL: A red rose or several small carnations were sure to enhance the beauty of the arrangement. **14.** MODEL: Several small carnations or a red rose was sure to enhance the beauty of the arrangement.

24

Verb Agreement: When Words Intervene Between Subject and Verb

After writing your answer(s) in the right-hand column, check this column to see whether you have responded correctly. If you have made a mistake, or if you need more practice, do whatever is asked below the dotted line in each answer frame.

Answers to questions for added practice can be found at the end of each lesson.

Understanding and Applying the Principles

1

$$\overset{s}{\overbrace{\text{The canary}}} \overset{v}{\overbrace{\text{was}}} \text{ hungry.}$$

The canary was hungry.

(s = subject, v = verb)

In the sentence above, the subject is _____ [*singular* or *plural?*], and the verb is therefore also _____. [*singular* or *plural?*]

Answers and Added Practice

1

singular, singular

. . . .

Captain Grimes is ready.

In that sentence the verb is _____
_____. [*singular* or *plural?*]

2

$$\overset{s}{\overbrace{\text{The canary}}} \overset{v}{\overbrace{\text{was}}} \text{ hungry, as well as the}$$

The canary was hungry, as well as the goldfish.

In that sentence the subject and the verb are still _____. [*singular* or *plural?*]

2

singular

. . . .

Captain Grimes is ready, as well as Lieutenant Foley.

In that sentence the verb is still _____. [*singular* or *plural?*]

3

$$\overset{s}{\overbrace{\text{The canary}}}\text{, as well as the goldfish, } \overset{v}{\overbrace{\text{was}}}$$

The canary, as well as the goldfish, was hungry.

In the sentence above, the words *as well as the goldfish* have been placed between the subject and the verb. The subject and the verb are _____ [*the same* or *not the same?*] as in Frames 1 and 2.

3

the same

· ·

Captain Grimes, as well as Lieutenant Foley, is ready.

In that sentence the subject and the verb are _____ [*the same* or *not the same*?] as in Answer Frames 1 and 2.

4

Many persons become confused by a sentence like the example in Frame 3. They argue that because two pets were hungry, the verb should be plural. However, the subject is still the singular noun *canary*. The phrase *as well as the goldfish* is only a modifier, as it was in Frame 2.

To agree with the subject, therefore, the verb must be _____ _____ . [*singular* or *plural*?]

4

singular

· ·

Captain Grimes, as well as his eighty men, is ready.

Finish this sentence:

The verb *is* is still correct because _____

_____

_____.

5

Besides *as well as*, some other expressions that often come between subject and verb are *along with, together with, including, besides, especially, such as,* and *in addition to*. The principle is the same: The verb should agree with its _____ [What?], regardless of what words come between the subject and the verb.

5

subject

· ·

The eighty men, as well as Captain Grimes himself, are ready.

Finish:

The verb *are* is needed this time because _____

_____

_____ .

6

So we should write:

The dean, along with several professors, _____ [*has* or *have*?] drawn up a plan.

6

has

· ·

We should write:

Several professors, together with the dean, _____ [*has* or *have*?] drawn up a plan.

7

We should write:

Four professors, including Ms. Alexander, _____ [*was* or *were*?] not in class today.

7

were

· ·

We should write:

Ms. Alexander, besides three other professors, _____ [*was* or *were*?] not in class today.

8

should

· ·

We should write:

These colors, especially the deep blue at the far right, _____ [*is* or *are*?] among my favorites.

9

A. was   B. were

· ·

We should write:

Painting, much more than other arts, _____ [*was* or *were*?] affected by the impressionists.

10

A. is   B. are

· ·

Love of nature, as well as affection for the simple life, _____ [*is* or *are*?] steadily visible in Wordsworth's poems.

11

A. is

B. constitute

· ·

We should write:

Jakarta, as well as Surabaja and Bandung, _____ densely populated.

8

We have been saying that in deciding whether a verb should be singular or plural we _____ [*should* or *should not*?] ignore words such as *along with* or *as well as* that come between the subject and the verb.

9

In Frames 9–11, choose the correct verb in each sentence.

A. Claude Monet, along with Alfred Sisley and Berthe Morisot, _____ [*was* or *were*?] responsible for the first exhibition of impressionistic paintings.

B. Critics, as well as the general public, _____ [*was* or *were*?] at first highly displeased with the new style.

10

A. Grasmere, as well as other lakes in the Lake District, _____ [*is* or *are*?] almost as beautiful and unspoiled as it was in Wordsworth's day.

B. Coleridge and Southey, as well as Wordsworth, _____ [*is* or *are*?] included among the Lake Poets.

11

A. Java, besides Sumatra and Bali and thousands of other islands, _____ [*is* or *are*?] in the Indonesian Republic.

B. Exports, including much sugar, _____ [*constitutes* or *constitute*?] a large portion of the Javanese economy.

12

Write a sentence of your own. Start with the name of one course you are taking, add *as well as* and the names of some other courses, and use *is* or *are* (whichever is correct) in completing your sentence.

12

Model Answer

Biology, as well as English and trigonometry, is time consuming.

. . . .

Write a second sentence, similar but starting with the names of *two* courses.

13

Write a sentence starting with *Several European countries, including*. Then name one European country, and complete the sentence using *is* or *are* (whichever is correct).

13

Model Answer

Several European countries, including Italy, are havens for art lovers.

. . . .

Write a sentence starting with *No European country except Italy and France . . .*

14

Finish honestly: One thing I hope to remember from this lesson is that . . .

(In this frame, any answer that you consider honest and accurate is acceptable.)

Lesson 24: Answers to Questions for Added Practice

1. singular **2.** singular **3.** the same **4.** MODEL: . . . the subject is still *Captain Grimes*, a singular noun. **5.** MODEL: . . . the subject is *men*, a plural noun. **6.** have **7.** was **8.** are **9.** was **10.** is **11.** is **12.** MODEL: Biology and English, as well as trigonometry, are time consuming. **13.** No European country except Italy and France is willing to sign the agreement.

25

Verb Agreement:
With there, here, *and Other Inversions*

After writing your answer(s) in the right-hand column, check this column to see whether you have responded correctly. If you have made a mistake, or if you need more practice, do whatever is asked below the dotted line in each answer frame.

Answers to questions for added practice can be found at the end of each lesson.

Understanding and Applying the Principles

1

There was a wooden duck on the shelf.

A. Is that sentence about a *there* or about a *duck*? _____

B. The subject of the sentence is therefore _____ . [What word?]

Answers and Added Practice

1

A. a duck   B. *duck*

....

There is also a wooden chicken.

In that sentence the subject is _____ . [What word?]

2

In most sentences, the subject comes before the verb. For instance:

$$\overset{\text{s} \qquad \text{v}}{\overbrace{\textbf{The duck is}}} \textbf{ wooden.}$$

A. In the boldface sentence in Frame 1, the verb is _____ . [What word?]

B. That verb comes _____ [*before* or *after*?] the subject.

2

A. *was*   B. before

....

In *There is also a wooden chicken,* the verb comes _____ [*before* or *after*?] the subject.

3

Often, especially after *there* or *here,* the usual positions of the subject and the verb are reversed. Instead of Subject–Verb the order is *There*—Verb—Subject.

Here is that duck.

In that sentence the order is _____ —_____ —_____ .

3

Here—Verb—Subject

....

Where is that duck?

In that example the order is

_____ — _____ —

_____ .

4

All this wouldn't matter except that the verb must agree with its subject. So we have to note whether the out-of-place subject is singular or plural.

  A. In *There was a duck on the shelf*, the subject is _____
    _____ . [*singular* or *plural?*]
  B. In *There were two ducks on the shelf*, the subject is _____
    _____ . [*singular* or *plural?*]

4

  A. singular   B. plural

....

Which is correct?

  A. Here is some chickens.
  B. Here are some chickens.

_____ [A or B?]

5

Besides there and *here*, other introductory words may result in a similar reversal of subject and verb.

  A. In *Nor was that announcement the only surprise*, the subject
    is _____ . [What word?]
  B. In *Nor were those announcements the only surprises*, the sub-
    ject is _____ . [What word?]
  C. In A, which has a singular subject, the verb is _____
    _____ . [*singular* or *plural?*]
  D. In B, which has a plural subject, the verb is _____
    _____ . [*singular* or *plural?*]

5

  A. *announcement*
  B. *announcements*
  C, singular
  D. plural

....

Which is or are correct?

  A. Neither is your presence
    welcome.
  B. Neither are your presents
    welcome.

_____ [A, B, or A *and* B?]

6

Most question words, especially *when, where, why,* and *how,* also often result in a reversal of subject and verb.

  A. We say *Where is my shoe?* and *Where* _____ [What
    verb?] *my shoes?*
  B. We say *When is she arriving?* and *When* _____ [What
    verb?] *they arriving?*
  C. We say *Why is the sky blue?* and *Why* _____ [What verb?]
    the skies blue?

6

  A. are   B. are   C. are

....

  A. Why _____ [*is* or *are?*]
    your shoe untied?
  B. Why _____ [*is* or *are?*]
    your shoes untied?
  C. How _____ [*is* or *are?*]
    their names pronounced?

7

Sometimes a *group* of words at the start of a sentence results in an inversion (a reversal of the subject-verb order).

  A. We say *In New York is my favorite museum*, and *In New York*
    _____ [What verb?] *my favorite museums.*
  B. We say *Early in the morning was heard a familiar sound*, and
    Early in the morning _____ [What verb?] *heard some fa-
    miliar sounds.*

7

A. are B. were

· ·

A. After the dancing _____

_____ [*comes* or
come?] the remembering.

B. After the dance _____
[*comes* or *come?*] the mem-
ories.

8

In summary, in a sentence with *there* or other words that result
in reversal, we need to locate the subject and then note whether
it should be singular or plural. As usual, a singular subject
requires a _____ verb, and a plural subject requires
a _____ verb.

8

singular, plural

· ·

Underline the subject in each sentence:

A. Where are the snows of
yesteryear?

B. Why does love so often
fade?

9

In Frames 9–11, write the correct verb in each blank.

A. Here _____ [*is* or *are?*] two eggs in a nest.

B. Where _____ [*has* or *have?*] the parent birds gone?

C. There _____ [*is* or *are?*] some birds in that tree.

9

A. are B. have C. are

· ·

A. There _____ [*hasn't*
or *haven't?*] been a close
race in recent years.

B. In fact, there _____
[*hasn't* or *haven't?*] ever
been any close races.

10

A. In the woods _____ [*was* or *were?*] a tiny hermitage.

B. In the woods _____ [*was* or *were?*] a tiny hermitage
and an old-fashioned well.

C. In the woods _____ [*was* or *were?*] a tiny hermitage
with an old-fashioned well beside it.

10

A. was B. were C. was

· ·

Three fat robins, wondering
what to do.
One flew away, and then there
_____ [*was* or *were?*]
two.

11

A. When _____ [*do* or *does?*] the next flight leave for
El Paso?

B. When _____ [*do* or *does?*] the next flights leave for
El Paso?

C. In El Paso _____ [*lives* or *live?*] my dearest friends.

11

A. does B. do C. live

· ·

A. Here _____ [*is* or *are*?] news of some pleasant developments.

B. Here _____ [*is* or *are*?] some new developments.

12

Make up a sentence starting with *There* followed by *was* or *were*, whichever is correct, and tell about two accidents on Fifth Street.

12

Model Answer

There were two serious accidents on Fifth Street this morning.

· ·

Finish this sentence:

On Fifth Street _____

[*was* or *were*] _____

_____ .

13

A. Complete: Near the bottom of the fire escape is _____

_____ .

B. Complete: Near the bottom of the fire escape are _____

_____ .

13

Model Answer

A. a small fenced-in area.

B. a narrow sidewalk and a street.

· ·

Complete: On top of the hill were

_____

_____ .

14

Finish honestly: One thing I hope to remember from this lesson is that . . .

(In this frame, any answer that you consider honest and accurate is acceptable.)

Lesson 25: Answers to Questions for Added Practice

1. *chicken* **2.** before **3.** Where—Verb—Subject **4.** B **5.** A and B **6.** A. is B. are C. are **7.** A. comes B. come **8.** A. snows B. love **9.** A. hasn't B. haven't **10.** were **11.** A. is B. are **12.** MODELS: On Fifth Street was a serious accident. On Fifth Street were two serious accidents. **13.** MODEL: On top of the hill were three tumbledown shanties.

26

Verb Agreement: *The Jury* is *or the Jury* are?

After writing your answer(s) in the right-hand column, check this column to see whether you have responded correctly. If you have made a mistake, or if you need more practice, do whatever is asked below the dotted line in each answer frame.

Answers to questions for added practice can be found at the end of each lesson.

Answers and Added Practice

1

　　singular

. . . .

Now think of an orchestra rather than a jury.

　　The orchestra _____ [*is* or *are*?] playing Beethoven's Sixth Symphony.

2

　　plural

. . . .

Think again of the orchestra.

　　The orchestra _____ [*is* or *are*?] tuning their instruments.

Understanding and Applying the Principles

1

Secluded in a jury room, members of a jury have weighed the evidence and finally voted. As is necessary in most trials in the United States, the verdict is unanimous. As a unit the jury—well, let's see.

The jury reports its decision that the defendant is guilty.

Because the jury is acting as a unit, a _____ [*singular* or *plural*?] verb has been used in the example.

2

In the course of that particular trial, the jury members have had to be "sequestered"—kept away from outsiders. For one or more nights they are taken to rooms in a local hotel. Obviously, they do not sleep in one room or sleep as a unit.

The jury have been locked in their rooms for the night.

Because the jury members were doing things individually rather than as a unit, a _____ [*singular* or *plural*?] verb such as *have, are,* or *sleep* is needed.

3

A noun that names a collection of people or things is called a *collective noun.* Among the familiar collective nouns are *class, committee, jury, team, audience, band, crowd,* and *herd.*
　　Which of these collective nouns can you name?

　　A. a _____ of pigeons
　　B. a _____ of quail
　　C. a _____ of whales
　　D. a _____ of fish
　　E. a _____ of bees

3

Most Likely Answers

    A. flock   B. covey or bevy

    C. pod   D. school or shoal

    E. swarm or hive

································

Try these:

    a *pack* of _____

    a *gaggle* of _____

    a *drove* of _____

4

Perhaps about four times out of five we treat a collective noun as a unit. When bees are swarming, for instance, we see not the individual bees but the whole swarm moving like a dark, humming little cloud at treetop level. So, of course, we say,

    A swarm of bees _____ [*was* or *were?*] passing over the Jordan house.

4

    was

································

Write a sentence about a *school* of small fish (considered as a unit.) Use *darts* or *dart*, whichever is correct.

5

Usually a band acts as a unit:

    The band _____ marching onto the field.

But sometimes the band members act as individuals:

    The band _____ walking or riding toward their homes.

    A. In the first example a _____ [*singular* or *plural?*] verb is required.

    B. In the second, the verb should be _____. [*singular* or *plural?*]

5

    A. singular   B. plural

································

Write a sentence in which *class* is likely to take a plural verb.

6

    POOR: **The band *has* now stopped playing and are leaving for their homes.**

In the first part of that sentence, the band is considered as _____ [*a unit* or *individuals?*], but in the second the emphasis is on _____. [*unit action* or *individual actions?*]

    Treating the band as both singular and plural in the same sentence results in awkwardness.

6

a unit
individual actions

....

Try to write an improved version of the boldface sentence in Frame 6.

7

Let's recapitulate:

A. When a collective noun used as a subject is regarded as a unit, it takes a _____ [*singular* or *plural?*] verb.

B. When the individual parts of the collection are emphasized, the noun takes a _____ [*singular* or *plural?*] verb.

C. Treating a collective noun as both a singular and plural in the same sentence is _____. [*wise* or *unwise?*]

7

A. singular
B. plural
C. unwise

....

Which verb?

The audience _____ [*is* or *are?*] talking, standing in the aisles, or struggling toward the refreshment stand.

8

In his "Elegy Written in a Country Churchyard" English poet Thomas Gray included this line: "The lowing herd wind slowly o'er the lea." Maybe he used the plural verb *wind* because most British people say things like "The Government are . . ." But perhaps Gray knew cows well. Often, as they walk single-file along their crooked paths through a meadow, some of them moo loudly or softly, and one occasionally stops to nip a blade of grass, another kicks at an annoying fly, another butts her neighbor in front, and so on. Gray realized that cows _____ _____ [*usually act* or *seldom act?*] as a unit.

8

seldom act

....

James Russell Lowell criticized people who have no goals or dreams as "The unmotived herd that only sleep and feed." His verbs show that he was thinking of a herd as _____ _____. [*a unit* or *individuals?*]

9

Write a sentence of your own starting with *The committee.* Tell of something that a committee does as a unit. Do you need a singular verb, such as *is, has,* or *approves;* or a plural verb such as *are, have,* or *approve?* _____ [*Singular* or *Plural?*]

9

Model Answer

 The committee quickly passes
 the motion. Singular

....

Write a similar sentence starting
with *The Rotary Club.*

10

Again start a sentence with *The committee.* This time tell of
things that members of the committee may do as individuals
during the deliberations. Use a clearly plural verb.

10

Model Answer

 The committee have doodled,
 argued, looked out the window,
 yawned, and argued some
 more.

....

Write a similar sentence about the
Rotary Club or some other club.
Again emphasize the actions of in-
dividuals.

11

Finish honestly: One thing I hope to remember from this lesson
is that . . .

(In this frame, any answer that you consider honest and accurate is acceptable.)

Lesson 26: Answers to Questions for Added Practice

1. is **2.** are **3.** wolves, geese, cattle (Some other answers are possible.) **4.** MODEL: A school of minnows
darts toward the shelter of a large rock. **5.** MODEL: The class are finishing their essays and preparing
to turn them in. **6.** MODEL: The band has now stopped playing, and its members are leaving for their
homes. **7.** are **8.** individuals **9.** MODEL: The Rotary Club has decided to contribute a hundred dollars.
10. The Rotary Club were straggling two by two into the meeting room. (*More likely:* The Rotary Club
members . . .)

▰▰27▰ Principal Parts: The i, a, u, *Verbs and the* -en *Verbs*

After writing your answer(s) in the right-hand column, check this column to see whether you have responded correctly. If you have made a mistake, or if you need more practice, do whatever is asked below the dotted line in each answer frame.

Answers to questions for added practice can be found at the end of each lesson.

Understanding and Applying the Principles

1

begin   drink   ring   sing   sink   swim

Only one letter is the same in all six of those verbs. What is that letter? _____

Answers and Added Practice

1

i

. . . .

The six verb forms have something else in common; each is in the present tense: *I begin now, I drink now, now I sing,* and so on.

2

When you look at the past tense forms of the same six verbs (for example, **Yesterday the children** *began* **to complain**), you will note that they all share another letter.

began   drank   rang   sang   sank   swam

That shared letter is _____ .

2

a

. . . .

Note: Most modern dictionaries also list *sung* and *sunk* as the past tense forms of *sing* and *sink.* Conservative users of the language prefer *sang* and *sank* for the past tense, as in *Cleo sang a solo while the ship sank.*

3

Finally, when you use *has, have,* or *had* with these verbs (*has begun,* for example), you note that they share still another letter:

(has) **begun   drunk   rung   sung   sunk   swum**

This time the shared letter is _____ .

These three basic forms of a verb are called its *principal parts.* The principal parts of *begin,* for example, are identified in this way:

Present tense	**Past tense**	**Past participle**
begin	began	(has) begun

3

u

....

In comparing the second principal part (the past tense) with the third (the past participle), we note that only the _____ [*second* or *third*?] should be used after *has, have,* or *had.*

Note: *shrink* (shrank, shrunk) and *spring* (sprang, sprung) are also *i, a, u* verbs but are not treated in this lesson. *Swing* (swung, swung) does not fit the pattern.

4

The principal parts we have been looking at have that name because they are the principal, or chief, forms of the verbs, on which the other forms are based.

> The principal parts of *begin* are, as we observed, *begin, began,* and *(has) begun.*

A. The principal parts of *drink* are _____, _____, and *(has)* _____.

B. Of *ring*: _____, _____, and *(has)* _____.

C. Of *sing*: _____, _____, and *(has)* _____.

D. Of *sink*: _____, _____, and *(has)* _____.

E. Of *swim*: _____, _____, and *(has)* _____.

4

A. drink, drank, drunk

B. ring, rang, rung

C. sing, sang, sung

D. sink, sank, sunk

E. swim, swam, swum

....

Say to yourself several times:

began	have begun
drank	have drunk
rang	have rung
sang	have sung
sank	have sunk
swam	have swum

5

drive	**drove**	(has) **driven**
eat	**ate**	(has) **eaten**
ride	**rode**	(has) **ridden**
speak	**spoke**	(has) **spoken**
write	**wrote**	(has) **written**

A. The words in the third column share what two letters? _____

B. So, as you might expect, these verbs may be called the _____ [What two letters?] verbs.

Note: Other *-en* verbs, not treated here, include *break (broke, broken), choose (chose, chosen), fall (fell, fallen),* and *give (gave, given).*

5

A. *en*   B. *-en*

....

Say to yourself several times:

drove	have driven
ate	have eaten
ride	have ridden
spoke	have spoken
wrote	have written

6

The chief problem with both the *i, a, u* verbs and the *-en* verbs is the confusing of the second and third principal parts.

The second principal part is the past tense (*swam* and *wrote,* for instance). It never needs the help of another verb and will cause some people to object if one is used. So we write

I *swam* across the lagoon.

She _____ [past tense of *write*] a sonnet. We _____ [past tense of *drink*] two quarts of milk after our hike.

6

wrote, drank

. . . .

Write the past tense of each verb:

She _____ [*speak*] in a monotone.

He _____ [*eat*] the sardines.

The waterlogged board _____ _____ [*sink*].

The chimes _____ [*ring*].

The fight _____ [*begin*] at Clancy's.

7

But if we have a helping verb (usually *has, have, had, is, are, was,* or *were*) we use instead the third principal part, the past participle. So we write

   A. I have _____ [a form of *swim*] across the lagoon.

   B. Her sonnet was _____ [a form of *write*] late at night.

   C. We have _____ [a form of *drink*] two quarts of milk.

7

A. swum   B. written
C. drunk

. . . .

Write the correct form of each verb.

She has never _____ [*speak*] to me.

All the sardines have been _____ . [*eat*]

Has the board _____ ? [*sink*]

Have the chimes _____ ? [*ring*]

Has the fight _____ ? [*begin*]

8

To summarize: When you are uncertain whether to use the second or the third principal part of a verb, follow these two simple guides:

   A. If there is not a helping verb, choose the _____ [*second* or *third*?] principal part.

   B. If there is a helping verb (usually *has, have, had, is, are, was,* or *were*), choose the _____ [*second* or *third*?] principal part.

8

A. second   B. third

. . . .

Write a short original sentence with the third principal part of each *-en* verb in Answer Frame 7.

9

If any of the *i, a, u* verbs or the *-en* verbs cause you trouble, the best way to master them is oral. Make up a short sentence with the past tense form and a similar sentence with a helping verb and the third principal part.

   For example: *I rode the horse. I have ridden the horse.*

Say the two sentences several times, aloud if possible. Repeat several more times if the problem recurs.

   Try that—right now—with all the *i, a, u,* or *-en* verbs that you cannot use confidently. (Nothing to write here.)

9

No Written Answer

....

Repeat the oral practice as necessary.

10

In Frames 10–12 choose between the past tense and the past participle of the verb in brackets.

A. They _____ [*begin*] to pray.
B. They have _____ [*begin*] to pray.
C. She _____ [*drink*] some sangria.
D. She has _____ [*drink*] some sangria.
E. We _____ [*ring*] the bell.
F. The bell was _____ [*ring*].
G. Children _____ [*sing*] the old ballad.
H. Children have _____ [*sing*] the old ballad.

10

A. began	B. begun
C. drank	D. drunk
E. rang	F. rung
G. sang	H. sung

....

Write an original sentence using one of the verbs above that you find difficult.

11

A. The bottle _____ . [*sink*]
B. The bottle has _____ . [*sink*]
C. She _____ [*swim*] for an hour.
D. She had _____ [*swim*] for an hour.
E. We _____ [*drive*] all night.
F. We have _____ [*drive*] all night.
G. We _____ [*eat*] lunch early.
H. We have not _____ [*eat*] lunch yet.

11

A. sank	B. sunk
C. swam	D. swum
E. drove	F. driven
G. ate	H. eaten

....

Write an original sentence using one of the verbs above that you find difficult.

12

A. Kelly _____ [*ride*] a unicorn.
B. The unicorn had never been _____ [*ride*] before.
C. She _____ [*speak*] in monosyllables.
D. Her words were _____ [*speak*] haltingly.
E. In high school we _____ [*write*] too seldom.
F. In college I have _____ [*write*] two long term papers.

12

A. rode   B. ridden
C. spoke   D. spoken
E. wrote   F. written

. . . .

Write an original sentence using one of the verbs above that you find difficult.

13

Finish honestly: One thing I hope to remember from this lesson is that . . .

(In this frame, any answer that you consider honest and accurate is acceptable.)

Lesson 27: Answers to Questions for Added Practice

3. third **6.** spoke, ate, sank, rang, began **7.** spoken, eaten, sunk, rung, begun **8.** MODEL: I have seldom spoken in public. MODEL: Mice have eaten some of the flour.

═══28═══

Principal Parts: come, do, draw, fly, go, grow, *and* see

After writing your answer(s) in the right-hand column, check this column to see whether you have responded correctly. If you have made a mistake, or if you need more practice, do whatever is asked below the dotted line in each answer frame.

Answers to questions for added practice can be found at the end of each lesson.

Understanding and Applying the Principles

1

Present Tense	Past Tense	Past Participle
come	came	(have) come

Ruth *came* back last week.
Ruth had not *come* back before.

Many of the troubles with the seven verbs in this lesson arise from confusing the past tense with the past participle.

The examples above show that the past tense _____

_____ [*takes* or *does not take*?] a helping

verb, but that the past participle _____ .
[*does* or *does not*?]

Answers and Added Practice

1

does not take, does

. . . .

A. Is *Pete come home* correct? _____

B. Is *Pete had came home* correct? _____

C. Is *Pete had come from Memphis* correct? _____

D. Is *Pete came from Memphis* correct? _____

2

The principle illustrated with *come* in Frame 1 applies to other irregular verbs.

Present Tense	Past Tense	Past Participle
do	**did**	(have) **done**
draw	**drew**	(have) **drawn**
fly	**flew**	(have) **flown**
go	**went**	(have) **gone**
grow	**grew**	(have) **grown**
see	**saw**	(have) **seen**

The past tense uses no helper, but the past participle does. So it is easy to choose the correct verb in each of these sentences:

A. Rae had _____ [*did* or *done?*] her best.

B. She had _____ [*drew* or *drawn?*] the picture.

C. She had _____ [*flew* or *flown?*] to New York with it.

D. She had never _____ [*went* or *gone?*] to New York before.

E. She had _____ [*grew* or *grown?*] up in the Midwest.

F. She had never _____ [*saw* or *seen?*] a city larger than Dayton.

2

A. done	B. drawn
C. flown	D. gone
E. grown	F. seen

. . . .

Choose the correct form of the verb (past tense or past participle.)

A. [*do*] I _____ it this morning.

B. [*draw*] He _____ a number.

C. [*fly*] Have you ever _____ ?

D. [*go*] We _____ yesterday.

E. [*grow*] The tree _____ fast.

F. [*see*] I _____ it first!

3

The helping (or auxiliary) verbs used with a past participle are usually *has, have, had, is, are, was,* or *were. Be* or *been* may also appear in such combinations as *could be seen* or *has been done.*

A. [*see*] An oriole was _____ in the orchard.

B. [*do*] All the work has been _____ .

C. [*draw*] Have the papers been _____ up?

D. [*fly*] Have the birds _____ away?

E. [*come*] Has the postman _____ yet?

F. [*go*] Has the postman _____ yet?

3

    A. seen   B. done
    C. drawn   D. flown
    E. come   F. gone

. . . .

More practice:

    A. [*grow*] How that girl has ___ _____ !
    B. [*fly*] Who has _____ to Anchorage recently?
    C. [*do*] Granny _____ all the work.

4

Summary:

Underline the verb in each pair that may be correctly used with a helping verb.

    come, came   done, did   drawn, drew
    flew, flown   went, gone   grew, grown
    seen, saw

4

come, done, drawn, flown, gone, grown, seen

. . . .

Write sentences using three of those verbs.

5

If you find it difficult to remember the proper use of any of the verbs in this lesson, the best way to master them is oral. Make up pairs of similar sentences with the past tense and the past participle of each troublesome verb.

    For example: *I saw a purple cow. I have never seen a purple cow.* Say the two sentences several times, aloud if possible, and repeat several more times if the problem recurs.

    Try that—right now—with all the verbs in this lesson that you cannot use confidently.

(Nothing to write here.)

5

No Written Answer

. . . .

As a doctor's prescription sometimes says, *Take additional doses as necessary.*

6

In Frames 6–7 write the proper form—past tense or past participle—of the verb.

    A. [*do*] I _____ it!
    B. [*do*] Never had I _____ it before.
    C. [*fly*] I had never _____ a model plane successfully.
    D. [*grow*] I had _____ accustomed to defeat.
    E. [*come*] I could hardly wait until Dad _____ home.

6

A. did   B. done   C. flown
D. grown   E. came

....

More of the same:

A. [*grow*] Have you ever _____
   _____ house ferns?

B. [*come*] Last year mine _____
   _____ up all right but
   didn't flourish.

C. [*see*] I'm glad you haven't
   _____ my ferns.

7

A. [*go*] Have you ever _____ to San Francisco?
B. [*fly*] Yes. I have _____ there three times.
C. [*see*] Have you _____ the Golden Gate Bridge?
D. [*see*] Of course I _____ that!
E. [*grow*] Has the city's population _____ steadily?
F. [*go*] No. It _____ down between 1950 and 1980.
G. [*draw*] It has _____ numerous Spanish speakers in recent years.

7

A. gone   B. flown   C. seen
D. saw   E. grown   F. went
G. drawn

....

**I came home, did some work,
and went away again.**

Rewrite that sentence, inserting *had* after *I* and making other necessary changes throughout.

8

Choose from the seven verbs in this lesson one that you or some of your friends misuse. Write a sentence using its past tense form. Then rewrite the sentence, this time with a helping verb and the past participle.

8

Model Answer

I drew a winning number. I have seldom drawn winning numbers.

....

Repeat Frame 8 with a different one of the seven verbs.

9

Repeat, with a different one of the seven verbs, what you did in Frame 8. This time use the past participle in your first sentence.

9

Model Answer

You've come a long way, Ma'am!

You came a long way, Ma'am!

....

Repeat Frame 9 with a different one of the seven verbs.

10

Finish honestly: One thing I hope to remember from this lesson is that . . .

(In this frame, any answer that you consider honest and accurate is acceptable.)

Lesson 28: Answers to Questions for Added Practice

1. A. No B. No C. Yes D. Yes **2.** A. did B. drew C. flown D. went E. grew F. saw **3.** A. grown B. flown C. did **6.** A. grown B. came C. seen **7.** I had come home, done some work, and gone away again. **8.** MODELS: She saw a pigeon. She has seen a pigeon. **9.** MODELS: She had gone to the store. She went to the store.

══════29══════

Principal Parts:
sit, set; lie, lay; rise, raise

After writing your answer(s) in the right-hand column, check this column to see whether you have responded correctly. If you have made a mistake, or if you need more practice, do whatever is asked below the dotted line in each answer frame.

Answers to questions for added practice can be found at the end of each lesson.

Understanding and Applying the Principles

1

    s   v

Betty sat on the tuffet.

    s   v   o

Betty set the box on the tuffet.

(s = subject, v = verb, o = object)

In the first sentence, Betty did not place anything on the tuffet (except herself).

In the second, she placed the _____ on the tuffet.

Answers and Added Practice

1

box

. . . .

Betty unwisely set the plastic dish on the stove.

In that sentence, label the subject *s*, the verb *v*, and the object *o* (the name of what she set).

2

catalog

. . . .

Frieda lays her magenta dress across the bed.

Label the three parts as in Answer Frame 1.

3

cup

. . . .

Marta slowly and quietly raises the window beside her bed.

Again, label as in Answer Frame 1.

4

box, catalog, cup

. . . .

From Answer Frames 1, 2, and 3 copy the three verbs with the object of each.

2

    s   v
Freda lies on the sofa.

    s   v   o
Freda lays the catalog on the sofa.

In the first sentence, Freda does not place anything on the sofa (except herself).

In the second, she places the ＿＿＿＿＿＿＿ on the sofa.

3

    s   v
Marta rises at nine on Sundays.

    s   v   o
Marta raises the cup to nose level.

In the first sentence, Marta does not lift anything (except herself).

In the second, she lifts the ＿＿＿＿＿ .

4

The first three frames have illustrated the fact that when we use a form of *set, lay,* or *raise,* we need always to name what is set, laid, or raised. In other words, the verbs *set, lay,* and *raise* take grammatical objects—names of *real* objects that someone sets, lays, or raises.

    In Frames 1, 2, and 3, the objects are labeled *o*. List those three objects.

＿＿＿＿＿＿＿ ＿＿＿＿＿＿＿ ＿＿＿＿＿＿＿

5

If you do not know whether to use a form of *set, lay,* or *raise* or a form of *sit, lie,* or *rise,* think about whether something (or someone) is being placed or lifted.

A. If something (or someone) is being placed or lifted, a form of *set,* ＿＿＿＿＿＿ , or ＿＿＿＿＿＿ [What two verbs?] should be used.

B. If nothing is being placed or lifted, a form of *sit,* ＿＿＿＿ ＿＿＿＿＿＿ , or ＿＿＿＿＿＿ should be used.

5

    A. lay, raise

    B. lie, rise

....

In each sentence, is something being placed or lifted?

    A. She sets the dishes down.

        ————————

    B. The dog lies in the shade.

        ————————

    C. She raised her hand.

        ————————

6

Principal Parts of *sit* and *set*

Present Tense	Past Tense	Past Participle
I *sit* here.	I *sat* here	I have *sat* here.
I *set* it here.	I *set* it here.	I have *set* it here.

    A. We should say, "I _____ [*sat* or *set*?] on this hillside last week."

    B. We should say, "I have often _____ [*sat* or *set*?] on this hillside."

6

    A. sat B. sat

....

    A. I am _____ [*sitting* or *setting*?] near a window.

    B. I have _____ [*sat* or *set*?] here for a month.

    C. I enjoy _____ [*sitting* or *setting*?] records for _____ [*sitting* or *setting*?]

7

Principal Parts of *lie* and *lay*

Present Tense	Past Tense	Past Participle
I *lie* here now.	I *lay* here yesterday.	I have *lain* here.
I *lay* it here.	I *laid* it here.	I have *laid* it here.

    A. We should say, "She _____ [*lay* or *laid*?] on the hillside for an hour yesterday."

    B. We should say, "She has _____ [*lain* or *laid*?] on the hillside for an hour."

7

    A. lay B. lain

....

    A. The cat _____ [*lies* or *lays*?] near the fire.

    B. She is _____ [*lying* or *laying*?] there now.

    C. She has _____ [*lain* or *laid*?] there nearly an hour.

8

Principal Parts of *rise* and *raise*

Present Tense	Past Tense	Past Participle
I *rise*.	I *rose*.	I have *risen*.
I *raise* it.	I *raised* it.	I have *raised* it.

    A. We should say, "I _____ [*rose* or *raised up*?] too quickly."

    B. We should say, "My hand had _____ [*risen* or *raised*?] involuntarily."

8

A. rose   B. risen

. . . .

A. Don't _____ [*rise* or *raise?*] up now.

B. He _____ [*rose* or *raised?*] the window.

C. The window _____ [*rose* or *raised?*] mysteriously.

9

In Frames 9–11, test each sentence to observe whether something is being placed or lifted. If so, choose a suitable form of *set, lay,* or *raise.* Otherwise choose a suitable form of *sit, lie,* or *rise.*

A. [*sit, set*] Bob _____ the bust of Caruso on the shelf.

B. [*sit, set*] It has _____ there ever since.

C. [*sit, set*] Bob likes to _____ here admiring it.

D. [*lie, lay*] Now he is _____ on the couch looking at the bust of his idol. [Use an *-ing* form.]

9

A. sets (present) or set (past)

B. sat

C. sit

D. lying (Note the spelling.)

. . . .

A. Don't just _____ [*sit* or *set?*] there.

B. _____ [*Lie* or *Lay?*] down, Spot!

C. I decided to _____ [*lie* or *lay?*] down for a while.

10

A. [*lie, lay*] Bob _____ here each afternoon.

B. [*lie, lay*] He has _____ here every day.

C. [*lie, lay*] Today he has _____ a clean pillow on the couch.

D. [*rise, raise*] A few minutes ago he _____ up angrily because of a noisy neighbor.

10

    A. lies (present) or lay (past)

    B. lain C. laid D. rose

. . . .

    A. _____ [*Sit* or *Set?*] down, please.

    B. It's not easy to _____ [*sit* or *set?*] still.

    C. They _____ [*lay* or *laid?*] on the cots.

11

Write short sentences correctly using each of the following verbs:

    A. has risen

    B. have lain

    C. lying

    D. laying

    E. sits

    F. set

11

Model Answers

    A. The moon has risen

    B. The seeds have lain dormant.

    C. Sid is still lying there.

    D. Masons are laying bricks.

    E. She sits on the floor.

    F. I set the tuffet there for her.

. . . .

Use these correctly:

lay (past tense of *lie*)

lays (a present tense form of *lay*)

12

Follow the instructions in Frame 11.

    A. was sitting

    B. was setting

    C. was lying

    D. had been lying

    E. raised

    F. rose

12

Model Answers

   A. She was sitting in an odd position.

   B. We were setting the pieces on the chessboard.

   C. A five-dollar bill was lying in the gutter.

   D. It had been lying there unnoticed.

   E. Our opponents raised several questions.

   F. We rose to answer them.

13

Follow the instructions in Frame 11.

   A. lay (a form of *lie*)

   B. laid

   C. lain

   D. sitting, lying

   E. setting, raising

13

Model Answers

   A. Tom lay there stunned and unmoving.

   B. I laid my hand on his chest.

   C. How long had he lain there?

   D. I had been sitting at home while he was lying here.

   E. Lucy had been setting the table and nobody thought about where Tom might be.

14

A college president once remarked, "I can tell whether a person is a college graduate by noticing whether he or she uses *lie* and *lay* correctly." Probably his observation was neither scientific nor completely accurate.

   Nevertheless, a careless or an uneducated person is _____ _____ [*likely* or *unlikely*?] to use all forms of the two verbs properly.

14

unlikely

....

Do you ever judge a person—whether fairly or unfairly—by the kind of language he uses?

15

If you find it difficult to remember the proper uses of some of the verbs in this lesson, the best way to master them is oral. Make up short sentences in which you correctly use the forms that give you trouble.

For example: **She was *lying* down. She *lay* there for ten minutes. Then she *sat* up. She had not *lain* there long. Now she is *sitting* up.**

Say the sentences several times, aloud if possible, and repeat them each time the problem recurs.

Try that—right now—with any of the verb forms that you cannot use confidently. (Nothing to write here.)

15

No Written Answer

....

Oral repetition of language forms and patterns is the best way to make them stick. After enough repetition, one no longer needs to think about them but automatically speaks or writes them.

16

Finish honestly: One thing I hope to remember from this lesson is that . . .

(In this frame, any answer that you consider honest and accurate is acceptable.)

Lesson 29: Answers to Questions for Added Practice

1. Betty (s), set (v), dish (o) **2.** Frieda (s), lays (v), dress (o) **3.** Marta (s), raises (v), window (o) **4.** set dish, lays dress, raises window **5.** A. Yes B. No C. Yes **6.** A. sitting B. sat C. setting, sitting **7.** A. lies B. lying C. lain **8.** A. rise B. raised C. rose **9.** A. sit B. Lie C. lie **10.** A. Sit B. sit C. lay **11.** MODELS: The injured player lay still for at least a minute. The judge lays his gavel down. **12.** (Personal opinion)

═30═

Future Tense: Does Anybody Still Say shall?

After writing your answer(s) in the right-hand column, check this column to see whether you have responded correctly. If you have made a mistake, or if you need more practice, do whatever is asked below the dotted line in each answer frame.

Answers to questions for added practice can be found at the end of each lesson.

Understanding and Applying the Principles

1

A story about an ultraconservative English teacher of yester-year: He saw a woman struggling in deep water and heard her shouting: "I will drown! Nobody shall save me!"

The English teacher said to himself, "What a pity that she has determined to drown!"

Why do you suppose he said that? _____
_____
_____

Answers and Added Practice

1

Model Answer
He thought that the woman's use of *shall* (with *I*) and *will* (with *nobody*) showed determination. (Count any other answer as correct.)

· ·

If you were the swimmer, what might you yell?

2

Actually, future time is often shown without *shall* or *will*, as in *I am going to . . .* , or *I plan to . . .* , or *I am about to . . .* , or the like. Sometimes we even use present tense verbs to mean future time.

For instance, *She arrives Friday* means that she will _____
_____ . [What two words?]

2

arrive Friday

....

Write two short sentences illustrating future time, the first by using *She expects to*, the second by using a present tense verb.

3

People sometimes worry about whether to use *shall* or *will* to indicate future time. However, except in very formal circumstances, *will* is used today in most statements in which the choice exists and is used also in questions (except those like *Shall I cook some parsnips?*)

So, worrying about *shall* is largely _____.
[*necessary* or *needless*?]

3

needless

....

Write a sentence, probably but not necessarily a question, in which you normally use *shall.*

4

Until early in this century, books prescribed rigid rules for *shall* and *will*. Today, unless we are writing something for extremely conservative readers, few people are likely to follow those rules.

However, in case you ever *do* feel yourself needing highly formal language, it is _____ [*wise* or *unwise*?] to know a little about the rules.

4

wise

....

Language changes. A new word may be invented, may flourish, and then may die. Pronunciations change. Grammatical patterns slowly alter. A usage that is standard in one century may become nonstandard in another, or vice versa.

5

So, in brief, here they are:

(1) In simple statements about the future, use *shall* with *I* or *we* (first person pronouns), and use *will* with nouns and all other pronouns.

(2) In statements making a promise or expressing determination, reverse what was said in (1).

A. In formal situations, then, for a simple statement we should say, "We _____ [*shall* or *will*?] discuss the matter further tonight."

B. Also, "They _____ [*shall* or *will*?] discuss the matter further tonight."

C. To show determination or promise, "We _____ [*shall* or *will*?] succeed," and "They _____ [*shall* or *will*?] not cross our border!"

5

    A. shall
    B. will
    C. will, shall

. . . .

Look back at Frame 1. The swimmer seemed to be _____ _____ _____ .

[*making a simple statement,* or *showing determination?*]

6

In selecting *shall* or *will* for each of these sentences, make the highly formal choice.

    A. I _____ need considerable reassurance.
    B. He _____ fly tomorrow from Washington to New Delhi.
    C. Do not be afraid. No one _____ harm you.

6

    A. shall B. will C. shall

. . . .

    A. Sentences A and B in Frame 6 express _____ _____ .

      [*simple statements* or *determination or promise?*]
    B. Sentence C expresses _____ _____ .

7

Interestingly, some prominent persons in our century have turned the old rules around. Early in World War II Prime Minister Winston Churchill told the British people, "We shall fight on the beaches . . . we shall fight in the fields and on the streets . . . we shall never surrender." And American General Douglas MacArthur, retreating from Corregidor, said, "I shall return."

    Churchill and MacArthur were each using *shall* with the first person to _____ _____ . [*make a simple statement* or *express determination or promise?*]

7

    express determination or promise

. . . .

Note the reversal. Ordinarily, as we have seen, formal language would employ _____ [*shall* or *will*] with *I* or *we* to show determination.

8

Finish honestly: One thing that I hope to remember from this lesson is that . . .

(In this frame, any answer that you consider honest and accurate is acceptable.)

Lesson 30: Answers to Questions for Added Practice

1. (Personal preference, but "Help!" seems most likely) **2.** MODELS: Ms. Randolph expects to have new merchandise soon. She makes the announcement tomorrow. **3.** MODEL: Shall I leave the car where it is? **5.** showing determination **6.** A. simple statements B. promise (possibly determination, too) **7.** will

═31═

Undesirable Shifts in Verbs: Tense, Voice, and Mood

After writing your answer(s) in the right-hand column, check this column to see whether you have responded correctly. If you have made a mistake, or if you need more practice, do whatever is asked below the dotted line in each answer frame.

Answers to questions for added practice can be found at the end of each lesson.

Understanding and Applying the Principles

1

An old wisecrack that you can repeat while driving quickly through a small town: "This is a pretty little town, wasn't it?"

In that joke, *is* is in the present tense: it refers to present time. *Was* is in the past tense: it refers to _____ time.

Answers and Added Practice

1

past

. . . .

The chief tenses are present (*see* or *sees*), past (*saw*), and future (*will see*). Others include present perfect (*has* or *have seen*), past perfect (*had seen*), and future perfect (*will have seen*).

2

Usually there's nothing funny about changes in tense. They may be not only unnecessary but also ridiculous.

> **Dapper Don Donegal strode into the saloon, and the first person he sees is Dangerous Dan Devore.**

A. In that sentence there is no reason at all to shift from the past tense *strode* to the present tense _____ and _____ .

B. The present tense verbs should be changed to _____ and _____ .

2

    A. sees, is

    B. saw, was

. . . .

Don scowled at Dan, and reaches instinctively toward his holster.

The present tense verb _____ _____ should be changed to the _____ tense verb _____ .

3

Sometimes a shift in tense *is* needed.

> I *read* (past tense) in the paper that three more satellites *will be launched* (future tense) soon.
>
> The woman at the ticket window *told* (past tense) me that the tickets *are* (present tense) no longer available.
>
> Galileo *believed* (past tense) that the earth *is* (present tense) not the center of the universe.

As those illustrations show, you may shift tense if there is a good _____ for doing so.

3

    reason

. . . .

Explain briefly why the shifts in Frame 3 are justified.

4

Mavis opened the door, and on the lawn two kittens were seen.

In that example, the undesirable shift is in voice, from active to passive. *Opened* tells what act the subject (Mavis) performed.

Does *were seen* tell what act the subject performed? _____

4

    No

. . . .

Which sentence is better?

    A. **We hurried, and soon reached the cabin.**

    B. **We hurried, and soon the cabin was reached.**

    _____

5

In the *active voice*, the subject of the verb does something. In the *passive voice*, something is done to the subject.

> The example in Frame 4 has the verb *opened* in the _____ _____ [Which?] voice, and the verb *were seen* in the _____ voice.

5

    active, passive

. . . .

Rewrite: **My father wanted to fly to Detroit, but that suggestion was vetoed by my mother.**

6

To avoid the unnecessary shift in voice in Frame 4, we could write this:

> Mavis _____ [What verb?] the door, and on the lawn she _____ [What verb?] two kittens.

6

opened, saw

....

Rewrite to correct two shifts:

The cats frisked about, but are startled by a hawk.

7

Look in the drawer, and you may then take out the smaller package.

Shifts in mood, as in that example, may be less awkward than shifts in tense and voice. The first clause in the example gives a command and is in the *imperative mood*.

Does the second clause also give a command? _____

7

No

....

Mood is sometimes called *mode*. The most common mood, the *indicative*, makes a statement. The *imperative* mood expresses a command or a request. The *subjunctive* mood usually expresses a wish or condition contrary to fact. (See Lesson 32.)

8

To avoid the shift in mood in Frame 7, we can simply omit two or three words in the second clause. The sentence will then read:

_____

_____

8

Look in the drawer, and (then) take out the smaller package.

....

Rewrite: **I recommend that Gordon be re-elected, and besides, he deserves a raise.**

9

To summarize: Avoid unnecessary shifts in the _____ , _____ , or _____ of verbs. (If necessary, review Frames 2, 4, and 7.)

9

tense, voice, mood

. . . .

Rewrite: **I wish that I could be living in the eighteenth century, and some of the gowns of that period would be spectacular to wear.**

10

In Frames 10 and 11, choose the preferable word(s) for each blank.

A. Jerry lit a fire in the fireplace, and soon the cabin _____ [*is* or *was?*] warm.

B. He found more wood, and in a little while _____ _____ [*laid it* or *it was laid?*] onto the lively blaze.

C. That pleasant fire _____ [*comforts* or *comforted?*] not only our bodies but also our spirits.

10

A. was

B. laid it

C. comforted

. . . .

Finish:

The reason for *comforted* in sentence C is that _____ _____ _____ _____

11

A. We begin our closing sprint, and now the finish line _____ _____ [*is* or *was?*] only a hundred meters away.

B. The spectators rise to their feet and _____ _____ _____ [*are excited by the tightness of the race* or *roar encouragement to the three runners now side by side?*]

C. "Run, Charley, and _____ _____ " [*it will be possible for you to win!* or *win!*]

11

A. is B. roar encouragement . . . C. win!

. . . .

In sentence C, *win!* is not only in the same mood as *Run!*, but also, in the circumstances, it seems more _____ .

12

Make up a pair of sentences about a scary scene in a movie. Use the same tense, voice, and mood in both.

12

Model Answer

> The door slowly opened and the barrel of a shotgun emerged. Somewhere else, a rifle cracked.

....

Add another sentence to what you wrote.

13

Compose a compound or complex sentence. Tell someone how to go to a certain room or building on campus.

13

Model Answer

> Go straight ahead to the corner, walk left for a block, and then go left for a half block.

....

Compose a sentence about three things that you did earlier today. Avoid shifts.

14

Finish honestly: One thing I hope to remember from this lesson is that . . .

(In this frame, any answer that you consider honest and accurate is acceptable.)

Lesson 31: Answers to Questions for Added Practice

2. *reaches*, past, *reached* **3.** MODELS: The reading and the launching occur at different times. The telling and the availability occur at different times. The present tense (*is, are, am,* etc.) is used for something that is lastingly true—"the eternal present." **4.** A **5.** My father wanted to fly to Detroit, but my mother vetoed that suggestion. **6.** The cats frisked about, but a hawk startled them. **8.** MODEL: I recommend that Gordon be re-elected and given a raise. **9.** MODEL: I wish that I could be living in the eighteenth century and (be) wearing some of the spectacular gowns of that period. **10.** MODEL: The tense agrees with the tense used in the previous sentences. **11.** MODEL: appropriate **12.** MODEL: A woman screamed. **13.** MODEL: I woke up early and almost bright, whistled all the way to my first class, and knew all the answers to the test questions.

32

The Subjunctive Mood: If I Were a Peanut

After writing your answer(s) in the right-hand column, check this column to see whether you have responded correctly. If you have made a mistake, or if you need more practice, do whatever is asked below the dotted line in each answer frame.

Answers to questions for added practice can be found at the end of each lesson.

Understanding and Applying the Principles

1

> **If George Washington were alive, our foreign policy would be different.**

Is President George Washington alive? _____

Answers and Added Practice

1

No

. . . .

If I were a peanut, I'd grow underground.

If I were a marble, I'd be nice and round.

Am I a peanut or a marble? _____

2

The example in Frame 1 illustrates the most frequent use of the *subjunctive mood* in modern English. It occurs in a clause starting with *if*, it appears in a statement that is contrary to fact, and (with a singular subject) it uses the verb _____ [which word?] rather than *was*.

Note: Not all *if*-clauses are contrary to fact; some are not and so should not be treated as subjunctive. For instance, in *If it was raining, we stayed indoors*, the meaning is "During the times when it was raining . . ."—not at all contrary to fact.

2

were

. . . .

Look again at Answer Frame 1. Note that the two opening clauses meet the three conditions mentioned in Frame 2.

3

> **I wish I were a songbird.**

A. When we make a wish, the thing we are wishing _____ [*is* or *is not*?] now true. For that reason the subjunctive is customarily used for wishes: they are at the time of the wish contrary to fact.

B. In the example of the subjunctive above, the verb _____ _____ is used instead of *was*, which would be used in the indicative mood.

3

A. is not   B. were

· ·

Finish each clause, using *were* and something contrary to fact.

A. If my mother _____

_____

_____ .

B. I wish my mother _____

_____

_____ .

4

The most important characteristic of the majority of subjunctives is the use of *were* instead of *was* in clauses that express wishes or show something else that is contrary to fact.

(In older times, *be* was used in the subjunctive instead of *is*. Patrick Henry, for instance, said, "If this *be* treason, make the most of it." That usage has almost died out.)

Write two sentences using the subjunctive, one beginning with *If he* . . . , and the other with *I wish he* . . .

4

Model Answers

If he were a good surveyor, he could determine the boundary. I wish he were knowledgeable about surveying.

· ·

In the sentences above, could *I*, *she*, or *Mr. Green* each be substituted for *he*? _____

5

I move that the motion *be* adopted.

Resolved, that a constitutional change *be* considered.

I urge that the council *learn* more about the case.

It is necessary that at least two employees *be* laid off.

Aside from contrary-to-fact statements, the subjunctive *be* and verb forms such as *learn* instead of a customary *learns* are used, as in the examples above. These most often appear in *that-*clauses for moving, resolving, recommending, urging, insisting, requesting, or demanding something, or in sentences beginning *It is necessary* (*essential, desirable*) *that* . . .

Finish each sentence, using words different from those in the examples:

A. I move that _____

_____ .

B. Resolved, (or *Be it resolved*,) _____

_____ .

C. We recommend that _____

_____ .

5

Model Answers

   A. I move that this body vote for impeachment.

   B. Resolved, that John Wright be commended for his long service.

   C. We demand that the committee reconsider its proposal.

. . . .

As the models above suggest, such subjunctive forms are often used in formal business meetings or in other formal discussions.

6

     Perish the thought.   God bless America.
     If need be , . . .   Come what may , . . .
     Be that as it may , . . .

Finally, a few old subjunctive forms survive in such expressions as those above. They seldom cause problems.

   Use *If need be* and *Come what may* in separate sentences.

6

Model Answers

   If need be, we can bring helicopters into the flooded area. Come what may, the people still here must be protected.

. . . .

Perish the thought is sometimes written as a complete sentence, but also may appear followed by a *that*-clause.

7

Summary: Although the subjunctive is used in English much less than formerly, it still appears in these instances:

   A. In wishes and in *if*-clauses about something that is

     _____ ____ _____ .

   B. In *that*-clauses for moving, _____ ,

     _____ , _____ ,

     _____ , or demanding, or in statements about necessity. (See Frame 5 if necessary.)

   C. In a few old, idiomatic expressions such as _____

     _____ .

7

   A. contrary to fact

   B. resolving, recommending, urging, insisting, requesting,

   C. *If need be*, and so forth

. . . .

Write a motion that you might make in a business meeting of an organization.

8

In Frames 8–10 assume you are writing in a formal situation. Choose for each sentence the verb that is in the subjunctive mood.

   A. John wished that the plane _____ not late.

   B. If Sandra _____ here, she would be resentful.

   C. I request that he _____ [*act* or *acts*?] at once.

   D. If I _____ you, I would stay in school.

8

A. were
B. were
C. act
D. were

....

A. If I _____ he, I'd take more chemistry.
B. I recommend that this rule _____ amended.

9

A. If need _____ , I can lend you the money.
B. It is essential that an answer _____ dispatched within an hour.
C. If your friend _____ completely loyal, he would have told you about the scheme.
D. I wish that a robot _____ as useful as science fiction writers predicted.

9

A. be
B. be
C. were
D. were

....

A. I wish that Aunt Tilly _____ rich.
B. It is necessary that I _____ excused.

10

A. It is desirable that Dr. Ray _____ [*resign* or *resigns*?] now.
B. Sidney urged that no new steps _____ taken.
C. Far _____ it from me to be critical.
D. Sometimes she wished that she _____ a peanut.

10

A. resign   B. be   C. be   D. were

....

A. Lois requested that the motion _____ tabled.
B. Resolved, that this club _____ its deep sympathy to the bereaved.

11

Finish honestly: One thing I hope to remember from this lesson is that . . .

(In this frame, any answer that you consider honest and accurate is acceptable.)

Lesson 32: Answers to Questions for Added Practice

1. No (presumably) **3.** MODELS: A. If my mother were here, she would disapprove. B. I wish my mother were not a worrier. **4.** Yes **7.** MODEL: I move that the minutes be approved as read. **8.** A. were B. be **9.** A. were B. be **10.** A. be B. MODEL: extend (*not* extends)

33

Pronoun Case: Subjects and Objects

After writing your answer(s) in the right-hand column, check this column to see whether you have responded correctly. If you have made a mistake, or if you need more practice, do whatever is asked below the dotted line in each answer frame.

Answers to questions for added practice can be found at the end of each lesson.

Answers and Added Practice

1

   She, him

. . . .

A subject often shows who or what performed an action. A direct object often shows who or what received that action. (The same pronouns are also used for other kinds of objects.)

In the sentence **He helped her,** the subject is _____ and the direct object is _____ .

Understanding and Applying the Principles

1

      (s = subject, v = verb, o = object)

In the sentence above, the subject is the word _____ , and the direct object is the word _____ .

2

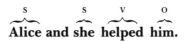

The sentence above has two subjects instead of one. The addition of another subject _____ [*does* or *does not?*] make it necessary to change the word *she* to something else.

2

does not

· ·

The point is that in choosing a pronoun, we should ignore any additional subject, such as *Alice*. Try
these:

A. He helped me. Jane and
_____ [*he* or *him*?] helped
me.

B. I helped her. Jane and ____
_____ [*I* or *me*?] helped
her.

3

The sentence in Frame 2 shows that when we have two subjects,
such as *Alice* and *she*, of which at least one is a pronoun, we use
the same pronoun as we would if it stood by itself as subject. In
other words, we say **She helped him,** and also:

Alice and _____ [*she* or *her*?] helped him.

3

she

· ·

A. I like him. Ray and _____ [*I*
or *me*?] like him.

B. She rented a horse. They
rented a horse. _____
[*She* or *Her*?] and _____
[*they* or *them*?] rented a
horse.

4

s v   o   o
She helped Lois and him.

The sentence above has two direct objects instead of just one.
We would say **She helped him**. The addition of another object,
Lois, _____ [*does* or *does not*?] make it necessary to
change the word *him* to something else.

4

does not

· ·

The point is that in choosing a pronoun, we should ignore any additional object, such as *Lois*. Try
these:

A. We saw her. We saw Mae
and _____ . [*she* or *her*?]

B. We saw her in the playpen.
We saw _____ [*she* or
her?] and the toys in the
playpen.

5

The sentence in Frame 4 shows that when we have two objects,
such as *Lois* and *him*, of which at least one is a pronoun, we use
the same pronoun as we would if it stood by itself as an object.
In other words, we say **She helped him**, and also:

She helped Lois and _____ [*he* or *him*?]

5

him

....

A. The dog bit me. The dog bit both Ralph and _____. [*I* or *me?*]

B. Bees sting her. Bees sting me. Bees sting _____ [*she* or *her?*] and _____. [*I* or *me?*]

6

These five personal pronouns, as well as *you* and *it*, may be used as subjects:

    I, we, he, she, they

What are the seven personal pronouns that may be used as subjects? _____

6

I, we, he, she, they, it, you

....

Use two of those pronouns in each sentence.

A. _____ and _____ played tennis.

B. _____ and _____ enjoy picnics.

C. _____ and _____ solved the puzzle.

7

These five personal pronouns, as well as *you* and *it*, may be used as objects:

    me, us, him, her, them

What are the seven personal pronouns that may be used as objects? _____

7

me, us, him, her, them, you, it

....

Use two of those pronouns in each sentence.

A. Please help _____ and _____ .

B. The police chased _____ and _____ .

C. The rattlesnakes alarmed _____ and _____ .

8

Frames 1–7 have shown that when we have two subjects or two objects, the pronouns we use are the same as if they stood by themselves as subject or object.

    So, since we write **I bought a present for her**, we also write:

Max and _____ [*I* or *me?*] bought a present for you and _____ . [*she* or *her?*]

8

I, her

....

A. Helen and _____ [*he* or *him?*] gave Glenn and _____ [*I* or *me?*] a gift.

B. _____ [*He* or *Him?*] and _____ [*she* or *her?*] like to skate with the Eliots and _____ . [*we* or *us?*]

9

Choose the proper pronoun for each blank.

A. Perry and _____ [*I* or *me?*] found some sand dollars.

B. We showed them to Bet's father and _____ . [*she* or *her?*]

C. _____ [*He* or *Him?*] and _____ [*she* or *her?*] said that few sand dollars are found on this beach.

9

    A. I B. her C. He, she

································

    A. My mother and _____ [*I* or *me?*] went shopping.

    B. We selected some clothes for my sister and _____ . [*I* or *me?*]

10

    A. She B. I C. We

································

(For more about such expressions as *we Graysons*, see Lesson 34.)

    A. _____ [*He* or *Him?*] and _____ [*I* or *me?*] will study chemistry next term.

    B. Lab work may be difficult for _____ [*he* or *him?*] and _____ . [*I* or *me?*]

11

    A. They B. me C. I

································

    A. Sam and _____ [*I* or *me?*] will take Sally and _____ [*she* or *her?*] with us.

    B. We think they'll enjoy going with _____ [*we* or *us?*] Phi Sigs.

12

Model Answer

    Lee and she [or *I, we, you, he, they*] saw bloody pawprints in the snow.

································

Using a personal pronoun, finish this sentence by saying something about walking in moonlight:

    Kathy and _____

    _____

    _____ .

10

Choose the proper pronoun for each blank.

    A. _____ [*She* or *Her?*] and Jack excel in foreign languages.

    B. Both are much better linguists than Tom and _____ [*I* or *me?*] are.

    C. _____ [*We* or *Us?*] Graysons are usually good students.

11

Choose the proper pronoun for each blank.

    A. _____ [*They* or *Them?*] and several of their friends bought lottery tickets.

    B. My own parents urged my sister and _____ [*I* or *me?*] not to gamble.

    C. Clare and _____ [*I* or *me?*] had to admit that state lotteries are gambling games.

12

Write a sentence starting with *Lee and,* followed by a personal pronoun. Tell what Lee and the other person saw in the snow.

13

Write a sentence starting with *The discovery surprised Lee and . . .* Follow with a personal pronoun and a few other words that fit.

13

Model Answer

The discovery surprised Lee and her [or *me, us, you, him, them*] because Rover seemed unhurt.

. . . .

Finish, using a personal pronoun and other appropriate words:

The incident unnerved Lee and ——————————

——————————

—————————— .

14

Start a sentence with *Lee and . . .* followed by a personal pronoun. Tell what Lee and the other person told *you and . . .* (followed by another personal pronoun).

14

Model Answer

Lee and she [or *I, we, he, they*] told *you* and *me* [or *us, her, him, them*] that we were mistaken.

15

Finish honestly: One thing I hope to remember from this exercise is that . . .

(Any answer that you consider honest and accurate is acceptable.)

Lesson 33: Answers to Questions for Added Practice

1. *He, her* **2.** A. he B. I **3.** A. I B. She, they **4.** A. her B. her **5.** A. me B. her, me **6,7** (Any of the given list may be used.) **8.** A. he, me B. He, she, us **9.** A. I B. me **10.** A. He, I B. him, me **11.** A. I, her B. us **12.** MODEL: Kathy and I enjoy walking in the moonlight. **13.** MODEL: The incident unnerved Lee and me so much that we hurried home.

≡34≡

Appositives and Predicate Nominatives: (we, us) *Girls Thought It Was* (he, him)

After writing your answer(s) in the right-hand column, check this column to see whether you have responded correctly. If you have made a mistake, or if you need more practice, do whatever is asked below the dotted line in each answer frame.

Answers to questions for added practice can be found at the end of each lesson.

Understanding and Applying the Principles

1

> **Hawaii, the youngest state, is the only one that is not on the North American continent.**

In that example, *the youngest state* is called an appositive, from Latin words meaning "placed next to." It is in apposition with *Hawaii* and, in effect, supplies another name or identification for it.

Why is *appositive* a good name for such a construction? _____

_____

_____

_____

Answers and Added Practice

1

Model Answer

> *The youngest state* is placed next to *Hawaii* and tells something else that Hawaii can be called.

· ·

> **The Volunteer State, Tennessee, got its nickname because 30,000 Tennesseans volunteered to serve in one of America's early wars.**

Which word is the appositive in that sentence? _____

2

> **We Hawaiians had no contact with Europeans until 1778, when Captain James Cook came to the islands.**

Appositives are not likely to cause difficulty unless the appositive or the word next to it is a pronoun—specifically, *I* or *me*, *she* or *her*, *he* or *him*, *we* or *us*, *they* or *them*.

A. In the example, which word is the appositive? _____

_____

B. If that appositive were not present, would we start the sentence with *We* or *Us*? _____

C. Does the presence of the appositive change the pronoun we should use? _____

2

A. *Hawaiians*   B. *We*

C. No

· ·

We Tennesseans are proud of the diversity of our state.

In that sentence, is the first word changed because an appositive is next to it? _____

3

Cook's arrival had both good and bad consequences for us Hawaiians.

A. In that sentence, which word is the appositive? _____
_____

B. Without the appositive, the last word of the sentence would be _____.

C. Does the presence of the appositive change the pronoun we should use? _____

3

A. *Hawaiians*   B. *us*   C. No

· ·

Among us Tennesseans are many descendants of Revolutionary War soldiers.

If the appositive *Tennesseans* were not in that sentence, the second word of the sentence would be _____. So, the presence of the appositive _____ [*changes* or *does not change?*] the pronoun.

4

Our family, my parents and I, are descended from the ancient Hawaiians, who were probably Polynesians.

A. The four-word appositive in that sentence is _____
_____ .

B. If we leave out *Our family*, is *I* still the correct pronoun? _____

C. Again, we see that a pronoun _____ [*is* or *is not?*] changed because of the existence of an appositive.

4

A. *My parents and I*

B. Yes   C. is not

· ·

We—my brothers and I—hope that Tennessee's future will never involve another war.

Why is *I* correct in that sentence?

5

Today life is changing rapidly for Hawaiians, both us and the latecomers.

A. The five-word appositive is _____
_____ .

B. If we leave out *Hawaiians*, is *us* still the correct pronoun? _____

C. Once more we see that a pronoun _____ [*is* or *is not?*] changed because of an appositive.

5

A. *both us and the latecomers*
B. Yes C. is not

....

Modern war seems suicidal to us—my brothers and me.

Why is *me* correct in that sentence?

6

 ← This is a panda. →
this = panda

The sentence and the equation show that verbs like *is* (*are, was, were, has been,* and so forth) are often similar in meaning to equal signs. That is, the things named on the two sides often are different names for _____ [*the same* or *different*?] meanings.

6

A. the same

....

My brother was once a sailor.

In that sentence, the two words that have the same meaning are _____ and _____ .

7

He was the messenger.   he = messenger
The messenger was he.   messenger = he

A. The sentences above also show equality. *He was the messenger* means that *he* and *the messenger* are the same, and *The messenger was he* means that *the messenger* and _____ [Who?] are the same.

B. Since we say *He was the messenger*, when we turn the equation around we should say, The messenger was _____ . [*he* or *him*?]

7

A. he B. he

....

Choose the formally correct pronouns.

A. That is _____ . [*he* or *him*?]

B. That was _____ . [*she* or *her*?]

C. It is _____ [*they* or *them*?] who deserve the praise.

D. It is _____ [*we* or *us*?] who deserve the blame.

8

s   v   pn   s   v
He was the messenger. The messenger was

pn s v pn
he. It was she who received the message.

(s = subject, v = verb, pn = predicate nominative)

In these examples, *messenger, he,* and *she* are called *predicate nominatives*. Predicate nominatives appear in the predicate (the verb part) of a sentence, and in formal circumstances they are in the nominative case (*I, he, she, we, they*)—the same case as is used for subjects.

Copy the two predicate nominatives from the examples in Frame 7. _____ _____

8

messenger   he

. . . .

Again, choose the formally correct pronouns.

    A. Can it be _____ [*she* or *her?*] who betrayed us?

    B. Probably it was _____ [*she* or *her?*]. The traitor certainly is not _____. [*he* or *him?*]

9

In ordinary conversation most speakers say things like *The messenger was him* or *It's me.* Even Sir Winston Churchill used to say "It was me." In formal writing, however, most teachers and editors and many business people prefer the predicate nominative.

The same personal pronouns that are used as subjects are used as predicate nominatives.

To review, they are *I, y___ __, h__, s___ __, i__, w__,* and *t___ __ __.*

9

you, he, she, it, we, they

. . . .

Make up a short sentence similar to *He was the messenger.* Label the subject (S) and the predicate nominative (PN). Then rewrite it, interchanging the two labeled parts. Note that the pronoun is the same, whether it is S or PN.

10

Look back at the subtitle of this lesson. Copy it, using the formal choices.

10

We Girls Thought It Was He.

. . . .

Now try this:

It was _____ [*they* or *them?*] who annoyed _____ [*we* or *us?*] boys.

11

In Frames 11–12 are sentences containing appositives. Choose the correct pronoun for each.

    A. _____ [*We* or *Us?*] Hawaiians mingle easily with the other Americans and the many foreigners who live in Hawaii.

    B. That is not difficult for _____ [*we* or *us?*] Hawaiians because we are naturally friendly.

    C. In effect we say to everyone, "Let's you and _____ [*I* or *me?*] be friends." [Hint: *Let's* means "Let us," and *you* and the missing word are in apposition to *us.*]

11

    A. We B. us C. me

....

A remark by a coward:

    "Let's you and _____ [*he* or *him*?] fight."

12

    A. us B. me C. I

....

Explain why, in Frame 12, *me* is the correct answer for B, but *I* is correct for C.

13

    A. I   you   he   she
    B. we   you   they

....

Follow the instructions in Frame 13 for this:

    One of the owners is _____

    _____ _____ _____ .

14

    A. I   he   she
    B. we   you   they

....

Now this:

    It was _____ _____ _____

    _____ _____ _____

    who solved the problem.

12

    A. Learning languages is easy for many of _____ [*we* or *us*?] Hawaiians.
    B. Our teachers commended two of us, Leilani and _____. [*I* or *me*?]
    C. Each day many Hawaiians, Leilani and _____ [*I* or *me*?], for example, hear several languages besides English.

13

In formal English each sentence in Frames 13–14 requires a predicate nominative. From the following list of pronouns, choose *all* that might be used.

    I   me   you   he   him   she
    her   we   us   they   them

    A. The owner is _____ _____ _____ _____ .
    B. The owners are _____ _____ _____ .

14

    A. It was _____ _____ _____ who was named by the State Department.
    B. It was _____ _____ _____ who were named by the State Department.

15

Finish honestly: One thing I hope to remember from this lesson is that . . .

(In this frame, any answer that you consider honest and accurate is acceptable.)

Lesson 34: Answers to Questions for Added Practice

1. *Tennessee* **2.** No **3.** *us*, does not change **4.** MODEL: It is in the same case as the subject, *we*. **5.** MODEL: It is in the same case as *us*. **6.** *brother, sailor* **7.** A. he B. she C. they D. we **8.** A. she B. she, he **9.** MODEL: She (S) was the soloist (PN). The soloist (S) was she (PN). **10.** they, us **11.** him **12.** MODEL: In B, *me* is in the same case as *two of us*, with which it is in apposition. In C, *I* is in apposition with the subject, *Hawaiians*. **13.** I, you, he, she **14.** I, you, he, she, we, they

═35═

Two Troublesome Pronouns: Toom Am I Speaking Toom?

After writing your answer(s) in the right-hand column, check this column to see whether you have responded correctly. If you have made a mistake, or if you need more practice, do whatever is asked below the dotted line in each answer frame.

Answers to questions for added practice can be found at the end of each lesson.

Understanding and Applying the Principles

1

If we are deciding whether *who* or *whom* is correct in a given sentence, the wise old owl is right more often than not.

For instance, when a secretary asks on the phone, "May I tell Mr. Grant [*who* or *whom*] is calling?" the proper choice is

_____ .

Answers and Added Practice

1

   who

. . . .

Do you prefer *who* or *whom* in each of these?

  A. _____ is calling, please?

  B. Tell me _____ let the cat out.

  C. The man _____ asked that question was an officer.

2

If you positively cannot decide whether *who* or *whom* is better in a sentence, it's safer to use *who*. But as a college student and a literate adult, you will find that occasionally a properly placed *whom* will be expected of you. For instance, "To who" is not bad for an owl, but for an educated human being, "____ _____" is preferable.

2

To whom

....

Similarly, we say *to her, to him, for them, with us,* and the like. We use these forms when the pronouns are objects of prepositions.

3

Who is used as the subject of a sentence or of a clause.

    A. In *Who is calling?* the pronoun _____ [Which word?] is the subject of the sentence.

    B. In *May I tell Mr. Grant who is calling?* _____ [Which word?] is the subject of a clause.

    C. In *Who shall I say is calling?* the word *Who* is correct because it is the _____ [*subject* or *object*?] of *is calling.*

3

    A. *Who*　B. *who*　C. subject

....

If C in Frame 3 puzzles you, try omitting *shall I say* when you read it. Then you can easily see that _____ is the subject of the sentence.

4

Whom is not used as a subject but, especially in formal writing, is used as any kind of object.

                             s   v

  (1) **The plaintiff told the jury he had seen**

         do

      her in the tree.

                           do   s

  (2) **The plaintiff told the jury whom he**

         v

      had seen in the tree.

    (s = subject, v = verb, do = direct object)

    A. In (1) we say, of course, "he had seen *her*" (not *she*). The pronoun *her* is the direct object.

    B. In (2) we find the same structure, even though the word order is different. The pronoun *whom* is the _____ _____ .

4

direct object

. . . .

Try these:

A. The plaintiff told the jury _____ [*who* or *whom?*] was in the tree.

B. The plaintiff told the jury _____ he suspected.

5

In Frame 2 we saw that in formal English *to whom* is preferred instead of *to who*. *To* is a preposition. Similarly, *whom* serves as the object of other prepositions. For example:

from whom   after whom   with whom

Write the obvious choice in each blank:

near _____   by _____   through _____

5

whom, whom, whom

. . . .

A. Part of the service in many churches includes singing a doxology, "Praise God from whom all blessings flow." Explain why *whom* is correct.

B. Some legal documents or letters begin, "To whom this may concern." Why *to whom?*

6

Most difficulties with *who* and *whom* can be eliminated if you thoroughly understand the difference between these two constructions:

(1) The person *whom Bonnie called* was named Plum.

(2) The person *who called Bonnie* was called Plum.

A. In (1), Bonnie did the calling: *Bonnie called whom*. Like the word *her* in *Bonnie called her*, the word *whom* is the _____ [*subject* or *object?*] in that clause.

B. In (2), somebody else called Bonnie. Like the word *she* in *She called Bonnie*, the word *who* is the _____ [*subject* or *object?*] of that clause.

6

A. object   B. subject

· ·

Choose *who* or *whom.*

A. The woman _____ scored highest was Melba Downey.

B. The woman _____ the crowd preferred was Gladys Rosen.

7

Tell *whoever called Bonnie* not to call again.

Tell *whomever Bonnie called* that she apologizes.

Whoever is used like *who; whomever,* like *whom.* That is, *whoever* may be used as _____ [*a subject* or *an object*?], and *whomever* may be used as _____ . [*a subject* or *an object*?]

7

a subject, an object

· ·

Choose *whoever* or *whomever.*

A. The accused must work with _____ the court appoints.

B. The accused must work with_____ is appointed.

Note: An entire clause can be the object of a preposition.

8

Here is an example of a kind of sentence that tricks some radio and television announcers:

The player *who you said was ineligible* has just scored a touchdown.

Who is correct in that sentence. Some persons are confused by inserted words such as *you said, she insisted, you believe,* and so forth. In the example, *you said* does not alter the structure of the basic clause, *who was ineligible.* In that clause, the word *who* is the _____ . [*subject* or *object*?]

8

subject

· ·

Choose *who* or *whom.*

A. Her brother _____ she swore was twenty-two is actually a minor.

B. George McKay, _____ Dodson thought should be appointed, was not chosen.

9

In Frames 9–11, assume you are writing in a formal situation. Choose *who* or *whom* for each blank in Frames 9 and 10.

A. From _____ did Scott get the information?

B. _____ supposedly sent it to him?

C. The person _____ sent it may have been a detective.

D. No person _____ Scott knows well could have done it.

E. No person _____ knows Scott well could have done it.

9

   A. whom B. Who
   C. who   D. whom
   E. who

. . . .

Explain the answers to D and E.

10

   A. The man _____ drives the snowplow is an Italian.
   B. The man _____ Mr. Connor said drives the snow-plow is an Italian.
   C. The man _____ Mrs. Knight was thinking about is a Greek.
   D. The man _____ is Greek does not drive a snow-plow.
   E. The man _____ Mrs. Knight said is Greek does not drive a snowplow.

10

   A. who B. who C. whom
   D. who E. who

. . . .

Explain the answers to C and E.

11

Choose *whoever* or *whomever*.

   A. Arrest _____ was in the house at the time of the murder.
   B. Arrest _____ you find in the house.
   C. _____ is in the house is a suspect.
   D. _____ you find is a suspect.

11

   A. whoever B. whomever
   C. Whoever D. Whomever

. . . .

Explain the answer to A.

12

Look back at the subtitle of this lesson.

   A. Obviously the first *Toom* is intended to mean "_____." [What two words?]
   B. Is *To whom* correct in that question? _____
   C. What should be done to the second *Toom*? _____
   _____

12

    A. To whom B. Yes
    C. Delete it (or the equivalent)

. . . .

In most telephone conversations, "To whom am I speaking?" may seem stiff and unnatural. What would you say if you believed the person on the line was a fellow student?

What would you say if you thought it was someone from the Dean's office?

13

Finish honestly: One thing I hope to remember from this lesson is that . . .

(In this frame, any answer that you consider honest and accurate is acceptable.)

Lesson 35: Answers to Questions for Added Practice

1. A. Who B. who C. who **3.** Who **4.** A. who B. whom **5.** MODELS: A. *Whom* is the object of the preposition *from*. B. *Whom* is the object of the preposition *to*. **6.** A. who B. whom (object of *preferred*) **7.** A. whom ever (object of *appoints*) B. whoever (subject of *is appointed*) **8.** A. who (subject of *was*) B. who (subject of *should be appointed*) **9.** MODELS: In D, *whom* is the object of *knows*. In E, *who* is the subject of *knows*. **10.** MODELS: In C, *whom* is the object of the preposition *about*. In E, *who* is the subject of *is*. **11.** MODEL: *Whoever* is the subject of *was*. **12.** (Probable answers) "Who is this?" for an informal situation. "Who is this, please?" or "To whom am I speaking, please?" for a formal one.

36

Pronoun Order: My Dear,
you *Should Go Ahead of* him *and* me

After writing your answer(s) in the right-hand column, check this column to see whether you have responded correctly. If you have made a mistake, or if you need more practice, do whatever is asked below the dotted line in each answer frame.

Answers to questions for added practice can be found at the end of each lesson.

Answers and Added Practice

1

   he, I

. . . .

You should write:

   _____ [*You, She,* or *I*?], _____
   _____ [*you, she,* or *I*?], and
   _____ [*you, she,* or *I*?] have
tickets.

2

   A. you, I
   B. you, he, I
   C. they, we
   D. you, they, we
   E. you, William, I

. . . .

Write short sentences using your correct answers for two of the groups.

Understanding and Applying the Principles

1

In arranging personal pronouns as subjects, to be polite you should put yourself last. Here is the polite arrangement:

1	2	3
you	she	I
	he	we
	they	

So you should write:

You, _____ [*he* or *I*?], and _____ [*he* or *I*?] stayed together.

2

Write each group of pronouns in the polite arrangement. In one group, a person's name has replaced a pronoun.

   A. *I, you*   _____ _____
   B. *he, I, you*   _____ _____ _____
   C. *they, we*   _____ _____
   D. *they, you, we* _____ _____ _____
   E. *I, William, you* _____ _____ _____

3

In the following sentences, use any personal pronouns (except *it*) that are acceptable as subjects. (See Frame 1.) Place them in the polite order.

   A. _____ and _____ will sing at the party.
   B. _____, _____, and _____ will sing at the party.
   C. I hope that _____ and _____ can be there.

3

Model Answers
    A. You, I   B. You, she, I
    C. you, he

. . . .

Any of the pronouns in Frame 1 may be used in your answer here, but they should be in the order listed.

4

So much for subjects. If we use two or more pronouns together as *objects*, it is polite to put them in this order:

1	2	3
you	her	me
	him	us
	them	

Which is polite, A or B? _____
A. Lettie called you and me.
B. Lettie called me and you.

4

        A

. . . .

Which is most polite?

    A. Lettie called me, Nancy, and you.
    B. Lettie called you, Nancy, and me.
    C. Lettie called Nancy, me, and you. _____

5

Write the pronouns in the polite arrangement. In one group a person's name has replaced a pronoun.

    A. *me, you*   _____ _____
    B. *him, me, you*   _____ _____ _____
    C. *them, us*   _____ _____
    D. *them, you, us*   _____ _____ _____
    E. *me, Wilma, you* _____ _____ _____

5

    A. you, me   B. you, him, me
    C. them, us   D. you, them,
    us   E. you, Wilma, me

. . . .

Write three short sentences using your correct answers for three of the groups.

6

In the following sentences, use any personal pronouns (except *it*) that are acceptable as objects. (See Frame 4.) Place them in the polite order.

    A. The present is for _____ and _____.
    B. No, it is for _____, _____, and _____.
    C. Dad brought _____ and _____ another package.
    D. He asked _____ and _____ to divide it between _____ and _____.

6

Model Answers

   A. you, me

   B. you, him, me

   C. them, us

   D. you, me, them, us

. . . .

Any of the pronouns in Frame 4 may be used, but should be in the order listed there.

7

Finish honestly: One thing I hope to remember from this lesson is that . . .

(In this frame, any answer that you consider honest and accurate is acceptable.)

Lesson 36: Answers to Questions for Added Practice

1. You, she, I **2.** MODELS: You and I saw the exhibit. You, they, and we share the credit. **4.** B **5.** MODELS: Jane called both you and me. In fact, she called you, him, and me. Why did she call them and us?

37

Possessives with -ing-words: A moose Attacking or a moose's Attacking?

After writing your answer(s) in the right-hand column, check this column to see whether you have responded correctly. If you have made a mistake, or if you need more practice, do whatever is asked below the dotted line in each answer frame.

Answers to questions for added practice can be found at the end of each lesson.

Answers and Added Practice

1

    A. No B. Yes

. . . .

    Her baby's being in danger alarms almost every mother.

Is that sentence good or poor? ____

____

2

    A. No B. Yes
    C. *Jack's*

. . . .

    A. **Katy being alarmed is understandable.**
    B. **Katy's being alarmed is understandable.**

Is A or B the better sentence? ____

____

Understanding and Applying the Principles

1

    POOR: **A moose attacking a truck is not an infrequent occurrence.**

    GOOD: **A moose's attacking a truck (*or* A moose's attack on a truck) is not an infrequent occurrence.**

A. In the poor sentence we seem to be saying that a moose is not an infrequent occurrence. Does that make sense?

    _____

B. In the good sentence, readers readily understand that a moose's attacking (or attack) is not infrequent. Does that make sense? _____

2

    (Jack or Jack's) telling moose stories was a highlight of our camping trip in Alaska.

A. Was Jack a highlight? _____
B. Was his telling stories a highlight? _____
C. So, _____ [*Jack or Jack's?*] is the better word to use in the example.

3

    (1) **We liked the man narrating moose stories one after another.**
    (2) **We liked the man's narrating moose stories one after another.**

Both of those sentences make sense. Both are good sentences, but they have different meanings.

A. In (1), we liked _____.
B. In (2), we may or may not have liked the man, but we definitely liked _____

_____ .

3

    A. the man

    B. the man's narrating moose stories one after another

. . . .

Katy had had a bad dream about _____ [*Billy* or *Billy's?*] falling off a cliff.

4

When you are using a noun or a pronoun followed by an *-ing*-word, think for a moment about whether or not a possessive such as *moose's* or *Jack's* or *his* should be used with it. Ask your-self, "Which word says what I intend to say?"

    A. In Frame 3, *man* makes sense if we mean that we like

    _____ .

    B. In (2) of Frame 3, *man's* makes sense if we mean that we liked _____ .

4

Model Answers

    A. the narrator

    B. his storytelling

. . . .

Now, if Katy rushed up the stairs, she would run the risk of _____ _____ [*Billy* or *Billy's?*] leaning toward her and losing his balance.

5

In Frames 5–7, choose the word that best brings out the prob-able meaning.

    A. I always enjoy_____ [*you* or *your?*] singing of the old favorites.

    B. I always enjoy _____ [*you* or *your?*] singing.

    C. The sound was off, but I saw _____ [*you* or *your?*] singing on television.

5

    A. your B. your C. you

. . . .

She moved cautiously upward, tak-ing advantage of _____ [*him* or *his?*] glancing in other directions.

6

    A. _____ [*He, Him,* or *His?*] playing the violin so calmly helped us all to relax.

    B. We were moved by _____ [*him* or *his?*] playing.

    C. I had seen _____ [*him* or *his?*] playing once before.

6

    A. His B. his C. him

. . . .

_____ [*Katy* or *Katy's?*] slow moving paid off and prevented _____ [*him* or *his?*] toppling over and tumbling down the steep stairs.

7

    A. _____ [*Warner* or *Warner's?*] handling of the huge crane is very deft.

    B. I like to watch its gigantic _____ [*arm* or *arm's?*] reaching out to put a beam precisely in place.

    C. _____ [*Crowds* or *Crowds'?*] watching him do not bother Warner at all.

7

    A. Warner's   B. arm
    C. Crowds

. . . .

    A. **Jennie liked the nurse caring for her during the day.**

    B. **Jennie liked the nurse's caring for her during the day.**

Do both A and B have the same meaning? _____

Which means that Jennie liked the care she received? _____

8

Write a sentence in which you tell of someone who was scrambling (maybe after a football or away from some bees, for instance). Write it in such a way that a possessive is *not* necessary. Perhaps start with *I saw.*

8

Model Answer

    I saw at least six players scrambling after the fumbled ball.

. . . .

In that model answer the emphasis is on the _____

_____ . [*number of players* or *scrambling*?]

9

Rewrite the sentence you wrote for Frame 8. This time word it in such a way that a possessive is necessary before *scrambling.*

9

Model Answer

    The six players' scrambling after the fumbled ball was a comic sight.

. . . .

In that model answer the emphasis is on the _____

_____ . [*number of players* or *scrambling*?]

10

Finish honestly: One thing I hope to remember from this lesson is that . . .

(In this frame, any answer that you consider honest and accurate is acceptable.)

Lesson 37: Answers to Questions for Added Practice

1. Good **2.** B **3.** Billy's **4.** Billy's **5.** his **6.** Katy's, his **7.** No, B **8.** number of players **9.** scrambling

38

Pronoun Reference: Which One Do You Mean?

After writing your answer(s) in the right-hand column, check this column to see whether you have responded correctly. If you have made a mistake, or if you need more practice, do whatever is asked below the dotted line in each answer frame.

Answers to questions for added practice can be found at the end of each lesson.

Understanding and Applying the Principles

1

> **Laura and Linda were going shopping. She said that she did not like the sweater she had bought last time, and if she agreed with her, she would exchange it, unless she wanted it herself.**

Do you understand that? _____

Answers and Added Practice

1

No

. . . .

Are you sure that you understand this one? _____

> **After you have taken the old shirt out of the box, throw it away.**

2

Do you know for sure what each of the following sentences means?

A. When Dr. Rome was in the dentist's office, he told him some funny stories about dentistry. _____ [*Yes* or *No*?]

B. Louise told Yolanda that she could not continue having dates with Tom because she did not like him. _____

C. The visitor, whom the host had been arguing with, left because he became angry. _____

2

    A. No (Who told the stories?)

    B. No (Who is *she*?)

    C. No (Who became angry?)

· ·

    Cathy's mother told her that she might be too busy to attend the concert.

Do you know who may be too busy?

_____

3

The examples in Frames 1 and 2 have shown that in using pronouns (especially *she, her, he, him, it, they, them, which,* and sometimes the possessive forms *her, hers, his, its, their,* and *theirs*) we need to make clear which of two persons or things we mean. Otherwise, people may ask us, "_____?" [If you don't know, look at the subtitle of this exercise.]

3

    Which one do you mean?

· ·

    Fritz told his father that he had a hole in his sock.

On hearing that you might ask, "Who had the holey sock, _____ _____ or _____?"

4

When we find that we have written a sentence in which a pronoun may refer to more than one person or thing, we can usually correct the sentence rather easily. For example:

    When Dr. Rome was in the dentist's office, he told him some funny stories about dentistry

can be corrected by changing *he* to either _____ or _____.

4

    Dr. Rome, the dentist

· ·

    When the students and the teachers went on a field trip, one of them was too ill to go.

Which word in that sentence is unclear? _____

5

    The visitor, whom the host had been arguing with, left because he became angry.

Two ways to correct that:

    A. The visitor left when his _____ became angry during an argument.

    B. The visitor left after _____ [What pronoun?] became angry during an argument with his host.

5

    A. host B. he

· ·

    The lawyer talked with the doctor when he needed advice.

Rewrite that sentence to make the meaning clear.

6

    Louise told Yolanda that she could not continue having dates with Tom because she did not like him.

When we are reporting conversation, we can often clear up faulty pronoun reference by using a direct quotation, like this:

    Louise told Yolanda, "I will not _____."

    [Complete the sentence.]

6

continue having dates with Tom because I [or *you*] do not like him

....

Mickey told his father that he had used his razor.

Rewrite, using a direct quotation.

7

The keepers are careful about when they feed the animals and about when they need medical attention.

A. Which *they* is unclear, the first or the second? _____

B. What words may be substituted for the unclear *they*?

_____

7

A. Second

B. *the animals* (or *the zoo inhabitants*, etc.)

....

Mother plays both the piano and the violin. Maybe that fact explains why I like it so well.

Rewrite the second sentence, making clear what *it* means.

8

When the natives and the invaders fought a pitched battle, several of them were killed.

Rewrite and clarify the last part of that sentence.

8

several of the natives [*or* invaders] were killed, *or* several on each side were killed.

....

The Indians said that they had found two bears but that they had run away at once.

Rewrite, making clear who ran away.

9

After you take the papers from the boxes, burn them.

Rewrite the sentence to clarify what should be burned.

9

Model Answer

Burn the boxes after you remove the papers.

. . . .

Many snakes live in the tropics, which may be dangerous.

Rewrite so that *which* refers clearly to snakes, or so that you need not use *which*.

10

Write a sentence containing the words *coach, pitcher,* and *he.* Be sure that the meaning of *he* is clear.

10

Model Answer

The coach, as he walked to the mound, was deciding whether to remove the pitcher.

. . . .

Write a sentence in such a way that *which* clearly refers to potatoes.

11

Write a sentence containing the words *kitchen, dining room,* and *it.* Be sure that the meaning of *it* is clear.

11

Model Answer

Although the kitchen is larger than the dining room, it looks smaller because of the cabinets.

. . . .

Write a sentence using *hat, coat,* and *it.* Be sure that the meaning of *it* is clear.

12

Her mother told Jeannine that she had to visit her sister and that she would meet her at her house.

Rewrite the example, using a direct quotation, as in Frame 6. (Note that the sentence above has several possible meanings.)

12

Model Answer

Her mother told Jeannine, "I have to visit my sister. I'll see you at her house."

. . . .

Jeannine told her cousin that her mother was expecting visitors.

Rewrite, clarifying the second *her.* Use a direct quotation.

13

Finish honestly: One thing I hope to remember from this lesson is that . . .

(In this frame, any answer that you consider honest and accurate is acceptable.)

Lesson 38: Answers to Questions for Added Practice

1. No. **2.** No **3.** Fritz, his father **4.** *them* **5.** MODEL: When the lawyer needed advice, he talked with the doctor. **6.** Mickey told his father, "I used your razor." (*Or* . . . "You used my razor.") **7.** Maybe that fact explains why I like music (*or* the piano *or* the violin *or* playing . . .) **8.** MODEL: The Indians said that they had found two bears, which had run away at once. **9.** MODEL: Many possibly dangerous snakes live in the tropics. **10.** MODEL: We bought three large potatoes, which we intended to bake. **11.** MODEL: My hat was ready to be thrown away, but because my cashmere coat was almost new, I hated to lose it. **12.** Jeannine told her cousin, "My mother is expecting visitors." (*Or* . . . "Your mother is expecting visitors.")

39

Pronoun Reference: Vague Shapes in the Fog

After writing your answer(s) in the right-hand column, check this column to see whether you have responded correctly. If you have made a mistake, or if you need more practice, do whatever is asked below the dotted line in each answer frame.

Answers to questions for added practice can be found at the end of each lesson.

Understanding and Applying the Principles

1

They have many trout in these streams.

In the sentence above, do you know who *they* are? _____

Answers and Added Practice

1

No

....

They have many excellent highways in the South.

Do you know who *they* are? _____

2

Among the most common pronouns are *she, her, he, him, it, they,* and *them,* and *which, that,* and *this.* Whenever we use one of these pronouns, we should be certain that everyone can immediately understand what we mean.

In Frame 1, the pronoun that is not clear is _____.

2

They

....

In many games, the eyes must be kept on the ball. If he does not do so, he will probably not play well.

The pronoun that is not clear is

_____.

3

To make clear a sentence like the example in Frame 1, we must reword it. Two ways to reword that example are:

A. Many _____ [What?] live in these streams.

B. _____ [Who?] catch many trout in these streams.

3

    A. trout

    B. Fishermen (*or* People, etc.)

. . . .

Reword the example in Answer Frame 1.

4

Jim opened one eye, which showed us that he was conscious.

    A. In that sentence, *which* seems at first to refer to *eye*. However, it really refers to the fact that Jim _____ _____ . [Did what?]

    B. One way to reword the sentence is: Jim's _____ _____ [Doing what?] showed us that he was conscious.

    C. Another way: When Jim opened one eye, _____ [Who?] knew that _____ . [What?]

4

    A. opened one eye

    B. opening one eye

    C. we, he was conscious

. . . .

Reword to show what *it* means:

    You should be sure to boil it before you drink it.

5

To summarize: When we use the pronouns *she, her, he, him, it, they,* or *them,* or *which, that,* or *this,* we must be sure that everyone can easily understand what we mean. In other words the meaning of a pronoun _____ [*must* or *need not?*] be instantly clear.

5

    must

. . . .

Reword the example in Answer Frame 2. The change may be made in either the first or the second sentence.

6

    A. They had little machinery in pioneer days.

    B. Pioneers had little machinery.

Which sentence is more clear, A or B? _____

6

B

. . . .

A. My father likes to follow tradition, which I believe is a good thing.

B. My father, wisely I believe, likes to follow tradition.

Which sentence is more clear, A or B? _____

7

A. Lin Yutang's *The Wisdom of China and India* is a collection of Oriental classics. He was an authority on the subject.

B. Lin Yutang's *The Wisdom of China and India* is a collection of Oriental classics. Lin was an authority on the subject.

Which sentence is more clear, A or B? _____

7

B (A pronoun should usually not refer to a possessive.)

. . . .

A. My firing quickly at the target was a mistake.

B. I fired quickly at the target, which was a mistake.

Which sentence is more clear, A or B? _____

8

A. The television weather forecaster said that we'll have more rain.

B. It said on television that we'll have more rain.

Which is more clear, A or B? _____

Note: In a few sentences, such as **It is going to snow,** the pronoun *it* does not need to refer to anything definite. In most sentences, though, we have to be sure that a reader or a listener can understand at once what each pronoun refers to.

8

A

. . . .

A. It says in the paper that Sholem's is having a shoe sale.

B. The paper has an advertisement about a shoe sale at Sholem's.

Which sentence is more clear, A or B? _____

9

Use the word *which* in a sentence in such a way that it refers clearly to respect for ancestors.

9

Model Answer

Respect for ancestors, which was long typical of the Chinese, was discouraged in the early years of the Communist regime.

. . . .

Make up a sentence about Florida weather. Use *they* in your sentence, but be sure that the meaning is clear.

10

In Frames 10–12, write a better version of each sentence.

It says in a newspaper column by Sheila Martin that wigs are less popular this year.

10

Model Answer

Sheila Martin says in a newspaper column that wigs are less popular this year.

. . . .

Rewrite:

I don't believe the astrological predictions in the newspaper. He always writes generalities.

11

I felt a tug on my line, which was very sudden.

11

Model Answer
  I felt a sudden tug on my line.
. . . .

Rewrite:

With the job half done, I lost my enthusiasm, and I kept postponing it.

12

I ate another large tomato. That is an old weakness of mine.

12

Model Answer
  I ate another large tomato. Inability to resist tomatoes is an old weakness of mine.
. . . .

Rewrite:

Because Jean could neither read well nor spell well, this was a handicap.

13

Finish honestly: One thing I hope to remember from this lesson is that . . .

(In this frame, any answer that you consider honest and accurate is acceptable.)

Lesson 39: Answers to Questions for Added Practice

1. No **2.** *he* **3.** MODEL: Many excellent highways are in the South. (*Or* The South has many excellent highways.) **4.** MODEL: You should be sure to boil the water before you drink it. **5.** MODEL: . . . If a player does not do so, he will probably not play well. **6.** B **7.** A **8.** B **9.** MODEL: Not all the Floridians enjoy the warm weather to which they awaken every morning. **10.** MODEL: . . . The columnist (*or* The astrologer, etc.) always writes generalities. **11.** MODEL: With the job half done, I lost my enthusiasm, and I kept postponing the second half. **12.** MODEL: Jean was handicapped by being unable to read well or spell well.

40

Pronoun Shift: she *Isn't* you, *Is She?*

After writing your answer(s) in the right-hand column, check this column to see whether you have responded correctly. If you have made a mistake, or if you need more practice, do whatever is asked below the dotted line in each answer frame.

Answers to questions for added practice can be found at the end of each lesson.

Understanding and Applying the Principles

1

I wondered whether a person should spend all her time seeing horror movies when you have so many other kinds available.

The sentence above starts with the pronoun *I*, shifts to *a person* spending *her* time, and then _____ [Who?] have so many other kinds available.

Answers and Added Practice

1

    you

. . . .

Note the shifts:
I (first person) → *a person, her* (third person) → *you* (second person)

2

One way to improve the example in Frame 1 is to write:

I wondered whether I should spend all _____ [Whose?] time seeing horror movies when _____ [Who?] have so many other kinds available.

2

    my, I

. . . .

The last part of the example in Frame 1 could also be written:

When so many _____

_____

_____

_____

_____ .

[Finish the sentence.]

3

The point is that we should avoid *unnecessary* shifts in the person of pronouns. Personal pronouns are often classified like this:

First person: **I, me, my, mine, we, us, our, ours**

Second person: **you, your, yours**

Third person: **she, her, he, him, it, hers, his, its, they, them, theirs**

Indefinite pronouns such as *somebody* or *everyone*, as well as all nouns, such as *a man* or *a person*, are treated as third person.

We _____ [*should* or *should not?*] shift unnecessarily from one person to another.

3

> should not

. . . .

> **A parent should not assume that your child is always a little angel.**

Does that sentence contain an unnecessary shift? _____

4

Obviously, sometimes a shift is necessary. For instance, if *you* do one thing and *he* or *she* does another, a shift is justified. Is it justified in the following sentence?

> **You went to the library while she went to her locker.**

_____ [*Justified* or *Unjustified*?]

4

> Justified

. . . .

> **You strengthened your mind and she revitalized her body.**

Is that shift justified? _____

5

Many shifts involve *someone* or *somebody* or *a person*, which may unwisely be changed to *you*. For example:

> **A person may come from Crawfordsville by canoe, if you wish.**

The shift from _____ to _____ is _____
_____ . [*justified* or *unjustified*?]

5

> *a person, you,* unjustified

. . . .

> **If somebody wants fresh air, you can open a window.**

The shift from _____

to _____ is _____

_____ .

[*justified* or *unjustified*?]

6

In England, if one is unfortunate enough to start one's sentence with *one*, one is expected to continue using *one* to the end of one's sentence. In the United States, however, a shift to *he* or *his* or *she* or *her* (but not to *you* or *your*) is permissible, because *one*, *he*, and *she* are all third person. So Americans may write

> One should do _____ [*his* or *your*?] work as well as _____ [*he* or *you*?] can.

6

> his, he

. . . .

Copy the final sentence from Frame 6, but start with *You* rather than *One*. Complete the sentence in the way that is now necessary.

7

In summary, we _____ [*should* or *should not*?] shift to a different person unless we have a good reason for doing so.

7

should not

. . . .

Repeat what you wrote in Answer Frame 6, but this time start with *Everyone*.

8

In Frames 8–10, copy the better choice in each blank.

   A. If a customer sees clerks standing around and talking instead of working, _____ [*you get* or *he gets?*] a bad impression of the store.

   B. If clerks are standing and talking instead of working, _____ [*you* or *they?*] give customers a bad impression of the store.

8

   A. he gets B. they

. . . .

When students cut across lawns, _____ [*you* or *they?*] make homeowners justifiably angry.

9

   A. When you are watching a race on a large track, _____ _____ [*you* or *a person?*] should have binoculars.

   B. When a person is watching a race on a large track, _____ _____ [*you* or *he or she?*] should have binoculars.

9

   A. you B. he or she

. . . .

In reading *Moby Dick* I learned that a sailor's life was hard when _____ _____ [*you were* or *he was?*] on a whaler.

10

   A. When you arrive at the door of a Japanese house, _____ _____ [*you* or *one* or *a person?*] should remove _____ [*your* or *his?*] shoes.

   B. When a person arrives at the door of a Japanese house, _____ [*you* or *he?*] should remove _____ [*your* or *his?*] shoes.

10

   A. you, your
   B. he, his

. . . .

When you first observe these carvings, _____ [*you notice* or *one notices?*] that the grain is very slightly raised.

11

Make up a sentence about how to choose a sweater. Start it like this:

    When you choose a sweater, . . .

Write the entire sentence.

11

Model Answer

When you choose a sweater, you should consider warmth and practicality, not just color and stylishness.

. . . .

Finish this:

When a girl is choosing a sweater, . . .

12

Make up a sentence about what one should do before repairing an electrical outlet. Start it like this:

When a person is repairing an electrical outlet, . . .

Write the entire sentence.

12

Model Answer

When a person is repairing an electrical outlet, he or she should first turn off the electricity.

. . . .

Finish this:

If you hope to do well in college, . . .

13

Finish honestly: One thing I hope to remember from this lesson is that . . .

(In this frame, any answer that you consider honest and accurate is acceptable.)

Lesson 40: Answers to Questions for Added Practice

2. MODEL: When so many kinds of movies are available, I wondered whether I should spend all my time watching horror films. (*Or* . . . whether a person should spend all her time watching horror films.) **3.** Yes **4.** Yes **5.** *somebody, you,* unjustified. **6.** You should do your work as well as you can. **7.** Everyone should do his (*or* her) work as well as he (*or* she) can. **8.** they **9.** he was **10.** you notice **11.** MODEL: When a girl is choosing a sweater, she should consider warmth and practicality, not just color and stylishness. **12.** MODEL: If you hope to do well in college, you will need to develop good study habits.

══41══

Pronoun Agreement:
someone *Can't Be* they, *Can He?*

After writing your answer(s) in the right-hand column, check this column to see whether you have responded correctly. If you have made a mistake, or if you need more practice, do whatever is asked below the dotted line in each answer frame.

Answers to questions for added practice can be found at the end of each lesson.

Understanding and Applying the Principles

1

This lesson concerns the formal use of other words with *someone* and similar pronouns. In informal use, greater freedom exists.

Somebody is peering out that window.

A. In that sentence, only _____ [How many?] person(s) is (are) peering out.

B. That appears to be true because a _____ [*singular* or *plural*?] verb is used.

Answers and Added Practice

1

    A. one B. singular

· ·

Someone is creeping up behind us.

In that sentence, only _____ [How many?] person(s) is (are) creeping?

2

Somebody, then, refers to only one person. Which of the following sentences should we write?

A. Somebody is guarding *their* own property. [Note that *their* refers to more than one person.]

B. Somebody is guarding *his* own property. [Note that *he* or *his* refers to only one person.]

____ [A or B?] is preferable.

2

    B

· ·

Someone is afraid that _____ [*his* or *their*?] own belongings may be stolen.

3

We should write *Somebody is guarding his own property* because *his*, like *somebody*, refers to only _____ [How many?] person(s).

3

one

....

Someone said that her children were in danger,

This sentence is correct because *her*, like *someone*, _____

_____

_____ . [Finish the sentence.]

4

More than one

....

Someone, like *somebody*, is singular, and *her* (or *his*) is also singular. If we used *their* instead of *her* or *his*, we would be mixing a plural with a

_____ .

5

his

....

In writing anything formal, careful writers use _____ [*her* or *their*?] to refer to *someone*, *somebody*, and similar words when the gender is female.

6

A. his   B. her

....

Similarly we should write:

A. Has any contestant brought

_____ [*his* or *their*?] computer?

B. Each girl sang _____ [*her* or *their*?] solo.

4

Somebody and *his* (or *her*) agree in number. Each is singular, referring to only one person.

Does *their* refer to one person or more than one? _____

_____

5

So **Somebody is guarding their own property** is not logical, although it or something similar is often heard in informal speech. In most writing, therefore, it is considered better to use _____ [*his* or *their*?] to refer to *somebody*.

6

Other singular words like *somebody* include *someone, anyone, anybody, nobody, no one, everybody,* and *each*. Almost always, *either* or *neither* is also singular. Notice that all these words except *each, either,* and *neither* end in the singular *one* or *body*.

Because they are singular, a singular word like *his* should be used to refer to them. So we should write

A. Has anyone brought _____ [*his* or *their*?] computer?

B. Each of the girls sang _____ [*her* or *their*?] solo.

7

If both males and females are in a group, we may use the inclusive phrase *his or her* along with a word like *somebody*. When that is awkward, *his* is usually acceptable. (See also Lesson 62, Sexist Language.) So the first example in Frame 6 may be written:

Has anyone brought _____ [*his or her,* or *their*?] computer.

7

his or her

. . . .

Each of the vocalists sang _____ _____ [*his or her*, or *their?*] solo.

8

A. their B. their

. . . .

A. A singular such as *somebody* is referred to by the singular possessive _____ or _____ .

B. A plural such as *both* or *all* is referred to by the plural possessive _____ .

9

A. his B. her C. their

. . . .

A. Everyone must supply _____ _____ [*his, his or her*, or *their?*] own equipment.

B. Nobody can be entirely freed from _____ [*his, his or her*, or *their?*] responsibilities.

10

A. his (*or his or her*)
B. his (*or his or her*)
C. their

. . . .

A. Everybody is most interested in _____ [*his, his or her*, or *their?*] own destiny.

B. All are most interested in _____ [*his or her* or *their?*] own destinies.

8

Obviously *both* and *all* are plural, not singular, and so should be followed by the plural *their*.

A. Both of the men were dressed in _____ [*his or their?*] best clothes.

B. All the men were dressed in _____ [*his or their?*] best clothes.

9

In Frames 9–10, write in each blank the word considered best in formal writing.

A. No one lost _____ [*his or their?*] way.

B. Each of the girls lost _____ [*his, her*, or *their?*] way.

C. Both of the girls lost _____ [*her or their?*] way.

10

A. Everybody has _____ [*his, his or her*, or *their?*] opinions.

B. Anybody has a right to _____ [*his, his or her*, or *their?*] own opinions.

C. All have a right to _____ [*his, his or her*, or *their?*] opinions.

11

The principle we have been observing applies also when the word referring to *someone*, etc., is not possessive. You can easily make the choice in these sentences:

A. Neither of them is allowed to choose the steak that _____ _____ . [*he prefers* or *they prefer?*]

B. Nobody received what _____ [*he or they?*] requested.

C. Did everybody get the magazines that _____ [*she or they?*] requested?

11

A. he prefers
B. he
C. she

· ·

A. Each of the would-be angels told St. Peter what _____ _____ [*she* or *they*?] had done on earth.

B. All of them may have exaggerated what _____ [*she* or *they*?] had accomplished.

12

Student or *person* or any other singular word obviously refers to only one person, just as *someone* does. So we should write:

A. A student sometimes asks for help with _____ [*his or her* or *their*?] spelling.

B. A doctor sometimes consults _____ [*his or her* or *their*?] colleagues.

12

A. his or her   B. his or her

· ·

A college teacher may have to write a book before _____ [*he or she* or *they*?] can become a professor.

13

Compose a sentence starting with *Someone tried* and using *he* or *his*.

13

Model Answer

Someone tried to open the safe, but he could not do so.

· ·

Compose a sentence starting with *Everybody likes* and using *she* or *her*.

14

Compose a sentence starting with *Each of the girls* and using *she, her, they,* or *their* (whichever is correct in formal writing).

14

Model Answer

Each of the girls chose the costume that she liked best.

. . . .

Compose a sentence starting with *No one in the audience* and using *his, her,* or *their* (whichever is correct in formal writing).

15

Compose a sentence in which you use *a person* and a pronoun that agrees with it.

15

Model Answer

A person must make up his own mind.

. . . .

Compose a sentence in which you use *a woman* and a pronoun that agrees with it.

16

Finish honestly: One thing I hope to remember from this lesson is that . . .

(In this frame, any answer that you consider honest and accurate is acceptable.)

Lesson 41: Answers to Questions for Added Practice

1. one **2.** his **3.** MODEL: refers to only one person **4.** singular **5.** her **6.** A. his B. her **7.** his or her **8.** A. his, her B. their **9.** A. his (*or* his or her) B. his (*or* his or her) **10.** A. his (*or* his or her) B. their **11.** A. she B. they **12.** he or she **13.** MODEL: Everybody likes to recall her first date, if only to laugh about it. **14.** MODEL: No one in the audience has left his (*or* her *or* his or her) seat. **15.** MODEL: A woman today has much more personal freedom than her mother or grandmother had.

====42====

Degree in Comparisons: Sometimes better *Is Better than* best

After writing your answer(s) in the right-hand column, check this column to see whether you have responded correctly. If you have made a mistake, or if you need more practice, do whatever is asked below the dotted line in each answer frame.

Answers to questions for added practice can be found at the end of each lesson.

Understanding and Applying the Principles

1

Kevin   **Jason**

A. Kevin is the _____ [*taller* or *shorter?*] of the two boys.
B. Jason is the _____ [*taller* or *shorter?*] of the two.

Answers and Added Practice

1

   A. taller   B. shorter

   . . . .

   A. Kevin is the _____ [*larger* or *smaller?*] of the two.
   B. Jason is the _____ [*larger* or *smaller?*] of the two.

2

Kevin   **Jason**   **Chris**

A. Of these three boys, who is tallest? _____
B. Who is the shortest of the three? _____

2

    A. Kevin B. Chris

. . . .

    A. Kevin is the _____
       _____ [*largest* or
    smallest?] of the three.

    B. Chris is the _____
       _____ [*largest* or
    smallest?] of the three.

3

    A. We say that Kevin is the *taller* when we are talking about
      _____ [How many?] boys.

    B. We say that Kevin is the *tallest* when we are talking about
      _____ [*two* or *three or more?*] boys.

3

    A. two B. three or more

. . . .

    A. We say that Kevin is the *larger* when we are talking about _____ [How many?] boys.

    B. We say that Kevin is the *largest* when we are talking about _____ [How many?] boys.

4

    A. With words like *tall, short, large,* or *small,* we add *-er* when we are comparing _____ [How many?] persons or things.

    B. With the same words, we add *-est* when we are comparing _____ [How many?] persons or things.

4

    A. two B. three or more
    (*or* more than two)

. . . .

Add *-er* or *-est,* as needed:

    the strong _____ of the two
    the weak _____ of the six
    the long _____ of two lines
    the bright _____ of the stars
    in the Big Dipper

5

Some adjectives and adverbs, like *beautiful* and *quickly,* do not add *-er* and *-est.*

    A. Instead of *beautifuler* and *beautifulest,* we say _____ [m - - -?] *beautiful* and _____ [m - - -?] *beautiful.*

    B. Instead of *quicklier* and *quickliest,* we say _____ *quickly* and _____ *quickly.*

Note: In general, *more* and *most* are used with adverbs ending in *-ly,* with adjectives of three syllables or more, and with two-syllable adjectives ending in *-al* [*fatal*], *-ed* [*hated*], *-en* [*wooden*], *-er* [*eager*], *-ful* [*blissful*], *-ic* [*hectic*], *-id* [*candid*], *-il* [*civil*], *-ile* [*agile*], *-ing* [*sparkling*], *-ish* [*foolish*], *-ive* [*pensive*], *-om* [*random*], *-ose* [*verbose*], *-ous* [*famous*], *-que* [*oblique*], *-st* [*earnest*], and *-ure* [*mature*].

5

    A. more, most

    B. more, most

....

Put a check before each word with which *more* and *most* are needed instead of *-er* and *-est*.

_____ carefully	_____ lazy
_____ cheerful	_____ strenuous
_____ bright	_____ frantic
_____ waspish	_____ rabid
_____ strange	_____ earnest

6

More, like the ending *-er*, is used in comparing two things. *Most*, like the ending *-est*, is used in comparing three or more things. So we say:

    A. I think that yours is the _____ [*more* or *most?*] attractive of the two paintings.

    B. Of the two women, she reacts _____ [*more* or *most?*] quickly.

6

    A. more B. more

....

    A. Of the two solutions, yours is the _____ [*more* or *most?*] complicated.

    B. Peerless was the _____ [*more* or *most?*] awkward of the two colts.

7

Using any one of the words listed in Answer Frame 5, complete each of these sentences, adding *more*, *most*, *-er*, or *-est* (whichever is correct).

    A. Charles is the _____ of the two men.

    B. Miranda is the _____ of the five children.

    C. His temperament is the _____ of the two.

7

    A. (a word with *more* or *-er*)

    B. (a word with *most* or *-est*)

    C. (a word with *more* or *-er*)

....

Follow the directions in Frame 7.

    A. Leo thought about Glenna and Faye and decided that Faye was the _____
_____ .

    B. But considering Alice as well as the other two, Leo thought Alice was the _____
_____ .

8

Complete the following sentence, saying something that will require you to use an adjective or an adverb with *-er*, *-est*, *more*, or *most* (whichever is correct).

    Of the two mechanics, he . . .

[Write the entire sentence.]

8

Model Answer

    Of the two mechanics, he is the more experienced.

· ·

Follow the directions in Frame 8.

    A. Of the two clarinetists, she _____

        _____ .

    B. Of all the band members, she _____

        _____ .

9

Supply a suitable beginning for the following sentence, using an appropriate adjective with *-er, -est, more,* or *most.*

    . . . of the four tame rabbits.

[Write the entire sentence.]

9

Model Answer

    Speckly is the oldest of the four tame rabbits.

· ·

Follow the directions in Frame 8.

_____

_____

of the two tame rabbits.

10

A Harvard football coach finished a pre-game speech by saying, "May the best team win!"

    A Yale man asked him, "Don't you mean the *better* team?"

    "No," said the Harvard coach. "I brought sixty-six men. That's six teams."

Why, in your opinion, did the Yale man ask his question?

10

Model Answer

    The Yale man thought of only two teams, Yale and Harvard, and assumed an error on the part of the Harvard coach.

11

Finish honestly: One thing I hope to remember from this lesson is that . . .

[In this frame, any answer that you consider honest and accurate is acceptable.]

Lesson 42: Answers to Questions for Added Practice

1. A. larger B. smaller **2.** A. largest B. smallest **3.** A. two B. three or more **4.** stronger, weakest, longer, brightest **5.** more carefully, more cheerful, more strenuous, more frantic, more waspish, more rabid, more earnest **6.** A. more B. more **7.** A. *more* (and any listed word appropriate for describing girls) B. *most* (and any appropriate word from the list) **8.** MODELS: A. Of the two clarinetists, she achieves the clearer tone. B. Of all the band members, she is the most dependable. **9.** MODEL: Hippity is the friskier (*or* more frisky) of the two tame rabbits.

═══43═══

Modifiers After Verbs of the Senses: How Does the Dog Smell?

After writing your answer(s) in the right-hand column, check this column to see whether you have responded correctly. If you have made a mistake, or if you need more practice, do whatever is asked below the dotted line in each answer frame.

Answers to questions for added practice can be found at the end of each lesson.

Understanding and Applying the Principles

1

We'll find out whether strawberries taste *sweet* or *sweetly* and whether a dog smells *bad* or *badly* or possibly both. First, a bit of useful grammar: We use most adjectives to describe something or someone, to tell how it *is* or *seems*.

> **Claribel is *tall*.**
> **Elephants seem *huge*.**

Vinegar is _____ . [Tell how vinegar tastes. The word you use is an adjective.]

Answers and Added Practice

1

    sour (*or* tart, etc.)

· ·

Write a suitable adjective in each blank.

    A. Grass is _____ .

    B. Brown grass seems _____

        _____ .

    C. Your lawn is _____ .

2

Most adverbs, unlike most adjectives, end in *-ly*. We generally use an adverb to tell how somebody *does* something.

> **Jack does his work *rapidly*.**
> **Claribel sleeps *soundly*.**

Crows caw _____ . [Tell how they caw. The word you use is an adverb.]

2

noisily (*or* raucously, loudly, etc.)

....

Write a suitable adverb in each blank. (It will probably end in -*ly*.)

A. Jack types _____ .

B. He proofreads _____

_____ .

C. He seals the letter _____

_____ .

3

Now let's go back to the strawberries. Remember that we want to find out whether they taste *sweet* or *sweetly*.

A. Do the strawberries themselves taste anything? _____

B. Do we want to say that the strawberries *are* or *seem to be* something? _____

3

A. No B. Yes

....

In *The strawberries smell fresh,* do the strawberries themselves smell anything?

_____ [*Yes* or *No?*]

4

Because we want to say that the strawberries are or seem to be sweet, we should write:

The strawberries taste sweet.

or

The strawberries taste sweetly.

Copy the correct sentence.

4

The strawberries taste sweet.

....

Copy the correct sentence:

The strawberries smell freshly.
The strawberries smell fresh.

5

"Oh, your roses smell so sweetly!" a dear lady exclaimed.

She should have said what?

5

"Oh, your roses smell so sweet!"

....

Was the lady right when she said a moment later, "And your whole garden looks beautiful!"?

_____ [*Yes* or *No?*]

6

Now about that dog. Pooch has been out in the rain. So we say:

A. Pooch seems wet. Yes, Pooch is wet.

B. Pooch looks _____ . [*wet* or *wetly?*]

C. Pooch smells _____ . [*wet* or *wetly?*]

D. Pooch smells _____ . [*bad* or *badly?*]

Milady sprays Pooch with the dog's cologne, or some of her own, and then

E. Pooch smells _____ . [*good* or *well?*]

6

B. wet   C. wet
D. bad   E. good

....

A. The medicine tastes _____ _____ . [*bitter* or *bitterly*?]
B. The soft music sounded _____ . [*pleasant* or *pleasantly*?]
C. Rotten eggs smell _____ _____ . [*bad* or *badly*?]

7

When we tell how something *is* or *seems* instead of how somebody *does* something, we need an adjective rather than an adverb. The verbs of the senses are often used as substitutes for *is* or *seem*. Those verbs are *taste, smell, look, sound,* and *feel*.

Look refers to the sense of sight, *sound* to the sense of _____ _____ , *feel* to the sense of _____ , *smell* to the sense of _____ , and *taste* to the sense of _____ .

7

hearing, feeling (*or* touch), smell, taste

....

We use *look* to refer to things that we *see, sound* for things we _____ _____ , *smell* for things that have an _____ , *taste* for things we put into our mouths, and *feel* for things we _____ .

8

So, after a verb of the senses we usually place an adjective. Strawberries taste *sweet* or *good* or *delicious,* and wet Pooch smells *unpleasant* or *bad*.
   But consider this:

Pooch smells the bone cautiously.

A. Are we saying that Pooch *is* or *seems* something? _____
B. Are we saying that he *does* something? _____

8

A. No.   B. Yes

....

Bossie looked proudly at her calf.

A. Are we saying that Bossie *was* or *seemed* something? _____
B. Are we saying that she *did* something? _____

9

When we say that Pooch or any other living being performs the act of smelling, tasting, looking, feeling, or sounding, we need an adverb rather than an adjective.

A. So Pooch smells the bone *cautiously,* or _____ , or _____ . [Supply two other possible adverbs.]
B. Pooch has a keen sense of smell. When he lifts his nose into a light breeze and sniffs, he is probably smelling very _____ . [*good* or *well*?]

9

    A. hesitantly, quickly (or any other suitable adverbs)

    B. well

. . . .

A person may

    A. feel an object _____ _____ [*real careful* or *very carefully?*],

    B. look _____ [*curious* or *curiously*] at the object, and

    C. taste the object _____ _____ . [*quick* or *quickly?*]

10

If you are ever in doubt about whether to use an adjective or an adverb after a verb of the senses, try using *is, are, seems,* or *seem* in the place of the verb. If it makes fairly good sense, use the adjective.

    For instance, when faced with a choice between *The water tastes bad* or *The water tastes badly,* you could use *seems: The water seems bad.*

    A. Does *The water seems bad* make sense? _____

    B. So you choose *The water tastes* _____ . [*bad* or *badly?*]

10

    A. Yes   B. bad

. . . .

Mark each sentence right or wrong:

    A. The juggler looks unpleasantly. _____

    B. The music sounds pleasant. _____

    C. The surface feels smooth. _____

11

Bad and *badly* are the words most likely to cause trouble after verbs of the senses. The general principle applies to them as to other modifiers: Use the adjective *bad* if *is, are, seems,* or *seem* makes sense, and use the adverb *badly* only if somebody is performing badly the act of smelling, feeling, or the like.

    A. The meat tastes _____ . [*bad* or *badly?*]

    B. My fingers are usually sensitive, but that day they were feeling the surfaces _____ . [*bad* or *badly?*]

11

    A. bad   B. badly

. . . .

    A. Did Little Boy Blue probably sound his horn *bad* or *badly?* _____

    B. Did his music sound *bad* or *badly?* _____

12

Make up two sentences.

    A. In the first, tell about the feel of tree bark.

    B. In the second, tell about the appearance of your sister on her wedding day. Use *looked.*

12

Model Answers

    A. The tree bark felt rough. [An adjective is required.]

    B. My sister looked beautiful on her wedding day. [An adjective is required.]

13

    A. Write a sentence about the smell of freshly baked cookies.

    B. Write a sentence about how a small boy smells the cookies.

13

Model Answers

    A. The cookies smell spicy. [Adjective required.]

    B. The little boy smells the cookies delightedly. [Adverb required.]

14

Finish honestly: One thing I hope to remember from this lesson is that . . .

(In this frame, any answer that you consider honest and accurate is acceptable.)

Lesson 43: Answers to Questions for Added Practice

1. MODELS: A. green B. dead C. attractive **2.** MODELS: A. expertly B. carefully C. immediately **3.** No **4.** The strawberries smell fresh. **5.** Yes **6.** A. bitter B. pleasant C. bad **7.** hear, odor, touch (*or* feel) **8.** A. No B. Yes **9.** A. very carefully B. curiously C. quickly **10.** A. Wrong B. Right C. Right **11.** A. Badly B. Bad

44

Adjectives Vs. Adverbs: If You Make Good Candy, You Make Candy Well

After writing your answer(s) in the right-hand column, check this column to see whether you have responded correctly. If you have made a mistake, or if you need more practice, do whatever is asked below the dotted line in each answer frame.

Answers to questions for added practice can be found at the end of each lesson.

Understanding and Applying the Principles

1

You make good candy.

(adj = adjective, n = noun)

The arrow in the sentence shows that the adjective *good* modifies (tells something about) the noun _____ . [What word?]

Answers and Added Practice

1

candy

....

Our store prides itself on selling good merchandise.

In that sentence the adjective _____ tells something about the noun _____ .

2

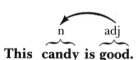
This candy is good.

Once more the arrow shows that the adjective *good* modifies the noun _____ [What word?], used here as the subject of the sentence.

2

candy

....

The cutlery is especially good.

In that sentence the adjective *good* tells something about the noun _____ .

3

You make candy well.

(v = verb, adv = adverb)

This time nothing is said about the quality of the candy. Instead, as the arrow shows, we are told how the act of making the candy is performed. That is, the adverb *well* modifies the verb _____ . [What word?]

3

make

. . . .

Other adverbs than *well* could be used in the same sentence. For instance, you make candy *efficiently*. List two other adverbs that fit. _____

_____ _____

4

make

. . . .

The answer is satisfactory.

In that sentence the adjective _____

_____ modifies

the noun _____ .

5

A. No   B. Yes   C. *evenly*

. . . .

A. The doctor examined him

_____ .

[*thorough* or *thoroughly*?]

B. The doctor examined him

_____ . [*good* or *well*?]

6

conquered, sinks, spoke, have offered

. . . .

Write a sentence using one of the verbs of action from Frame 6. Use a suitable adverb to modify it.

4

The sentences we have been examining illustrate the most important difference between an adjective, like *good*, and an adverb, like *well*. To choose between an adjective and an adverb, we need to know whether it modifies a word used as a noun (like *candy* in Frames 1 and 2), or a verb (like _____ [What word?] in Frame 3).

5

Let's see how we can decide whether to use the adjective *even* or the adverb *evenly* in this sentence:

   Mother divided the pie _____ .

   A. Are we saying that the pie was even? _____
   B. Are we saying that the dividing was done evenly? _____
   C. So we need an adverb to modify the verb *divided*. The word needed in the example is _____ . [*even* or *evenly*?]

6

In summary, we use an adverb to modify a verb showing action, as *make* and *divide* do. A verb of action tells what someone is doing, was doing, or will be doing.

   Copy the four of the following verbs that show action.

   **is   conquered   sinks   seems
   spoke   have been   have offered**

7

Most adverbs, like *evenly*, *quickly*, and *carelessly*, end in *-ly*, but not all of them do. Such words as *well*, *hard*, *better*, *straight*, *fast*, *high*, *late*, *low*, and *right* may be used as either adjectives or adverbs.

   A. In **The shelf is straight**, the word *straight* modifies the noun _____ and is an _____ . [*adjective* or *adverb*?]
   B. In **The ball went straight down the fairway**, the word *straight* modifies the verb _____ and is an _____ . [*adjective* or *adverb*?]

7

A. *shelf*, adjective
B. *went*, adverb

· ·

A. In *Hit the hard ball, hard* is an
_____ .[*adjective*
or *adverb?*]
B. In *Hit the ball hard, hard* is an
_____ . [*adjective*
or *adverb?*]

8

In Frames 8–9, tell whether an adjective or an adverb is needed
in each sentence.

A. His reply was _____ .   _____
B. The plane departs _____ .   _____
C. The crowd shouts _____ .   _____

8

A. Adjective   B. Adverb
C. Adverb

· ·

Copy the three sentences from
Frame 8, completing each with any
word that makes sense and is grammatically correct.

9

A. The dress seems _____ .   _____
B. The soldiers fought _____ .   _____
C. My sister became _____ .   _____

9

A. Adjective   B. Adverb
C. Adjective

· ·

Proceed as in Answer Frame 8,
completing the sentences from
Frame 9.

10

One of the most persistent errors of some students involves the
use of *good* where *well* is required. Oral practice is the best way
to master the correct form. Read each of the following sentences several times, aloud if possible. Repeat if the problem
recurs at any time.

You make candy well. You do many things
well. You swim well. You play tennis well. You
sing fairly well. Sometimes you write rather
well. I am proud of how well you do so many
things.

10

No Written Answer

. . . .

Add to the group in Frame 10 three other practice sentences using *well* correctly.

11

Make up a sentence in which you tell how you do an important task.

11

Model Answer

I take care of my little brother very regularly.

. . . .

What are three adverbs besides *well* that could replace *regularly* in the sentence above? _____ ,

_____ , _____ .

12

Write another sentence. This time use the adverb *well* to explain how thoroughly you understand the use of adverbs.

12

Model Answer

I understand the use of adverbs very well.

. . . .

I can make a dress _____ .

What are three adverbs which will fit that sentence?

13

Finish honestly: One thing I hope to remember from this lesson is that . . .

(In this frame, any answer that you consider honest and accurate is acceptable.)

Lesson 44: Answers to Questions for Added Practice

1. *good, merchandise* **2.** *cutlery* **3.** MODELS: easily, frequently **4.** *satisfactory, answer* **5.** A. thoroughly B. well **6.** MODEL: The doctor spoke very softly. **7.** A. adjective B. adverb **8.** MODELS: A. His reply was brief. B. The plane departs immediately. C. The crowd shouts boisterously. **9.** MODELS: A. The dress seems tight. B. The soldiers fought gallantly. C. My sister became pregnant. **10.** MODELS: You speak well. You also drive well. I wish I could do so many things so well. **11.** MODELS: often, gladly, reluctantly **12.** MODELS: skillfully, easily, occasionally

═══45═══

Double Negatives: When You Say "No," Once Should Be Enough

After writing your answer(s) in the right-hand column, check this column to see whether you have responded correctly. If you have made a mistake, or if you need more practice, do whatever is asked below the dotted line in each answer frame.

Answers to questions for added practice can be found at the end of each lesson.

Understanding and Applying the Principles

1

In French it is correct to say *Je ne sais pas*. Translated exactly, that means "I not do know not."

Is **I not do know not** good English? _____

Answers and Added Practice

1

> No

· ·

English isn't French. A sentence form that is perfectly correct in one language may be quite wrong in another.

2

> One

· ·

In the incorrect sentence **I do not know no French**, how many words are negatives? _____

3

> Two

· ·

How many negatives are in each sentence?

  A. I saw nobody. _____

  B. I didn't see nothing.

  _____

  C. I didn't see anything.

  _____

4

> She did not hear any noise (*or*)
> She heard no noise.

· ·

This sentence has three negatives:

  I can't see none nowhere.

Rewrite it with only one negative.

2

The French *Je ne sais pas* has two words, *ne* and *pas*, that are negatives, meaning "no" or "not."

> In the correct English sentence **I do not know** how many words are negatives? _____

3

In modern English, unlike French, one negative is almost always enough, and two negatives are generally considered wrong.

> How many negatives are in the following incorrect sentence? **I did not see nobody.** _____

4

Because **I did not see nobody** has two negatives, the form **I did not see anybody** is preferred in modern English. How can the following sentence be improved?

  She did not hear no noise.

_____

5

If you have hardly any money, you do not have much money. The word *hardly*, then, is another negative, comparable to *not* or *no*. If you said **I don't have hardly any money**, you would be unwisely using _____ [How many?] negatives; and if you said **I don't hardly have no money**, you would be using _____ . [How many?]

5

two, three

. . . .

Improve the example in Frame 5. You may want to use *almost* or *much* in your sentence.

6

Scarcely, like *hardly*, has a negative meaning. *Scarcely any* and *hardly any*, for instance, mean "not much."

Which should you say to avoid a double negative?

A. I have scarcely any money.

B. I don't have scarcely any money.

C. I have scarcely no money.

D. I don't scarcely have no money.

_____ [A, B, C, or D?]

6

A

. . . .

Use *scarcely* and three other of these words to write a good four-word sentence:

    have   anything   eaten
    ate   nothing   ate   you
    not

7

Neither, meaning "not either" or "not one or the other," is also a negative. Which should you say to avoid a double negative?

A. I didn't neither.

B. I didn't either.

_____ [A or B?]

7

B

. . . .

Rewrite to get rid of two negatives:

Sam didn't bring no matches neither.

8

In summary, six of the most used negatives are *not* (or *n't*), *none*, *hardly*, *scarcely*, *neither*, and *no* (which sometimes appears by itself and sometimes in *nobody*, *no one*, *nothing*, and *nowhere*).

Ordinarily, no more than _____ [How many?] of those words should appear in a single clause or sentence.

8

one

· ·

What should we say instead of each of these?

    A. *not nobody:* nobody or not

    — — — — — — — —

    B. *not nothing:* nothing or not

    — — — — — — — —

    C. *not nowhere:* nowhere, or not

    — — — — — — — —

9

    A. 1   B. 2

· ·

Which is correct?

    A. I hardly think so.

    B. I don't hardly think so.

    _____

10

    A. 2   B. 2

· ·

Rewrite, correcting each error:

    A. I don't like you, neither.

    _____

    _____

    B. She hasn't hardly enough to
    live on. _____

    _____

    _____

11

    A. 2   B. 1

· ·

Rewrite, correcting each error:

    A. There aren't no plans yet.

    _____

    _____

    B. She didn't scarcely have no
    food. _____

    _____

    _____

9

In Frames 9–11, choose the correct sentence in each pair.

    A. 1. She didn't hear anything.
        2. She didn't hear nothing.
        _____ [1 or 2?]
    B. 1. Susan didn't hardly believe your story.
        2. Susan hardly believed your story.
        _____ [1 or 2?]

10

    A. 1. He hasn't neither courage nor wisdom.
        2. He has neither courage nor wisdom.
        _____ [1 or 2?]
    B. 1. There wasn't hardly anybody in the room.
        2. There was hardly anybody in the room.
        _____ [1 or 2?]

11

    A. 1. We haven't scarcely seen Max all week.
        2. We have scarcely seen Max all week.
        _____ [1 or 2?]
    B. 1. This isn't a picture of any place I've seen.
        2. This isn't a picture of no place I've seen.
        _____ [1 or 2?]

12

Write a sentence of your own to express the fact that no voices could be heard. Start with *I couldn't hear.*

12

Model Answer

I couldn't hear any voices from the next room.

. . . .

Write a sentence about friends. Start with *Mary doesn't have.*

13

Rewrite your sentence for Frame 12 to express the same meaning in a different way. This time start with *I heard.*

13

Model Answer

I heard no voices from the next room.

. . . .

Rewrite your sentence from Answer Frame 12. Start with *Mary has.*

14

Write a sentence in which you use the word *hardly* correctly. You may want to say something about having enough time.

14

Model Answer

We have hardly enough time to get to school. [Not *haven't hardly!*]

. . . .

Write a sentence about buying Christmas presents. Use *scarcely.*

15

If undesirable double negatives or multiple negatives occur in your speaking or writing, oral practice can be most helpful. Write down a dozen or so correct examples of the sort that you sometimes mistake, and read them several times, preferably aloud. Your sentences should be short, like these:

I don't see them anywhere.

We do not have any.

If the problem recurs, repeat as often as necessary, perhaps adding other correct examples.

15	16
No written answer ·	Finish honestly: One thing I hope to remember from this lesson is that . . . (In this frame, any answer that you consider honest and accurate is acceptable.)

Lesson 45: Answers to Questions for Added Practice

2. Two **3.** A. One B. Two C. One **4.** I can't see any anywhere. (*Or, less likely:* I can see none anywhere.) **5.** MODEL: I have almost no money. (*Or* I do not have much money.) **6.** You ate scarcely anything. **7.** Sam didn't bring any matches either. (*Or* Sam brought no matches either.) **8.** A. anybody B. anything C. anywhere **9.** A **10.** A. I don't like you, either. B. She has hardly enough to live on. **11.** A. There are no (*or* There aren't any) plans yet. B. She had scarcely any food (*or* almost no food). **12.** MODEL: Mary doesn't have any friends. **13.** MODEL: Mary has no friends. **14.** We have scarcely any money for Christmas presents.

▰▰▰46▰▰▰

Conjunctions: Making the Best Connections

After writing your answer(s) in the right-hand column, check this column to see whether you have responded correctly. If you have made a mistake, or if you need more practice, do whatever is asked below the dotted line in each answer frame.

Answers to questions for added practice can be found at the end of each lesson.

Understanding and Applying the Principles

1

In this lesson we'll examine a few conjunctions (connecting words) that are sometimes slightly confusing. (For overuse of the conjunction *and*, see Lesson 8.)

> **Either the troops on the left flank or those in the center must be driven back.**
> **Neither the troops on the left flank nor those in the center are experienced in combat.**

Those examples show that *either* teams with *or* and that *neither* teams with _____ . [What word?]

Answers and Added Practice

1

nor

....

Remember the two *n*'s:
neither . . . nor.

2

Is the following sentence, then, correct or incorrect?

**Neither the soldiers on the left flank or those
in the center can be considered reliable.**

_____

2

Incorrect

....

Choose: Neither the artillery fire
_____ [*or* or *nor*] the tanks are
successful.

3

Other conjunctions that are sometimes confused or misused
include *while, since,* and *as.*

**While Dad was cleaning the basement,
Mother was complaining that he didn't help
enough around the house.**

Think about the word *while* as it is used in that sentence.

A. Are you sure that you know what it means as used
there? _____

B. Probably it means "although" or "even though" or "despite the fact that." But possibly it means _____ .

3

A. Probably not (but any answer is satisfactory)

B. When (*or* during the time
that)

....

In some sentences, *while* is completely clear. For example,

**While Dad was sweeping the
floor, I burned the trash.**

4

If you ever feel that *while* is ambiguous (has two possible meanings) in a sentence of your own, use a more precise word or
phrase instead—perhaps *although* or *when* or *during the few minutes that.*

_____ [*While* or *Although*?] she has red hair, she
controls her temper better than redheads are said to do.

4

Although

....

In the example, *While she has red
hair* is somewhat ambiguous. It
could mean "When she has red
hair"—because hair color is often
changed.

5

**As a wren began to sing, Ann remembered
her dead canary.**

In that example, *as* may mean "because," although probably
it means _____ . That is, it may either show a reason or
refer to time.

5

When (*or* Whenever)

....

Try to think of a sentence in which *as* almost certainly means "because."

6

Since, also, may either show a reason or refer to time, and for that reason the word is sometimes ambiguous. Mark each of these sentences *Shows reason*, *Refers to time*, or *Is ambiguous*.

A. Since the year began, Adco's profits have dropped.

_____

B. Since profits depend on sales, the company is examining its selling practices. _____

C. Since its sales have plummeted, the per-share price of Adco's stock has declined and stockholders have become unhappy. _____

6

A. Refers to time
B. Shows reason
C. Is ambiguous

....

In Example C in Frame 6, what word should be substituted for *Since* if the writer's intent is to show a reason? _____

7

Complete each sentence:

A. Do not confuse *nor* with _____ .

B. Sometimes, for clarity, it is desirable to use *although* or *when* instead of _____ .

C. Sometimes, for clarity, it is desirable to use *because* or a time-word like *when* or *after* instead of _____ or

_____ .

7

A. *or*   B. *while*   C. *as, since*

....

Choose:

A. I want neither riches _____ [*nor* or *or*?] fame.

B. _____ [*While* or *Although*?] the ore was mined in Minnesota, it was processed in Pennsylvania.

C. _____ [*As* or *Because*?] the tree started falling toward me, I ran for safety.

8

Choose the unambiguous conjunction in each sentence.

A. _____ [*As* or *When*?] the tree started falling toward me, I ran for safety.

B. _____ [*Since* or *Because*?] the divers had found the gold coins, they had argued that the money was theirs.

C. _____ [*Since* or *After*?] the divers had found the gold coins, they had argued that the money was theirs.

8

A. When (Compare with C in Answer Frame 7.) B. Because C. After

· ·

Since Sam's wife left him, he has become rich.

Substitute first *After* and then *Because* for *Since*. Which word suggests more strongly that the wife was a hindrance? _____

_____

9

Write a sentence using *neither* and the word that often teams with it. You may want to say something about junipers and rose bushes.

9

Model Answer

Neither the junipers nor the rose bushes need trimming.

· ·

Make up another sentence with *neither . . . nor.*

10

Write a sentence using *while* to mean "during the time that." Be sure that no confusion with the meaning of *although* is likely. You may want to say something about a battle.

10

Model Answer

While the enemy advanced slowly, the Americans were digging trenches.

· ·

Write a sentence in which *While* means "although."

11

Write a sentence using *as* meaning "while" or "when"—that is, as a time word. Be sure that no confusion with the meaning of *because* is likely. You may want to say something about the noise of hammering.

11

Model Answer

> As the noise continued, I decided that it was the sound of hammering.

. . . .

Write a sentence in which *as* means "because."

12

Write a sentence using *since* to refer clearly to time. Be sure that no confusion with the meaning of *because* is likely. You may want to say something about World War II.

12

Model Answer

> Since World War II ended, world tensions have been steady.

. . . .

Write a sentence in which *since* means "because."

13

Finish honestly: One thing I hope to remember from this lesson is that . . .

(In this frame, any answer that you consider honest and accurate is acceptable.)

Lesson 46: Answers to Questions for Added Practice

2. nor **5.** MODEL: As the car is a complete wreck, we'll have to walk for a while. **6.** *Because* **7.** A. nor B. Although C. Because **8.** *Because* **9.** MODEL: I prefer neither the red nor the blue curtains. **10.** MODEL: While you may disagree, I believe that the Dolphins are the strongest team in the league. **11.** MODEL: As Craig is not eligible for re-election, he should have little voice in next year's budget. **12.** MODEL: Since the receiver dropped the ball and there was no interference, there can be no touchdown.

47

Definitions:
Is a Tiger When a Cat Has Stripes?

After writing your answer(s) in the right-hand column, check this column to see whether you have responded correctly. If you have made a mistake, or if you need more practice, do whatever is asked below the dotted line in each answer frame.

Answers to questions for added practice can be found at the end of each lesson.

Understanding and Applying the Principles

1

"What's a tiger?" asked Baby Sue. From the height of his superior knowledge, Sue's six-year-old brother, Bobby Don, answered, **"Aw, Stupid, a tiger is when a big cat has got stripes."**

    A. Is a tiger a member of the cat family? _____

    B. Does a tiger have stripes, and is it large? _____

Answers and Added Practice

1

    A. Yes B. Yes

. . . .

Try writing your own definition of *tiger*.

2

Bobby Don's definition of *tiger* was accurate but—as may be expected of a six-year-old—not quite standard in form. Let's see first what was good about it.

    A. Does it show the group or family to which the tiger belongs? _____

    B. Does it suggest ways in which a tiger differs from other cats? _____

2

    A. Yes B. Yes

. . . .

Look at your own definition of *tiger*. Does it also show the group to which the tiger belongs, and differentiate the tiger from other cats?

_____

3

Each good definition of a thing (a noun) places it into a CLASSIFICATION. It also provides DIFFERENTIATION to show how the thing differs from others in the same classification.

    A. In Bobby Don's definition the tiger is placed in the _____ classification. [What family?]

    B. Bobby Don tells Sue two things that differentiate tigers from other cats. These are the tiger's _____ and its _____ .

3

A. cat   B. size (*or* bigness), stripes

....

A monarchy is a form of government in which one person rules.

A. The classification is _____

_____ .

B. The differentiation is _____

_____ .

4

In form, Bobby Don's definition has a not uncommon flaw.

A. Is a tiger a *when*? _____

B. Do you know what a "when" is? _____

4

A. No   B. No

....

A monarchy is when one person rules.

What's wrong with that definition?

5

By age twelve or eighteen, Robert Donald has become more sophisticated. Now he defines *tiger* in this way:

A tiger is a large, fierce Asiatic cat with yellow fur striped with black.

A. The classification is the _____ family.

B. The words showing differentiation from most other cats are

1. _____   2. _____

3. _____   4. _____

5. _____

5

A. cat

B. 1. large 2. fierce
   3. Asiatic 4. with yellow fur 5. striped with black

....

How does your definition of *tiger* (Answer Frame 1) differ from Robert Donald's?

6

Because a thing is not a *when*, it should not be defined as a *when*. Similarly, a thing is not a *where*.

Poor: **A simile is where two unlike things are compared.**

Mature: **A simile is a comparison generally introduced by *like* or *as* and suggesting a relationship between two basically unlike things.**

In the mature definition we avoid the unwise use of _____

_____ [What word?] and we indicate clearly the

c _____ and the marks of

d _____ .

6

where, classification, differentiation

....

An oligarchy is where a few people rule.

Rewrite that definition, eliminating *where*.

7

The reason for our defeat is because our quarterback was injured.

Although the sentence above is not a definition, the construction *the reason is because* is similar to *the* (something) *is when* (or *where*).

The example may be rewritten:

A. The reason for our defeat is that _____ _____ . [Finish the sentence.] *Or,*

B. Our defeat was caused by _____ _____ . *Or, perhaps best:*

C. Injury to our quarterback _____ _____ .

7

A. our quarterback was injured.
B. the injury of our quarterback.
C. caused our defeat.

....

The reason I voted Democratic is because my parents are Democrats.

Rewrite that sentence.

8

Summary:

A. Avoid defining a thing as a _____ or a _____ .

B. In defining a word used as a noun, show its _____ _____ and its marks of _____ .

C. Avoid *the reason is* _____ .

8

A. *when, where*
B. classification, differentiation
C. *because*

....

Larceny is when you steal something.

Rewrite that sentence in three words.

9

A lanyard is where you have a short rope to tighten or tie down something on a ship.

Rewrite that sentence.

9

Model Answer

A lanyard is a short rope used on a ship to tighten or tie down something.

. . . .

Lassitude is where a person feels tired or lazy.

Rewrite in five words, the fourth of which is *or.*

10

A morganatic marriage was when a nobleman's lower-class wife and her children could not inherit his rank and property.

Rewrite the first part of that definition.

10

Model Answer

A morganatic marriage was a form of marriage in which . . .

. . . .

A pungent smell is when it hurts the inside of your nose.

Rewrite.

11

The reason the Supreme Court overturned the decision was because the precedent cited did not apply.

Instead of *because,* the word _____ should be used, especially in formal writing.

11

that

. . . .

The reason I am calling you is because one of your clients has entered a formal protest against our firm.

Rewrite.

12

Finish honestly: One thing I hope to remember from this lesson is that . . .

(In this frame any answer that you consider honest and accurate is acceptable.)

Lesson 47: Answers to Questions for Added Practice

1. (Personal response) **2.** (Personal response) **3.** A. form of government B. rule by one person **4.** MODEL: A monarchy is not a *when.* **5.** (Personal evaluation) **6.** MODEL: An oligarchy is a form of government in which a few people rule. **7.** MODEL: I voted Democratic because my parents are Democrats. **8.** MODEL: Larceny is stealing. **9.** MODEL: Lassitude is tiredness or laziness. **10.** MODEL: A pungent smell is one that hurts the inside of your nose. **11.** The reason I am calling you is that one of your clients has entered a formal protest against our firm. (*Or* I am calling you because . . .)

Mastery Test
Usage

For directions, see page 101.

21. a. A junior and a senior have applied for the job of student assistant. A U

    b. Only one of the applicants know how to type. A U

    c. The junior or the senior is being interviewed this morning. A U

22. a. Everyone in both study groups was ready to take the test. A U

    b. Each student in both groups is strong in a different subject. A U

    c. Because of the makeup of our groups, everybody benefits. A U

23. a. Neither my roommate nor I were able to afford new textbooks last semester. A U

    b. My electronics text and my chemistry lab manual were marked up. A U

    c. Neither my composition text nor my paperback novels were marked up in any way. A U

24. a. Disney World and several other attractions in Florida are on our list of places to visit during the spring break. A U

    b. SueAnn Smith, along with several other girls from my residence hall, is helping to share expenses. A U

    c. Lookout Mountain, as well as Mammoth Cave and Gatlinburg, is on our list of places to visit on our return trip. A U

25. a. There is three books and a notebook somewhere in this room. A U

    b. Under those dirty clothes and pizza boxes is one book. A U

    c. Here is a notebook and two books in the bathroom. A U

26. a. When we arrived, the stage crew was still checking the lights, arranging furniture, and attending to their other duties. A U

    b. During the entire play, the audience was absolutely quiet. A U

    c. After the play, the audience were talking excitedly among themselves, shaking hands with the director, and picking up extra copies of the playbill. A U

27. a. Fortunately I have never rode in a car with a drunken driver. A U

    b. In my opinion, any driver who has drunk too much is a very dangerous person. A U

    c. I have broken several friendships because people have chose to drink and drive. A U

28. a. Mark, who is a major in aviation technology, has already flew a plane. A U

    b. I have never went up with him, but I hope he asks me to go. A U

c. I have never seen the campus from the air.   A   U

29. a. A student was just laying on the bench fast asleep.   A   U

b. In a few minutes, he stirred and tried to sit up, but soon he lay back with his eyes shut.   A   U

c. Suddenly he rose and dashed off toward the chemistry building.   A   U

30. a. After the distinguished-looking gentleman picked up the fragile Chinese vase, the clerk asked, "Shall I wrap it for you, sir?"   A   U

b. The gentleman looked up and asked, "Will you also put packing material around it?"   A   U

c. The clerk, who seemed to dislike the question, answered, "I will give this elegant piece my usual professional attention."   A   U

31. a. Randy drove past the stop sign, and the first person he sees is a campus police officer driving toward him.   A   U

b. As soon as he saw the officer, Randy panics and steps on the accelerator pedal.   A   U

c. Randy's car leaped ahead and plows right into the police car.   A   U

32. a. If this were not such a formal occasion, we could have some fun.   A   U

b. I wish I were on the beach playing volleyball rather than in this reception line shaking hands.   A   U

c. Be that as it may, we must do this or simply vanish socially.   A   U

33. a. Jill and I caught the flu from Sue and Helen.   A   U

b. They should not have invited Jill and me to study with them.   A   U

c. Sue sneezed on Jill and me at least six times as we all sat around the table.   A   U

34. a. We southerners have to stick together in this northern city college.   A   U

b. Our very small group, my friends and I from Georgia, shouldn't have to apologize for our dialect.   A   U

c. It is we who think northerners have a strange way of talking.   A   U

35. a. Our social affairs committee added the names of all distinguished guests who we thought should sit at the head table.   A   U

b. All members of this committee were seniors in whom we had complete confidence.   A   U

c. Unfortunately, they forgot to arrange a place for the keynote speaker whom I had personally invited.   A   U

36. a. The coach has added you, him, and me to the starting lineup.   A   U

b. I always believed that I, you, and he would be first-string players.   A   U

c. Now you and I are in competition with him.   A   U

37. a. Paul's spinning the wheels resulted in our getting stuck deeper.   A   U

b. You coming when you did saved the day.   A   U

c. My signaling to passing motorists didn't do us any good.   A   U

38. a. John will sit next to Bob at the game, but he doesn't know that his parents will be there also.   A   U

b. Bob's parents wanted to go with John's parents, but they had to stay at home.   A   U

c. John told Bob that he had left his binoculars in the car.   A   U

39. a. They were distributing programs at the door of the theater, which looked more attractive this year.   A   U

b. It said in the program that the variety show would begin in twenty minutes.   A   U

c. When I finally walked up to my friends with copies of the program, one of them was missing.   A   U

40. a. Before a student turns in a paper, they should proofread it carefully.   A   U

b. If a student writes an essay outside class, you have no excuse for many errors.   A   U

c. No student should assume that your paper is free of errors.   A   U

41. a. The bus driver said that somebody in our fraternity group forgot to pay their restaurant bill.   A   U

b. Everybody had to find their receipt to prove that they had paid.   A   U

c. Nobody was allowed to leave until he could find his receipt.   A   U

42. a. Of these two sports cars, the yellow one is the newest.   A   U

b. The black car is the best one of the two mechanically.   A   U

c. The yellow car may look more attractive than the black one, but it will be the most expensive of the two to drive.   A   U

43. a. After being closed up during spring break, our room smelled badly.   A   U

b. Joe, my roommate, opened the refrigerator and smelled inside cautiously.   A   U

c. I could tell from across the room that the cheese, milk, and fish smelled bad.   A   U

44. a. I have studied hard, so I should do good on the test.   A   U

b. To make a good grade on a microbiology test, a student has to prepare well.   A   U

c. I didn't do very well on the last test because I didn't review my notes thoroughly.   A   U

45. a. Cindy was so hungry that she couldn't hardly sit still.   A   U

b. She said that she arrived at the cafeteria late and couldn't buy scarcely enough to stay alive.   A   U

c. We knew that if we didn't take her out for a snack we wouldn't hardly have any peace and quiet in the room.   A   U

46. a. While the used biology textbook had two missing pages, it was still a bargain.   A   U

b. I was lucky that neither the sociology text or the paperback dictionary was damaged.   A   U

c. While I was in the bookstore, other students were complaining about messy used texts.   A   U

47. a. Endnotes are when references are placed toward the end of a paper.   A   U

b. Footnotes are where references are placed at the bottom of a page.   A   U

c. In-text citations are short parenthetical references placed within the text of a paper.   A   U

Answers to this test can be found on p. 511.

Diction
and Style

Diagnostic Test
Diction and Style

Directions

Because each test item consists of three parts, a, b, and c, you will have three chances to test your knowledge of each principle. You must decide quickly whether or not the word choice and arrangement in each sentence convey the writer's feelings and ideas accurately and appropriately. Is the language direct, clear, and engaging? Is it vigorous enough to provide the emphasis each sentence needs? Does the language heighten your interest and satisfaction, or leave you indifferent or even hostile? If you believe that the language in a sentence is effective, circle the letter A. *If even one word is weak, unclear, inaccurate, or otherwise ineffective, circle the letter* U.

Sample Item

1. a. All of the gum was chewed by me.   A   (U)
   b. Sometimes when I chew my gum fast, I bite my tongue.   (A)   U
   c. During the horror movie last night, my tongue was bitten.   A   (U)

Note: *The writing in* a *was marked U for unacceptable because it is passive, wordy, and weak.* I chewed all of the gum *would describe this action directly and emphatically with fewer words. The writing in* c *was marked U because it doesn't tell clearly who bit the tongue.* I bit my tongue *would be a stronger main clause to end the sentence.*

How to Use the Test

Like the lessons in this book, this diagnostic test is self-instructional. When you have finished it, score it with the key provided on page 511. The test will measure your awareness of the diction and style generally expected in college essays. Each test item will give you three chances to recognize acceptable diction and style.

If you miss one or more of the three chances, you should plan to do the corresponding lesson in the pages that follow. For example, making one or more errors in test item 59 means that you should do Lesson 59.

At the end of this group of lessons, on page 329, is a matching Mastery Test. Take that test after you have completed the needed lessons. It will show you the items in which you have improved and those in which you need further work. Study once more the lessons corresponding to the missed items.

48. a. Alice she is going to Nassau for spring break.   A   U
    b. When she returns back from vacation, she will tell me that the water was blue in color and very warm.   A   U
    c. Maybe in future years to come I'll be able to visit places like that.   A   U

49. a. I like the story "The Open Window" more than Lucy.   A   U

b. Short stories appeal to me more than any type of literature.   A   U

c. The characters in a short story seem more vivid than poetry.   A   U

50. a. I hear lectures, which usually make me sleepy, will be given only once a week in Speech 103.   A   U

b. I have heard nothing but lectures in Math 160, Biology 150, Economics 100, and wonder how I'll remember everything.   A   U

c. My roommate has already noticed most of my notebooks are full and the batteries in my recorder are weak.   A   U

51. a. Those two guards were quick and our quarterback slow.   A   U

b. Our quarterback never has and never will make up his mind in time.   A   U

c. He just keeps backing up with his arm poised, and players catching him behind the line of scrimmage.   A   U

52. a. A considerable amount of money was earned last semester by Jill and Mary.   A   U

b. Typing and filing were done by them in the English Department office.   A   U

c. Their resident hall counselor told them about these jobs.   A   U

53. a. There are several men in halls on our campus who could be strong contestants in the Ugliest Man contest.   A   U

b. One resident in our hall definitely looks like winner.   A   U

c. There is a belief held by most students that some   A   U

comic relief is needed in the middle of a semester.

54. a. Some professors scold a student for calling them at home, even when the student's classes conflict with the professor's office hours, according to my friends.   A   U

b. Berating a student who calls as a last resort about something important is poor behavior for a teacher, it seems to me.   A   U

c. Although some professors rebuke students for such calls, most are too considerate to treat students this way.   A   U

55. a. In the accident Becky broke her hip, her wrist, and her watch.   A   U

b. The mechanic said that her car needed a new front bumper, a new radiator, and a new motor.   A   U

c. While recuperating, Becky acquired six new boyfriends, a new watch, and a little insight.   A   U

56. a. From his tiny perch by the window, my aging canary, Chirpie, watched me passively, his eyes twinkling occasionally in the faltering rays of a gorgeous sunset.   A   U

b. Beneath that little pile of noble plumage, bronzed by the light, beat a heart which still filled my dreary life with joy and love.   A   U

c. With a little shiver, diminutive Chirpie stiffened and then fell on his side, lost forever to me but wrapped in clouds of eternal light.   A   U

57. a. I envy people who write excellent themes, but I am beginning to realize that good writers work hard.   A   U

b. A theme that looks as slick as a whistle is probably written by the sweat of the brow. A U

c. It goes without saying that teachers take a dim view of any theme that I write on the spur of the moment. A U

58. a. When the professor called on me, my face fell a mile and my mind felt as empty as the Grand Canyon. A U

b. My eyes fell to the floor, but I could sense that the professor's eyes were glued on me. A U

c. I died right there; that was a moment to end all moments. A U

59. a. Mark thought that campus politics was a green pasture, but he discovered that it was really a jungle. A U

b. When he crossed the bridge from common student to campus politician, he bit off more than he could chew. A U

c. We decided to keep him in the dark as long as he was basking in a ray of sunshine. A U

60. a. Our star campus reporter said that six swimmers slipped on the side of the swimming pool. A U

b. His clever story about this sport was the funniest I've seen of any sort. A U

c. His accurate account of this accident deserves some acclaim or accolade. A U

61. a. The nature of the last scene in this stage representation of a drama is such as to warrant its being performed under other conditions. A U

b. I suggest that we change the lighting to darker tones of red and also play somber background music to accen-

tuate Macbeth's despair and melancholy.

c. Unfortunately, it will be less difficult to emit the sound symbols to describe the changes we must make than it will be to perform the physical motions necessary to accomplish the tasks so described. A U

62. a. Secretaries and other women were always surprised to discover that the dean's receptionist was a tall, handsome man. A U

b. Caught between office cuties who thought he was a hunk and visitors who looked amazed to see him behind a typewriter, Tom began feeling frustrated. A U

c. Tom had simply answered an advertisement for a student assistant who could type forty words a minute and schedule appointments. A U

63. a. Irregardless of the consequences, some students try and party alot every weekend. A U

b. It's a fact that too much partying has its price. A · U

c. A hour or two of studying between parties will lead to disaster for most students. A U

64. a. A winning football season shouldn't effect my grades, but it always does. A U

b. Just when I am already to study, my mind becomes occupied with tailgate parties and victory celebrations. A U

c. A winning season raises my moral, but it lowers my grades. A U

65. a. By changing the topic of conversation to my missing A U

watch, I didn't mean to infer that one of my friends was a thief.

b. No less than twelve people were in my room that night.   A   U

c. To accuse anyone unless I could cite conclusive evidence would be against my principles.   A   U

66. a. Some college students have the delusion that soon after graduation they will be successful and wealthy.   A   U

b. These credulous students apparently believe that a college degree guarantees success.   A   U

c. They are very anxious to be instant leaders of business and industry.   A   U

Answers to this test can be found on Page 511.

Wordiness and Repetition:
My Cousin, He Repeats Himself
Over and Over—Repeatedly

After writing your answer(s) in the right-hand column, check this column to see whether you have responded correctly. If you have made a mistake, or if you need more practice, do whatever is asked below the dotted line in each answer frame.

Answers to questions for added practice can be found at the end of each lesson.

Answers and Added Practice

1

    shorter

. . . .

About how long was the longest speech, lecture, or sermon you ever listened to?

2

    cut

. . . .

What two words should be cut from the subtitle of this lesson?

Understanding and Applying the Principles

1

Some oldtime political orators spoke for an hour, two hours, or even more. Ministers' sermons sometimes outlasted two hour-glasses.

Today's political speeches and sermons are usually _____ _____ [*shorter* or *even longer*?]

2

Today's good speakers and writers include facts and ideas that they consider important, they think of good examples, and they use all the words needed to express themselves clearly. But they also try to be concise. The last part of *concise* comes from a Latin word meaning "to cut."

Concise speakers and writers _____ [Do what?] unnecessary words and pointless repetition of information and opinion.

3

   **My mother she thinks that the Republicans
   will win.**

A. Which two words refer to the same person? _____
   _____

B. The unnecessary word in the example is _____ .

3

    A. *mother, she*
    B. *she*

. . . .

My mother she is a "double subject." Other examples: *my father he, that old car it, our friends they.*

    Write another example, then cross out the unneeded word.

4

In my report I reported on a topic related to the topic of the report that Archer made.

    A. What two words are repeated awkwardly in that sentence? _____ , _____
    B. Rewrite the sentence in eight words, starting with *I reported.* Use *topic* only once, and *report* not at all. _____

_____

4

    A. *report, topic*
    B. I reported on a topic similar to Archer's.

. . . .

Sometimes we recall the times when we had such good times together.

Rewrite, using the word or syllable *times* only once.

5

This is an apple that is too green.

    A. Is it really necessary to tell most people that "This is an apple"? _____
    B. Rewrite, starting with *This apple.* Eliminate three-eighths of the words in the original sentence. _____

_____

5

    A. No
    B. This apple is too green.

. . . .

    A. **We were driving in a driving rain.**

The second *driving* may be changed to _____ .

    B. **The last part of the show is less interesting than the first part of the show.**

Four words that may be cut out are

_____ .

6

His success in the speaking line seemed to indicate the desirability of his planning to enroll in a college of some kind somewhere in order to develop further the kind of talent that seemed to be his strongest asset.

    A. Do you believe that the thirty-nine words of the example can be reduced to about fifteen? _____
    B. Try to reduce them without losing their meaning. _____

_____

_____

_____

6

A. (Any answer is acceptable, especially if it is *Yes.*)

B. **Model Answer**

His success in speaking indicated that he should enroll in college as a speech major.

. . . .

Some of my problems in writing are due to the fact that my vocabulary of words is small.

Rewrite in about twelve words.

7

Meanings, as well as words, should not be repeated unnecessarily.

The street was slick and slippery.

A. In that sentence, what two words mean about the same thing? _____ , _____

B. Rewrite the sentence, eliminating one-third of the words. _____

7

A. *slick, slippery*

B. The street was slick (*or* slippery).

. . . .

This little pamphlet is one that I found listed in a list of books and pamphlets in a bibliography.

Rewrite in seven words.

8

In Frames 8–10, reduce each sentence by the number of words shown in brackets.

A. Please repeat that again. [1] _____

B. The tracks of the bear had been covered by new snow that had fallen recently. [4 or 6] _____

_____

_____

8

    A. Please repeat that.

    B. The tracks of the bear (*or* The bear's tracks) had been covered by new snow.

....

A topic sentence of a paragraph is a summary of the paragraph all summed up in a single sentence.

Rewrite in about six words.

9

    A. Cadiz has a population of two thousand people [1 or 3]

_____

    B. Redwood trees may live to be the age of three thousand years old. [6] _____

_____

9

    A. Cadiz has a population of two thousand (*or* has two thousand people).

    B. Redwood trees may live three thousand years.

....

In the present time of today, now and then an occasional glimmer of hope for the future in years to come glimmers into our consciousness.

Rewrite in about thirteen words, starting with *Today*.

10

    A. Finally, the detective she had all the necessary information that she needed. [3 or 4] _____

_____

_____

    B. The cause of the accident was due to the fact that it had been raining, and as a result the pavement was wet from the water on it. [23] [Hint: Start your five-word sentence with *Wet.*] _____

_____

10

   A. Finally, the detective had all the necessary information (*or* all the information she needed).

   B. Wet pavement caused the accident.

· ·

My experiments in the pitching line sometimes caused me to be in possession of a sore pitching arm.

Rewrite in about nine words.

11

   A. Compose a wordy sentence in which you use the word *college* three times. _____
_____
_____
_____

   B. Rewrite your sentence in fewer words. Do not change the meaning, but use *college* only once. _____
_____
_____
_____

11

Model Answer

   A. As a college student, I find that college lives up to many of my expectations of college.

   B. As a student I find that college lives up to many of my expectations.

· ·

Write a wordy sentence in which you use *class* three times. Then write an improved version.

12

   A. Compose a wordy sentence in which you use *cause* or *caused, due to the fact that, today,* and *this modern world.*
_____
_____
_____

   B. Rewrite your sentence. Do not change the meaning, but reduce the repetition and wordiness as much as possible.
_____
_____
_____

12

Model Answers

    A. In this modern world of to-day, the cause of many of our troubles is due to the fact that most people are too selfish.

    B. Today, many of our troubles are caused by selfishness.

13

Finish honestly: One thing I hope to remember from this lesson is that . . .

(In this frame, any answer that you consider honest and accurate is acceptable.)

Lesson 48: Answers to Questions for Added Practice

1. (Personal estimate) **2.** *He, Repeatedly* (and perhaps *Over and Over*) **3.** MODEL: Jack's horse it (Cross out *it.*) **4.** MODEL: Occasionally we recall the times when we had such fun together. **5.** A. *pouring* (or *heavy*, etc.) B. *part of the show* **6.** MODEL: My limited vocabulary causes some of my problems in writing. **7.** This pamphlet was listed in a bibliography. **8.** A topic sentence summarizes a paragraph. (*Or* A topic sentence is a paragraph summary.) **9.** MODEL: Today a glimmer of hope for the future occasionally shines into our consciousness. (*Or, perhaps better:* Today we are sometimes aware of a glimmer of hope for the future.) **10.** MODEL: My experiments in pitching sometimes made my arm sore. **11.** MODEL: This class is a better class than any other class I have ever been in. This class is the best I have ever been in.

══49══

Comparisons: Where Is Phoenix?

After writing your answer(s) in the right-hand column, check this column to see whether you have responded correctly. If you have made a mistake, or if you need more practice, do whatever is asked below the dotted line in each answer frame.

Answers to questions for added practice can be found at the end of each lesson.

Understanding and Applying the Principles

1

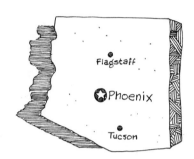

Phoenix is larger than any city in Arizona.

If Phoenix is larger than any city that is in Arizona, then it must not be in Arizona. In what state do you believe Phoenix to be?

_____

Answers and Added Practice

1

(The best bet is Arizona, although smaller Phoenixes are in Maryland, New York, and Oregon.)

. . . .

Do you believe that Rhode Island is smaller than any state? _____ Why or why not?

2

Because Phoenix really *is* a city in Arizona, we may say that it is larger than any *other* city in that state. So we should alter the sentence in Frame 1 to read:

Phoenix is larger than _____

_____ . [Finish]

2

any other city in Arizona

. . . .

Rhode Island is smaller than _____
_____ [*any* or *any other*?] state.

3

San Diego is larger than any city in Arizona.

A. In what state is San Diego? _____
B. Is the example correct without *other*? _____
C. Is it correct to say that Phoenix is larger than any city in New Mexico? _____

3

    A. (California has a large San Diego, Texas a small one.)

    B. Yes C. Yes

. . . .

Finish logically:

    A. I like *Huckleberry Finn* more than _____ _____ book by Mark Twain.

    B. I like *Hamlet* better than _____ plays by Shakespeare.

4

Like *other*, *else* is sometimes needed to complete a comparison logically.

    A. Mathematics is harder for me than any _____ subject.

    B. Mathematics is harder for me than anything _____ .

    C. Mathematics is harder for me than for anyone _____ _____ in my class.

4

    A. other B. else C. else

. . . .

Complete:

    A. Eileen got to this class before anyone _____ now in the room.

    B. Tomatoes are better than anything _____ that grows in the garden.

5

Linda likes hamburgers more than her brother.

    A. Is the meaning of that sentence completely clear? _____

    B. The probable meaning is that Linda likes hamburgers more than her brother _____ .

    C. An unlikely but possible meaning: Linda likes hamburgers more than she _____ her brother.

5

    A. No B. does C. likes (*or* does)

. . . .

Clarify:

Rawk Moz ate more than his little sister.

6

Speak Toothpaste gets teeth whiter.

The sentence above is similar to many other sentences used in advertising. What makes it meaningless? _____

6

Model Answer

Whiter that what—snow or coal? The statement provides no basis for comparing.

. . . .

The Ford Motor Company once used the slogan "Ford Trucks Last Longer." Try to think of other advertising that uses unfinished comparisons.

7

Plant life in the West differs from that in the East.

Explain in your own words why the sentence above would not be logical if *that in* were omitted.

7

Model Answer

It is not possible to compare plant life with the East.

. . . .

Finish properly:

Today the cost of a good new dress is greater than _____

_____

_____

_____ .

8

All our examples in this lesson have shown that we should not omit needed words in a comparison. Among words often unwisely omitted are modifiers like *other* and *else*, verbs like *do* or *does*, pronouns like *that* or *those*, and words needed to finish a

_____ in a sentence like

Speak Toothpaste gets teeth whiter.

8

comparison

. . . .

Add the missing word(s).

A. I envy Marge more than _____ _____ Flavia.

B. I envy Marge more than Joan _____ _____ .

9

In Frames 9–11, supply the word or words needed to complete each comparison logically.

A. I like Fido better than my mother _____ .

B. Orville's hair is longer than _____ _____ the other man.

C. I prefer *Macbeth* to any _____ Shakespearean play.

9

A. does B. that of C. other

. . . .

Add the missing words:

A. Improbable: Clarence likes hamsters more than _____ _____ his mother.

B. Probable: Clarence likes hamsters more than his mother _____ .

10

A. Our left tackle is shorter than anyone _____ on our team.

B. Our left tackle is shorter than any _____ player on our team.

C. The shoes of our backs are different from _____ _____ our linemen.

10

A. else   B. other   C. those of

....

Add the missing words:

A. The cost of some radios is greater than _____ _____ some television sets.

B. Save more at our store ____ _____ _____ _____ .

11

A. Pacer Pens last longer _____ .

B. I enjoy ice cream more than anything _____ .

C. The working hours in the factory were longer than _____ ____ most other places.

11

A. than ever (*or* than most others, etc.)

B. else   C. those in

....

Add the missing words:

A. A pipe organ is larger than any _____ musical instrument.

B. The American president has greater responsibilities than anyone _____ in the United States.

12

Write a sentence in which you compare how well you and Clancy like butter pecan ice cream. Start with *I like butter pecan ice cream better than* . . .

12

Model Answer

I like butter pecan ice cream better than Clancy does.

....

Write a sentence in which you compare how intensely you and a friend dislike something.

13

Compare Professor Waxly with other of your professors in some respect, such as sense of humor.

13

Model Answer

Professor Waxly's sense of humor is more obvious than that of my other professors.

. . . .

Try to think of a possibly honest way to finish this advertising slogan for a motor oil:

Tuffoil is tougher _____

_____

_____ .

14

Finish honestly: One thing I hope to remember from this lesson is that . . .

(In this frame, any answer that you consider honest and accurate is acceptable.)

Lesson 49: Answers to Questions for Added Practice

1. No. MODEL: It is smaller than any *other* state, but it cannot be smaller than itself. **2.** any other **3.** A. any other B. other **4.** A. else B. else **5.** Rawk Moz ate more than his little sister did. **6.** EXAMPLE: Stores' advertising which assures us that we can "Save more during our giant clearance sale." **7.** MODEL: Today the cost of a good new dress is greater than the cost of two dresses a few years ago. **8.** A. I do B. does **9.** A. he does (*or* he likes) B. does **10.** that of (*or* the cost of) B. MODEL: than you can anywhere else in the city **11.** A. other B. else **12.** MODEL: I dislike loud music much more intensely than Beverly does. **13.** MODEL: than any ordinary motor oil

═50═

Faulty Omission: Add a Word, Help a Reader

After writing your answer(s) in the right-hand column, check this column to see whether you have responded correctly. If you have made a mistake, or if you need more practice, do whatever is asked below the dotted line in each answer frame.

Answers to questions for added practice can be found at the end of each lesson.

Understanding and Applying the Principles

1

> **We had forgotten Mother, who usually came home at five, had told us not to expect her before six.**

A. No doubt you misread the sentence above, at least for a moment. At first glance, it seems that we had forgotten

_____ .

B. A once-popular song was called "What a Difference a Day Makes!" Sometimes in a sentence, "What a difference a word makes!" The sentence at the top can be made clear immediately by adding the word _____ before *Mother*.

Answers and Added Practice

1

    A. Mother   B. *that*

. . . .

The defense attorney repeated the testimony of the plaintiff was false.

To make the sentence immediately clear, the word _____ should be added after _____

_____ .

2

Obviously, we should not toss in *that*'s or other words unless they are needed.

> **Mother said (that) she had told us twice.**

Is that sentence completely clear without *that*? _____

2

    Yes

. . . .

Mother said (that) the delay was unavoidable.

Is *that* needed? _____

3

> **Summers Pat likes to bicycle across the countryside.**

What word before *Summers* would make that sentence slightly easier for a reader to understand at once? _____

3

In (or *During*)

. . . .

I need to earn money summer vacations.

The word _____ should be added before _____

_____ .

4

Leah was fond and affectionate toward her brother.

A. Is one fond *toward* someone? _____
B. One is fond _____ someone.
C. So it would be better to write **Leah was fond _____ and affectionate toward her** brother.
D. Leah was fond _____ her brother and affectionate _____ him. [This is smoother than C because the phrase *of her brother* is not divided.]

4

A. No B. of C. of D. of, toward

. . . .

Ben's faith and devotion to his country are unquestionable.

A. One has faith _____ one's country, not faith *to* it.
B. An improved sentence: Ben's faith _____ _____ _____ and devotion to _____ are unquestionable.

5

Working in the garden were Helga, Nyssa, Hans, and Jens was busy in the orchard.

For a moment, that sentence seems to mean that four persons were working in the garden.

A. How many were actually doing so? _____
B. Adding the word _____ before *Hans* would make the meaning immediately clear.

5

A. Three B. *and*

. . . .

I have sometimes gone swimming with Jack, Pete, Ossie, and Hank has been my swimming companion many times.

The word _____ should be added before _____ .

6

Janet is as intelligent, or even more intelligent, than her sister.

A. Is it correct to say that one person is *as intelligent than* another? _____
B. Clearly a second *as* is needed, perhaps like this: Janet is _____ intelligent _____ her sister, or even more so.

6

A. No B. as, as

. . . .

Frank is as tall, or even taller, than Glenn.

Better: Frank is _____ tall _____ Glenn, or even taller.

7

The chief purpose of writing is to convey meanings from one mind to another. A writer is responsible for expressing those meanings so clearly that they can be immediately understood.

One way to help the reader is to avoid the _____ of such little words as *that, and, in,* and *as* in places where they may help to make meaning clear. (If you need a clue, see the title of this lesson.)

7

omission

· ·

Have you sometimes had to read a sentence two or three times to understand it, even though all the words were familiar? _____

If so, how did you feel? _____

_____

8

In Frames 8–11, add the words necessary to help readers understand at once.

A. I believe the girls, who have been working in the kitchen, will bring in some refreshments. [Add _____ after _____ .]

B. Sally dreams of rubies, pearls, diamonds, and wonders whether she will ever have any. [Add _____ after _____ .]

8

A. *that, believe*

B. *and, pearls*

· ·

We brought wieners, buns, mustard, and started off to our picnic. [Add _____ after _____ .]

9

A. My father noticed one of his socks, which he had been wearing all day, was blue and the other was red. [Add _____ after _____ .]

B. April we expect to go to Albuquerque. [Add _____ before _____ .]

9

A. *that, noticed*

B. *In, April*

· ·

These trees grow both in valleys and hills. [Add _____ after _____ .]

10

A. I took the test which I was not ready. [Add _____ after _____ .]

B. What sort vegetable do you prefer? [Add _____ after _____ .]

10

A. *for, test* (or possibly *for, ready*)   B. *of, sort*

· ·

Our cabin burned down my first day in camp. [Add _____ after _____ .]

11

A. The canned food was in a box and some shelves. [Add _____ before _____ .]

B. I wonder what type people professors are. [Add _____ after _____ .]

11

A. *on, some*   B. *of, type*

· ·

I found the rabbits, which Lois had penned up, had escaped. [Add _____ after _____ .]

12

Helen is as slim, if not slimmer, than Paula.

Review Frame 6 and then rewrite the sentence above. _____

_____

_____

12

Model Answer

Helen is as slim as Paula, if not slimmer.

· ·

George is as strong, if not stronger, than Ralph.

Rewrite.

13

Write a sentence in which you use the words *interested* and *ignorant* to describe your feeling about some topic. Do not omit a necessary preposition after each of those words. _____

_____

_____

13

Model Answer

I am interested in prehistoric animals but rather ignorant about them.

· ·

To describe your reaction to some news, write a sentence containing the words *alarmed* and *afraid*.

14

After the words *I bought*, list several things that you purchased recently. Add *and sold*, and name something that you sold. Do not omit a necessary *and*. _____

_____

_____

14

Model Answer

I bought flour, sugar, and salt, and sold a case of eggs.

· ·

Write a similar sentence using *Gloria brought . . . and Virginia brought . . .*

15

Finish honestly: One thing I hope to remember from this lesson is that . . .

(In this frame, any answer that you consider honest and accurate is acceptable.)

Lesson 50: Answers to Questions for Practice

1. *that, repeated* **2.** No **3.** *in* (or *during*), *summer vacations* **4.** A. *in* B. *in his country, it* **5.** *and, Ossie* **6.** *as, as* **7.** (Personal opinion) **8.** *and, buns* **9.** *on, and* **10.** *on* (or *during*), *down* **11.** *that, found* **12.** George is as strong as Ralph, if not stronger. **13.** MODEL: I was alarmed by the dictator's action and afraid of the possible consequences. **14.** MODEL: Gloria brought meat, salad, and dessert, and Virginia brought only her knitting.

≡51≡

Faulty Omission of Verb Parts: The Cars Was Whizzing?

After writing your answer(s) in the right-hand column, check this column to see whether you have responded correctly. If you have made a mistake, or if you need more practice, do whatever is asked below the dotted line in each answer frame.

Answers to questions for added practice can be found at the end of each lesson.

Answers and Added Practice

1

    A. One   B. More than one
. . . .

Rereading the example in Frame 1, can you already see what is wrong with it? _____

Understanding and Applying the Principles

1

    A bus was grinding along the street, and cars whizzing past it.

    A. How many buses were grinding along? _____
    _____ [*One* or *More than one*?]
    B. How many cars were whizzing past it? _____
    _____ [*One* or *More than one*?]

2

In Frame 1, *A bus was grinding along the street* is all right, because only one bus was there. But the word *was* does not fit here with *whizzing,* for we would not say cars *was* whizzing past.

    A. The verb form that would fit with *cars* is _____ .
    B. Copy the whole sentence, adding the missing verb form.

2

    A. *were*

    B. A bus was grinding along the street, and cars were whizzing past it.

....

The sky was becoming darker, and a few plump raindrops plopping down.

The verb form _____ should be added after _____

_____ .

3

    Colleen never has and never will dance the polka.

That sentence seems to say **Colleen never has *dance* the polka.**

That is not a good sentence because _____

_____ .

3

Model Answer
    dance should be *danced.*

....

    Jordan never has and probably will not now vote for Armbruster.

Is that a good sentence? _____

4

Let's try to improve the example in Frame 3.

    A. Colleen never has danced and never will dance the polka. [Not very good. It sounds as though Colleen _____ .]

    B. Let's try again: Colleen never has _____ the polka and never _____ do so. [That's better, isn't it?]

4

    A. never has danced

    B. danced, will

....

Rewrite the Jordan sentence from Answer Frame 3.

5

    This clipper allows the hair be cut long, short, or medium.

Part of the infinitive *to be cut* has been left out of that sentence.

    What word should be inserted? _____

5

    to

....

    Your brakes need adjusted.

The words _____ _____ should be inserted after _____ .

6

    The prize was awarded to the painter who had and was doing the most original high-quality work.

    A. In that sentence the word _____ should be added after *had.*

    B. A smoother form of the sentence is this: The prize was awarded to the painter who had _____

_____

    and was still _____ .

6

    A. *done*

    B. done the most original high-quality work, doing so

....

I have never and do not expect to see the Taj Mahal.

Rewrite.

7

In verbs consisting of two or three words, writers sometimes carelessly omit one or more of the words.

    The point of this lesson is that no verb part should be _____ _____ if it is logically and grammatically required.

7

    omitted

....

Old-fashioned fountain pens were expensive and messy but still fondly remembered by many people.

Is the missing verb form more likely *were* or *are*? _____

8

In the following sentence the omission of verbs in two parts of the sentence is satisfactory:

    Nancy was elected president; Tom, treasurer; and Laverne, secretary.

The two words omitted after *Tom* are _____ _____ , and those omitted after *Laverne* are also _____ _____ . Repeating them would have been awkward.

8

    was elected, was elected

....

Because the two omitted words are the same as those after *Nancy,* and because the meaning is clear and repetition would be awkward, the sentence is satisfactory.

9

In Frames 9–11, add the missing verb forms.

    A. Doves were cooing and a mockingbird singing. [Add _____ after _____ .]

    B. A butterfly was posing, with its wings forming a V, on one lily, and bees standing on their heads as they sipped nectar deep inside several other lilies. [Add _____ after _____ .]

9

    A. *was, mockingbird*

    B. *were, bees*

....

The short stories are amusing and the novel suspenseful. [Add _____ after _____ .]

10

    A. A squirrel was chattering angrily in the tree, and two catbirds hopping excitedly from branch to branch. [Add _____ after _____ .]

    B. Two catbirds were hopping excitedly from branch to branch, and a squirrel chattering angrily. [Add _____ after _____ .]

10

A. *were, catbirds*
B. *was, squirrel*

. . . .

The novel is suspenseful and the short stories amusing. [Add _____ after_____ .]

11

A. A team member may leave or a new member added at any time. [Add _____ after _____ .]
B. My term paper needs retyped. [Add _____ after _____ .]

11

A. *may be, member*
B. *to be, needs*

. . . .

A prisoner may have escaped and a guard wounded during the blackout. [Add _____ _____ after _____ .]

12

An author who has or is writing a play understands the difficulties of this literary form.

Review Frames 3 and 4, and then rewrite the sentence above.

12

Model Answer

An author who has written a play or who is now writing one understands the difficulties of this literary form.

. . . .

I have always and will always fear control of the nation by a few rich people.

Rewrite.

13

While the chemistry teacher was _____ _____

and the students _____ _____ , some phosphorus in the sink caught fire.

Tell what was being done by the teacher and by the students. Do not omit any needed word.

13

Model Answer

lecturing on photosynthesis, were trying to stay awake

....

Write a sentence about something being done by some cats and something else by a dog.

14

Look back at the boldface sentence in Frame 3. Compose a similar—but correct—sentence beginning, *I never have . . .*

14

Model Answer

I never have caught a tarpon and probably never will catch one.

....

15

Finish honestly: One thing I hope to remember from this lesson is that . . .

(In this frame, any answer that you consider honest and accurate is acceptable.)

Lesson 51: Answers to Questions for Added Practice

1. (Personal opinion) **2.** *were, raindrops* **3.** No **4.** MODEL: Jordan never has voted for Armbruster and probably will not do so now. **5.** *to be, need* **6.** MODEL: I have never seen the Taj Mahal and never expect to see it (*or* do so). **7.** *are* **9.** *is, novel* **10.** *are, stories* **11.** *may have been, guard* **12.** MODEL: I have always feared control of the nation by a few rich people and will always do so (*or* harbor that fear, etc.). **13.** MODEL: Several cats were yowling, and a dog was barking in protest.

52

Unnecessary Passive Voice: Is It Better to Do or to Be Done Unto?

After writing your answer(s) in the right-hand column, check this column to see whether you have responded correctly. If you have made a mistake, or if you need more practice, do whatever is asked below the dotted line in each answer frame.

Answers to questions for added practice can be found at the end of each lesson.

Answers and Added Practice

1

No

. . . .

According to the example in Frame 1, who moved from farm to farm? _____

_____

Who did the harvesting? _____

_____

2

Model Answer
Threshing crews moved from farm to farm, harvesting the wheat.

. . . .

Which has fewer words, (A), the example in Frame 1, or (B) your rewritten sentence? _____

Understanding and Applying the Principles

1

Wheat was harvested by threshing crews as farm after farm was moved to by them.

The sentence above is not grammatically wrong, but it is weak and unemphatic. It uses the *passive voice*. That is, the subject does not act but is acted upon.

Did the wheat and the farms do anything? _____

2

Rewrite the example in Frame 1, starting it with *Threshing crews moved.*

3

Your revised sentence is in the *active voice*. That is, you told what the subject did. Ordinarily the active voice is shorter, stronger, and more emphatic than the passive. The active voice straightforwardly tells who did what.

The passive voice, in contrast, tells what was _____ by _____ .

3

done, whom (*or* somebody)

....

Prayers for good weather are said by them.

Rewrite, starting with *They pray.*

4

Sometimes, it is true, we need the passive voice. For instance, if a murder has been committed and the murderer is unknown, we cannot say who performed the act. Instead we generally say something like this:

A. A murder has been _____ . (*Or*)

B. A body has been _____ . (*Or*)

C. The battered body of James Carson, 41, was _____ by searchers Tuesday night beside Solemn Creek.

4

A. committed   B. found (*or* discovered, etc.)   C. found (*or a similar word*)

....

A. **President Garfield was assassinated.**

B. **Charles Guiteau assassinated President Garfield.**

Here the sentence with the passive voice, _____ [A or B?], is more likely because the president is more important than the assassin.

5

A. I must call my brother at once.

B. My brother must be called by me at once.

Which is more emphatic, A or B? _____

5

A

....

A. **A good time was had by all at the party.**

B. **Everybody enjoyed the party.**

Which is more emphatic? _____

6

A. The song that was sung by Rosemary was applauded by all her friends.

B. All Rosemary's friends applauded her song.

Which is more emphatic, A or B? _____

6

B

....

A. **You should return the books within two weeks.**

B. **The books should be returned by you within two weeks.**

Which is more emphatic? _____

7

A. In the first six frames, we have seen that the _____ voice is ordinarily more emphatic than the _____ voice.

B. However, the _____ voice is necessary or at least preferable when the person or thing performing the action is unknown or relatively unimportant.

7

    A. active, passive

    B. passive

....

The Pulitzer Prizes are awarded in honor of Joseph Pulitzer, a famous journalist.

Explain why the passive voice is satisfactory in that sentence.

8

In Frames 8–9, decide which is the better sentence of the two.

    A. Monte passed me the ball, but the speedy right end from Corvallis tackled me immediately.

    B. The ball was passed by Monte to me, but I was tackled immediately by the speedy right end from Corvallis.

    ——

8

    A

....

    A. **I wrote the first draft of the paragraph.**

    B. **The first draft of the paragraph was written by me.**

Which version is better? _____

9

    A. Kathryn made the pie filling, but Myra baked the pie.

    B. The pie filling was made by Kathryn, but the pie itself was baked by Myra.

    ——

9

    A

....

    A. **The rifle was aimed carefully and the trigger was squeezed.**

    B. **Bart aimed the rifle carefully and squeezed the trigger.**

Which version is better? _____

10

Write a short sentence starting with *John* and telling about his mowing the lawn. Tell whether you used the active or the passive voice.

10

Model Answer

    John mowed the lawn. [Active]

....

Follow the instructions in Frame 10, but write about Jack and a sandwich.

11

Rewrite the sentence you wrote for Frame 10, but use the other voice. Tell which sentence seems stronger.

11

Model Answer

    The lawn was mowed by John.
(The sentence with active voice
is stronger.)

· ·

Change your sentence in Answer
Frame 10 to the other voice. Tell
which is stronger.

12

Assume that you are writing a sentence about tsetse flies, which
carry a protozoan that causes sleeping sickness. Decide
whether, in light of the fact that you are concentrating on tsetse
flies, the sentence is most likely to start with *Tsetse flies, A protozoan,* or *Sleeping sickness.* Write the sentence.

12

Model Answer

    Tsetse flies carry a protozoan
that causes sleeping sickness.

13

Finish honestly: One thing I hope to remember from this lesson
is that . . .

(In this frame, any answer that you consider honest and accurate is acceptable.)

Lesson 52: Answers to Questions for Added Practice

1. Threshing crews, Threshing crews **2.** B **3.** They pray for good weather. **4.** A **5.** B **6.** A **7.** MODEL:
Joseph Pulitzer did not perform any action. **8.** A **9.** B **10.** MODEL: Jack ate a Reuben sandwich. (Active)
11. MODEL: A Reuben sandwich was eaten by Jack. (Passive. The sentence with active voice is stronger.)

53

The There Is *Sentence: Often a Weakling*

After writing your answer(s) in the right-hand column, check this column to see whether you have responded correctly. If you have made a mistake, or if you need more practice, do whatever is asked below the dotted line in each answer frame.

Answers to questions for added practice can be found at the end of each lesson.

Understanding and Applying the Principles

1

> **There were a number of convincing arguments presented by the district attorney.**

The sentence above is not grammatically wrong. It is not a bad sentence, but it is weaker than it needs to be. One reason for the weakness is the way it starts.

> When you read *There were*, have you any idea of what the sentence will be about? _____

Answers and Added Practice

1

No

. . . .

Good writers often have remarked that every sentence and every paragraph should be especially strong at the beginning and at the end.

2

A sentence that starts with *there were* (or *there is, there was, there may be, there might have been,* and so forth) is often weak because the opening is only an empty filler, signifying nothing. A sentence usually should start with something important to the meaning.

> In the example in Frame 1, two parts are especially important. One is the convincing arguments. The other is the reference to the _____ _____.

2

district attorney

. . . .

Note that the "empty" *there* we are discussing is different from *there* meaning "in that place," as in *There he stands.*

3

Either of two revisions will get rid of the *there were* opening in the example and replace it with an important part:

A. Many convincing _____ were presented by the district attorney.

B. The _____ _____ presented many convincing arguments.

3

    A. arguments
    B. district attorney

....

**There are two scissortails
near that tree.**

In this sentence the two most important words are probably _____
_____ and
_____.

4

Of the two strengthened sentences in Frame 3, the first is less
strong than the second because it uses the passive voice, in
which something is done to the subject. (See Lesson 52.)
    Copy the stronger of the two sentences.

4

    The district attorney presented
many convincing arguments.

....

A good way to revise the sentence
in Answer Frame 3 is this:

    Two _____
    _____
    _____.

5

    **There are numerous small lakes and several
small mountains that England's Lake Poets
described in their verses.**

Shorten and improve that sentence by rewriting. Start with
England's.

5

England's Lake Poets described
in their verses numerous small
lakes and several small mountains.

....

**There are also a number of
mockingbirds nearby.**

By starting that sentence with *Several,* we can save _____
[How many?] words.

6

Summary: Although sentences starting with *There is* and similar
expressions are sometimes needed, we should usually start our
sentences with something _____ [*more* or *less*?] important.

6

more

....

There were many fascinating birds we saw near Lake Texoma.

Rewrite, starting with *We*.

7

There are a number of students who have trouble with chemistry.

Rewrite that sentence, starting with *Many* and using only six words instead of the eleven in the original.

7

Many students have trouble with chemistry.

....

Rewrite again the sentence in Answer Frame 6. Start with *Near* and omit *There were*.

8

There is a belief held by some people that the rotary engine can reduce air pollution.

Rewrite that sentence, starting with *Some* and using only eleven words instead of the sixteen in the original.

8

Some people believe that the rotary engine can reduce air pollution.

....

How many words did you save in your rewritten versions in answer Frames 6 and 7? _____ _____

9

Compose a sentence about a store in your community. Start with *There is*.

9

Model Answer

    There is a store on K Street that sells only batteries.

. . . .

Compose a sentence about two museums. Start with *There are*.

10

Now rewrite your sentence in Frame 9, eliminating *There is*. How many words do you save?

10

Model Answer

    A store on K Street sells only batteries.
    Three

. . . .

Rewrite your sentence from Answer Frame 9, eliminating *There are*.

11

Compose a sentence about swans. Start with *There were*. Then rewrite your sentence, eliminating *There were*.

11

Model Answer

    There were four swans cruising majestically on the pond.
    Four swans were cruising majestically on the pond.

12

Finish honestly: One thing I hope to remember from this lesson is that . . .

(In this frame, any answer that you consider honest and accurate is acceptable.)

Lesson 53: Answers to Questions for Added Practice

3. scissortails, tree **4.** Two scissortails are near that tree. **5.** Three **6.** We saw many fascinating birds near Lake Texoma. **7.** Near Lake Texoma we saw many fascinating birds. **8.** Two in each **9.** MODEL: There are two museums in particular that you must see in London. **10.** MODEL: You must see two museums in particular in London.

≡54≡

Weak Sentence Endings: Fading into Nothingness

After writing your answer(s) in the right-hand column, check this column to see whether you have responded correctly. If you have made a mistake, or if you need more practice, do whatever is asked below the dotted line in each answer frame.

Answers to questions for added practice can be found at the end of each lesson.

Answers and Added Practice

1

strong
....

The end of a joke is sometimes called the "punch line." Why is that appropriate?

Understanding and Applying the Principles

1

> **A question in an examination was "How may a person get good posture?"**
>
> **One small farm boy wrote, "Keep the cows off, and give the grass a chance."**

Many people have said that a joke should end with a bang. That means that the end should be ＿＿＿＿＿. [*weak* or *strong*?]

2

> **Once a small farm boy didn't know the difference between *posture* and *pasture*, and he wrote that you should keep the cows off it if you want good posture, but of course he was thinking about pasture.**

That version of the joke is not very effective for two reasons: The beginning gives away and spoils the punch line, and the ending is ＿＿＿＿＿. [*weak* or *strong*?]

2

weak

....

Strong finishes are desirable not only in jokes, but also in _____. [Name one other thing.]

3

A sentence, like a joke, should have a strong ending.

The Senate should act at once, it seems to me.

The ending of that sentence is _____. [*weak* or *strong*?]

3

weak

....

A loud voice and much shouting often indicate insecurity, on the other hand.

That sentence ends _____. [*strongly* or *weakly*?]

4

When we end a sentence with a wishy-washy expression such as *it seems to me* or *perhaps* or *on the other hand*, we should think first about whether we really need it. Sometimes it can be cut out without doing any harm. If we do need it, we can usually bury it somewhere inside the sentence.

The example in Frame 3 could be written:

The Senate, _____ _____ _____ _____, should act at once.

4

it seems to me

....

Rewrite the sentence in Answer Frame 3, moving the last four words to the interior of the sentence.

5

The later paintings of Degas greatly influenced Gauguin and Picasso, it is believed.

A. Unless we can indicate who "believed," the last three words of that sentence _____ [*are* or *are no*?] stronger than *perhaps* would be.

B. The three words add _____ [*a fair amount* or *almost nothing*?] to the meaning of the sentence.

C. They probably should be _____. [*kept* or *deleted*?]

D. If they are not deleted, they should be placed after _____ _____. [What word?]

5

A. are no   B. almost nothing
C. deleted D. *Degas*

....

His paintings of dancers may be the ones for which Degas is best remembered, in all probability.

Are the last three words needed?

_____

6

I looked at my father's workbench, which I hoped to find a hammer on.

Once most textbooks said that it is wrong to have a preposition (a word that functions like *on, to, from,* or *between*) at the end of a sentence. Today most of them say that a preposition at the end is not wrong but that it often weakens a sentence. A preposition should appear at the end only if no other location is suitable.

One way to strengthen the example is to put the word *on* before _____. [Which word?]

6

which

....

His paintings of dancers were what Degas earned most of his fame from.

Rewrite, using the phrase *the ones from which*.

7

Another way to strengthen the example in Frame 6 is to omit *which* and *on* and place *where* after the word _____.

7

workbench

....

Once more rewrite the sentence from Answer Frame 6. This time start with *Degas earned*.

8

In summary, good writers usually avoid _____ [What kind of?] sentence endings.

8

weak *(or a synonym)*

....

A. **she thoroughly enjoyed the play**

B. **although she was sleepy at the beginning**

If we combine these clauses, _____ [A or B?] should come first.

9

The president may speak on television about the bill, perhaps.

The word *perhaps* is not needed because in that sentence the word _____ carries a similar meaning.

9

may

....

It is possible that the whole postal system will undergo revolutionary change, it is felt.

The last three words should be _____ _____. [*kept* or *deleted?*]

10

Perhaps the president will speak publicly in support of the bill, or he may simply try to exert pressure on Congress, on the other hand.

What words in that sentence are not needed? _____

_____

10

on the other hand

. . . .

I doubt that electronic mail will ever replace paper and ink, but maybe I'm wrong, of course, but that's what I think.

A good writer would delete _____ _____[How many?] words.

11

The president's speech brought a flood of supportive letters, although it was not one of his best.

Tell what might be done to that sentence without deleting any words.

11

Model Answer
The *although*-clause might be placed after *speech*.

. . . .

This levee will withstand the highest and fiercest flood-waters, according to experts.

Perhaps that sentence is not bad. However, *according to experts* could easily be placed after _____ [What word?]

12

Meridian Park is an ideal place to bring toddlers to.

The preposition at the end of that sentence is _____ _____. [*necessary* or *unnecessary*?]

12

unnecessary

. . . .

A. **Where is he at?**
B. **Where did he go to?**
C. **Where did he come from?**

In ____ and ____, the preposition at the end is unnecessary.

13

The police barricaded all roads which the suspects might leave town by.

The preposition at the end of that sentence should be placed before _____.

13

which

. . . .

If you say "Where is he at?" and "Where did he go to?" repeat aloud, a dozen times or more, "Where is he?" "Where did he go?"

14

A. Write a sentence giving an opinion concerning a recent event on your campus. End it with *it seems to me*.

B. Decide whether you really need *it seems to me*. If it is true that other persons could strongly support a different opinion, keep *it seems to me* but move it from the end.

14

Model Answers

A. The firing of Coach Clayton is indefensible, it seems to me.

B. The firing of Coach Clayton, it seems to me, is indefensible.

15

Finish honestly: One thing I hope to remember from this lesson is that . . .

(In this frame, any answer that you consider honest and accurate is acceptable.)

Lesson 54: Answers to Questions for Added Practice

1. MODEL: The ending hits hard, like a sudden punch. **2.** races (*or* novels *or* most contests, etc.) **3.** weakly **4.** A loud voice and much shouting, on the other hand, often indicate insecurity. **5.** No **6.** His paintings of dancers were the ones from which Degas earned most of his fame. **7.** Degas earned most of his fame from his paintings of dancers. **8.** B **9.** deleted **10.** eleven **11.** *levee* **12.** A, B. (In C, "From where did he come?" is possible, but today seems awkward and unnatural.) **13.** (No written answer)

≡55≡

Climax in a Series: Build Up, Not Down

After writing your answer(s) in the right-hand column, check this column to see whether you have responded correctly. If you have made a mistake, or if you need more practice, do whatever is asked below the dotted line in each answer frame.

Answers to questions for added practice can be found at the end of each lesson.

Understanding and Applying the Principles

1

When the house caught fire, Mrs. Vandergould managed to save her jewelry, her paintings, and her canned food.

Why do you feel a letdown when you reach the end of that sentence?

_____

_____

Answers and Added Practice

1

Model Answer

The canned food is probably less valuable than the jewelry and the paintings.

....

She bought a new dress, a new coat, and some thread.

Another letdown feeling? _____

2

A. The example in Frame 1 contains a series naming three items: _____ , _____ , and _____ .

B. The subtitle of this lesson suggests that in a series it is usually desirable to build up to the most important item. Jewelry and paintings are likely to be _____ [*more or less*?] important to Mrs. Vandergould than canned food is.

2

A. jewelry, paintings, canned food

B. more

....

In the example in Answer Frame 1, which of the items in the series may deserve no mention at all? _____

_____

3

A. Assuming that Mrs. V's canned food is not very special, it _____ [*may* or *should not*?] be omitted entirely.

B. If her jewelry is rather ordinary but her paintings include one Old Master and a Picasso, the _____ should be the item named last in the series.

3

A. may   B. paintings

....

In the woods Susan was afraid of three things:

wolves

mosquitoes

bears

Which item should probably *not* be placed in the climactic position? ___

_____

4

The principle we have been establishing is that when two or more items are named one after another, as in a series, the _____ [*most* or *least?*] important should usually be placed last, as a climax.

4

most

....

In Answer Frame 3, assume that local mosquitoes have been found to carry a deadly disease. Which item is now likely to belong in the climactic position? _____

5

In New York the Jackson family saw the United Nations in action, saw and heard *Rigoletto* at the Metropolitan Opera, and bought a present for little Tommy.

Explain in your own words why the items in the series, as named above, are probably not placed in the best order.

5

Model Answer

Buying the present is probably less important than visiting the United Nations or going to the Metropolitan Opera.

....

Professor X is writing a reference to help you get a job. Would you prefer that he mention as a climax in his summary

(A) that you are moderately attractive,

(B) that you are completely reliable, or

(C) that you are reasonably studious? _____

6

Assume that the Jacksons are devoted to opera. If you are Mrs. Jackson, writing to a friend about the trip to New York, which item in the series are you likely to name as a climax? _____

_____

6

the Metropolitan Opera

....

At a county fair you spent most of your time watching auto races. You also rode on a Loop-the-Loop and ate hot dogs and cotton candy. Write a sentence about your day, building to a climax.

7

Now make a different assumption. The present for "little Tommy" is a very expensive Porsche. Does the series order as printed in Frame 5 now appear good or poor? _____

Obviously, the circumstances must be considered in deciding what is most important.

7

Good

....

Assume that for some reason the cotton candy was the highlight of your trip to the fair. Rewrite the sentence you wrote in Answer Frame 7.

8

I lost my chewing gum, my candy, and my poise.

The sentence above (unless it is intended to be funny) is poor for a reason other than importance or climax or emphasis. Gum and candy are actual, concrete things: one can see and touch them. Poise is abstract: it cannot be seen and touched.

The example illustrates the fact that items in a series or other list normally should be in the same general category. For instance, it should not consist of a mixture of c_____ and a _____ things.

8

concrete, abstract

....

At camp the boy found helpful counselors, adventurous friends, and a pet squirrel.

Which item does not belong in that series? _____

9

Write a sentence in which you name three things that you like about your college. Put last the one that is most important to you.

9

Model Answer

In my school I like the athletic program, the teachers, and especially my housemates.

. . . .

Write a sentence concerning three things you like or dislike about a sport. Put at the end the item you think most important.

10

Write a sentence in which you tell of three things that you hope to gain from being in college. Put last the one that is most important to you.

10

Model Answer

From college I hope to gain new friendships, help toward my future career, and knowledge in many fields in which I am ignorant.

. . . .

Write a sentence characterizing in a series someone you know or have read about. Put at the end the item you consider most important.

11

Finish honestly: One thing I hope to remember from this lesson is that . . .

(In this frame, any answer that you consider honest and accurate is acceptable.)

Lesson 55: Answers to Questions for Added Practice

1. Yes **2.** Thread **3.** Mosquitoes **4.** Mosquitoes **5.** B **6.** MODEL: At the county fair I enjoyed eating hot dogs and cotton candy, the Loop-the-Loop made my heart beat fast, but the auto races gave me the most thrills. **7.** MODEL: At the county fair I was interested in the auto races, was excited by the Loop-the-Loop, but was especially delighted by some unusually delectable cotton candy. **8.** Squirrel **9.** In soccer I like the speed, the sudden turns in the action, and particularly the often superb defensive plays. **10.** MODEL: George Washington was a fairly competent general, a good leader of men, and a better-than-average president.

56

Flowery Writing: Some Flowers Are Weeds

After writing your answer(s) in the right-hand column, check this column to see whether you have responded correctly. If you have made a mistake, or if you need more practice, do whatever is asked below the dotted line in each answer frame.

Answers to questions for added practice can be found at the end of each lesson.

Answers and Added Practice

1

No (If you answered *Yes*, you need this lesson very much.)

....

Tall trees tower high above a serene little cabin, embowered in a lush valley, with peaceful ripplets laving its feet.

Flowery writing is often excessively sweet—like saccharine. Is the sentence above too sweet? _____

2

Exaggerated

....

A. Does the example in Answer Frame 1 tell us what variety of trees? _____

B. Does it identify the valley? _____

C. Does it tell us what body of water has ripplets? _____

D. Have you ever seen a cabin getting its feet laved? _____

Understanding and Applying the Principles

1

    My grandmother is a lovely little old lady with flowing white locks, exquisite eyes of purest aquamarine, and a darling, darting smile that twinkles on and off like a flashing neon sign.

Do you like the description above? _____

2

Writing like that in Frame 1 is often called "flowery" writing. An occasional flower is delightful, but in most writing we need good, healthy grass. Flowery writing is often exaggerated rather than true to life.

    Is the description of Grandmother true to life or exaggerated? _____

3

    In a lovely, peaceful nook by the sun-kissed sea, where the painful cares of the unblessed world touch us not, we spend summers filled with bliss.

A. Is that sentence true to life or exaggerated? _____
_____

B. Is it tasteful or much too sweet? _____

3

    A. Exaggerated
    B. Much too sweet

. . . .

Norway pines tower more than a hundred feet above the two-room cabin in the Marquette Valley. A few feet in front of the cabin, Colusa Creek dances and sparkles.

Do you prefer this description or that in Answer Frame 1? _____

4

Look again at the example in Frame 3.

    A. Can you be sure what a *peaceful nook* is? _____
    B. Do you know what sea is near the nook? _____
    C. Do you know why the summers are so blissful? _____
    D. You conclude that the flowery passage is too _____ _____ . [*vague* or *specific*?]

4

    A. (Probably not)
    B. No
    C. No (not exactly)
    D. vague

. . . .

    A. Does the example in Answer Frame 3 tell us what kind of trees? _____
    B. Does it identify the valley? _____

5

The cottage where we spend our summers is on the Florida Keys. To the east we see the Atlantic; to the west, the Gulf of Mexico. We can relax in those balmy, palmy surroundings, untroubled by many of the cares that annoy us the rest of the year.

    A. Is that description true to life or exaggerated? _____ _____

    B. Is it tasteful or much too sweet? _____

5

    A. True to life   B. Tasteful

. . . .

Read again the example in Answer Frame 3.

    A. Does it identify the body of water? _____
    B. Do you prefer (1) a cabin that is getting its feet washed or (2) a cabin with a creek dancing and sparkling nearby? _____

6

    A. In Frame 5, are we told what waters are near the cottage? _____
    B. Are we given any hints as to why summers in that area are pleasant? _____
    C. The passage in Frame 5 is _____ [*more* or *less*?] specific than that in Frame 3.
    D. The passage in Frame 5 seems _____ [*more* or *less*?] natural and honest than that in Frame 3.

6

A. Yes   B. Yes
C. more   D. more

....

Flowery writing often makes use of wornout expressions such as *peaceful nook* and *sun-kissed sea*. It may also use ridiculous comparisons, as in Frame 1, where Grandmother's smile is said to resemble a flashing neon sign.

7

Obviously we should try to make our writing interesting, colorful, original. But:

A. It _____ [*should* or *should not?*] be gushy and saccharine.
B. It _____ [*should* or *should not?*] be flowery.
C. It _____ [*should* or *should not?*] be true to life, specific, filled with facts and details.

7

A. should not   B. should not
C. should

....

Note the specific details in Frame 5 and in Answer Frame 4. Often, specific details are the main things needed to provide color and interest.

8

The storm broke with fury. Wind and rain lashed our frail craft like angry giants determined to send us to abysmal depths.

That description is _____. [*good* or *flowery?*]

8

flowery

....

Out on the hardwood arena, our white-clad knights faced their gigantic opponents, ready to battle unto death for the glory of our institution of learning.

That description is _____.
[*good* or *flowery?*]

9

After the gray clouds blackened, we lowered the sails. Suddenly the storm struck. The rain blinded us, and the wind stirred up six-foot waves that bounced and twisted our tiny Star.

That passage is better than the one in Frame 8 because [Check all that apply]:

_____ A. It provides details about clouds, wind, and waves, and the effects of the storm.
_____ B. It avoids overworked expressions such as *broke with fury* and *angry giants*.
_____ C. It seems honest, not overdrawn.

9

A, B, C

. . . .

On the basketball floor our five players, dressed in white with red numbers and our school's emblem, awaited the center jump against their taller opponents.

A. Does Answer Frame 8 or Answer Frame 9 provide more specific details? _____

B. Which one has more over-worked expressions? _____

C. Which seems more honest and realistic? _____

10

Write a sentence of twenty or more words, describing a marching band. (If possible, try to recall a particular band.) Try to write colorfully but avoid flowery writing.

10

Model Answer

Vigorously playing the school song, the band, attired in bright blue uniforms with white plumes, gloves, and shoes, marched on in an I-formation that changed abruptly to *HELLO* and then to *ALUMS*.

11

Finish honestly: One thing that I hope to remember from this lesson is that . . .

(In this frame, any answer that you consider honest and accurate is acceptable.)

Lesson 56: Answers to Questions for Added Practice

1. Yes **2.** A. No B. No C. No D. (Probably not) **3.** This one. (If you answered "Frame 1," you have a little problem.) **4.** A. Yes B. Yes **5.** A. Yes B. (2) **8.** flowery **9.** A. 9 B. 8 C. 9

57

Trite Expressions: Almost as Old as the Hills

After writing your answer(s) in the right-hand column, check this column to see whether you have responded correctly. If you have made a mistake, or if you need more practice, do whatever is asked below the dotted line in each answer frame.

Answers to questions for added practice can be found at the end of each lesson.

Answers and Added Practice

1

Yes (but this is a free country).
. . . .

Playful language, even puns, may sometimes be vivid. William Lyon Phelps, for instance, once said, "A cold can be either positive or negative: sometimes the eyes have it and sometimes the nose."

2

stale (*or* trite, old, worn out, hackneyed, etc.)
. . . .

"The rosy-fingered dawn" was a beautiful description when someone first used it—over two thousand years ago. But now it too is
_____ .

Understanding and Applying the Principles

1

Almost everyone enjoys vivid language. When someone observed, for example, that crowds sometimes ooze from subways like toothpaste, his readers perhaps chuckled appreciatively.

Do you like Oscar Wilde's statement about a certain woman, that **"Her line of conversation was as interesting as a laundry list"?** _____

2

Unfortunately, vivid language loses its freshness when often repeated, as a bright seashell loses much of its luster after long exposure on the shore. Whoever first referred to *a bolt from the blue* created a fine symbol for "surprise"—a lightning bolt suddenly appearing when the sun was still shining.

But after many repetitions that expression has become _____
_____ . [Supply an appropriate adjective]

3

Trite, meaning "overused" or "stale," is derived from the Latin word *tritus*, meaning "worn out" or "rubbed away"—perhaps like the shine on the seashell.

In your own words tell why it is appropriate to refer to some language expressions as *trite*.

3

Model Answer

Some expressions lose their attractiveness by being "rubbed" so often.

. . . .

Check each expression that you have often heard:

_____ makes my blood boil

_____ few and far between

_____ busy as bees

_____ walk on air

_____ off the beaten track

4

In time of peril, amid the roar of battle, soldiers have little time to wonder whether sudden death is their destiny.

Two trite expressions from that sentence are _____ and _____ .

4

time of peril, roar of battle

. . . .

Again, check each that you have often heard:

_____ little bundle of joy

_____ hoping against hope

_____ fair sex

_____ view with alarm

_____ point with pride

5

This modest violet, who was fair as the dawn, in her child-like innocence was now walking on air.

Copy four trite expressions from that sentence.

5

modest violet, fair as the dawn, child-like innocence, walking on air

. . . .

Check as before:

_____ follow in the footsteps

_____ as cold as ice

_____ in the last analysis

_____ nipped in the bud

_____ priceless

6

Some phrases, as everyone realizes, must be used over and over. (Examples are *as everyone realizes* and *over and over*.) The phrases we should try to avoid, the truly trite ones, are those that were colorful when they were first used, but shine no more.

It is better to employ a straightforward and unfigurative expression than a _____ one.

6

trite (*or* stale, etc.)

....

One final group from a list that could reach into the next county:

_____ selling like hot cakes

_____ happy as a lark

_____ better half (wife)

_____ the Grim Reaper

_____ every waking hour

7

Last but not least, we partook of delicious refreshments.

To eliminate trite expressions, such as the two in that sentence, we sometimes can use simple, ordinary words such as *finally* or *at the end*, and sometimes we can provide specific details, such as the names of some of the refreshments.

Using those hints, rewrite the example.

7

Model Answer

Near the end of the party, we enjoyed finger sandwiches, chiffon pie, and pink lemonade.

....

Rewrite in a straightforward way, in nine words if you can:

The bridegroom clasped his blushing bride to his manly chest and tasted her ruby lips.

8

It goes without saying **that** *at long last* **everyone realized that Jed was** *as green as grass.*

Write a straightforward version of the example, avoiding use of the italicized expressions.

8

Model Answer

Of course, everyone finally realized that Jed was very naive.

....

Each waking hour Mrs. Ames devoted to worthy causes.

Rewrite, eliminating *each waking hour*, and making *worthy causes* specific.

9

At the *ripe age* **of fifty-seven, this lady of** *sterling character* **repeated the marital vows and** *embarked upon* **the** *stormy sea of matrimony.*

Follow the instructions in Frame 8.

9

Model Answer
This virtuous lady married at fifty-seven.

· ·

Rewrite, avoiding use of the italicized expressions:

In the *storied past, far off the beaten track* in the *windswept heights* of the Himalayas, lived this *hardy race.*

10

If you are lucky enough to be one of those too rare persons who frequently can think of fresh and colorful expressions, do so.

Write a sentence using a fresh way to say *sun-kissed land, rock-bound coast, crack of dawn, rolling prairie, white as a sheet, quick as a flash, stick to your guns.* (Choose one.)

10

Model Answer (for *sun-kissed land*)
The sunlight brightened the field of wheat as polish restores tarnished copper. (Give yourself credit if you made an attempt.)

· ·

Try to think of a fresh substitute for any of the trite expressions in Answer Frames 3–6.

11

Finish honestly: One thing I hope to remember from this lesson is that . . .

(In this frame, any answer that you consider honest and accurate is acceptable.)

Lesson 57: Answers to Questions for Added Practice

2. stale (*or a synonym*) **3–6.** (Personal responses) **7.** MODEL: The bridegroom hugged his bride and kissed her gently. **8.** MODEL: Mrs. Ames devoted her spare time to the Girl Scouts and to helping runaway children. **9.** MODEL: These sturdy people lived long ago in the Himalayas, far from well-populated areas.

58

Far-fetched Figures: The Dangers of Hyperbole

After writing your answer(s) in the right-hand column, check this column to see whether you have responded correctly. If you have made a mistake, or if you need more practice, do whatever is asked below the dotted line in each answer frame.

Answers to questions for added practice can be found at the end of each lesson.

Understanding and Applying the Principles

1

The reaching fingertips of the tallest pines probed the hidden secrets of the sky.

A good writer would not write that sentence because even a very tall pine could not _____

_____ . [Finish the sentence.]

Answers and Added Practice

1

Model Answer
   probe very far into the sky

. . . .

The little girl's tears descended in mighty torrents.

Why wouldn't a good writer write that?

2

The sweet, high notes of the flute pierced the eardrums of everyone in the huge audience.

A good writer would not write that because _____

_____ .

2

Model Answer
The sound of a flute would not really pierce eardrums. (Also, the idea of piercing contradicts the idea of sweetness.)

. . . .

Her eyes were glued to the ceiling, and then they fell to the floor.

Why don't you like that?

3

Figures of speech are imaginative comparisons. Writing that employs figures of speech is enjoyable if they are not trite (see Lesson 57), mixed (see Lesson 59), or far-fetched (that's what we are dealing with now).

What word do you know that means "far-fetched"? _____

_____

3

Unlikely (*or* Exaggerated *or a synonym*)

. . . .

Does *far-fetched* accurately describe the comparisons in Frames 1 and 2 and Answer Frames 1 and 2? _____

4

A synonym for *exaggeration* is *hyperbole* (pronounced high-PURR-bo-lee). Hyperbole is useful: The humor of Mark Twain and of most TV comedians depends on it.

But if we are not trying to be funny, unintentional hyperbole may make our readers laugh when they're not supposed to. It may make them laugh _____. [*at us* or *with us*?]

4

at us

. . . .

An example of good hyperbole: "[Italians] spell it Vinci and pronounce it Vinchy; foreigners always spell better than they pronounce."
—Mark Twain

5

The Astorbilts' new automobile was about a block long. The family needed a telephone to talk to the chauffeur.

A. Was the automobile really "about a block long"? _____
B. May the telephone be in the car for a reason other than the one given? _____

5

     A. No B. Yes

. . . .

The ears of corn ready for the picker were as numerous as the sands on all the world's seashores.

A. Is it appropriate to compare the number of ears of corn with the number of grains of sand on seashores? _____

B. Is the statement even approximately true? _____

6

Rewrite the first sentence of the example in Frame 5. Assuming that no humor is intended, use straightforward language or think of a more realistic comparison.

6

Model Answer

    The Astorbilts' new automobile was about five feet longer than my father's one-ton pickup truck.

. . . .

Try to rewrite the sentence in Answer Frame 5.

7

So far in this lesson we have seen that, although good figures of speech are worth seeking, we should normally avoid those that are improbable and _____.

7

    farfetched (*or* exaggerated *or* hyperbolic, etc.)

. . . .

Another example of Mark Twain's use of hyperbole for humorous purposes: "The educated Southerner has no use for an *r*, except at the beginning of a word."

8

Which do you like best?

A. The mathematics examination consisted of oceans of problems.
B. The mathematics examination had about a million problems.
C. The mathematics examination was so long that a young Einstein would have had to work on it until midnight.

I like _____ [A, B, or C?] best because _____

_____

_____.

8

Model Answer

C, though imaginative, it is less far-fetched than A or B.

. . . .

During my week of illness I endured 999,999 TV commercials.

I _____ [*like* or *don't like*?] that because _____

_____

_____ .

9

Model Answer

B (imaginative but not too exaggerated)

C (rather dull, but better than the too-exaggerated A)

. . . .

During my week of illness, the medical advertising on TV made me think I had several additional ailments.

I _____ [*like* or *do not like*?] that because _____

_____

_____ .

10

Model Answer

C (imaginative and maybe only only a little exaggerated)

B (dull, but better than the too-exaggerated A)

. . . .

Try your hand at describing a fat man in bathing trunks.

9

Which is best, and which is second best?

A. Wearing our clogs, the two of us clattered along the boardwalk like twenty-seven elephants.

B. Wearing our clogs, the two of us tap-tapped along the boardwalk like a nervous drummer.

C. Our steps sounded loud as the two of us slapped along the boardwalk on clogs.

I like _____ [A, B, or C?] best and _____ [A, B, or C?] second best.

10

Which is best, and which is second best?

A. In her bulky red sweater she looks as big as an oldfashioned one-room schoolhouse.

B. Her bulky red sweater hardly makes her look slim.

C. In her bulky red sweater she could serve as a stop sign a block away—if she were octagonal.

I like _____ [A, B, or C?] best and _____ [A, B, or C?] second best.

11

Imagine a class concentrating on an important examination. Suddenly and unexpectedly, a loud bell rings. Write a sentence in which you greatly exaggerate the sound of the bell or its effect on the students. Make this sentence far-fetched and unbelievable.

11

Model Answer

The sudden bell sounded like the blare of a thousand Chinese gongs in our startled ears.

. . . .

What is bad about the Model Answer above?

12

Now rewrite the sentence you wrote for Frame 11. Though still using, if possible, a figure of speech, try this time to make it effective and believable.

12

Model Answer

The sudden clangor of a bell exploded the silence.

. . . .

What is good about that Model Answer?

13

Finish honestly: One thing I hope to remember from this lesson is that . . .

(In this frame, any answer that you consider honest and accurate is acceptable.)

Lesson 58: Answers to Questions for Added Practice

1. MODEL: Even abundant tears do not fall in torrents. **2.** MODEL: Both the gluing and the falling sound painful. **3.** Yes **5.** A. No B. No **6.** MODEL: The ears of corn ready for the picker were as numerous as the blades of grass on our lawn. **8.** (Either *like* or *don't like* is acceptable. The number 999,999 is a little more imaginative than the overused "a million this" or "a million that.") **9.** MODEL: like, it is amusing but also true to life **10.** MODEL: His belly lapped over his belt, his navel gazing at the ground. **11.** "A thousand Chinese gongs" is not only too exaggerated but also too painful to contemplate. **12.** "Exploded the silence" is more imaginative than "broke the silence" would be.

59

Figures of Speech: Don't Mix Them

After writing your answer(s) in the right-hand column, check this column to see whether you have responded correctly. If you have made a mistake, or if you need more practice, do whatever is asked below the dotted line in each answer frame.

Answers to questions for added practice can be found at the end of each lesson.

Answers and Added Practice

1

    No

....

    The gaps in my knowledge of botany stand out like sore thumbs.

A. Do gaps "stand out"? _____
B. Are gaps like thumbs? _____

2

Model Answer
    The search for wealth became Rex's guiding star (*or* goal).

....

    That snake in the grass is barking up the wrong tree.

Do snakes bark? _____

Understanding and Applying the Principles

1

    The wheels of commerce became Rex's guiding star.

Do wheels become stars? _____

2

One thing wrong with the language in Frame 1 is that the figures of speech are trite (worn out; see Lesson 57). Another is that they are mixed. It is possible that commerce or the search for wealth may become a guiding star, but wheels do not become stars.

    Using those hints, rewrite the sentence in Frame 1.

3

A mixed figure starts out with one image (mental picture) and then shifts abruptly to one or two ridiculously different ones.

    In your own words, tell what shift occurs here:

    A gossip is like a busy little bee, always sharpening her claws for her next victim.

3

Model Answer

First the gossip is compared to a bee, then to some creature that constantly sharpens claws and searches for victims.

. . . .

Bees really spend most of their time searching for _____, not for victims.

4

Often the best way to correct a mixed figure is to leave out some of the images. Rewrite the example in Frame 3, leaving out the least desirable part.

4

Model Answer

A gossip is always sharpening her claws for her next victim.

. . . .

The little electric motor hummed erratically like a bee that isn't quite hitting on all cylinders.

What's wrong with that?

5

The boy plinked the keys of the piano with as much enthusiasm as a hen in a rainstorm.

In Frames 1 and 3, the figures of speech were rather trite as well as mixed. The sentence above shows that comparisons may be faulty even when they are not worn out. Explain what makes the sentence somewhat ridiculous.

5

Model Answer

A hen in a rainstorm has no apparent relationship to playing a piano.

. . . .

Rewrite the example in Answer Frame 4, getting rid of the bee, the cylinders, or both.

6

In Jack's search for greener pastures he was often in troubled waters.

What was unusual about Jack's search for greener pastures?

6

Model Answer

In searching for a pasture, one ordinarily would not look in water, troubled or otherwise.

. . . .

Rewrite the sentence in Frame 6.

7

Summarize in your own words the purpose of the first six frames.

7

Model Answer

The purpose is to show that figures of speech should be sensible and plausible, and not mixed.

. . . .

The two roosters roared into battle, tooth and spurs.

Rewrite. (Hint: chickens have no teeth.)

8

Lem threw caution to the winds but weathered every gale, although he found that he was really fighting a tempest in a teapot.

Rewrite that sentence, making it less windy.

8

Model Answer

Lem went ahead boldly and survived stormy days, but found later that he had been unnecessarily worried.

. . . .

That dog in the manger is just trying to feather his own nest.

Does a dog generally make much use of feathers? _____

9

When opportunity knocks, you must take the bull by the horns and answer the call.

The person best able to follow that advice is an understudy for a wounded matador.

Rewrite the advice in ordinary language by adding two words:

When you have a good chance, _____ _____ .

9

take it

....

Every piece of our delicious candy comes with an iron-clad guarantee.

Does that include dental insurance? (You needn't answer that.)

10

For Kathy, being as playful as a kitten is as natural as falling off a log.

Rewrite that sentence, trying to find something unmixed (and preferably not trite) to say about Kathy's playfulness. Begin with the words *Kathy is as playful as . . .*

10

Model Answer

Kathy is as playful as a monkey at a lunch counter.

....

One of the worst (or best) examples of mixed figures:

She felt like a ship on the stormy sea of life, floating on a cloud. She could hitch her wagon to a star and plow a straight course across the dreary landscape on an even keel.

11

Finish honestly: One thing I hope to remember from this lesson is that . . .

(In this frame, any answer that you consider honest and accurate is acceptable.)

Lesson 59: Answers to Questions for Added Practice

1. A. No B. No **2.** No **3.** food (*or* nectar) **4.** MODEL: Bees don't have cylinders. **5.** MODEL: The little electric motor hummed erratically, pausing now and then for reassurance. **6.** MODEL: Jack's search for a better job often led him into trouble. **7.** MODEL: The two roosters began leaping at each other, ripping with beaks and spurs. **8.** No

60

Euphony: Let's Make Beautiful Music

After writing your answer(s) in the right-hand column, check this column to see whether you have responded correctly. If you have made a mistake, or if you need more practice, do whatever is asked below the dotted line in each answer frame.

Answers to questions for added practice can be found at the end of each lesson.

Understanding and Applying the Principles

1

The sorrowful stranger's certainly extravagant tastes certainly distressed us.

The sound of the letter _____ appears so frequently in that sentence that it is annoying.

Answers and Added Practice

1

s

....

The four fluffy little foxes fought in fun for fifteen minutes.

In that sentence the _____-sounds are too numerous.

2

For literary reasons, a poet may intentionally repeat a sound, as Edgar Allan Poe, for instance, often did. That is, he or she uses *alliteration*. But in ordinary prose, a sound repeated many times in one sentence or so may be mildly disturbing. A sound of *s* occurs about a dozen times in the nine words of the example in Frame 1.

Try rewriting that example with no more than six or seven *s* sounds.

2

Model Answer

The sorrowful stranger's desire for high living greatly annoyed us.

....

Rewrite the example in Answer Frame 1.

3

This peppermint mint has an unusually strong mint flavor.

A. What word in that sentence is annoyingly repeated?

_____

B. Rewrite the sentence without using *mint* more than once.

3

A. *mint*

B. **Model Answer**

This peppermint has an unusually strong flavor.

....

This coin is the oldest coin in my coin collection.

Rewrite, using *coin* only once.

4

We searched throughout the house, trying in vain to find the mouse.

Unintentional rhymes are considered bad because they may distract readers or cause unwanted amusement.
    Rewrite the example to avoid rhyming words.

4

Model Answer

We searched all the rooms, trying in vain to find the mouse.

....

We heard a crash and a clatter, and rushed out to see what was the matter.

To avoid the rhyme, we may write

_____

instead of *what was the matter.*

5

Tabasco, in southeastern Mexico, which, in 1524, was crossed by Cortez, is a jungle plain, but laced with rivers, and containing many swamps.

In your own words, tell what makes that sentence unpleasant to read.

5

Model Answer

The sentence is jerky because of being chopped into many small parts.

. . . .

Ecuador, which means "equator," is on the equator, in South America, and is crossed, twice in fact, by ranges of mountains, the Andes.

That sentence also is _____ .

6

Rewrite the example in Frame 5 to make it flow more smoothly.

6

Model Answer

When Cortez in 1524 crossed Tabasco in southeastern Mexico, he found that it is a jungle plain, but laced with rivers and containing many swamps.

. . . .

Try to rewrite the example in Answer Frame 5.

7

Euphony means "pleasantness of sound." *Cacophony* (accent the second syllable) means almost the opposite: "unevenness or unpleasantness of sound."

Reread the boldface sentences in Frames 1, 3, 4, and 5. To you, which one seems most cacophonous? _____

7

(Personal opinion. Some persons are bothered most by the hissing sounds of 1, some dislike repetition or rhyme, and some are disturbed by the choppiness of 5.)

. . . .

We have noted three of the causes of the lack of euphony: repetition of the same _____ or _____ _____ , unintentional _____ _____ , and a _____ effect from dividing a sentence into too many small parts.

8

"The Merry Musicians" made marvelous music Monday.

Rewrite, reducing the number of *m*'s.

8

Model Answer

"The Merry Musicians" played unusually well on Monday.

. . . .

Plenty of parties put pleasure into pretty Patty's vacation.

Rewrite, eliminating some p's.

9

We rented a car and then drove far into the hills of Miramar.

Rewrite, eliminating the rhymes and making the rhythm less regular.

9

Model Answer

We rented an automobile and then drove far back into the hills of Miramar.

. . . .

I fed the cat, put on my hat, and went to eat at the Automat.

Now improve on that.

10

I played an old long-playing record of the musical play *Chorus Line*, which played a record number of times on Broadway.

Rewrite, eliminating unnecessary repetition.

10

Model Answer

I played an old LP recording of the musical *Chorus Line*, which has set a record for consecutive Broadway performances.

. . . .

This story is a story about the history of the early days of the Southern Pacific Railroad.

Rewrite to reduce undesirable repetition.

11

July, our seventh month, but the fifth month, called Quintilis, in ancient Rome, was named for Julius Caesar, born in that month.

Smooth that. Perhaps you should use two sentences.

11

Model Answer

July, our seventh month, was named for Julius Caesar, who was born in that month. In ancient Rome it was the fifth month and was called Quintilis.

. . . .

As the example shows, a long, choppy sentence should often be divided.

12

Finish honestly: One thing I hope to remember from this lesson is that . . .

(In this frame, any answer that you consider honest and accurate is acceptable.)

Lesson 60: Answers to Questions for Added Practice

1. *f* **2.** MODEL: The four soft fox cubs wrestled playfully for a quarter of an hour. **3.** This is the oldest coin in my collection. **4.** MODEL: what had happened **5.** jerky (*or* choppy *or a synonym*) **6.** South America's Ecuador, named for the equator on which it lies, is crossed twice by ranges of the Andes Mountains. **7.** sound, word, rhyme, jerky (*or* choppy, etc.) **8.** MODEL: Patty, a lovely girl, enjoyed her party-filled vacation. **9.** MODEL: After feeding Tabby, I put on my hat and coat and went to eat at the Automat. **10.** MODEL: This story tells about the early days of the Southern Pacific Railroad.

═══61═══

Vague Words: Woolly, Flabby, and Dull

After writing your answer(s) in the right-hand column, check this column to see whether you have responded correctly. If you have made a mistake, or if you need more practice, do whatever is asked below the dotted line in each answer frame.

Answers to questions for added practice can be found at the end of each lesson.

Understanding and Applying the Principles

1

Now here is a young man named Timothy. The nature of the circumstances makes his case hopeless.

A. Have you any idea about what makes Timothy's "case" hopeless or even what his "case" is? _____

B. What group of five words in the example is especially vague in meaning? _____

Answers and Added Practice

1

    A. No (unless by intuition).

    B. *The nature of the circum-*
       stances.

. . . .

Would it help to add in Frame 1,
Conditions have made it so? _____

2

Imagine Timothy, a flesh-and-blood young man, surrounded
by—even engulfed in—"the nature of the circumstances"!
What an uncertain fate! Readers can't possibly estimate how
horrible the "circumstances" are. Is he in trouble with the law?
Is he about to fail in all his courses? We do not know.

So let's think of some possible "circumstances" that make
his "case" hopeless. For example, perhaps Timothy has spent
all his money and his father won't lend him any for a big
week-end.

Write two more imaginary "circumstances" to fit with that
one.

2

Model Answer

    Timothy has been fired from
his job. He already owes money
to his best friend.

. . . .

Are your own answers more definite than "the nature of the circumstances"? _____

3

We rewrite the example in Frame 1, getting rid of the vague
words:

    Now here is a young man named Timothy. Broke and with a
    father who won't lend him any money, he . . . [Finish the
    sentence with your imaginary "circumstances."]

3

Model Answer

    regrets that he has been fired
and that his credit isn't good.

. . . .

Read your revised sentence about
Timothy. Doesn't it tell you more
about him than the sentence in
Frame 1 does? _____

4

Nouns like some of those in Frame 1 are difficult to understand
or to define. They are shapeless, weak, flabby, woolly, hard to
grasp—and dull to read or hear.

    The three especially vague words in Frame 1 are _____

_____, _____, and _____.

4

nature, circumstances, case

....

In Answer Frames 1 and 2 we noted these other often vague words:

_____ ,

_____ .

5

The character of Gray's work in the mining line led to a condition of near physical exhaustion.

Three nouns in the sentence above add so little to the meaning that they may be omitted.

A. *The character of Gray's work* can be shortened to _____

_____ .

B. *In the mining line* can be shortened to _____ _____

_____ .

C. *A condition of near physical exhaustion* can be shortened to

_____ _____ _____ .

5

A. *Gray's work*
B. *in mining*
C. *near physical exhaustion*

....

A. Is it better to spend a dollar or a quarter for the same result? _____

B. Is it better to spend four words or one for the same result? _____

6

Try to rewrite the example in Frame 5, eliminating the words *character, line,* and *condition.* It may help to name Gray's work specifically. For example, he may have been a "loader" or a "shooter."

6

Model Answer

Gray's work as a loader almost exhausted him physically.

....

Jones is in the hardware line.

Say the same thing in three words:

_____

_____

7

Often the vague nouns are the six we have noted: *case, character, circumstance, condition, line,* and *nature.* Sometimes, however, they are "big" words that say no more than ordinary words but are harder to understand.

Here, for instance, is a vague way to express a familiar four-word proverb:

It is indubitably desirable for you to observe with considerable carefulness ere you propel yourself forward precipitately.

What is the proverb? (It starts with *Look.*)

7

Look before you leap.

· ·

Remember: The purpose of communication is to convey meaning, not to conceal it.

8

Each individual entity that coruscates brightly may not with any degree of certainty be identified as that metal which in chemistry is designated as *aurum*.

That sentence hides this familiar six-word statement of Shakespeare's:

All that _____ .

8

All that glitters is not gold. (Shakespeare actually wrote *glisters*, but that word is now seldom used.)

· ·

Translate this proverb into eleven one-syllable words:

A single member of the feathered tribe that one clutches in his hand is the equivalent of double that number which are situated in a specimen of short, branched vegetation:

A bird _____

_____

_____ .

9

Which is better, A or B?

   A. Simple, direct, precise language
   B. Big words chosen to impress people

_____

9

A

· ·

Translate in four words this statement about a road:

The thoroughfare on which vehicular traffic flows heavily was in a condition marred by the circumstance that precipitation had fallen in frozen form, resulting in a slippery encrustation.

10

Translate this sentence into about ten simple words:

In order to withdraw the cylindrical stopper made of the outer tissues of the cork oak from the rigid, narrow-necked glass container, the nature of the circumstances requires the insertion and lateral rotation of a pointed, spiral-shaped metallic object.

To remove _____

_____

10

Model Answer

> To remove the cork from the bottle, use a corkscrew.

· ·

State this clearly in four words:

> **In the case of Simon Legree, it may be said with but slight fear of successful contradiction that a pronounced tendency toward cruelty was characteristic of his nature.**

11

Finish honestly: One thing I hope to remember from this lesson is that . . .

(In this frame, any answer that you consider honest and accurate is acceptable.)

Lesson 61: Answers to Questions for Added Practice

1. No **2.** (Personal evaluation) **3.** Yes. (It should.) **4.** condition(s), character **5.** A. Quarter B. One **6.** Jones sells hardware. **8.** A bird in the hand is worth two in the bush. **9.** MODEL: The highway was icy. **10.** Simon Legree was cruel.

═══62═══

Reducing Sexist Language: Not Only All Men Are Created Equal

After writing your answer(s) in the right-hand column, check this column to see whether you have responded correctly. If you have made a mistake, or if you need more practice, do whatever is asked below the dotted line in each answer frame.

Answers to questions for added practice can be found at the end of each lesson.

Understanding and Applying the Principles

1

A well-known textbook publisher (McGraw-Hill) tells its authors, "Men and women should be treated primarily as people, and not primarily as members of the opposite sexes."

Do you believe that would be a good rule for society in general to follow? _____

Answers and Added Practice

1

(Give yourself credit for either answer, but the rest of this lesson will be easier for you if your answer was *Yes*.)

....

On the beach, Jane and Barbara saw this sign:

DANGER
MAN-EATING
SHARKS

"Well," Jane said, "I guess *we* are safe."

Was she right? _____

2

The National Council of Teachers of English (NCTE) names three major (and often overlapping) kinds of sexist language: 1. that which omits women; 2. that which demeans women (or men); and 3. that which presents unfair stereotypes of women (or men). In this lesson we'll look at all three.

Here are some pairs of terms. In each pair, underline the term that clearly does *not* omit women or men.

A. postmen   mail carriers
B. human achievements   Man's achievements
C. the common man   the average person

2

A. <u>mail carriers</u>   B. <u>human achievements</u>   C. <u>the average person</u>

....

Proceed as in Frame 2.

A. stewardesses   flight attendants
B. firemen   fire fighters
C. police officers   policemen

(Instead of starting most speeches with "Ladies and Gentlemen," perhaps speakers should sometimes say "Gentlemen and Ladies.")

3

Concerning demeaning, NCTE says, "Men and women should be treated in a parallel manner, whether the description involves jobs, appearance, marital status, or titles."

In each pair below, underline the expression that treats both sexes equally.

A. a doctor   a lady doctor
B. Candidates are Jack Jones, captain of the football team, and Jill Smith, a pretty senior.
   Candidates are Jack Jones, captain of the football team, and Jill Smith, first flutist in the orchestra.
C. Senator Lowell and Mrs. Green
   Senator Lowell and Representative Green
D. Signs on restroom doors:
   WOMEN   MEN   LADIES   MEN
E. Lynne Peterson, a poet   Lynne Peterson, a poetess

3

A. <u>a doctor</u>   B. . . . <u>Jill Smith,
first flutist</u> . . .   C. . . . <u>Repre-
sentative</u> . . .   D. <u>WOMEN
MEN</u>   E. . . .<u>a poet</u>

. . . .

Proceed as in Frame 3.

A. lawyers and their spouses
   lawyers and their wives

B. (I now pronounce you:)
   man and wife   husband
   and wife

4

Stereotyping is pretending or believing that all members of a
group are alike (for instance, women, men, blondes, Italians,
blacks, Chinese). Men, for example, are often depicted in TV
commercials as bumbling near-idiots, and women in commercials and elsewhere as persons primarily concerned with how
they look, how to catch and hold a man, and how to polish the
furniture or do the laundry.

In each pair, which expression is more fair? (Answer A. 1 or
A. 2, etc.)

A. 1. You ladies who are going shopping . . .
   2. You shoppers . . .   _____

B. 1. elementary school teachers . . . they . . .
   2. an elementary school teacher . . . she . . .   _____

C. 1. principals . . . they . . .
   2. a principal . . . he . . .   _____

4

A. 2   B. 1   C. 1

. . . .

Proceed as in Frame 4.

A.1. the ladies chattered

A.2. the women talked _____

B.1. Men spend their autumn
     Sundays watching foot-
     ball on TV

B.2. Many   men   spend . . .

     _____

C.1. Businessmen often ne-
     glect their wives and chil-
     dren.

C.2. Business   people   often
     neglect their families. ___

     _____

5

In your opinion, does each of the following examples show 1.
omission of women or men, 2. demeaning of women or men,
or 3. stereotyping?

Write 1, 2, or 3 in each blank. Sometimes two answers are
possible.

A. airline pilots and other men   _____

B. librarians, as well as other women   _____

C. a baby sitter . . . she . . .   _____

D. blonde cutie Mitzi Mayfair and straight-A student
   Ralph Short   _____

E. a lady druggist   _____

5

Probable Answers

A. 3 or 1   B. 3 or 1
C. 3 or 1   D. 2   E. 2 or 3

. . . .

A. Are good athletes always male? _____

B. Are "homemakers" always women? _____

C. Was there "primitive woman" as well as "primitive man"? _____

D. Instead of "the best man" for the job, we may say "the best p _ _ _ _ n" or "the best ca _ _ _ _ _ _ e" for the job.

6

Each student cast his vote in the election, and Sally Graham won.

Some feminists and other people object to *his* and *he* when the reference is to both males and females. They recommend *his or her* and *he or she,* or else a recasting of the sentence—possibly *All students cast their votes* . . . or *All students voted* . . .

Other people argue that for centuries *his* and *he,* in sentences like the example, have been understood to include both sexes.

Present-day usage is divided. One solution is to use *his or her* and *he or she,* or to recast the sentence, but when either of those results in awkwardness, to use the long-established *his* and *he.*

How would you write the example?

Why?

6

Personal preference

. . . .

In some instances the use of *they* or *he or she* is impracticable. For instance, in explaining what each student in a mixed group should do as an individual in following a long series of instructions, *they* is impossible, and *he or she* might have to be repeated many times. However, when a plural form is possible and appropriate, it should usually be chosen. For example, saying *students* or *the students* or *all students* makes possible the use of *they* instead of *he or she.*

7

Dear Miss (or Mrs. or Ms.) Simon:

Some people point out that *Mr.* does not indicate a man's marital status, and say that it is discriminatory to address a woman as *Miss* or *Mrs.,* titles which force such an indication for women. These people often prefer the noncommittal *Ms.* Many women, however, prefer to be addressed as *Miss* or *Mrs.*

One partial solution: Use *Miss* or *Mrs.* when a woman's marital status is known or when she has shown (as in signing a letter) what title she prefers. Otherwise use *Ms.*

What is your own solution?

7

Personal preference

. . . .

As part of the signature of a business letter, a thoughtful woman indicates in parentheses the one of the three titles that she prefers.

8

In Frames 8–13, some obviously sexist language is used. Rewrite each example to remove the sexist implications.

The center, Bob Jackson, is the weak sister on the team.

8

Model Answer

. . . is the poorest player . . .

. . . .

In Answer Frames 8–13, proceed as in Frame 8.

A businessman, on the telephone:

"All right, Mr. Forbes, I'll have my girl take care of it tomorrow."

9

Amelia Earhart, a noted aviatrix, disappeared mysteriously.

9

Model Answer

Amelia Earhart, a noted aviator (*or* pilot *or* flier) . . .

. . . .

A woman's work is never done.

10

Like other men, he spends his weekends fiddling with his car and watching sports.

10

Model Answer

    Like many (*or* some) other men. . . .

. . . .

Frank Marston is a college professor, and his wife, Louise, is an attractive redhead.

11

    Each secretary is also given suggestions about care of her hands, practical hair styling for the office, and intelligent use of makeup.

11

Model Answer

    . . . suggestions about personal grooming.

. . . .

"I left my ball and chain at home."
"My old man left me at home."

12

    Gateway is the store where you can choose from hundreds of dolls and nurse's kits for your little girl, and hundreds of trucks and doctor's kits for your little boy.

12

Model Answer

    . . . hundreds of dolls, trucks, and nurse's and doctor's kits for your children.

. . . .

Although she is a woman, she manages the office efficiently.

13

    "All men are created equal."

That quotation from the Declaration of Independence offers a good start for a class discussion. Did the signers of the Declaration, all of whom were men, mean males only? Equal in what ways? Were the signers sexist?

    How would you have written the sentence at the top?

13

Model Answer

All human beings are created equal. (Yes, most or all the signers of the Declaration were sexist.)

. . . .

(Swords cut two ways. The League of Women Voters encourages men to become dues-paying members, but its officers have voted down proposals to change its name.)

14

Finish honestly: One thing I hope to remember from this lesson is that . . .

(In this frame, any answer that you consider honest and accurate is acceptable.)

Lesson 62: Answers to Questions for Added Practice

1. No (Sharks seem indifferent to the sex of their meals.) **2.** A. <u>flight attendants</u> B. <u>fire fighters</u> C. <u>police officers</u> **3.** A. <u>lawyers and their spouses</u> B. <u>husband and wife</u> 4. A. 2 B. 2 C. 2 **5.** A. No B. No C. Yes D. person, candidate **8.** MODEL: . . . "I'll have my secretary (*or* assistant, etc.) . . . **9.** MODEL: No one's work is ever done. **10.** MODEL: . . . and his wife, Louise, is a part-time librarian. **11.** "I left my wife at home." (*Or probably better:* "My wife stayed at home.") "My husband left me at home." (*Or probably better:* "I decided to stay at home.") **12.** She manages the office efficiently.

63

A Few "Which Ones?" and a Handful of "No-noes"

A, an;   than, then;   to, too, two;
their, there, they're;   its, it's;   whose, who's;
your, you're;   *and the Nonstandard* alot, busted,
being that, could of, he don't, has got, had ought,
irregardless, try and

After writing your answer(s) in the right-hand column, check this column to see whether you have responded correctly. If you have made a mistake, or if you need more practice, do whatever is asked below the dotted line in each answer frame.

Answers to questions for added practice can be found at the end of each lesson.

Answers and Added Practice

1

Model Answer

I hereby resolve to proofread carefully whatever I write so that I can correct obvious mistakes.

Understanding and Applying the Principles

1

Many of the misuses discussed in this lesson result from carelessness, which may cause up to half the little marks that instructors place on student compositions.

If you conscientiously can, finish this resolution about avoiding such carelessness:

I hereby resolve _____

_____

_____

2

a vs. *an*

An is used before a vowel sound, usually represented by *a, e, i, o,* or *u*:

> *an* **apple,** *an* **egg,** *an* **ice cube** or *an* **injury,** *an*
> **orange,** *an* **unlikely story.**

Sometimes a silent *h* appears in the spelling before the vowel: *an* hour, *an* honor.

A is used before a consonant sound: *a* **bird,** *a* **cow,** *a* **donkey.** A word like *union* or *university* starts with a consonant sound even though it is spelled with a vowel: *a* **union,** *a* **university.**

Write *a* or *an* in each blank:

A. _____ onion and _____ unusually large potato were lying on _____ table.

B. The onion said, "Soon we will form _____ union in _____ stew. That will be _____ honor for you."

2

A. An, an, a

B. a, a, an

. . . .

Supply *a* or *an*:

_____ university can be _____ attractive place. _____ older boy and I recently walked around _____ large campus for _____ hour. _____ extraordinary feature of the campus was _____ enormous planetarium.

3

than vs. *then*

Than is used in comparisons: **more beautiful *than* the moon, less desirable *than* it seems.**

Then rhymes with *when*, and both words refer to time: **When the sun rose, . . . *Then* the sun rose.**

Write *than* or *then* in each blank:

A. Your sister looks more relaxed _____ she did yesterday.

B. Yes, the coach talked to her. _____ she got a good night's sleep.

3

A. than   B. Then

. . . .

Supply *than* or *then*:

A. Alice grabbed a rebound and _____ started a fast break.

B. I have never seen the Tigers playing better _____ they are today.

C. Alice is passing more _____ _____ before.

D. She just made a beautiful pass to Betsy. _____ she took a return pass and scored.

4

to vs. *too* vs. *two*

To seldom causes trouble. It is used in infinitives such as ***to* buy** and ***to* eat**, and in phrases such as ***to* the museum**, or ***to* her and me**.

Too may mean "also," as in **Sandy cried, *too*,** or it may mean "excessively," as in **Don't walk *too* fast.**

Two is a number: ***two* letters.**

Write *to, too,* or *two* in each blank:

A. I make _____ many careless mistakes.

B. Dorothy had only _____ shots in the game.

C. We'll have _____ shoot better in the second half. I'll drive _____ the basket more often, _____ .

4

A. too   B. too   C. to, to, too

. . . .

Supply *to, too,* or *two*:

A. Kelly made _____ baskets in the first _____ minutes.

B. Lucy was playing well, _____ _____ , but I was still _____ careless.

C. "You'll have _____ think, Brenda," the coach said. "You're _____ often asleep out there."

5

their vs. *there* vs. *they're*

Their is a possessive, meaning "belonging to them." It is used before a noun or before *own*: ***Their* house is almost paid for. Soon it will be *their* own.**

There usually means "in that place": ***There* she stood. Was anyone else *there*?** Sometimes it is pronounced more lightly and is used only to get a sentence started: ***There* is a forestry display in the science museum.**

They're means "they are": **The boys are quick, but *they're* very small.**

Write *their, there,* or *they're* in each blank:

A. _____ was a bad accident. Several people were hurt _____ on that corner.

B. Are _____ injuries serious?

C. We don't know yet. _____ all in the hospital.

5

A. There, there B. their
C. They're

....

Supply *their*, *there*, or *they're*:

A. _____ is still some bread in Cheryl's pack.

B. Sally and Mona have none, and _____ canteens are empty.

C. _____ in worse trouble than Cheryl is.

D. _____ sure to ask Cheryl to come to _____ _____ rescue.

E. They will soon reach the Langtry cabin. Perhaps _____ _____ will be food and water _____.

6

A. its B. It's, its

....

Supply *it's* or *its*:

A. _____ a great day!

B. A crocus is pushing _____ yellow head up through the snow.

C. A light wind is blowing ___ _____ breath across the park.

D. _____ almost spring!

7

A. Who's, who's B. whose

....

Supply *who's* or *whose*:

A. _____ at the door?

B. It's the woman _____ been trying to sell us a parrot.

C. I don't want a parrot _____ _____ feathers look so bedraggled.

6

its vs. *it's*

It's, with an apostrophe, almost always means "it is," but sometimes "it has": ***It's*** (= it is) **fun to play table tennis, but *it's* (=** it has) **been a long time since I played.**

Its, without an apostrophe, means "belonging to it": **The monkey was swinging on *its* trapeze.** (We don't write *it's* here because we wouldn't say, "The monkey was swinging on it is trapeze.")

See Lessons 80 and 81 for more information about contractions and possessives.

Write *its* or *it's* in each blank.

A. The snake is darting out _____ tongue.

B. _____ amazing to see how fast _____ tongue moves.

7

whose vs. *who's*

Who's, with an apostrophe, means "who is" or "who has": ***Who's*** (= Who is) **there? *Who's* (= Who has) been eating my porridge?"**

Whose, without an apostrophe, is a possessive meaning "belonging to whom": ***Whose* porridge did she eat?**

Write *whose* or *who's* in each blank:

A. _____ the rascal _____ been eating my porridge?

B. I'm the one _____ porridge has been eaten.

8

your vs. *you're*

You're, with an apostrophe, means "you are": ***You're* sure, aren't you?**

Your, without an apostrophe, means "belonging to you": **Is this *your* final offer?**

Write *your* or *you're* in each blank:

A. _____ at the top of _____ game now.

B. Thanks for _____ compliment. _____ not doing badly yourself.

8

A. You're, your   B. your,
You're

....

Supply *you're* or *your*:

A. _____ next patient
is here, Doctor, whenever
_____ ready.

B. _____ very efficient,
Miss Adams. I'm grateful
for _____ help.

C. Thanks, Doctor. _____
as kind to me as you are
to _____ patients.

9

No-noes: *alot, being that, bust*

Frames 9–11 deal briefly with several expressions that are considered nonstandard.

A lot, an informal expression, is two words, not one. **There's not *a lot* of time.**

Being that is a nonstandard substitute for *because.*

Bust is nonstandard for the meanings "burst" or "break": **The balloon *burst*. The balloon has *burst*. The tie rod is *broken*.**

Choose the standard form for each blank:

A. _____ [*Alot* or *A lot?*] of money will be needed for the hospital bill.

B. Both of Walt's legs are _____ . [*broken* or *busted?*]

C. _____ [*Being that* or *Because?*] he has no medical insurance, we'll have to help him _____ . [*alot* or *a lot?*]

9

A. A lot   B. broken
C. Because, a lot

....

Choose the standard form:

A. You ought to forgive him

_____

[*being that* or *because?*] he is your brother.

B. He couldn't keep the bag from _____ .
[*breaking open* or *busting?*]

C. _____ [*Alot* or *A lot?*] of corn spilled out.

10

No-noes: *could of, he don't, has got*

Could of is a mistaken spelling for *could've*, the contraction of the more formal *could have*. *Of* is similarly misused after *may, might, must, should,* and *would.*

Don't is nonstandard after *he, she, it,* or a singular noun, such as *elephant.* It means "do not," and obviously we'd not say "she do not" or "an elephant do not." Use *doesn't* instead, or *does not* in formal writing.

Has got (or *have got*, etc.) is not standard formal American usage, although frequent in the British Isles. Say **He *has* a toothache**, not **He *has got* (or He's got) a toothache.** Say **We *must* hurry**, not **We've got to hurry.**

Choose the standard form for each blank:

A. He _____ [*has* or *'s got*] a severe nosebleed.

B. He may _____ [*of* or *have?*] broken his nose.

C. It _____ [*doesn't* or *don't?*] look broken to me.

10

A. has B. have C. doesn't

· ·

Choose the standard form:

A. They_____ [*'ve got to* or *must*?] finish by four o'clock, so they _____ [*haven't* or *haven't got*?] much time.

B. It _____ [*don't* or *doesn't*?] look promising.

C. They _____ [*should have* or *should of*?] started earlier.

11

No-noes: *had ought, try and, irregardless*

Had ought is nonstandard. *Ought* is enough: **They *ought* to reconsider.**

One does not *try and* do something: One *tries to:* **Try to remember what happened.**

Irregardless is a longer and nonstandard substitute for *regardless*: **I'll complain *regardless* of the consequences.**

Choose the standard form for each blank:

You _____ [*ought* or *had ought*?] to _____ _____ [*try and* or *try to*?] call her, _____ [*irregardless* or *regardless*?] of what she said.

11

ought, try to, regardless

· ·

Choose the standard form:

A. Ideally lawyers _____ _____ [*had ought* or *ought*?] to try _____ [*to* or *and*?] discover truth and falsehood, innocence and guilt, _____

_____ [*regardless* or *irregardless*?] of legal technicalities.

B. They _____ [*had ought* or *ought*?] to try _____ [*and* or *to*?] attain truth and rightness, not necessarily victory.

12

Finish honestly: One thing I hope to remember from this lesson is that . . .

(In this frame, any answer that you consider honest and accurate is acceptable.)

Lesson 63: Answers to Questions for Added Practice

2. A, an, An, a, an, An, an **3.** A. then B. than C. than D. Then **4.** A. two, two B. too, too C. to, too **5.** A. There B. their C. They're D. They're, their E. there, there **6.** A. It's B. its C. its D. It's **7.** A. Who's B. who's C. whose **8.** A. Your, you're B. You're, your C. You're, your **9.** A. because B. breaking open C. A lot **10.** A. must, haven't B. doesn't C. should have **11.** A. ought, to, regardless B. ought, to

=64=

Words Frequently Confused (I)
Accept, except;   advice, advise;   affect, effect;
all ready, already;   alumnus *and related words;*
breath, breathe;   conscience, conscious;
device, devise;   dual, duel;   emigrate, immigrate;
moral, morale;   prophecy, prophesy;
wreath, wreathe

After writing your answer(s) in the right-hand column, check this column to see whether you have responded correctly. If you have made a mistake, or if you need more practice, do whatever is asked below the dotted line in each answer frame.

Answers to questions for added practice can be found at the end of each lesson.

Understanding and Applying the Principles

1

accept vs. *except*

Accept is a verb meaning "to receive something that is given or paid": **The captain *accepted* the trophy for her team.**

Except is usually a preposition. It means "leaving out" or "with the exception of": **Everyone *except* one girl is in line.**
Write *accept* or *except* in each blank:

A. Please _____ this gift from the class, Mrs. Lang.

B. The flood damaged all the houses _____ the Ludwigs'.

Answers and Added Practice

1

    A. accept   B. except

. . . .

Supply *accept* or *except:*

    A. I cannot _____
       your apology.

    B. Frost killed all the vege-
       tables _____ the peas.

    C. We ate all our meals, _____
       _____ breakfast,
       on the trail.

    D. Uncle Ray was so poor that
       we hated to _____
       a present from him.

2

advice vs. *advise*; *device* vs. *devise*; *prophecy* vs. *prophesy*

Nouns	**Verbs**
Dads give advi**c**e.	Please advi**s**e me.
What is this devi**c**e?	Try to devi**s**e a plan.
What is your prophe**c**y?	To prophe**s**y well is hard.

The easiest way to recall the three pairs of words in this frame is to remember that those used as nouns are spelled with a *c* and those used as verbs are spelled with an *s*.

    The nouns *advi e, devi e,* and *prophe y* are spelled with a _____ , and the verbs (to) *advi e,* (to) *devi e,* and (to) *prophe y* are spelled with an _____ . [Fill in the letters.]

2

    c c c c, s s s s

. . . .

Supply *advice, advise, device, devise, prophecy,* or *prophesy:*

    A. I _____ you not
       to take this _____
       out of your shop.

    B. I _____
       that every _____
       you invent will fail.

    C. I admit that people seldom
       follow my _____
       and that my _____ ies
       are usually wrong.

3

affect vs. *effect*

Affect is a verb usually meaning "to influence or change": **Sunspots *affect* the weather on Earth.**

    Effect is usually a noun meaning "result": **The effect of the professor's announcement was the cancelation of our class.**

    Write *affect* or *effect* in each blank:

    A. No one can describe the full _____ of the
       storm.

    B. A blizzard can _____ the lives of millions of
       people.

3

A. effect B. affect

· ·

Supply *affect* or *effect*:

A. One _____ of last night's rain is deeper water in the creek.

B. The depth of water can ___ _____ canoeing.

Note: *Effect* can also be a verb, meaning "to cause or bring about." For example, **The President's speech** *effected* **a change in some people's awareness of the problem.**

4

all ready vs. *already*

"Is Cathy here?"
"No. She has *already* gone."
"That's too bad. I was *all ready* to come over, but my car wouldn't start."

A. Apparently _____ [*all ready* or *already*?] means "before this time."

B. _____ seems to mean "completely ready" or "completely prepared."

C. Cathy had been _____ before Dan arrived.

D. When he arrived, it was _____ too late for the show.

4

A. already B. All ready
C. all ready D. already

· ·

Supply *all ready* or *already*:

A. The band members were _____ to leave.

B. A busload of other students had _____ gone.

C. One band member called, "We're _____ to go _____ !"

5

alumnus and Related Words

AN ALUMNUS   TWO ALUMNI   AN ALUMNA

TWO ALUMNAE   SEVERAL ALUMNI

Write *alumni* or *alumnae* in each blank:

A. Men who attended the University of Maine are _____ _____ of that institution.

B. Women who once studied at Texas State College for Women are among its _____

C. Men and women who attended Lakeland Community College are _____ of that institution.

5

A. alumni B. alumnae
C. alumni

....

Supply *alumnus, alumna, alumni,* or *alumnae*:

A. An _____ (male)
B. An _____ (female)
C. Two _____ (female)
D. Two _____ (male)
E. Two _____ (a
female and a male)

6

breath vs. *breathe; wreath* vs. *wreathe*

Breath (brĕth) and *wreath* (rēth) both end with the *th* sound of *thin* and are spelled without a final *e*. Besides, both are nouns: **to take a deep *breath*, to lay a holiday *wreath*.**

Breathe and *wreathe* both end with the *th* sound of *there*, have a final *e*, and are verbs: **to *breathe* deeply; A vine had *wreathed* itself around the tree trunk.**

Supply one of the four words in each blank:

A. It's good to _____ this clean air.
B. Let's go out for a _____ of fresh air.
C. Jean consciously tries to _____ her face with a big smile.
D. The President laid a _____ at the tomb.

6

A. breathe B. breath
C. wreathe D. wreath

....

Supply *breath, breathe, wreath,* or *wreathe*:

A. a holly _____ for the holidays
B. her sweet-smelling _____ _____
C. a skirt _____ d with a flowery belt
D. hardly able to _____

7

conscience vs. *conscious* and *consciousness*

My *conscience* told me not to do that.
Were you really *conscious* of doing wrong?
Yes, but my *consciousness* of the harm I might do was not very great.

Study the way that the italicized words above are used. Then complete each of the following by writing one of the three words:

A. _____ seems to mean "aware," but it can also mean "awake."
B. _____ means "awareness."
C. My _____ hurts me when I know that I have done something wrong.

7

A. Conscious   B. Consciousness   C. conscience

. . . .

Supply *conscious, consciousness,* or *conscience*:

A. I did no wrong. My _____ is clear.

B. Slowly I returned to _____ .

C. Jeff remained _____ after his fall.

D. Does your _____ ever hurt you?

8

dual vs. *duel*

Dual is an adjective meaning "double." Many driver-training cars have *dual* controls so that in an emergency the instructor can take over.

Duel is usually a noun, sometimes a verb. It means "a battle (occasionally pre-arranged) between two persons, animals, holders of certain beliefs, etc.": **The duke and the count fought a *duel*. They *dueled* for ten minutes.**

A. *Dual* pumps means _____ [How many?] pumps.

B. Is it correct to say that four teams are *dueling* for first place? _____

C. An automobile may have a _____ [*dual* or *duel*?] braking system.

8

A. two   B. No   C. dual

. . . .

Supply *dual* or *duel*:

A. Burr killed Hamilton in a _____ .

B. My first sports car had _____ carburetors.

C. The law has a _____ purpose: to beautify the park and to protect wildlife.

D. _____ing is illegal here.

9

emigrate and *emigrant* vs. *immigrate* and *immigrant*

Immigrants immigrate   Emigrants emigrate

Patrick and Colleen Doyle's ancestors *emigrated* from Ireland over a century ago. From the standpoint of Ireland, they were *emigrants*. The *e* in *emigrate* and *emigrant* means "out" or "away from."

The Doyles *immigrated* into the United States, where they were *immigrants*. The *im* in those two words means "into."

Using at least two of our four words, write one or more sentences about your ancestors or others who have come from abroad to live in the United States.

9

Model Answer

My ancestors emigrated from Denmark in 1870 and were among the first Danish immigrants to settle in northwestern Iowa.

·····························

Supply *emigrate, immigrate, emigrant,* or *immigrant*:

A. Millions of _____ s entered the United States from 1890 to 1914.

B. Most of them _____ _____ d from southern or central Europe and were happy that Americans allowed them to _____ .

C. Italians who remained at home were sorry to see the _____ s leave.

10

moral vs. *morale*

Morale (məRAL), with an *e*, means "the condition of one's spirits," as shown in such things as cheerfulness and willingness to work. It is a noun.

Moral (MORəl), with no *e*, has several meanings, usually referring to goodness or badness. It may be either an adjective or a noun. The plural *morals* often means "standards of conduct": **She has high morals.**

Supply *moral, morals,* or *morale* in each blank:

A. A person who makes a _____ judgment judges in terms of good and evil.

B. A group with low _____ is not likely to be cheerful.

C. She had a bad reputation. "She has the _____ of an alley cat," gossips asserted.

10

A. moral   B. morale
C. morals

·····························

Supply *moral, morals,* or *morale*:

A. Is Jack a _____ person?

B. Yes. He has excellent _____ .

C. He looks sad today. Is his _____ low?

D. Perhaps I have a _____ obligation to cheer him up.

11

Finish honestly: One thing I hope to remember from this lesson is that . . .

(In this frame, any answer that you consider honest and accurate is acceptable.)

Note: If, after completing Lessons 64–66, you still confuse any of the pairs of words, construct some short original sentences with the troublesome words and repeat them orally at intervals. *Hearing* the correct uses may help you to remember.

Lesson 64: Answers to Questions for Added Practice

1. A. accept B. except C. except D. accept **2.** A. advise, device B. prophesy, device C. advice, prophecies **3.** A. effect B. affect **4.** A. all ready B. already C. all ready, already **5.** A. alumnus B. alumna C. alumnae D. alumni E. alumni **6.** A. wreath B. breath C. wreathed D. breathe **7.** A. conscience B. consciousness C. conscious D. conscience **8.** A. duel B. dual C. dual D. Dueling **9.** A. immigrants B. emigrated, immigrate C. emigrants **10.** A. moral B. morals C. morale D. moral

65

Words Frequently Confused (II)
Among, between;   amount, number;
avocation, vocation;   cite, sight, site;
complement, compliment;
disinterested, uninterested;   eminent, imminent;
fewer, less;   healthful, healthy;   imply, infer;
principal, principle;   stationary, stationery

After writing your answer(s) in the right-hand column, check this column to see whether you have responded correctly. If you have made a mistake, or if you need more practice, do whatever is asked below the dotted line in each answer frame.

Answers to questions for added practice can be found at the end of each lesson.

Understanding and Applying the Principles

1

among vs. *between*

The scientist placed a marble *between* the two cubes.

The scientist placed a marble *among* several cubes.

Judging from the example above, we should use _____ [*among* or *between*?] when we are talking about a group of three or more things or persons, and we should use _____ _____ [*among* or *between*?] when we are talking about only two.

Answers and Added Practice

1

among, between

. . . .

Supply *among* or *between*:

A. A small white house once stood _____ Manhattan's skyscrapers.

B. It was _____ a thirty-story and a forty-story building.

C. It remained there because of an argument _____ a strong-willed woman and a giant corporation.

D. Finally the woman died, and soon another tall building spired upward _____ New York's other towering buildings.

2

amount vs. *number*; *fewer* vs. *less*

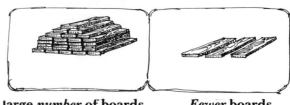

A large *number* of boards   ***Fewer* boards**

A large *amount* of sawdust   ***Less* sawdust**

A. Can you count sawdust? _____

B. Can you count boards? _____

C. If you cannot count something, you refer to its _____ _____ . [*amount* or *number*?]

D. If you can count something, you refer to its _____ . [*amount* or *number*?]

E. Is it correct to say *less* sawdust or *fewer* sawdust? _____ _____

F. Is it correct to say *less* boards or *fewer* boards? _____ _____

2

A. No B. Yes C. amount
D. number E. less F. fewer

. . . .

Supply *amount, number, fewer,* or *less*:

A. a large _____ of cans of oil

B. a large _____ of oil

C. _____ oil in this barrel

D. _____ cans of oil in this box

3

avocation vs. *vocation*

Your *vocation* is your job, your way of earning a living.

Your *avocation* is your hobby or sparetime activity. The *a* means "without," so an avocation is literally "without a job."

Laura Nichols is a member of a law firm. She is also a photographer and sometimes shows her pictures in amateur displays.

Is Laura's *avocation* law or photography? _____

3

photography

....

A. May one person's avocation be another's vocation? _____

_____

B. Give an example to show that your answer to question A is correct.

4

cite vs. *sight* vs. *site*

Cite is a verb with several meanings, three of which are illustrated here:

1. **To prove his point, Sam *cited*** [quoted, read from, summarized] **a paragraph from the textbook.**
2. **The lawyer *cited*** [called attention to] **a similar case.**
3. **Gordon Kranitz was *cited*** [given a special honor] **for heroic conduct.**

Sight as a verb means "to catch sight of": **We *sighted* a deer entering the grove.** As a noun it means "eyesight" or "something seen": **His *sight* is excellent. What a lovely *sight*!**

Site is ordinarily a noun, meaning "location": the *site* of the new church. Rarely, it may be a verb: **The church will be *sited*** [located] **at Oak and Market.**

Which, if any, of these words sometimes confuse you?

4

(Personal answer)

....

Supply *cite, sight,* or *site*:

A. The _____ of the house is on a hilltop.
B. The spring flowers are a pretty _____ .
C. I want to _____ two authorities.
D. Nancy was the first woman in her unit to be ____d for bravery.

5

complement vs. *compliment*

COMPLETE
COMPLETE
COMPLETE
COMPLETE
COMPLETE
COMPLETE
M
E
N
T

Complement (noun or verb) is always related to *complete*. Angles that *complement* each other *complete* a right angle. In sports a good defense may *complement* a good offense and thus *complete* a good team.

Compliment (noun or verb) involves saying something good about someone.

A. "What an attractive dress!" is a _____ .
B. A   The _____ of angle ABC is angle CBD.

C

B   D

5

    A. compliment
    B. complement

....

Supply *compliment* or *complement*:

    A. to pay an honest _____

    _____

    B. to _____
    one's wife on her good taste

    C. "We _____
    each other, Dear. I bring a
    hard business head to our
    marriage, and you bring
    culture."

6

disinterested vs. *uninterested*

Many careful speakers and writers are trying to preserve for *disinterested* its meaning of "impartial, favoring neither one nor another."

    Uninterested means "not interested."

    A. A baseball umpire should be _____

    but not _____ .

    B. I'm really _____ in
    baseball. It bores me.

6

    A. disinterested, uninterested
    B. uninterested

....

Supply *disinterested* or *uninterested*:

    A. A judge should be _____

    _____ .

    B. Pete is _____

    in chess. He goes to sleep.

7

eminent vs. *imminent*

Eminent means "famous, noted, highly respected": **an eminent aeronautical engineer.**

    Imminent means "on the verge of happening":
The two men were shouting angrily. A fight seemed *imminent*.

    A. Lightning was flashing. A storm was _____ .
    B. Barbara Tuchman, the author of several remarkable books, is an _____ historian.

7

    A. imminent B. eminent

....

Supply *eminent* or *imminent*:

    A. She became _____
    _____ while
    still young.

    B. When that driver ran the
    stop sign, a crash appeared
    _____ .

    C. A Democratic victory, I be-
    lieve, is _____ .

8

healthful vs. *healthy*

Most careful speakers and writers use *healthy* to mean only "having good health." They use *healthful* to mean "good for one's health."

    Which would they use to describe each of these?

    A. dishes of carrots and other vegetables _____
    B. a pleasant sea breeze _____
    C. most athletes _____
    D. an occasional vacation _____

8

    A. healthful   B. healthful
    C. healthy   D. healthful

Supply *healthful* and *healthy* to fit each of these:

    A. a vigorous spinach plant growing in the garden _____ _____

    B. spinach being eaten _____ _____

    C. a well person _____ _____

    D. Smoking and drinking are not _____ .

9

imply vs. *infer*

If you *imply* something, you hint it or say it indirectly: **The governor *implied* that taxes will be raised again.**

    It is the receiver of the message who *infers* something. That is, the listener or reader concludes that something is true even though not stated directly: **From what the governor said, we *inferred* that taxes will be raised again.**

    A. While you were speaking, I _____ed that you have an abnormal fear of crawling things.

    B. I didn't intend to _____ that. It is true, though, that I don't like snakes.

9

    A. inferred   B. imply

Supply *imply* or *infer*:

    A. When you said that, did you mean to _____ that snakes are worthless?

    B. No, you shouldn't _____ _____ that from what I said. I meant to _____ _____ only that I am afraid of them.

10

principal vs. *principle*

Principal comes from Latin *princeps*, meaning "chief." The *principal* of a school is its "chief" officer. The *principal* city in a state is its "chief" city.

    Principle means a "rule" or a "truth on which other truths may be based."

    A. "The _____ of the school is my *pal*," George said smugly.

    B. It helps to associate the *le* of *rule* with the *le* of _____ .

10

    A. principal   B. principle

Supply *principal* or *principle*:

    A. The _____ occupation in this area is coal mining.

    B. Every machine is based on at least one scientific _____ .

    C. The _____ _____ of this machine is that gravity pulls rather than pushes.

11

stationary vs. *stationery*

Stationary, spelled with *ary*, means "not moving": Cars in a traffic jam are *stationary*.

    Stationery, with *ery*, refers to writing paper, envelopes, and so on: Remember the *er* of *letter* and of *stationery*.

    A. The weather map shows a _____ front, which may not move at all today.

    B. Maybelle likes light-blue _____ with small flowers.

11

     A. stationary   B. stationery

· ·

Supply *stationary* or *stationery*:

    A. My father had some _____

     _____ printed with his name and address.

    B. A hummingbird sometimes appears to be _____

     _____ as it sips from a flower.

    C. Let's get Mom some _____

     _____ for her birthday.

12

Finish honestly: One thing I hope to remember from this lesson is that . . .

(In this frame, any answer that you consider honest and accurate is acceptable.)

Lesson 65: Answers to Questions for Added Practice

1. A. among B. between C. between D. among **2.** A. number B. amount C. less D. fewer **3.** A. Yes B. MODEL: For many people, fishing is an avocation, but for some it is a vocation. **4.** A. site B. sight C. cite D. cited **5.** A. compliment B. compliment C. complement **6.** A. disinterested B. uninterested **7.** A. eminent B. imminent C. imminent **8.** A. healthy B. healthful C. healthy D. healthful **9.** A. imply B. infer, imply **10.** A. principal B. principle C. principal principle **11.** A. stationery B. stationary C. stationery

═66═

Words Frequently Confused (III)
Allusion, delusion, illusion;   anxious, eager;
censor, censure;   climactic, climatic;
credible, creditable, credulous;   detract, distract;
genius, talent;   learn, teach;   noted, notorious;
respectable, respectful, respective

After writing your answer(s) in the right-hand column, check this column to see whether you have responded correctly. If you have made a mistake, or if you need more practice, do whatever is asked below the dotted line in each answer frame.

Answers to questions for added practice can be found at the end of each lesson.

Understanding and Applying the Principles

1

allusion vs. *delusion* vs. *illusion*

An *allusion* is an indirect reference or a brief mention; the word is related to the verb *allude*: **Senator Rand did not discuss the law, although he made an *allusion* to it.**

A *delusion* is a false and possibly harmful belief: **Some patients in mental hospitals have the *delusion* that they are Napoleon or even God.**

An *illusion* is a misleading appearance, often something that appears to be present but actually is not: Most magic tricks are *illusions*. A mirage is an *illusion*.

A. Ghosts, most modern people believe, are _____
_____ s .

B. Belief in ghosts is a(n) _____ .

C. Betsy made no _____ s to her former husband.

Answers and Added Practice

1

    A. illusions B. delusion
    C. allusions

. . . .

Supply *allusion, delusion,* or *illusion*:

    A. Belief in elves is, unfort-
       unately, a(n) _____
       _____ .

    B. Many of the things he saw
       were _____ s :
       apparitions, phantoms,
       specters.

    C. The story seems to contain
       several _____ s
       to the author's early life.

2

anxious vs. *eager*

An *anxious* person feels *anxiety.* He or she is worried or fearful that something bad may happen: **She is *anxious* about her grades. He's *anxious* about getting captured.**

    Eager is a more cheerful, more hopeful word. A person is *eager* for something awaited with pleasant expectation: **You are *eager* to be free. We are *eager* for some good home-cookin'.**

    A. Kenneth was _____ for the bus to come, because it would bring his best friend.

    B. Luella was _____ , because at two o'clock she would learn the results of her medical tests.

2

    A. eager B. anxious

. . . .

Supply *anxious* or *eager*:

    A. Probably most students be-
       come _____
       before important examina-
       tions.

    B. Probably most students are
       _____ for
       summer vacation.

3

beside vs. *besides*

Beside means "by the side of" or "next to": **Our kitten was lying *beside* two puppies.**

    Besides means "in addition (to)": **I was late; *besides,* my shoes were muddy. *Besides* muddy shoes, I was wearing soaking wet clothing.**

    A. _____ being adorable, the kitten is house-broken.

    B. It stands _____ the refrigerator and meows.

3

    A. Besides B. beside

. . . .

Supply *beside* or *besides*:

    A. I am tired, and hungry ____
       _____ .

    B. _____ being
       tired, I am hungry.

    C. I had to work _____
       a noisy engine all day.

4

censor vs. *censure*

The meaning of *censor,* both noun and verb, is most easily re-membered by its relation to *censorship*: A *censor censors* material that he or she believes other people should not see or hear.

    Censure, also a noun and verb, refers to blame, reprimand, or finding fault: **The court *censured* the defendant for arriving late.**

    A. Once plays were _____ ed if they contained profane or obscene language.

    B. The _____ s insisted that objectionable parts be cut out or modified.

    C. One author and director were legally _____ ed because they failed to make certain changes.

4

    A. censored B. censors

    C. censured

....

Supply *censor* or *censure*:

The legal _____
was given wide publicity in the
news media, which of course
could not print the scenes to
which the _____s
had objected.

5

climactic vs. *climatic*

Climactic means "pertaining to the climax": **At the *climactic* moment in our play, the gun that was supposed to shoot the villain didn't go off, so the heroine just said "Bang!"**

    Climatic means "pertaining to climate": *Climatic* **conditions vary considerably from Tucson to Flagstaff.**

    A. _____ conditions include temperature and precipitation as observed over a long period of time.

    B. A story is often most effective if it has a _____ arrangement.

5

    A. Climatic B. climactic

....

Supply *climatic* or *climactic*:

    A. The _____ scene of a play is not necessarily at the very end.

    B. The Weather Channel sometimes comments on _____ features of various places.

6

credible vs. *creditable* vs. *credulous*

A story or anything else that is believable is *credible*: **The judge shook his head as if he did not consider the testimony *credible*.**

    A *creditable* person or action is worthy of praise, worthy of being given credit: **Jill Sloan gave a *creditable* performance as Ophelia.**

    A *credulous* person is naive: he or she will believe almost anything.

    The negative forms, used about as often as the positive ones, are *incredible, uncreditable,* and *incredulous.*

    A. _____ people are sometimes left holding the bag in a snipe hunt.

    B. In Shakespeare's *As You Like It* the "bad guys" become "good guys" at the end. Such sudden reforms are not _____ .

    C. The pupils were commended for their _____ _____ attendance record.

6

    A. Credulous B. credible
    C. creditable

. . . .

Supply *credible, creditable,* or *credulous*:

    A. Never having been far from home, she was much too _____ .

    B. Stealing from one's own family is hardly a _____ _____ act.

    C. "Time passes so rapidly," the old man said. "It's in _____ that the century is already nearing its end."

7

detract vs. *distract*

Detract, usually followed by *from*, means "to take away, to reduce," especially something abstract, such as beauty or reputation: **Having too many gadgets on a car can *detract* from its appearance.**

    Distract means "to take attention away from something": **The flashing lights *distracted* Cal so much that he drove into a ditch.**

    A. Joe's nervousness _____ ed from the credibility of his story.

    B. While I was studying French, angry voices from next door _____ ed me.

7

    A. detracted B. distracted

. . . .

Supply *detract* or *distract*:

    A. Some people are more easily _____ ed by street noises than others are.

    B. His profane language _____ ed from his reputation.

8

genius vs. *talent*

Both *genius* and *talent* refer to inborn ability, but usually genius is considered stronger and even more praiseworthy. It refers to great powers of mind, or to creative power, or to one who has such powers.

    Talent is more restricted and does not necessarily suggest high intelligence or creative ability: **Rodney's basketball *talent* was obvious to the coaches.**

    A. Lucy's musical _____ became evident when she started playing a toy xylophone at the age of five.

    B. Marie Curie, who won a Nobel Prize for her discovery of metallic radium, was unquestionably a _____ .

    C. Her _____ was also shown in her innovative work on uranium and polonium.

8

   A. talent B. genius
   C. genius

....

Supply *genius* or *talent*:

   A. John Havlicek of the Boston Celtics had more basketball _____ than most other players of his time.

   B. Margaret Mead, the distinguished anthropologist, was certainly a person of

   _____ .

9

learn vs. *teach*

A learner *learns*: **In chemistry we are *learning* about the major elements.**
A teacher *teaches*: **Mr. Kalb is *teaching* us about the periodic table.**

   A. Our history teacher is _____ing us about life in Colonial days.

   B. She has _____ [*learned* or *taught*?] us about the Colonists' simple amusements.

9

   A. teaching B. taught

....

Supply *learn* or *teach*:

   A. Dad _____ [*learned* or *taught*?] us to identify several constellations.

   B. I'm going to _____ my friends to identify them.

10

noted vs. *notorious*

Noted has about the same meaning as *famous*. *Notorious* has about the same meaning as *infamous*: "well known for misdeeds or wickedness."

   A. People who do good things may become _____ .

   B. People who do evil things may become _____ .

10

   A. noted B. notorious

....

Supply *noted* or *notorious*:

   A. John Dillinger was a _____ bank robber.

   B. Lefty Gomez was a _____ baseball pitcher for the Yankees.

11

respectable vs. *respectful* vs. *respective*

A *respectable* person is decent, honest, and worthy of respect. *Respectable* clothing is modest and fairly good.

A *respectful* person shows respect and is normally polite and considerate.

Respective (a word often used when it is not really necessary) means "in the order mentioned": **The Dons and the Bruins were warming up by shooting at their *respective* baskets at our left and right.**

   A. The girl addressed the older woman courteously, in a _____ tone of voice.

   B. Her skirts were so short that the other women thought they were not _____ .

   C. When baseball announcer Dizzy Dean said, "The runners go back to their *respectable* bases," he meant _____ .

11

    A. respectful B. respectable
C. *respective*

. . . .

Supply *respectable, respectful,* or *respective*:

    A. The watch, the bracelet, and the necklace belong to Karen, Colleen, and Catherine _____ ly.

    B. The servants all bowed _____ ly as Sir Cedric entered.

    C. Banker Cartwright is considered one of the most _____ men in town.

12

Finish honestly: One thing I hope to remember from this lesson is that . . .

(In this frame, any answer that you consider honest and accurate is acceptable.)

Lesson 66: Answers to Questions for Added Practice

1. A. delusion B. illusions C. allusions **2.** A. anxious B. eager **3.** A. besides B. Besides C. beside **4.** censure, censors **5.** A. climactic B. climatic **6.** A. credulous B. creditable C. incredible **7.** A. distracted B. detracted **8.** A. talent B. genius **9.** A. taught B. teach **10.** A. notorious B. noted **11.** A. respectively B. respectfully C. respectable

Mastery Test
Diction and Style

For directions, see page 233.

48. a. My topic was a topic that was too big for an essay.   A U

    b. The tutor in the writing lab she agreed that my topic was too big.   A U

    c. One of my problems in the writing line is due to the fact that I can't reduce an idea down to something smaller in size.   A U

49. a. Jim Williams, our first-string quarterback, made more completions for more yardage than any quarterback in our conference.   A U

    b. Jim's brother kicked more field goals than any other place kicker in the conference.   A U

    c. I keep track of football statistics more than my roommate.   A U

50. a. Our communications professor remembered Carl, who had been absent, had not given his speech.   A U

    b. Carl is usually as convincing, or even more convincing, than anyone else I know.   A U

    c. Carl's speech stressed the importance of having a résumé in the placement office before graduating college.   A U

51. a. In the subway car today, ten men were sitting and an old, crippled woman standing.   A U

    b. The woman was carrying a bag of groceries and the men all pretending not to see her.   A U

    c. I guess that most men today never have and never will give up their seats.   A U

52. a. A sharp pain was felt by me as I walked across the dark room.   A U

    b. My shin was struck by a large object in the middle of the room.   A U

    c. Finally the light was turned on by me, and I could see that my roommate had not put the chair where it belonged.   A U

53. a. There were several hundred students waiting in line at the ticket window.   A U

    b. There are many students who will not bother to purchase their tickets early.   A U

    c. Several notices about early ticket sales appeared in the campus newspaper three weeks ago.   A U

54. a. The car was completely out of control, it seemed to us.   A U

    b. John, who was walking with me, saved my life.   A U

    c. John is more observant than I am when crossing the street, usually.   A U

55. a. While biking with my friends, I broke my leg, ripped my pants, and broke my shoelace.   A   U

    b. My friends cheered me up, hid my broken bike in some bushes, and pushed me on a good bike for six miles over country roads.   A   U

    c. From this experience I have learned that my friends can act in an emergency, know some good jokes, and know how to hide a bike.   A   U

56. a. Graduating from this college will be like dancing on the pink ruffles of clouds emblazoned by a gorgeous sunrise.   A   U

    b. I can see myself striding across the stage with a smile on my face and the diploma in my hand.   A   U

    c. I will be exquisitely intoxicated by the ambrosia that will exude from my own sense of academic achievement.   A   U

57. a. We are only two games into the season and already our team is as hot as a two-dollar pistol.   A   U

    b. Each one of our players is as sly as a fox and as quick as a wink in moving the ball around the court.   A   U

    c. In a nutshell, we will be the team to beat.   A   U

58. a. Marcee died at least a million times waiting for Roger to call.   A   U

    b. After Roger called, Marcee showered and dressed in a second and was downstairs in a flash.   A   U

    c. Marcee gets so hysterical over Roger that it kills me to watch her.   A   U

59. a. If Becky doesn't get a handle on her courses, she will soon go down the drain.   A   U

    b. The only way to earn a college degree is to put one's shoulder to the wheel and swim against the tide.   A   U

    c. When I have a rough row to hoe, I always try to keep my head above water.   A   U

60. a. When I was through working in the stacks, my friends asked me to go out for snacks.   A   U

    b. Chuck, Charlotte, and Charlie wanted to go out for chili and chips.   A   U

    c. Maybe I am cheap, but I would rather stay in my apartment and eat chilled chopped chicken and chunks of cheese than spend my money on chili and chips.   A   U

61. a. To stop a car equipped with a manual transmission, first move your right foot from the accelerator pedal to the brake pedal and press down until the car is traveling only about ten miles an hour.   A   U

    b. When the kinetic activity of your four-wheeled passenger vehicle has dissipated sufficiently to reduce the forward motion to the aforementioned rate, position your left transverse metatarsal arch on the clutch pedal with sufficient downward pressure to separate the power-transmitting coupling between the engine and the transmission.   A   U

    c. With your left foot still holding the clutch pedal down, gradually but firmly press down on the brake pedal with your right foot until the car stops.   A   U

62. a. Paul, my roommate, and I have Ms. Charlotte Adams as a teaching assistant for Engineering 212.   A   U

    b. For a lady instructor, she knows a lot about engineering.   A   U

    c. Having a man-to-man talk about engineering with a pretty blonde lady instructor is really strange.   A   U

63. a. At least once last week, I could of eaten mostaccioli.   A   U

    b. The cafeteria dietitians don't vary there weekly menus very much.   A   U

    c. An university as large as this one should offer more variety in the residence hall cafeterias.   A   U

64. a. Mr. James Crowe, an alumnus, and Ms. Mary Robertson, an alumna, spoke to our class during Career Week.   A   U

    b. They offered some good advise on applying for positions with industry after graduation.   A   U

    c. Although I am only a sophomore, I learned some facts that will affect my choice of electives.   A   U

65. a. The fall schedule contained a large amount of courses that interested me.   A   U

    b. My first problem was choosing three courses between six I needed for my major field.   A   U

    c. After I made this decision, I picked two courses that would complement my minor field.   A   U

66. a. In my opinion, the climatic scenes in many television dramas about criminals and police officers are too violent.   A   U

    b. Beside showing murders and rapes, these scenes often include police brutality.   A   U

    c. I don't believe in censoring television detective dramas to the point where they are no longer true to life, but I do support censuring television writers and producers who emphasize violence to win high viewer ratings.   A   U

Answers to this test can be found on page 512.

IV

Punctuation
and
Mechanics

Diagnostic Test
Punctuation and Mechanics

Directions

Because each test item consists of three parts, a, b, and c, you will have three chances to test your knowledge of each principle. In some items, a, b, or c will contain only one sentence or word group; in others each will include two or more sentences. In this test, you must decide quickly whether or not the punctuation, capitalization, and other mechanics in a, b, and c would be acceptable in a college essay. If you believe that the mechanics are acceptable in 1. a, for example, circle the letter A. If you believe that one or more of these mechanical features are unacceptable, circle the letter U.

Sample Item

1. a. John screamed, "Look out! You'll hit that dog!" U

   b. Mary said, "The light just turned red, George." U

   c. These are just two examples of the kinds of reaction my friends have when I drive them anywhere! A

Note: *The sample item tests acceptable uses of the exclamation mark. In sentence a, exclamation marks are appropriate after* out *and* dog *because John screamed these warnings. An exclamation mark is not needed after* George *in b because Mary has only made a statement. In c the exclamation mark is inappropriate because the statement is long and not highly emotional.*

Some items in this test go beyond the most common marks of punctuation and focus on such matters as parentheses, brackets, dashes, slashes, abbreviations, capitalization, underlining, and the appropriate ways to write numbers.

How to Use the Test

Like the lessons in this book, this diagnostic test is self-instructional. When you have finished it, score it with the key provided on page 512. The test will measure your awareness of the punctuation and mechanics generally expected in college essays. Each test item will give you three chances to recognize acceptable punctuation, capitalization, and other mechanics.

If you miss one or more of the three chances, you should plan to do the corresponding lesson in the pages that follow. For example, making one or more errors in test item 70 means that you should do Lesson 70.

At the end of this group of lessons, on page 505, is a matching Mastery Test. Take that test after you have completed the needed lessons. It will show you the items in which you have improved and those in which you need further work. Study once more the lessons corresponding to the missed items.

67. a. Will you please turn right on Stadium Avenue.   A   U

    b. Northwestern Avenue is closed to all traffic.   A   U

    c. In preparation for the pedestrian tunnel, engineers have already started excavating people will not be able to drive on Northwestern until next fall.   A   U

68. a. I wonder whether all the new construction will make the campus look more attractive?   A   U

    b. Will the new Electrical and Materials Engineering Building completely block any view of the fountain from Northwestern Avenue.   A   U

    c. Will the campus no longer have a scenic entrance?   A   U

69. a. "What a racket! Blast those air-hammers!" exclaimed Paul.   A   U

    b. "Look out. You're going to walk into that barricade," yelled Susie.   A   U

    c. "Ouch," screamed Terry. "That wind blew some dirt into my eyes."   A   U

70. a. While Jill was shooting another player hit Jill's arm.   A   U

    b. After Jill tripped the referee blew his whistle.   A   U

    c. Of their top five four players fouled out of the game.   A   U

71. a. That short, muscular freshman is the highest scorer on our team.   A   U

    b. He is usually able to confuse taller heavier players.   A   U

    c. His specialty is a long arching shot.   A   U

72. a. The library, a good place to meet people, is always crowded at night.   A   U

    b. My roommate, Joe claims that it is the best place on campus to find a date for the weekend.   A   U

    c. The Sweet Shop in the Union, however works best for me.   A   U

73. a. Every student who brings a car to the campus must register it with the campus police.   A   U

    b. This regulation which seeks to limit campus traffic to authorized vehicles certainly doesn't help a student to find a parking place.   A   U

    c. Most students, who drive around campus, agree that the parking permit is only a hunting license.   A   U

74. a. I had left my calculus, chemistry, sociology, and English books on the bus.   A   U

    b. Someone might have given them to the driver to turn in at the bus company but I couldn't take that chance.   A   U

    c. I stopped a taxi and told the driver that the bus would make its next stops at College, Madison, and Tenth.   A   U

75. a. Many new students, do not realize, that computers, are available to them, in several places on campus.   A   U

    b. Major public terminal rooms are available in several buildings, and, microcomputer systems are located in schools and departments.   A   U

c. For example, the Department of English has microcomputers in its Writing Laboratory, as well as in a special classroom where students can refine their word-processing skills. A U

76. a. Registering for classes early is a wise move, appointments with advisors are easier to arrange then, even the most popular classes are open. A U

b. I always intend to register early, however, I am easily distracted, so I usually end up taking courses I really don't want. A U

c. My friends can't understand why I register so late every semester; but they don't know that I am an incurable procrastinator. A U

77. a. Newly elected Student Senate officers are Chad Raper, President; Mary Miller, Secretary; and Jeff Zimmerman, Treasurer. A U

b. This year the big issues are a stronger student voice at meetings of the Board of Trustees; more parking spaces for commuting students; rising student fees, a matter that comes up every year; and changes in the process for appealing grades. A U

c. I am somewhat optimistic that the Student Senate will be able to do something about stronger representation, parking spaces, and grade appeals; although rising student fees, which result from rising administrative costs, seem inevitable. A U

78. a. In order to be considered for admission as a transfer student, I had to ask that my transcripts be sent from: Parkside Community College, Bradley University, and Northwestern University. A U

b. This statement in the University Bulletin caught me by surprise: "Grades are not transferred; only credit in the course is recorded." A U

c. After I saw this statement, I said in a quick note to Dad: "Well, it looks as though I'll have to prove myself all over again." A U

79. a. I had only ten minutes before the library closed, and I still hadn't referred to *Modern English: A Glossary of Literature and Language.* A U

b. The next day, though, I ran to the library at 8:00 a.m. and found the information before my class started. A U

c. Studying late, missing breakfast, doing an assignment at the last minute: those are facts of life for me this semester. A U

80. a. It's going to rain again, so he'd better not lecture past the class period. A U

b. He'll go on and on, and we'll get wet for sure, but he doesn't care. A U

c. No day is without it's problems. A U

81. a. Big Mouth's drive-in hamburger restaurant advertises students' favorites during the first week of each semester. A U

b. Tom's friends always order triple Belly Busters, but Jake's friends prefer the giant Frisbee Burgers from the Bunyan Burger carry-out restaurant.   A   U

c. My roommate and I wait for Bunyan Burgers' special on Babe's Cowchips, the biggest burgers around.   A   U

82. a. I finally learned the positions of all letters from the *a*'s to the *z*'s on most typewriters, and I even learned the positions of such symbols as the @'s and the +'s.   A   U

b. With this knowledge, I thought I could type easily on a computer keyboard, but I found *Esc*'s, *Ctrl*'s, *Alt*'s, and other strange-looking symbols.   A   U

c. Now I even have to worry about *f*'s all the way from *f1*'s to *f10*'s.   A   U

83. a. I asked my advisor whether I could drop Modern C-ommunications 110.   A   U

b. He said that it was too late to withdraw without my professor's signature.   A   U

c. I didn't want a failing grade to appear on my transcript, so I went through the process.   A   U

84. a. All twenty-three men in our fraternity worked on our display for the homecoming weekend.   A   U

b. The material cost us over one-hundred dollars, but at least we didn't have to pay for labor.   A   U

c. We also cooperated in funding the project by putting five- and ten-dollar contributions into a box in the hall.

85. a. Yesterday my campaign posters—but you probably know the story.   A   U

b. I tacked them up—the large yellow ones—in authorized spaces, but someone took them down.   A   U

c. From this experience I have learned that honesty and/or fair play is missing from our campus this 1988/89 school year.   A   U

86. a. Hugh didn't realize it (he was in a big hurry), but he left his books under his seat.   A   U

b. I made an effort to tell him, I even ran outside and looked in the parking lot, but I couldn't catch him.   A   U

c. I was stuck with more books than I could carry around all morning (fifteen, to be exact), so I left his books in the English office.   A   U

87. a. The University Bulletin says, "Also offered in the summer are intensive courses [four-week classes] and workshops."   A   U

b. The Summer Bulletin lists one interesting course as follows: "Engl. 302, Sports Lit., wks. 1–4, M–F 1:30–3:20, [Professor] A. R. Weeks."   A   U

c. I guess that even a university isn't perfect, because I found this statement in the catalog: "The usual semmer [*sic*] session is eight weeks."   A   U

88. a. As I left the room I said, "Have a nice weekend, Professor Smith."   A   U

b. With a smile, Professor Smith replied, "You have forgotten some unfinished business."   A   U

c. She said that my paper was due by noon.   A   U

89. a. Yesterday my roommate said, "Let's go on a double date this Saturday night".   A   U

b. "I realize," he said, "that we haven't gone on a double date this year."   A   U

c. Then he asked, "Does your girlfriend know of a girl who might like to go with me"?   A   U

90. a. Cary said, "Our campus disc jockey keeps playing the song 'Trash, Trash, Trash.'"   A   U

b. "I have heard," Paula chimed in, "'that a new group called The Garbage Collectors will have a concert here Friday night.'"   A   U

c. At that point, Tom smiled and asked, "Has anyone ever heard the expression 'One man's trash is another man's treasure'?"   A   U

91. (In a, b, and c, note especially the indentation and quotation marks in paragraphs of conversation.)

a.   "Please don't ask me about the test," Terry moaned. "I'm too exhausted to think about it."   A   U

   "By the way, are you hungry?" he went on.

b.   After about one second of silence, John replied, "I could never eat without knowing about the test."   A   U

   Sensing that Terry would also be tired after lunch, Tom added, "This will take only about five minutes."

c.   Paula, who had just walked up, said, "Well, Terry, how was the test? Tell us about it."   A   U

   "Are you prepared for the worst?" Terry grumbled.

92. a. The article "Thoreau and Human Nature" prompted me to read Thoreau's essay "Civil Disobedience."   A   U

b. The chapters in Thoreau's book Walden have such titles as *Sounds, Brute Neighbors,* and *Higher Laws.*   A   U

c. Thoreau's poem "Independence" is published in this anthology.   A   U

93. a. After explaining how comedy can result from using the wrong word, Professor Bower assigned Sheridan's play *The Rivals.*   A   U

b. Professor Bower went on to tell us that the name of Mrs. Malaprop, a character who mistakenly believed she spoke English *par excellence,* gave rise to the term *malapropism.*   A   U

c. The professor also told us that modern examples of malapropism, which is written with a small m, are often ridiculed in *The New Yorker* magazine.   A   U

94. a. Mr. Jonathan Kenner, Jr., received an invitation to attend a reception in Washington, D.C., with a request to R.S.V.P. by Saturday, August 10.   A   U

b. Mr. Kenner's secretary had scheduled a 10:30 a.m. flight on TWA 930, but Mr. Kenner canceled this arrangement and took one of his company's jets.   A   U

c. I guess it doesn't hurt to dream, but right now this undergraduate student has to get his book pack together & head for the library.   A   U

95. (In this item, a, b, and c are parts of a letter.)

a. Dear Dean Riley,   A   U

b.   Everyone in our class was astonished when Professor Brown said, "This will probably be my last year at State."   A   U

c.   All of us are of one opinion: Professor Brown is an excellent teacher who should be encouraged to stay at this university.
Sincerely Yours,   A   U

96. a. I grew up in the midwest, so I wanted to go to college in the east, the west, or the south.   A   U

b. I finally decided to attend the University of California at Davis, so I packed up and drove west in my restored Corvette.   A   U

c. I had read about the school in *A Guide To American Universities*.   A   U

97. a. My uncle, who served as a lieutenant in Vietnam, majored in Russian and political science in college.   A   U

b. Now he teaches military science in a college and has the military title of Colonel Anderson on his door.   A   U

c. Uncle John and Dad, who was a Sergeant in Vietnam, never talk about their war experiences.   A   U

98. a. Old Man Winter is especially unkind to us well-dressed women on campus.   A   U

b. Our high-heeled designer boots may look fashionable, but they are not very safe on icy walkways during the winter.   A   U

c. Vera, whose nicknames are Mademoiselle and Vera Vogue, doesn't let the ice spoil her image.   A   U

99. a. Center Community College on Sixth Street admitted its first students in the fall of nineteen hundred fifty-seven.   A   U

b. The total enrollment was only 675.   A   U

c. This fall, almost twenty thousand students are enrolled in twelve programs during the day, and in eight programs and ten non-credit classes during the evening.   A   U

100. a. At the end of play rehearsal Thursday, Dave still hadn't learned his short part, which began on line 33 in Act II, Scene 1 and included only six lines.   A   U

b. Friday afternoon, after calling him repeatedly at 352,7168 until 5:30 p.m., we stopped at his apartment at 1951 Vine Street.   A   U

c. When we arrived at the theater 30 minutes before curtain time, 2694 tickets had been sold, but no one had seen Dave.   A   U

Answers to this test can be found on page 512.

The Period:
Everything Must Stop Somewhere

After writing your answer(s) in the right-hand column, check this column to see whether you have responded correctly. If you have made a mistake, or if you need more practice, do whatever is asked below the dotted line in each answer frame.

Answers to questions for added practice can be found at the end of each lesson.

Understanding and Applying the Principles

1

If we had no periods or capital letters, sentences would be run together, like this:

> **she turned on the light and looked at the clock it was only three o'clock she yawned and wondered whether morning would ever come**

Are those unpunctuated lines *harder* or *easier* to read than most printed material? _____

Answers and Added Practice

1

Harder

. . . .

A. In Frame 1, insert the needed capitals and periods.

B. Do the same for this:

the doldrums are a belt of slight but shifty winds just north of the equator is the area in which they encircle the earth the tradewinds are on both sides of them

2

A period is used most often at the end of the kind of sentence that makes a statement. This is often called a *declarative sentence* because it "declares" something to be true.

In this frame, you have read two declarative sentences before this one.

A. The first of those declares that the most frequent place for a period is after _____ _____. [What?]

B. The second declares that the reason for the name *declarative* is that such a sentence _____ _____. [Does what?]

2

  A. a sentence that makes a statement

  B. "declares" something to be true

· ·

  A. In the example in Frame 1 are _____ [How many?] declarative sentences.

  B. How many are in the example in Answer Frame 1? _____

3

periods are useful in some cases they keep us from misreading a group of words that closes with a period is likely to be a declarative sentence

  A. The first sentence in that passage probably ends with _____ [What word?] but may conceivably end with _____ .

  B. The second sentence definitely ends with _____ .

  C. Does the passage illustrate the fact that periods sometimes prevent misreading? _____

3

  A. *useful, cases*

  B. *misreading*

  C. Yes

· ·

I finally found my present hidden under the tree was a tiny black box.

A period and a capital letter are needed after _____ . [What word?]

4

writing should be clear communication between writer and reader is the goal

  A. Did you misread the example—at least for a moment? _____

  B. Periods belong after the words _____ and _____ .

4

  A. (Probably)

  B. *clear, goal*

· ·

In Frame 4 the words _____ _____ and _____ should be capitalized.

5

Two or more sentences that are run together, like those in Frames 1, 3, and 4, are often called *run-on sentences*. The run-on sentence is generally considered a serious error. The chief reason is that run-on sentences are often _____ [*easy* or *difficult*?] to understand.

(Lesson 10 provides more information about run-on sentences and the similar comma splices.)

5

difficult

....

How can punctuation make this sentence more appetizing, or at least more clear?

Charlie went off by himself to eat the lizards squirming in the cage beside me spoiled my appetite.

6

Put a period after each sentence that makes a statement. Also, please put a period after each sentence that expresses a request or a mild command.

The two sentences above are requests or mild commands.

What punctuation mark is used after a request or a mild command? _____

6

period

....

please bring in firewood then start a fire

The words _____ and _____ _____ should be capitalized, and _____ [What marks?] should be placed after _____ and _____ .

7

Will you please think about your readers when you write.

Sometimes a request is worded like a question. The example shows that such a request is punctuated with a _____ .

7

period

....

Capitalize and punctuate the following:

capitalize each word that begins a sentence put in the necessary punctuation marks

---

8

To summarize:

   A. In Frame 2 we noted that a period should be used after a sentence making a _____ .

   B. In Frames 3–5, we saw that omission of punctuation can sometimes cause _____ .

   C. In Frame 6 we noted that a sentence making a _____ _____ or a _____ _____ should end with a period.

   D. In Frame 7 we observed that a request worded like a _____ should also be punctuated with a _____ .

Note: Incomplete sentences should not be confused with complete ones. See Lessons 1 and 2, which deal with fragments of sentences. For abbreviations, see Lesson 94.

8

    A. statement
    B. misreading
    C. request, mild command
    D. question, period

....

9

Using the letters *A*, *C*, and *D* for principles stated in Frame 8, tell why a period is at the end of each of the following sentences.

    A. Look at that covered wagon over there. _____
    B. Will you take a picture of it for me, please. _____
    C. Covered wagons were also called "prairie schooners." _____

9

    A. C B. D C. A

....

Write a mild command about anything at all. Punctuate correctly.

10

Write a sentence starting with *Please* and asking someone to do something. Punctuate correctly.

10

Model Answer

    Please send me your latest catalog.

....

Rewrite your sentence, omitting *Please*.

11

Rewrite your answer to Frame 10. This time start with *Will you*. Punctuate correctly.

11

Model Answer

Will you please send me your latest catalog.

. . . .

The reason for the period instead of a question mark is that such a sentence is actually a request rather than a question.

12

Here is a very old jingle that makes sense when correctly punctuated and capitalized. List the nine words that should be followed by periods.

> A funny old man told this to me
> I fell in a snowdrift in June said he
> I went to a ball game out in the sea
> I saw a jellyfish float up in a tree
> I saw some gum in a cup of tea
> I stirred my cream with a big brass key
> I opened my door on my bended knee
> I beg your pardon for this said he
> But tis true when told as it ought to be
> Tis a puzzle in punctuation you see

——————— ——————— ——————— ———————

——————— ——————— ——————— ———————

———————

12

me, snowdrift, game, float, gum, cream, door, be, see

13

Finish honestly: One thing I hope to remember from this lesson is that . . .

(In this frame, any answer that you consider honest and accurate is acceptable.)

Lesson 67: Answers to Questions for Added Practice

1. A. She   clock.   It   o'clock   She   come. B. The   winds.   Just   earth.   The them. **2.** A. three B. three **3.** present (*Possible but unlikely*: hidden) **4.** Writing, Communication **5.** Add a period after *eat*, and capitalize *the*. **6.** *please, then,* periods, *firewood, fire* **7.** Capitalize each word that begins a sentence. Put in the necessary punctuation marks. **9.** MODEL: Bring me some garlic, Mama. **10.** MODEL: Send me your latest catalog.

68

Question Marks: Did She Smile?
I Wonder Whether She Really Did.

After writing your answer(s) in the right-hand column, check this column to see whether you have responded correctly. If you have made a mistake, or if you need more practice, do whatever is asked below the dotted line in each answer frame.

Answers to questions for added practice can be found at the end of each lesson.

Understanding and Applying the Principles

1

When the British talk about marks of punctuation, they often call them "stops." In your own words, explain why that is a good name for them.

Answers and Added Practice

1

Model Answer

"Stops" is a good name because most punctuation marks tell the reader where to stop or at least to slow down.

. . . .

In Shakespeare's *Midsummer Night's Dream*, an amateur actor mangles his lines by pausing in the wrong places. An observer comments, "He knows not the stop."

2

One mark that tells the reader when to stop is a period, which the British may call a "full stop." Another stop is the question mark.

As that name suggests, a question mark is used after a _____

_____ .

2

question

. . . .

A question mark could also be called a "full stop," but it seldom is. It is sometimes referred to as an "interrogation point" because it follows an interrogation (a question).

3

Did Margo smile at me?

I wonder whether Margo smiled at me.

The sentences above show that there are two kinds of questions.

Which of them asks a question for which an answer is definitely expected? _____ [*First* or *Second*?]

3

First

. . . .

Two more examples:

> **Has Margo spoken of me?**
>
> **I wonder whether Margo has
> ever spoken of me.**

The _____ [*first* or *second*?]
of those sentences asks a question
directly.

4

A question like *Did Margo smile at me?* or *Has Margo ever spoken
of me?* is called a *direct* question. It asks directly for an answer.

If someone asks you, "Will you go?" you realize that an answer is expected and you answer "Yes" or "_____" or possibly
"_____."

4

No, Perhaps (*or* "Probably,"
etc.)

. . . .

A large proportion of questions ask
directly for *yes* or *no* responses.
Most of the others ask *Who? What?
When? Where? Why?* or a variant
such as *How much?*

5

An indirect question, though, actually makes a statement.

   A. In *I wonder whether Margo smiled at me*, the statement is
      that I _____ . [Do what?]

   B. Although someone may respond after hearing "I won-
      der whether Margo smiled at me," that sentence does
      not ask directly for an _____ .

5

A. wonder　B. answer

. . . .

Look again at the examples in Answer Frame 3.

The _____ [*first* or *second*?] does not ask directly for
an answer.

6

An indirect question often contains the clue-word *whether* (for
which *if* is sometimes substituted) and always is worded like a
statement.

> **I asked whether Margo is a good dancer.**

That indirect question uses the clue-word _____ ,
and it makes the statement that I _____ (something).

6

whether, asked

. . . .

> **I inquired about the time
> when her plane was due.**

That indirect question _____
[*has* or *has no*?] clue-word, but it is
worded as a statement telling
that I _____ .
[Did what?]

7

   A. We have seen that a _____ [What kind of?]
      question asks directly for an answer and that it is punc-
      tuated with a _____ _____ .

   B. An _____ [What kind of?] question is
      really a statement; it requires no answer. It is punc-
      tuated with a _____ .

7

A. direct, question mark
B. indirect, period

....

1. **I asked when her plane would arrive**
2. **"What gate will that be   "**
3. **I wondered whether her plane would be late**

A. Sentences _____ and _____ are indirect questions.
B. Punctuate the three sentences correctly.

8

Two infrequent uses of question marks:

1. **"Margo said that?" I asked in astonishment.**
2. **Geoffrey Chaucer, (A.D. 1340?–1400)**

A. In 1, *Margo said that?* is actually a _____ [*question* or *statement*?] although it is worded like a _____ _____ . [*question* or *statement*?]
B. In 2, the question mark indicates _____ [*certainty* or *uncertainty*?] about the date of Chaucer's birth.

8

A. question, statement
B. uncertainty

....

A. "You love her   " Sid asked incredulously.
B. Shakespeare was born April 23   , 1564. (His exact birthdate is not known.)

Punctuate those sentences correctly.

9

In Frames 9 and 10, write a question mark and the word *Direct* after each direct question. Write a period and the word *Indirect* after each indirect question.

A. Joan asked whether I had seen Margo lately __ _____

B. Joan wondered when I had last seen Margo __ _____

C. "When did you last see Margo __" Joan asked. _____

Note: For the order of quotation marks with other marks, see Lesson 89.

9

A. .   Indirect
B. .   Indirect
C. ?   Direct

....

Follow the instructions in Frame 9.

A. I wondered how she would greet me __ _____

B. Did the plane arrive on time __ _____

10

A. "Are you in love with her __" _____
B. Joan asked bluntly whether I love Margo __ _____

C. Joan wondered why I was so reluctant to answer __ __

10

    A. ?   Direct
    B. .   Indirect
    C. .   Indirect

· ·

Follow the instructions in Frame 9.

    A. Did you really smile at me that time, Margo __ _____

        _____

    B. I wonder whether you'll always smile so enigmatically

        __ _____

11

Write an indirect question about the location of a library. Start with the words *I wonder*, or *I asked*. Punctuate correctly.

11

Model Answer

    I wonder (*or* I asked) where the public library is.

· ·

Following the instructions in Frame 11, write an indirect question about the moon.

12

Rewrite the sentence you wrote for Frame 11. Leave out *I wonder* or *I asked*, and make the sentence a direct question. Punctuate correctly.

12

Model Answer

    Where is the public library?

13

Finish honestly: One thing that I hope to remember from this lesson is that . . .

(In this frame, any answer that you consider honest and accurate is acceptable.)

Lesson 68: Answers to Questions for Added Practice

3. first **5.** second **6.** has no, inquired (about something) **7.** A. 1, 3 B. arrive. be? late. **8.** A. her? B. (?) **9.** A. .   Indirect B. ?   Direct **10.** A. ?   Direct. B. .   Indirect. **11.** MODEL: I wonder whether the moon will be full tonight.

69

Exclamation Marks: Wow! What a Surprise!

After writing your answer(s) in the right-hand column, check this column to see whether you have responded correctly. If you have made a mistake, or if you need more practice, do whatever is asked below the dotted line in each answer frame.

Answers to questions for added practice can be found at the end of each lesson.

Understanding and Applying the Principles

1

Wonderful! You deserve a medal!

If someone *exclaims* something, he or she says it with strong feeling and probably in a voice louder than usual.

What have you done which made someone exclaim the words at the top of this frame?

Answers and Added Practice

1

(Here's your chance to be boastful. Any answer is correct.)

....

What word or words are you likely to exclaim when a friend does something remarkable?

2

Hurrah! What a play!

The punctuation marks used above and in Frame 1 are called *exclamation marks* (sometimes *exclamation points*).

That is obviously a good name because *Hurrah!* and *What a play!* are _____. [What?]

2

exclamations (*or* exclamatory)

······································

A. What might you shout during a game when something excites and pleases you? ___

_____

_____

B. What might you shout when displeased? _____

_____

3

Oh! You startled me!

An exclamation often shows surprise, although it may also show strong feelings of other kinds.

What might someone shout in response to each of the following? Write each with an exclamation mark. Answers will vary.

A. Pain _____
B. Anger _____
C. Sorrow or disappointment _____
D. Joy _____
E. Fear _____

3

Model Answers

A. Ouch! Ow! That hurt!
B. Stop that! Damn!
C. Oh, I'm sorry! What a shame!
D. Great! How splendid!
E. Oh! Get that thing out of here!

4

Oh, I don't believe so.
Well, no.

Some exclamations, often including *oh* and *well*, are spoken mildly, conversationally. A comma or a period indicates that fact.

In **Oh?** what does the question mark indicate?

4

Doubt (*or* Disbelief, Uncertainty, etc.)

······································

Punctuate to show each of the following:

Hesitation: Well ___ I'll need to think about it.

Indignation: Well ___

Questioning: Well ___

Fury: Oh ___ I'm so angry I could bite a grizzly ___

5

Wonderful! and *What a play!* and most other exclamations do not have subjects and verbs, as nearly all sentences have. Sometimes, though, a short sentence with a subject and a verb may be an exclamation.

Examples of such exclamatory sentences are _____

_____ [Which words?] in Frame 1 and

_____ in Frame 3.

5

> You deserve a medal!
> You startled me!

....

Write a short exclamatory sentence or phrase to fit each situation.

A. You see a lovely but expensive coat.

B. Your best friend tells you she (or he) has just become engaged.

6

Exclamatory sentences are seldom more than eight or ten words long, and usually shorter than that. The reason is that it is hard to hold through a long sentence the high pitch and excitement of an exclamation.

> **"How remarkable it is that you have recalled so clearly that first meeting of ours, which took place over ten years ago!"** he exclaimed.

Is that a likely exclamation? _____

6

> No

....

The exclamatory complete sentences in Frames 1 and 3 are only _____ and _____ [How many?] words long.

7

Some students use too many exclamation marks. Sentence after sentence of exclamation can become tiring. Like spices, exclamations should be used with moderation. An "exclamatory style" is seldom a good style.

In addition, despite the practice of comic strip artists, one mark after an exclamation is enough.

> We should not write *Wonderful!! You deserve a medal!!!* but simply *Wonderful __ You deserve a medal __*

7

> Wonderful! . . . medal!

....

> **I love Idaho! Its mountains! Its streams! I like the people! I like its cities and its wild forests! It's a wonderful state!**

Granted that such praise of Idaho may be deserved, is that style also praiseworthy? _____

8

Of the following sentences, the one most likely to be punctuated with an exclamation mark is _____.

A. How beautifully she plays the piano

B. She plays the piano exceptionally well

C. I am surprised that she has been taking piano lessons for only a year

8

A
....

Rewrite the example in Answer Frame 7, making enough changes so that no more than one exclamation mark is needed. (Hint: Three sentences may be best.)

9

A. In Frame 8, how many exclamation marks are needed after sentence A? _____

B. If either B or C in Frame 8 should be punctuated with an exclamation mark, the more likely choice is _____ .

9

A. One   B. B
....

You unexpectedly scored a goal in a soccer game. What might you shout?

10

You have become angry with your five-year-old brother, Tommy, because he has drawn pictures on your walls. Write a couple of exclamations you may use when you catch him. Punctuate correctly.

10

Model Answer
Tommy! You've ruined my room!

11

Finish honestly: One thing I hope to remember from this lesson is that . . .

(In this frame, any answer that you consider honest and accurate is acceptable.)

Lesson 69: Answers to Questions for Added Practice

1. (Personal answer) **2.** (Personal answer) **4.** Well, (*or* Well—) Well! Well? Oh! grizzly! **5.** A. MODEL: If only it didn't cost so much! B. MODEL: Great! I'm so happy for you! **6.** four and three **7.** No **8.** MODEL: I love Idaho with its mountains and streams and wild forests. I like its people and its cities, too. It's a wonderful state! **9.** (Personal answer)

═70═

Commas to Prevent Misreading: Does Everyone Know Charles Marvin?

After writing your answer(s) in the right-hand column, check this column to see whether you have responded correctly. If you have made a mistake, or if you need more practice, do whatever is asked below the dotted line in each answer frame.

Answers to questions for added practice can be found at the end of each lesson.

Answers and Added Practice

1.

    A. Charles Marvin
    B. Marvin, Charles
    C. comma

. . . .

As everyone knows Charles Marvin may be the better choice.

In that sentence, a comma after *knows* would make one meaning clear. A comma after _____ [What word?] would make a different meaning clear.

Understanding and Applying the Principles

1

    1. **Does anyone know Charles Marvin?**
    2. **Does anyone know Charles, Marvin?**

  A. In 1, the questioner asks whether anyone knows _____ _____ _____. [Whom?]

  B. In 2, he asks _____ [Whom?] whether anyone knows _____. [Whom?]

  C. That difference in meaning exists because of the presence of one little punctuation mark, a _____.

2

    After we had eaten a big bear from the park came nosing around our camp.

  A. In reading that sentence, did you for a moment have the impression that we had eaten a big bear? _____

  B. To prevent that impression, we should put a comma after the word _____.

2

    A. Yes. (Didn't you?)

    B. *eaten*

....

While the soldiers were walking on the sergeant went forward to ask the lieutenant a question.

A comma after _____ [What word?] would prevent a momentary misreading.

3

We are on the west side of the village square. Just opposite the church stands white and lovely.

    A. Because the second of those sentences has no comma, a reader is likely to read "Just opposite the church." Did you do that? _____

    B. A comma after _____ [What word?] would make the meaning clear.

3

    A. (Probably)   B. *opposite*

....

Before that Tuesday had always been my favorite day of the week.

A comma after the word _____ would prevent a possible momentary misreading.

4

Sitting on our front porch, cars and buses constantly zoom along the highway in front of our house.

The sentence above shows that a comma cannot make a bad sentence good. It sounds as if the cars and buses were sitting on the front porch.

    If a sentence is not clear even when properly punctuated, it must be rewritten. Rewrite the example above, starting it with *Sitting on our front porch, we.*

4

Model Answer

    Sitting on our front porch, we could see cars and buses constantly zooming . . .

....

Leaning over the edge of the cliff a tiny stream could be seen far below.

Rewrite that sentence, making clear that the stream was not leaning.

5

Even though a comma cannot make a bad sentence good, it often _____ [*may* or *may not?*] prevent misreading.

5

may

. . . .

While the defensive players were taking over an official was wiping the ball dry.

A comma after the word _____ would prevent a possible misreading.

6

In Frames 6–8, a comma may prevent momentary misreading of each sentence. Write the word after which a comma is needed.

    A. Although Jim was patiently waiting for Molly to be so late was unreasonable. _____

    B. Years before she had married Jim. _____

6

    A. waiting   B. before

. . . .

In Answer Frames 6, 7, and 8, follow the directions in Frame 6.

From Mary Murphy first got the news. _____

7

    A. While the troops moved along the road became dusty.

      _____

    B. Everyone was safe but sane advice was clearly needed.

      _____

7

    A. along   B. safe

. . . .

I am trying now and then I was too lazy. _____

8

    A. When Alice left George was very unhappy. _____

    B. The soldiers retreated slowly but steadily the feeling of imminent defeat increased. _____

8

    A. left   B. slowly

. . . .

While I was bathing my father began calling me. _____

9

Write a sentence of your own, starting with *When Kevin walked in the door.* Make *door* the subject of the sentence. Use punctuation to make sure that a reader cannot misunderstand.

9

Model Answer

When Kevin walked in, the door slowly swung shut behind him.

. . . .

Follow the instructions in Frame 9, but start with **Shortly before the flag**. Use *flag* as the subject.

10

Finish honestly: One thing I hope to remember from this lesson is that . . .

(In this frame, any answer that you consider honest and accurate is acceptable.)

Lesson 70: Answers to Questions for Added Practice

1. *Charles* **2.** *on* **3.** *that* **4.** MODEL: Leaning over the edge of the cliff, we could see a tiny stream far below. **5.** *over* **6.** Mary **7.** now **8.** bathing. **9.** MODEL: Shortly before, the flag had flown at half-mast.

71

Commas: Sometimes a Substitute for and

After writing your answer(s) in the right-hand column, check this column to see whether you have responded correctly. If you have made a mistake, or if you need more practice, do whatever is asked below the dotted line in each answer frame.

Answers to questions for added practice can be found at the end of each lesson.

Understanding and Applying the Principles

1

A yellowish, soggy dumpling swam sullenly in a greasy liquid.

When you read aloud the sentence above, do you notice a pause after *yellowish?* _____

Answers and Added Practice

1

Yes

· ·

**The cool, moist air flowed
down the valley.**

If you read that sentence aloud,
you pause after _____ .

2

**A yellowish egg dumpling swam sullenly in a
greasy liquid.**

When you read that sentence aloud, is the pause after *yellowish*
as great as in Frame 1? _____

2

No

· ·

**The cool night air flowed
down the valley.**

Is the pause after *cool* as great as in
Answer Frame 1? _____

3

In Frame 1, *yellowish* and *soggy* are both adjectives, modifying
dumpling. That example suggests, then, that when two consecutive adjectives modify a following word, we pause between
them when we speak, and in writing we place a _____
[What mark?] between them.

3

comma

· ·

In Answer Frame 1, *cool* and _____
_____ are both adjectives
modifying _____ .

4

In Frame 2, however, *yellowish* and *egg* are not the same kind of
word. *Yellowish* is an adjective, but *egg* is basically a noun, although used there to modify. *Yellowish* tells about *egg dumpling*,
not just about *dumpling*.

The example suggests that in speaking we hardly pause between such words, and that in writing we _____ [*put*
or *do not put*?] a comma between them.

4

do not put

· ·

In Answer Frame 2, *cool* modifies
_____ _____ . For that
reason, we do not put a _____
between *cool* and *night*.

5

If you are ever puzzled about whether to put a comma between
words like *yellowish* and *soggy* or *yellowish* and *egg*, three tests are
possible.

One, as we have seen, is to read the sentence (or sentence
part) aloud. A natural, distinct pause after the first of the two
words suggests that a comma _____ [*is* or *is not*?]
needed.

5

is

....

Try the pause test after each, and write *Comma* or *No comma* in each blank:

    A. a large brick house _____

        _____

    B. a small cozy house _____

        _____

    C. a loud shrill whistle _____

        _____

    D. a little tin whistle _____

        _____

6

A second test is to reverse the two words. If they still make good sense, use a comma.

    A. Does *a soggy, yellowish dumpling* make sense? _____

    B. Does *an egg, yellowish dumpling* make sense? _____

    C. So this test, too, shows that a comma _____ [*is* or *is not?*] needed in Frame 1 but _____ [*is* or *is not?*] needed in 2.

6

    A. Yes B. No C. is, is not

....

Try the reversal test on the four items in Answer Frame 5. Are the results the same? _____

7

A third test—perhaps the simplest—is to try putting *and* between the two words. If they still make sense, use a comma.

    A. Does *yellowish and soggy dumpling* make sense? _____

    B. Does *yellowish and egg dumpling* make sense? _____

    C. Does this test give the same results as those in Frames 1 and 2? _____

7

    A. Yes B. No C. Yes

....

Try the *and*-test on the four items in Answer Frame 5. Are the results the same? _____

8

Glaciers advance slowly, ponderously.

In that sentence, two adverbs, *slowly* and *ponderously*, both modify *advance*.

    A. Would the two adverbs make sense if reversed? _____

    B. Would they make sense with *and* between them? _____

    C. Those tests show that between such adverbs both modifying the same word, a _____ [What mark?] is used.

8

    A. Yes B. Yes C. comma

....

She dances gracefully brilliantly.

Should a comma be placed between the adverbs? _____

Note: Avoid frequent use of two *-ly* adverbs together without an *and*, because the combination sounds awkward.

9

In Frames 9–11, apply one or more of the three tests to see whether or not a comma is needed in each group of words. If it is, write *Comma* in the blank.

    A. an old television set _____

    B. an old ugly radio _____

    C. a maroon sports shirt _____

    D. a tiny timid smile _____

9

    B. Comma   D. Comma

. . . .

In Answer Frames 9–11, follow the instructions in Frame 9.

    A. a tiny red-coated soldier __

    _____

    B. A tiny tin soldier _____

10

    A. a light gray necktie _____
    B. the strong silent type _____
    C. a short stocky man _____
    D. a short lead pencil _____

10

    B. Comma   C. Comma

. . . .

    A. a careless slipshod writer

    _____

    B. this small flat key _____

    C. the tall filing cabinet _____

    _____

11

    A. Airplanes droned constantly annoyingly. _____
    B. Airplanes droned rather annoyingly. _____

11

    A. Comma

. . . .

    A. Slowly sullenly, the convict stood up. _____

    B. Extremely slowly, the convict stood up. _____

12

Write a sentence in which you use two consecutive adjectives before the word *potatoes*. Apply one or more of the tests (Frames 5–7), and use a comma if necessary.

12

Model Answer

    The lumpy, watery potatoes were far from appetizing. [A comma should be used.]

13

Write a sentence in which you place one adjective before *shoestring potatoes*. Apply one of the three tests (or two or three if you wish), and punctuate your sentence correctly.

13

Model Answer

The rubbery shoestring potatoes were inedible.
[No comma should be used.]

14

Finish honestly: One thing I hope to remember from this lesson
is that . . .

(In this frame, any answer that you consider honest and accurate is acceptable.)

Lesson 71: Answers to Questions for Added Practice

1. *cool* **2.** No **3.** *moist, air* **4.** *night air*, comma **5.** A. No comma B. Comma C. Comma D. No comma **6.** Yes
7. Yes **8.** Yes **9.** A. Comma B. No comma **10.** A. Comma B. Comma C. No comma **11.** A. Comma B. No
comma

===**72**===

Commas with Interpolations: Inserting Useful Details

After writing your answer(s) in
the right-hand column, check this
column to see whether you have
responded correctly. If you have
made a mistake, or if you need
more practice, do whatever is asked
below the dotted line in each answer frame.

Answers to questions for added
practice can be found at the end of
each lesson.

Understanding and Applying the Principles

1

The ancestor of *interpolation* is a Latin word meaning "polish."
In a sentence, details provide "polish" in the form of additional
information that is useful but may not be absolutely necessary.

> **Mount Everest, the world's tallest mountain,
> is in the Himalayas.**

A. In that sentence the interpolated element is _____
_____.

B. What punctuation marks are used with it? _____

Answers and Added Practice

1

    A. *the world's tallest mountain*
    B. Commas

. . . .

The Amazon River, South America's longest stream, has its source in Peru.

    A. In that sentence the interpolation is _____ _____ _____.

    B. The interpolation is punctuated with _____.

2

In Frame 1 and Answer Frame 1, the interpolations are *appositives*. An appositive, generally a noun, renames something that comes just before it in the sentence.

    We'll now glance at several other kinds of interpolations. Copy each interpolated element in the blank.

Date

    On February 12, 1809, Abraham Lincoln was born. _____

State or county

    His birthplace was a log cabin in Hardin County, Kentucky. _____

Each of those interpolated elements is punctuated with a comma or commas.

Note: Unless a specific date or place accompanies the year and the state, commas are not needed: *in early 1809, in northern Kentucky.*

2

1809, Kentucky

. . . .

On January 24, 1986, Voyager 2 took informative photographs of Uranus. It had left Cape Canaveral, Florida, over eight years earlier.

    A. The two interpolations are _____ and _____ _____.

    B. Each is punctuated with __ _____.

3

Transition: words used to show relationship between statements

    General Custer's men, however, were overconfident.

Qualification or emphasis

    A slogan, in my opinion, sways the emotions rather than the intellect. A slogan, I repeat, discourages thought.

    A. Copy the three interpolations. _____ _____ _____

    B. Each is punctuated with _____.

3

    A. *however, in my opinion, I repeat* B. commas

. . . .

A slogan, in consequence, affects the mindless rather than the thoughtful.

The interpolation, _____ _____ [What two words?] has a _____ on each side.

4

Explanatory words in conversation

    "While you were away," Louise said, "Betty had chicken pox."

Note: Commas and periods go inside closing quotation marks. See Lesson 89 for details.

Absolute phrase—noun plus participle

    Her friends being in school, she was lonely.

Adjectives following their noun

    Poor Betty, itching and uncomfortable, had a difficult few days.

    A. Copy the three interpolations. _____

_____

_____

    B. Each is punctuated with _____.

4

    A. *Louise said,   Her friends being in school,   itching and uncomfortable*
    B. commas

. . . .

"Tell me," John requested, "why some slogans are more influential than others."

This interpolation, _____ _____ _____ [What two words?] has a _____ and _____ _____ on each side.

5

Mild exclamation, or *yes* or *no*

    Well, I suppose you're right.

Names in direct address

    Your guess was better than mine, Tom.

    A. Copy the two interpolations. _____ _____

    B. Because these interpolations come at the beginning or the end of a sentence, obviously only one _____ is needed.

5

    A. *Well, Tom* B. comma

. . . .

Oh, can you stop at the bookstore for me, Nancy?

The interpolations, _____ and _____ _____ , are each set off by _____ .

6

The interpolations we have glanced at have two things in common. One is that each provides a little information or "polish" that is useful but not completely essential.

    The other is that they are set off by _____ . [What marks?]

6

commas

....

Referring if necessary to Frames 2–5, list ten kinds of interpolations.

7

In each sentence in Frames 7–10, insert a comma or commas to set off the interpolation. Do not add any other commas.

    A. James A. Garfield the twentieth President was shot by an office-seeker.

    B. The shooting occurred on July 2 1881.

    C. The assassin Charles J. Guiteau had failed to secure a political appointment.

7

    A. . . . Garfield, the twentieth President, . . .

    B. . . . July 2, 1881

    C. . . . assassin, Charles J. Guiteau, . . .

....

In Answer Frames 7–10, follow the instructions in Frame 7.

The sage grouse also called "cock of the plains" lives in the West.

8

    A. Garfield Heights Ohio is named for the twentieth President.

    B. Yes Garfield Heights is a suburb of Cleveland.

    C. Have you any other question George about Garfield?

8

    A. . . . Heights, Ohio, . . .

    B. Yes, Garfield . . .

    C. . . . question, George, . . .

....

The sage grouse I insist could not be seen in the Appalachians.

9

    A. "Lefty Grove" Grandpa said "was one of baseball's greatest pitchers."

    B. Grove won sixteen straight games a record number in his best year.

    C. His team having won the pennant he added two more victories in the World Series.

9

    A. . . . Grove," Grandpa said, . . .

    B. . . . games, a record number, . . .

    C. His team having won the pennant, . . .

....

A variety of ruffed grouse however does live in the East.

10

    A. A floodplain a deposit of sediment from a river is often very large.

    B. The floodplain of the Mississippi for instance is as much as eighty miles wide.

    C. The soil of a floodplain I should add is usually fertile.

10

    A. ... floodplain, a deposit ... river, is ...

    B. ... Mississippi, for instance, is ...

    C. ... floodplain, I should add, is ...

....

"I'd rather see a road runner instead of a grouse" Claire said.

11

Write a sentence starting with *Lake Superior.* After those words put an appositive to identify the lake further. Complete the sentence, punctuating correctly.

11

Model Answer

    Lake Superior, the largest of the Great Lakes, lies between the United States and Canada.

....

Write a similar sentence about the Mississippi River.

12

Write a sentence in which the words *Cletus said* appear near the middle. Use quotation marks around whatever Cletus said. Use commas as needed.

    (If necessary, refer to Frame 4 for correct placement of punctuation.)

12

Model Answer

    "The regular fullback," Cletus said, "has a sprained ankle."

....

Write a similar sentence using *Melba* and *commented* at the end.

13

Write a sentence in which you include the names of a city, a state, and a month, as well as a date (including the year). Punctuate correctly.

13

Model Answer

We moved to Spokane, Washington, on June 18, 1982.

. . . .

Write a similar sentence with different information.

14

Finish honestly: One thing I hope to remember from this lesson is that . . .

(In this frame, any answer that you consider honest and accurate is acceptable.)

Lesson 72: Answers to Questions for Added Practice

1. A. *South America's longest stream* B. commas **2.** A. *1986, Florida* B. commas **3.** *in consequence*, comma **4.** *John requested,* comma, quotation marks **5.** *Oh, Nancy,* a comma **6.** appositives, dates, states or counties, transitions, statements of qualification or emphasis, explanatory words in conversation, absolute phrases, adjectives following their nouns, mild exclamations, names in direct address **7.** . . . grouse, also . . . plains," lives . . . **8.** . . . grouse, I insist, could . . . **9.** . . . grouse, however, does . . . **10.** . . . grouse" Claire . . . **11.** MODEL: The Mississippi River, the greatest American river, has its source in northern Minnesota. **12.** MODEL: "That was an odd conversation," Melba commented. **13.** MODEL: From St. Joseph, Missouri, they left for Nevada on October 3, 1968.

73

Commas with Nonrestrictive Elements: Is That Clause or Phrase Essential?

After writing your answer(s) in the right-hand column, check this column to see whether you have responded correctly. If you have made a mistake, or if you need more practice, do whatever is asked below the dotted line in each answer frame.

Answers to questions for added practice can be found at the end of each lesson.

Understanding and Applying the Principles

1

> **Every student** *who did not pass his physical examination* **is ineligible for football.**
>
> **Aldo Marsh,** *who did not pass his physical examination,* **is ineligible for football.**

Both of those apparently similar sentences are correctly punctuated, even though the _____ [*first* or *second*?] has no commas and the other has two commas.

We'll see why in the next few frames.

Answers and Added Practice

1

first

∙∙∙∙∙∙∙∙∙∙∙∙∙∙∙∙∙∙∙∙∙∙∙∙∙∙∙∙∙∙

Any man *who has a lean and hungry look* is dangerous, Caesar believed. Cassius, *who had a lean and hungry look,* was a conspirator.

Note the difference in punctuation of the italicized clauses.

2

Read the first example in Frame 1. Then reread it, omitting the italicized words. Is the basic meaning almost exactly the same?

_____

2

No. (It is certainly not true that *every* student is ineligible for football.)

∙∙∙∙∙∙∙∙∙∙∙∙∙∙∙∙∙∙∙∙∙∙∙∙∙∙∙∙∙∙

In Answer Frame 1, if you omit the italicized words, the meaning of the first sentence is _____ [*the same* or *different*?]

3

Now read the second example in Frame 1, and then reread it, omitting the italicized words. Is the basic meaning almost exactly the same? _____

3

    Yes. (Both readings tell us that Aldo Marsh is ineligible for football.)

....

In Answer Frame 1, if you omit the italicized words, the basic meaning of the second sentence is _____ _____ . [*the same* or *different*?]

4

When a phrase or a clause, such as the *who*-clause in Frame 1, does not change the basic meaning of a sentence, it is called *nonrestrictive* or *nonessential*. Such a phrase or clause merely adds a little information.

    As the second example in Frame 1 shows, a nonessential phrase or clause _____ [*should* or *should not*?] be punctuated with commas.

4

    should

....

Which example in Answer Frame 1 contains a nonessential (nonrestrictive) clause? _____ [First or Second?]

5

If convenient, read *aloud* the two examples in Frame 1.

    Do you pause noticeably before and after

    A) the essential clause in the first, or

    B) the nonessential clause in the second?

    _____ [A or B?]

5

    B

....

If you read *aloud* the two examples in Answer Frame 1, do you naturally pause before and after the italicized clause in the *first* example or in the *second*? _____

6

Summary:

  A. If a phrase or a clause can be omitted without affecting the basic meaning of a sentence, it is nonessential and _____ [*should* or *should not*?] be punctuated with commas.

  B. If a reader would naturally make a noticeable pause before and after a phrase or a clause, he or she should recognize once more that it is nonrestrictive and requires _____ . [What marks?]

  C. In contrast, if omitting the phrase or clause considerably affects the meaning, and if a reader does not pause noticeably before and after it, it is essential (restrictive) and _____ [*should* or *should not*?] be punctuated with commas.

Note: Obviously, if the phrase or clause comes at the beginning or the end of the sentence, only one comma is needed, as this sentence itself illustrates.

6

A. should   B. commas
C. should not

. . . .

Look one more time at the second example in Answer Frame 1. The commas are there because

A. the italicized clause _____
_____ [*does* or *does not?*] affect the basic meaning of the sentence, and

B. a reader _____
_____ [*pauses* or *does not pause?*] before and after it.

7

In Frames 7–10, decide whether a comma or commas are needed with each of the italicized phrases or clauses. Test each in the ways summarized in Frame 6. Insert the comma or commas if needed; otherwise do nothing.

A. Everyone *in our class* was invited.

B. Janet Chester *who is a member of our class* was invited.

C. All students *who are members of our class* are invited.

7

(Only sentence B should have commas.)

. . . .

In Answer Frames 7–10, follow the instructions in Frame 7.

A. Someone *in this very room* is suspected of murder!

B. My sister Maxine *who is in this very room* is suspected of murder.

8

A. William Morris *who wrote a number of prose romances* believed that the lot of mankind could be improved by fiction.

B. Most people *who write prose romances* have less serious purposes.

C. *In the opinion of Professor Charles Johnson and others* prose romances should not be intended to teach.

8

(Sentence A should have two commas, B none, and C one.)

. . . .

A. Anyone *who supports Jones* will be rewarded liberally.

B. Frank Mills *who supported Jones* was rewarded liberally.

C. A liberal reward is given anyone *who supports Jones.*

9

A. I like to read a book *that develops at least one character fully.*

B. The book I have here *which is* Vanity Fair *by Thackeray* develops fully the character of an adventuress.

C. The adventuress *whose name is Becky Sharp* is clever and *it is evident* not at all scrupulous.

9

(Sentence A should have no commas, B two, C four.)

. . . .

A. Mr. Clancy *in the bow of the ship* saw the raft first.

B. A sailor *in the bow of the ship* saw the raft first.

10

A. Nancy saw a mouse *with unusually long ears.*

B. The mouse *that Nancy saw* had unusually long ears.

C. Nancy *with her unusually sharp eyes* saw a mouse.

10

(Sentence C should have two commas.)

. . . .

A. Do not use commas with a phrase *which is essential to the thought.*

B. The phrase in sentence C *which is not essential to the thought* should be set off by commas.

11

Write a sentence beginning with *Any girl who.* Punctuate correctly.

11

Model Answer

Any girl who wore makeup was considered bold and even vulgar. [No commas]

. . . .

Write a sentence beginning with *Two boys who.* Punctuate correctly.

12

Write a sentence beginning with *Clara Rice who.* Punctuate correctly.

12

Model Answer

Clara Rice, who wore makeup, was considered bold and even vulgar. [Commas required.]

. . . .

Write a sentence beginning with *Larry and Greg who*. Punctuate correctly.

13

Insert a suitable phrase or clause within the sentence *The child . . . was forgotten in the excitement*. Punctuate correctly.

13

Model Answer

The child at the top of the stairs was forgotten in the excitement, but not the other five children. [No commas] *Or*
The child, who kept perfectly quiet, was forgotten in the excitement in the saloon. [Commas required.]

. . . .

Insert a suitable phrase or clause within *A classroom . . . was especially cold that day.* Punctuate correctly.

14

Insert a suitable phrase or clause within the sentence *Alice . . . had many remarkable adventures*. Punctuate correctly.

14

Model Answer

Alice, who went through a hole made by a rabbit, had many remarkable adventures. [Commas required.]

. . . .

Insert a suitable phrase or clause within *This classroom . . . is unusually cold today.* Punctuate correctly.

15

Finish honestly: One thing I hope to remember from this lesson is that . . .

(In this frame, any answer that you consider honest and accurate is acceptable.)

Lesson 73: Answers to Questions for Added Practice

2. different **3.** the same **4.** Second **5.** Second **6.** A. does not B. pauses **7.** B. . . . Maxine, who . . . room, is . . . **8.** B. . . . Mills, who . . . Jones, was . . . **9.** A. . . . Clancy, in . . . ship, saw . . . **10.** B. . . . C, which . . . thought, should . . . **11.** MODEL: Two boys who were left behind had to hitchhike. **12.** MODEL: Larry and Greg, who were left behind, had to hitchhike. **13.** MODEL: A classroom on the north side was especially cold that day. **14.** MODEL: This classroom, which is on the north side, is unusually cold today.

▪74▪

Commas: In a Series and in Compound Sentences

After writing your answer(s) in the right-hand column, check this column to see whether you have responded correctly. If you have made a mistake, or if you need more practice, do whatever is asked below the dotted line in each answer frame.

Answers to questions for added practice can be found at the end of each lesson.

Understanding and Applying the Principles

1

Sue Arnold and Bob were present.

A. If the girl's name is Sue Arnold, then she and _____ [Who else?] were present.

B. If we are talking to Sue, we punctuate like this: **Sue, Arnold and Bob were present.** That means that _____ _____ and _____ were present.

C. But if a reader is uncertain whether or not we are talking to Sue, sentence B may be read as a series. If so, it means that _____ , _____ , and _____ were present.

D. To make completely clear that three people are named in a series, we can write **Sue, Arnold, and Bob were present.** Now the reader knows for sure that _____ , _____ , and _____ were present.

Answers and Added Practice

1

    A. Bob B. Arnold, Bob
    C. Sue, Arnold, Bob
    D. Sue, Arnold, Bob

. . . .

Our flag is red white and blue.

In that series, commas should be placed after _____ and _____ .

2

No firm rule dictates that a comma *must* precede *and* in a series. Because a comma in that place does occasionally prevent misreading, *The Writer's Tutor* recommends that it be used. (Your instructor may prefer that it be omitted, and some editors agree with that preference.)

One other example to support the use of that controversial comma:

A. If we read *Lenny cooked squash, beets, beans, and bacon,* we may rightly assume that Lenny used _____ [How many?] utensils, one for each kind of food.

B. But if we read *Lenny cooked squash, beets, beans and bacon,* we are left wondering whether he cooked the beans and bacon separately [using a total of _____ utensils] or together. [a total of _____ utensils]

2

    A. four B. four, three

....

Still another way out:

    Lenny cooked squash, beets, and beans with bacon.

(You may want to play with some other versions before you move on to *ice cream and cake*.)

3

A series may consist of three or more words (as in Frame 1), phrases, or dependent or independent clauses.

    Phrases: I like being with Joe **in classes, at home, and in the woods. Walking cautiously, avoiding dry twigs, and keeping every sense alert,** we watch for small animals.

In each sentence the phrases in the series are separated by _____ [What marks?]

3

    commas

....

    Fritz hurried down the street
    . . .

Add two more phrases to tell where else Fritz hurried. Punctuate correctly.

4

Dependent clauses:

    They asked **who the stranger was, what she wanted, and where she was going**.

Independent clauses:

    She came, I saw, and she conquered.

In each sentence the clauses in the series are separated by _____. [What marks?]

4

    commas

....

    When the leaves start turning
    . . .

    we know that winter is only a couple of months away.

Add two more *when-* clauses after *turning*. Punctuate correctly.

5

A compound sentence consists of two or more independent clauses, each of which could stand alone as a sentence. (See also Lessons 9 and 76.)

    The radio was blaring, but nobody answered my loud knocking on the door.

    A. Can the first four words stand alone as a sentence? _____

    B. Can the last nine words stand alone? _____

5

A. Yes B. Yes

. . . .

Marty sent word to Oscar . . .

Using a comma and *and* or *but*, add a clause to complete the sentence above.

6

Many compound sentences have two independent clauses joined by *and, but, for, or, nor, yet,* or *so.* Technically these are called *coordinating conjunctions*, but they can also be called *and*-words. When an *and*-word joins the parts of a compound sentence, we normally place a comma before it.

In the example in Frame 5, a _____ [What mark?] and _____ [What *and*-word?] join the parts of the compound sentence.

Note: If the *and*-word is not present, the punctuation is different. See Lessons 10 and 76.

6

comma, *but*

. . . .

Stay out long enough to get a light tan . . .

Using a comma and *but*, add a clause to complete the sentence above.

7

Summary:

A. In a series (say A B and C), the conventional punctuation is A___ B___ and C. [Supply the needed marks.]

B. In a compound sentence with the parts connected by *and, but, for, or, nor, yet,* and *so,* a _____ [What mark?] normally precedes the _____-word.

7

A. A, B, and C.

B. comma, *and*

. . . .

A compound sentence that has three or more independent clauses is obviously also a series. An example is in Frame 4.

8

In Frames 8 and 9, insert the commas missing in each series.

A. Helen Green Myra Blossom and Pauline Lentz are our candidates.

B. Red yellow and brown leaves adorn the trees.

C. The little boy's pockets contained three pencils a wrench with a broken end and a somewhat dried frog.

8

A. . . . Green, Myra Blossom, and . . .

B. . . . Red, yellow, and . . .

C. . . . pencils, a . . . end, and . . .

. . . .

In Answer Frames 8–12, insert the missing commas.

A. Taxis buses and private automobiles filled the streets.

B. The earth, wet black and glistening, rolled off the plow.

9

A. They slept in empty houses under bridges and on the beach.

B. We learned that Tolstoy was a Russian nobleman that he became deeply religious and that he wrote two of the world's greatest novels.

C. Clarinets pleaded caressingly saxophones sobbed a drum softly pulsed the rhythm and a flute cried shrilly above the other instruments.

9

A. ... houses, under ... bridges, and ...

B. ... nobleman, that ... religious, and ...

C. ... caressingly, saxophones sobbed, a ... rhythm, and ...

....

A. I would like to photograph lions in Africa ski in the Alps and swim the Hellespont.

B. You like ice cream I like pie Daddy likes you and I know why.

10

In Frames 10 and 11, insert commas where needed between the independent clauses in each sentence.

A. We ate all the sandwiches and the cookies remained in the basket.

B. You must have made the call for Tom would have told me otherwise.

C. Either he should apologize or you should withdraw your application.

10

A. ... sandwiches, and ...

B. ... call, for ...

C. ... apologize, or ...

....

A. Washington may not have cut down that cherry tree and he may not have thrown that dollar across the Potomac.

B. Emerson was a popular lecturer but Mark Twain drew even larger audiences.

11

A. Mark Twain was not a handsome man nor did he have an impressive bearing.

B. He often had serious points to make yet he kept his audiences laughing hilariously throughout his speeches.

C. Punctuation marks are intended to help make meaning clear and for that reason they should be used intelligently.

11

A. ... man, nor ...

B. ... make, yet ...

C. ... clear, and ...

....

A. Rabbits hopped through the dry grass and chipmunks scurried across the patio.

B. A bluejay squawked in the sunburst locust but a nearby cardinal ignored him.

12

Imagine that you are giving a younger student some advice about studying. Start with *To study effectively, you should,* and finish with a series of three suggestions. Punctuate correctly.

12

Model Answer

To study effectively, you should make a schedule, stick to it, and reject distractions.

· ·

Where he came from why he came and how long he expects to stay are all unknown.

13

Now imagine that you are the mayor of your town or city. You are giving a speech about its fine qualities. Write a sentence starting with *Ours is a city where we have*. Use a total of three *where*-clauses. Punctuate correctly.

13

Model Answer

Ours is a town where we have splendid parks, where we can be proud of our schools, and where neighbors are still neighborly.

· ·

Write a sentence starting with *I know that*, and finish it using three *that*-clauses.

14

Write a compound sentence. In the first clause tell what a friend of yours thinks about a play or a story. Use a comma and the conjunction *but*. In the second clause, tell someone else's opinion.

14

Model Answer

Harry likes the acting in *Southern Outlook*, but Lois thinks the characterization is unconvincing.

· ·

Write a compound sentence using *or* as the link between the independent clauses.

15

Write another compound sentence. In the first clause, tell one thing that a criminal did not do. Start the second clause with *nor did he*. Punctuate as shown in this lesson.

15

Model Answer

This criminal never carried a gun, nor did he ever inflict bodily injury.

16

Finish honestly: One thing I hope to remember from this lesson is that . . .

(In this frame, any answer that you consider honest and accurate is acceptable.)

Lesson 74: Answers to Questions for Added Practice

1. *red, white* **3.** MODEL: . . . across a parking lot, and into a yellow house. **4.** MODEL: . . . turning, when the nights are chilly, and when many birds have gone south, we know that winter is only a couple of months away. **5.** . . . Oscar, but the message was delayed. **6.** MODEL: . . . tan, but be careful not to burn. **8.** A. Taxis, buses, and . . . B. . . . wet, black, and . . . **9.** A. . . . Africa, ski in the Alps, and . . . B. . . . cream, I like pie, Daddy likes you, and . . . **10.** A. . . . tree, and . . . B. . . . lecturer, but . . . **11.** A. . . . grass, and . . . B. . . . locust, but . . . **12.** Where he came from, why he came, and . . . **13.** MODEL: I know that babies often cry, that they frequently keep their parents up at night, and that I'd like two or three anyway. **14.** MODEL: Karen may decide to fly, or she may come on a bus.

75

Commas: Avoid Too Much of a Good Thing

After writing your answer(s) in the right-hand column, check this column to see whether you have responded correctly. If you have made a mistake, or if you need more practice, do whatever is asked below the dotted line in each answer frame.

Answers to questions for added practice can be found at the end of each lesson.

Understanding and Applying the Principles

1

Some writers are "comma happy," sprinkling in commas (or perhaps dashes or other favorite marks) without any real reason. Using commas to set off essential parts of a sentence is as serious a mistake as omitting needed commas.

Which commas are not needed in the following sentence?

$$\overset{A}{\qquad} \overset{B}{\qquad}$$

These writers, do not realize, that excessive

$$\overset{C}{\qquad} \overset{D}{\qquad}$$

commas, reduce a reader's speed, and

comprehension.

_____ [Write the letters corresponding to unneeded commas.]

Answers and Added Practice

1

A, B, C, D

. . . .

Which commas are not needed?

$$\overset{A}{\qquad}$$

Ernest Hemingway, was an

$$\overset{B}{\qquad} \overset{C}{\qquad} \overset{D}{\qquad}$$

eminent, American, author, in

$$\overset{E}{\qquad} \overset{F}{\qquad}$$

his day, but, his future fame is

uncertain. _____

2

Frames 2–7 will consider five common instances of misused commas. A ● appears at each place where the presence of a comma ordinarily would be incorrect.

$$\overset{s}{\qquad} \overset{v}{\qquad}$$

The man with the straw hat● is Mr. Timm.

$$\overset{s}{\qquad}$$

Mr. Timm, who is wearing a straw hat,

$$\overset{v}{\qquad}$$

is standing in the front row.

(s = subject, v = verb)

The second example shows that sometimes an expression suitably fenced in by *two* commas may separate a subject and its verb.

The first example shows that an expression with only one comma ordinarily _____ [*should* or *should not?*] separate the subject and the verb.

2

should not

· ·

A. **One author whom we studied, was Ernest Hemingway.**

B. **One author, whose *The Old Man and the Sea* we read, was Ernest Hemingway.**

Sentence _____ [A or B?] is correctly punctuated.

3

When my sister married, one of her presents

v ⌢   pn ⌢

was• a set of crystalware.

v ⌢

Our aunt declared• that she had never seen a

do ⌢

lovelier gift.

(pn = predicate nominative, do = direct object)

The two sentences above show that a comma should not ordinarily be used between a _____ and a _____ _____ or between a _____ and a _____ _____ _____. [If you have forgotten what a predicate nominative is, see Lesson 34.]

3

verb, predicate nominative
verb, direct object

· ·

The chief problem is, that the roads are icy.

That sentence is _____ [*correctly* or *incorrectly?*] punctuated.

4

Violets usually are• blue, yellow, or white.

That sentence shows that a comma _____ [*should* or *should not?*] ordinarily precede a series. [See Answer Frame 5 for an uncommon kind of exception.]

4

should not

· ·

In the basket were lemons, kumquats, and papayas.

A comma _____ [*should* or *should not?*] be added after *basket.*

5

Violets usually are, as you have seen, blue, yellow, or white.

That correctly punctuated sentence is like the one in Frame 4 except that the clause *as you have seen* has been inserted and correctly marked as an interpolation.

It shows that two commas fencing in an insertion _____ [*are* or *are not?*] permissible.

5

are

· ·

In the basket were, unbelievably, lemons, kumquats, and papayas.

That punctuation is _____ _____. [*correct* or *incorrect?*]

6

Balboa discovered the Pacific, but• Keats gave the credit to Cortez.

The sentence above shows a comma correctly used in a compound sentence before *but.* (A comma would be used similarly before *and, for, or, nor, yet,* or *so.*)

The • shows that a comma ordinarily _____ [*should* or *should not?*] follow the conjunction.

6

should not

....

An open dictionary lay on the table, and, a one-volume encyclopedia stood nearby.

That punctuation is _____

_____. [*correct* or

incorrect?]

7

We follow the trail across the field• and through the pasture.

That sentence shows that when two phrases (or words) are joined by *and*, _____ [*a* or *no?*] comma is ordinarily desirable between them.

7

no

....

We walked along Wabash Avenue and across Grant Street.

Is a comma needed after *Avenue?*

_____

8

A final note: a comma should never be placed between an adjective and the noun it modifies. For example: *a dirty• spot.*

    In brief, we have seen in Frames 1–7 that _____

_____

_____ [Finish in your own words.]

8

Model Answer

    commas should not be used without a definite reason.

....

Commas or other punctuation marks should not be used excessively.
    What does *excessively* mean?

9

In Frames 9 and 10, copy the letters corresponding to the commas that should be deleted.

          A   B   C   D
    Ballet is, solo, or ensemble, dancing, that often

                              E   F
    tells a story. It was originally, a part of opera,

        G
    but, it was separated from opera in Paris in the

    sixteenth century. Great names in ballet

          H   I   J
    include, Diaghilev, Nijinski, and DeMille.

    _____

9

A, B, C, D, E, G, H
(The comma represented by J
is optional.)

· ·

In Answer Frames 9 and 10, follow
the instructions in Frame 9.

      A   B

Monrovia, was named, for

President James Monroe.

    C   D   E

This, small, city, which is now

             F

the capital of Liberia, was

      G

founded, in 1822. _____

10

         A   D

General Lee decided, that he should attack,

the forces of General Hooker near

            C

Chancellorsville, Virginia. General Thomas

        D   E

Jackson, who was known as "Stonewall," was

        F

successful, in flanking the Northern troops

          G

even though, he was wounded fatally. General

       H   I

Early, and General Stuart, completed Lee's last

important victory. _____

10

A, B, F, G, H, I

· ·

       A   B

Phosphorus, is used in,

        C   D

matches, certain poisons, and

                       E

fertilizers. It does not occur, by

    F   G

itself, but, it is found in a

number of compounds. _____

_____

11

Start a sentence with *Some of my friends are* . . . Then name three
or four of your friends. Punctuate correctly, not excessively.

11

Model Answer

Some of my friends are Karen, Ralph, Pauline, and Joe.

. . . .

Name three of your favorite sports. Start your sentence with *Three of my favorite sports are.*

12

Write a sentence beginning with *The professor announced.* Use *that* as the next word, and complete the sentence in a dozen words or more. Punctuate correctly, not excessively. (No quotation marks are needed.)

12

Model Answer

The professor announced that all students with a final grade of A, B, or C will be eligible for next summer's field trip to Sanibel island.

. . . .

Write a sentence starting with *The French teacher said.* Use *that* as the next word, and complete the sentence.

13

Write a sentence telling briefly why you oppose or favor capital punishment (execution of a condemned murderer, for example). Begin with *Two of my reasons are.* Punctuate correctly, not excessively.

13

Model Answer

Two of my reasons are that the Bible forbids killing and that the jury may have reached the wrong verdict.

. . . .

Write a sentence starting with *His excuse was.* As usual, punctuate correctly, not excessively.

14

Write a compound sentence. In the first main clause, tell briefly of one activity between halves of an athletic event. Use the conjunction *and.* In the second main clause, tell of a second activity. Punctuate correctly, not excessively.

14

Model Answer

The band flipped from one formation to another, and the twirler skied her baton higher than ever.

. . . .

Write a compound sentence. In the first main part, say something about some music you like. Use the conjunction *but.* In the second main part, tell of someone else's different reaction. Do not punctuate excessively.

15

Finish honestly: One thing I hope to remember from this lesson is that . . .

(In this frame, any answer that you consider honest and accurate is acceptable.)

Lesson 75: Answers to Questions for Added Practice

1. A, B, C, D, F **2.** B **3.** incorrectly **4.** should not **5.** correct **6.** incorrect **7.** No **8.** MODEL: "to an unreasonable degree" **9.** A, B, C, D, G **10.** A, B, E, G **11.** MODEL: Three of my favorite sports are tennis, swimming, and cross-country skiing. **12.** MODEL: The French teacher said that Paris is the most beautiful city in the world. **13.** MODEL: His excuse was that the other car had crossed the center line. **14.** MODEL: I like the music of Sibelius, but Marjorie prefers Grieg.

76

The Semicolon in a Compound or Compound-Complex Sentence: When You Shouldn't Use a Comma

After writing your answer(s) in the right-hand column, check this column to see whether you have responded correctly. If you have made a mistake, or if you need more practice, do whatever is asked below the dotted line in each answer frame.

Answers to questions for added practice can be found at the end of each lesson.

Answers and Added Practice

1

writer, authors

....

Goethe has been called a universal genius, for he was an author, a philosopher, an anatomist, and a botanist.

How can you tell that the sentence above is compound?

Understanding and Applying the Principles

1

Herman Melville through many years was almost ignored as a writer, but now he is considered one of the greatest American authors.

A compound sentence is in effect two (or possibly three or four) closely related simple sentences. In the example above, the first "sentence" begins with *Herman* and ends with _____ ; the second begins with *now* and ends with _____ .

2

To connect the two "sentences" (really, independent clauses) in the example in Frame 1, a _____ [What punctuation mark?] and the conjunction _____ [What word?] are used.

2

comma, *but*

....

In the example in Answer Frame 1, the first "sentence" ends with _____ _____. [What word?] Connecting the two "sentences" are a _____ _____ [What mark?] and the conjunction _____ .

3

One way to connect independent clauses in a compound sentence, then, is to use a comma and a conjunction of the kind called *coordinating*.

In Lesson 74 we also called it an *and*-word: *and, but, for, or, nor, yet,* or *so.*

Copy the seven *and*-words.

3

and, but, for, or, nor, yet, so

....

Memorize those words. If one of them is not the connecting link in a compound sentence that you write, you will need a different mark of punctuation.

4

Herman Melville through many years was ignored as a writer; now, though, he is considered one of the greatest American authors.

The example above is almost the same as that in Frame 1. However, an *and*-word is not used. Instead of a comma and an *and*-word, a _____ [What mark?] stands between the two clauses.

4

semicolon

....

Goethe has been called a universal genius; he was an author, a philosopher, an anatomist, and a botanist.

A. Is the first word in the second clause an *and*-word?

_____

B. The mark of punctuation needed is therefore a _____ _____ .

5

Herman Melville through many years was almost ignored as a writer; however, he is now considered one of the greatest American authors.

That sentence is another variation, but the principle is the same as that in Frame 4. When a word like *however* (*therefore, thus, moreover, nevertheless,* etc.) is used instead of an *and*-word, a _____ _____ [What mark?] is used instead of a _____ _____ . [What mark?]

5

semicolon, comma

....

Suppose that the second clause in the example in Answer Frame 4 started with *as evidence, he . . .* Would the punctuation be changed? _____

Note: *However* and the other words listed in Frame 5 are called *conjunctive adverbs.* When used as connectors of independent clauses, they require a longer stop than an *and*-word does. That is the reason for the semicolon.

6

Herman Melville, who wrote *Moby Dick* and other novels, through many years was almost ignored as a writer, but now he is considered one of the greatest American authors.

The sentence above is *compound-complex* rather than *compound,* for it contains a dependent clause (*who wrote* Moby Dick *and other novels*) as well as the two independent clauses. The principle is still the same, though. That is, a _____ [What mark?] and a(n) _____ [What kind of word?] stand between the two main parts of the sentence.

6

comma, coordinating conjunction (*or and*-word)

....

Goethe has been called a universal genius, and that title may be well deserved because he excelled in many fields.

If we delete *and,* the punctuation mark should be a _____.

7

Suppose that in the example in Frame 6 we substitute *however* for *but.* The punctuation needs to be changed from a _____ _____ to a _____.

7

comma, semicolon

....

In Answer Frame 6 the dependent clause is the group of words starting with *because.* Note that the semicolon separates two independent clauses, not an independent and a dependent clause.

8

To summarize:

A. When the two main parts of a compound or a compound-complex sentence are connected by *and, but, for, or, nor, yet,* or *so,* a _____ [What mark?] is used.

B. When those parts are not connected by an *and*-word, a _____ [What mark?] is used.

8

A. comma B. semicolon

....

Some students visualize this formula as a summary of the two principles: ☐ ; ☐ = ☐ , *and*-word ☐ .

9

In Frames 9–11, insert a comma or a semicolon (whichever is correct) above each caret.

A. Jesse Stuart was always a prolific writer‸ as an example, he wrote a college term paper of several hundred pages.

B. Stuart was also a teacher‸ and he often said that his heart was always in the classroom, even after he turned to other work.

9

    A. semicolon B. comma

. . . .

In Answer Frames 9–11, follow the instructions in Frame 9.

  A. Cheese has been a popular food for centuries‸ and to-day it exists in many varieties.

  B. Italy is known for Parmesan cheese‸ Holland is the home of Edam and Gouda.

10

  A. When *Webster's Third New International Dictionary* appeared, it was greeted with many hostile reviews‸ but slowly the turmoil subsided.

  B. The critics claimed that the dictionary lowered standards of usage‸ however, proponents argued that a dictionary should reflect standards, not try to set them.

10

    A. comma B. semicolon

. . . .

  A. *Caligula* was not the emperor's real name‸ he was really Caius Caesar.

  B. When Caius was a small boy, he delighted in wearing military boots‸ and *Caligula* means "little boots."

11

  A. The "paperback revolution" changed the publishing business greatly‸ for it made possible relatively inexpensive editions of thousands of books.

  B. Some of those books otherwise would not have become widely known, perhaps not even printed‸ the paperback editions, though, put them in the financial reach of many purchasers.

11

    A. comma B. semicolon

. . . .

  A. Junius and Edwin Booth built great reputations as actors‸ but John Wilkes Booth disgraced the family.

  B. Junius and Edwin Booth built great reputations as actors‸ however, John Wilkes Booth disgraced the family.

12

Write a compound or compound-complex sentence of your own, telling of two things you did this morning. Connect the two main parts with *and then*. Punctuate correctly.

12

Model Answer

    I went to French class during the first period, and then I spent an hour in the library.

. . . .

Write a compound or compound-complex sentence telling of a recent event at which you were present. Connect the two parts with *but soon*. Punctuate correctly.

13

Suppose that *and* is deleted from the model answer in Answer Frame 12. What change in punctuation is needed?

13

Model Answer

    A semicolon should replace the comma.

. . . .

In the sentence that you wrote for Answer Frame 12, delete *but*. What change in punctuation is needed?

14

Write a compound or compound-complex sentence giving two reasons why every American citizen of voting age should vote. Start the second part with *moreover*. Punctuate correctly.

14

Model Answer

    Only if everyone votes do we really hear the voice of the people; moreover, if voters are indifferent, democracy is endangered.

15

Finish honestly: One thing I hope to remember from this lesson is that . . .

(In this frame, any answer that you consider honest and accurate is acceptable.)

Lesson 76: Answers to Questions for Added Practice

1. MODEL: It appears to be two sentences connected by *for*. **2.** *genius*, comma, *for* **4.** A. No B. semicolon **5.** No **6.** semicolon **9.** A. (comma) B. (semicolon) **10.** A. (semicolon) B. (comma) **11.** A. (comma) B. (semicolon) **12.** MODEL: Our miler set the pace at first, but soon a Michigan man passed him. **13.** MODEL: The comma must be changed to a semicolon.

═77═

Semicolons: An Infrequent Use

After writing your answer(s) in the right-hand column, check this column to see whether you have responded correctly. If you have made a mistake, or if you need more practice, do whatever is asked below the dotted line in each answer frame.

Answers to questions for added practice can be found at the end of each lesson.

Understanding and Applying the Principles

1

  A. **Among the officers in attendance were Charles Hovey, president, Mildred Bray, secretary, Oscar Trapp, treasurer, and George Barth, a director.**

  B. **Among the officers in attendance were Charles Hovey, president; Mildred Bray, secretary; Oscar Trapp, treasurer; and George Barth, a director.**

The sentence that is easier to read and to understand immediately is _____ . [A or B?]

Answers and Added Practice

1

  B

. . . .

Note that in B the semicolons clearly set off each name with the appropriate title. In a longer list, this kind of punctuation would be even more helpful.

2

When there is a considerable amount of other punctuation (usually commas), we may sometimes use semicolons to separate equal parts of a sentence even though commas would otherwise be more normal.

In the Frame 1 examples, we have a series of names. What are the usual punctuation marks in a series? _____

2

Commas

....

In a series the parts are (or should be) grammatically equal: all nouns or all adjectives, for instance.

3

As we noted in Frame 2, semicolons may separate grammatically *equal* parts of a sentence that is punctuated more heavily than usual. In a compound sentence, the two or more independent clauses are grammatically equal. Semicolons should not be used to separate grammatically unequal parts, such as an independent and a dependent clause.

The punctuation in the following sentence is _____ _____. [*correct* or *incorrect*?]

> **The reds, yellows, and greens changed to pinks, oranges, and blues; but the original purples, blues, and aquas faded out completely.**

3

correct

....

Note that the example in Frame 3 is a compound sentence. The semicolon before *but* replaces the _____ _____[What mark?] that normally would appear in such a sentence.

4

The punctuation in the following sentence is _____. [*correct* or *incorrect*?]

> **The reds, yellows, and greens changed to pinks, oranges, and blues; although we saw no changes in the other colors.**

4

incorrect

....

The example in Frame 4 does not have two equal parts: it is complex rather than compound. The *although*-clause _____ [*is* or *is not*?] an independent clause.

5

In Frame 4 the material preceding the semicolon is an independent clause, and that following the semicolon is a dependent clause.

   A. In other words, those two parts are grammatically ____ _____. [*equal* or *unequal*?]

   B. Instead of the semicolon, a _____ should be used.

5

      A. unequal B. comma

. . . .

Should a semicolon or a comma be used at each caret?

> **Donnybrook is a suburb of Dublin, Ireland˄ whose name is familiar, even in the United States˄ because of a rowdy fair suppressed in 1855.**

    ———————   ———————

6

In Frames 6 and 7, write *Justified* or *Unjustified* to indicate whether a good reason exists for the semicolon(s) in each sentence.

    A. Meteorics, or meteoritology, as it is sometimes called, is the study of meteors; which, as knowledge of outer space increases, is becoming more and more important.

    ———————————————

    B. Iron meteorites contain an average of 90.8% iron, as compared with 4.7% in the earth's crust; 8.5% nickel, compared with 0.02%; 0.59% cobalt, compared with less than 0.001%; and 0.17% phosphorus, compared with 0.12%. ———————————

6

      A. Unjustified.
      B. Justified.

. . . .

In sentence A in Frame 6, suppose that the part after the semicolon is as follows: *and as knowledge of outer space increases, such study grows in importance.*

    The semicolon ———————
[*should* or *should not?*] be changed to a comma.

7

    A. I planted an oak tree, which would grow slowly and, in all probability, would long outlive me; a maple tree, which would grow more rapidly and might live fifty years; and a Chinese elm tree, which would grow fast but die young. ———————

    B. The Donner group of emigrants, heading for California, were caught by snow in mountain passes, and about half died of hunger; although the other half, sometimes because of luck or sturdiness, managed to survive. ————

7

      A. Justified.
      B. Unjustified.

. . . .

To justify a semicolon in B in Frame 7, we could delete *although*. A better solution, perhaps, is to use two sentences.

8

Finish honestly: One thing I hope to remember from this lesson is that . . .

(In this frame, any answer that you consider honest and accurate is acceptable.)

Lesson 77: Answers to Questions for Added Practice

3. comma **4.** is not **5.** comma, comma **6.** should

═══78═══

Colons Before Formal Quotations or Formal Lists: They Wear Business Suits

After writing your answer(s) in the right-hand column, check this column to see whether you have responded correctly. If you have made a mistake, or if you need more practice, do whatever is asked below the dotted line in each answer frame.

Answers to questions for added practice can be found at the end of each lesson.

Understanding and Applying the Principles

1

    A. The psychologist developed at some length this quotation from William Makepeace Thackeray: "Vanity is often the unseen spur."

    B. Jack said, "Let's meet at Bill's after lunch."

Sentence _____ [A or B?] seems more formal in tone.

Answers and Added Practice

1

    A

. . . .

    A. Then Mitzi chirped, "We've got to be ready in ten minutes, girls."

    B. Coleridge defined a picture in this way: "A picture is an intermediate something between a thought and a thing."

_____ [A or B?] is more formal.

2

    A. In sentence A in Frame 1, the quotation is rather formal, and it appears in a formal passage. The mark of punctuation preceding the quotation is a _____ .

    B. In sentence B, the situation and the quotation are obviously informal. The mark preceding the quotation is a _____ .

2

A. colon   B. comma

····························

In Answer Frame 1, the mark preceding the formal quotation is a _____ .

3

Colons are perhaps the most formal marks of punctuation. As the subtitle of this lesson suggests, they wear business attire rather than blue jeans. They are used, for instance, after the salutation of a letter to a corporate vice-president but not after the greeting in a billet-doux to an absent lover or spouse.

Frames 1 and 2 have shown that colons are often used also before _____ [*formal* or *informal*?] quotations.

3

formal

····························

For the colon to be appropriate, both the context and the quotation need to be relatively formal. A comma would be more appropriate in *Some old fellow named Coleridge said*, "A picture is an intermediate something between a thought and a thing."

4

A. **The states with the longest Atlantic coastlines are the following: Florida, North Carolina, Maine, and Massachusetts.**

B. **The states with the longest Atlantic coastlines are Florida, North Carolina, Maine, and Massachusetts.**

The tone of ____ [A or B?] seems somewhat the more formal. Partly for that reason, it is punctuated with a _____ .

4

A. colon

····························

Neither a colon nor a comma would be appropriate in B of Frame 4 because there is no natural pause after *are*.

5

Most hurricanes occur in these months: September, August, and October.

That sentence is not necessarily very formal. It ends with a list that is in apposition with *these months*. The sentence illustrates the fact that a list which is an appositive is generally preceded by a _____ . [What mark?]

5

colon

····························

When a list is introduced by *such as*, neither a colon nor a comma should be used.

6

A. We have seen that a _____ [*formal* or *informal*?] quotation in a _____ [*formal* or *informal*?] context is usually preceded by a colon.

B. A list introduced by *the following, as follows,* or *these* (or *these items,* etc.) is generally preceded by a _____ . [What mark?]

6

A. formal, formal   B. colon

....

Add at each caret the more likely mark, a colon or a comma, or none at all.

A. Tom said laughingly˄ "..."
B. The President stated˄ "..."
C. I ordered the following tools˄ ...
D. I ordered˄ a set of wrenches, ..., and ...

7

A. No mark   B. Colon
C. Colon   D. No mark

....

In Answer Frames 7–9, follow the instructions in Frame 7.

A. Among the industries of Dallas were˄ cotton processing, oil processing, and aircraft parts manufacturing. _____
B. The following are the chief cities of the Azores˄ Ponta Delgada, Angra do Heroísmo, and Horta. _____

8

A. colon   B. comma
C. colon   D. colon

....

A. The greatest novels of Dostoevsky are the following˄ *Crime and Punishment, The Idiot, The Possessed,* and *The Brothers Karamazov.* _____

B. Dostoevsky is famous for his novels, such as˄ *Crime and Punishment, The Idiot, The Possessed,* and *The Brothers Karamazov.* _____

[If in doubt about B, look at Answer Frame 5.]

7

In Frames 7–9, a caret is in each sentence. Indicate the punctuation you would place at that spot by writing in the blank *Colon, Comma,* or *No mark.*

A. Ralph purchased˄ a table, a cabinet, and a rug. _____

B. Mr. O'Dell purchased these items˄ a table, a cabinet, and a rug. _____
C. Military leaves are hereby granted to these sailors˄ Abrams, Grove, Monteith, and Welinski. _____
D. Military leaves were granted to˄ Abrams, Grove, Monteith, and Welinski. _____

8

A. Ward makes this statement in his *Technological History*˄ "During this period the number of blast furnaces in Pennsylvania decreased from 269 to 211." _____
B. Julia said˄ "I found that book dull."
C. Alfred, Lord Tennyson is the author of this paradoxical remark˄ "An obedient wife commands her husband."

D. McDowell had this to say about Emerson˄ "As prophet and spokesman of the Romantic generation, Emerson had the high distinction of writing their declaration of independence." _____

9

A. Ed reported˄ "We're almost broke, boys." _____
B. The treasurer reported˄ "Expenditures for the fiscal year have increased fourteen per cent. Income has increased only ten per cent." _____
C. The paintings of El Greco have these characteristics˄ elongated figures, sharp color contrasts, and religious significance. _____
D. Picasso's paintings are characterized by˄ dominant colors in his different periods, many angular designs, and highly impressionistic views of life. _____

9

    A. comma   B. colon
    C. colon   D. No mark

. . . .

    A. I said‸ "The skin-diving equipment isn't on board."

        ———————

    B. You of course remember these famous words of Patrick Henry‸ "Give me liberty or give me death!" ——

        ———————

10

Write a sentence in which you quote formally from any suitable book at hand. Begin in this way: [author] *states in* [book] . . . Punctuate correctly.

10

Model Answer

    Emerson states in his *Collected Essays*: "Every sweet has its sour; every evil, its good."

. . . .

In your own answer, a colon should precede the quotation, which should be in quotation marks.

11

Write a sentence beginning in this way: *A good athlete has these characteristics* . . . Complete the sentence by listing several appropriate items. Punctuate correctly.

11

Model Answer

    A good athlete has these characteristics: speed, keenness of vision, and good coordination.

. . . .

A colon should precede your list.

12

Finish honestly: One thing I hope to remember from this lesson is that . . .

(In this frame, any answer that you consider honest and accurate is acceptable.)

Lesson 78: Answers to Questions for Added Practice

1. B **2.** colon **6.** A. comma B. colon C. colon D. no mark **7.** A. No mark B. Colon **8.** A. Colon B. No mark **9.** A. Comma B. Colon

---

═══79═══

Colons: Eight Miscellaneous Uses

After writing your answer(s) in the right-hand column, check this column to see whether you have responded correctly. If you have made a mistake, or if you need more practice, do whatever is asked below the dotted line in each answer frame.

Answers to questions for added practice can be found at the end of each lesson.

Answers and Added Practice

1

colon

. . . .

Punctuate:

    1   16 a.m.

    11   26 a.m.

    9   00 p.m.

2

chapter, verse, colon

. . . .

Punctuate:

    Psalms 23   7

    John 3   16

Understanding and Applying the Principles

1

The party began at 9:30 p.m.

The sentence above shows that a _____ [What mark?] is used between figures designating hours and minutes.

Note: for an exact hour, 1:00 a.m., 1 a.m., and one a.m. are all acceptable.

2

The minister took as his text Psalms 52:2.

Bible citations show chapter and verse. In the example, the number 52 represents a _____ in the Book of Psalms in the Old Testament, and the number 2 represents a _____ _____. Those numbers are separated by a _____.

3

Dear Annie,
Dear Mr. Waddell:

As Lesson 78 indicates, a colon is a rather formal mark of punctuation. The first salutation above is suitable for a(n) ____ _____ [*formal* or *informal*?] letter. The second is appropriate for most _____ [*business* or *personal*?] correspondence.

3

informal, business

. . . .

The salutation of a letter to a prospective employer should normally be followed by a _____ .

4

colon

. . . .

After the phrase *See also:* a colon is appropriate if two or more references follow; if only one follows, no punctuation is needed.

N.B.: (from Latin words meaning "Note carefully") is another example.

5

colon

. . . .

Add a colon and two commas where they are needed.

"They tell us that capitalism is doomed Karl Marx I believe made the same announcement eighty years ago."—Sir C. P. Herbert

---

6

those, colon

. . . .

Punctuate completely:

Two dimes a comb and a book of matches my pockets contain nothing more

---

4

Note: A colon should not be used after the salutation of a friendly (personal) letter. In a business letter addressed to someone considered a personal friend, either a colon or a comma is acceptable.

The example above shows that a _____ [What mark?] is also used after a word such as *Note* that calls special attention to a following statement.

5

"A face which is always serene possesses a mysterious and powerful attraction: sad hearts come to it as to the sun to warm themselves again."—Joseph Roux

The sentence above illustrates the fact that a _____ [What mark?] may be used between two independent clauses when the second explains, rephrases, or elaborates on the first.

6

A hearty dinner, a warm fire, good conversation: those are the ingredients of a pleasant evening.

Many sentences end with a list. One like the above, however, starts with a list and then provides the subject of the sentence, which here is the word _____ . The list is separated from the following part by a _____ .

7

Stewart, George R. *American Place-Names*. New York: Oxford, 1970.

One frequently used style for listing a book in a bibliography is illustrated above. It includes a colon between the name of the _____ where the book was published and the name of the _____ .

7

city, publisher

. . . .

Using the example in Frame 7 as a model, punctuate completely:

Ripley Warren *Battleground* Charleston S C News & Courier and Evening Post 1983

8

One helpful reference book is Theodore Bernstein's *The Careful Writer: A Modern Guide to English Usage.*

That sentence illustrates the use of a colon between a _____ and a _____ .

8

title, subtitle

. . . .

Copy the title and the subtitle of this lesson.

9

We have noted in this lesson eight miscellaneous uses of the colon:

    A. to separate _____ and _____ in designating time; B. to separate _____ and _____ in Bible references; C. to follow the salutation in a _____ _____ letter; D. to follow an attention-calling word such as _____ ; E. to separate _____ [*dependent* or *independent*?] clauses when the second explains, rephrases, or elaborates the first; F. to follow a 1_____ at the start of a sentence; G. in a bibliography, to separate _____ and _____ ; H. to separate a title and a _____ .

9

  A. hours, minutes
  B. chapters, verses
  C. business
  D. *Note*
  E. independent
  F. list
  G. city, publisher
  H. subtitle

10

In Frames 10–12, insert colons where they are needed.

    A. 4 53 p.m.
    B. Luke 7 13
    C. Dear General Hahn
    D. Note The authorship is still in doubt.

10

  A. 4:53   B. 7:13
  C. Hahn: D. Note:

. . . .

Make up and write four examples of your own, similar to those in Frame 10.

11

  A. Swinburne loved to experiment with metrical forms he tried his hand at many of the elaborate and artificial French stanzas.
  B. Rondels, rondeaux, chansons he attempted them all.

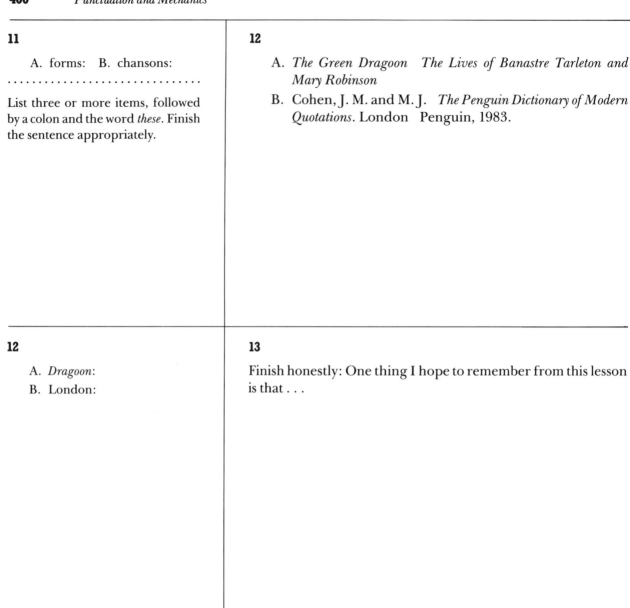

11

    A. forms: B. chansons:

....

List three or more items, followed by a colon and the word *these*. Finish the sentence appropriately.

12

    A. *The Green Dragoon The Lives of Banastre Tarleton and Mary Robinson*

    B. Cohen, J. M. and M. J. *The Penguin Dictionary of Modern Quotations*. London Penguin, 1983.

12

    A. *Dragoon*:

    B. London:

13

Finish honestly: One thing I hope to remember from this lesson is that . . .

(In this frame, any answer that you consider honest and accurate is acceptable.)

Lesson 79: Answers to Questions for Added Practice

1. 1:16 11:26 9:00 **2.** 23:7 3:16 **3.** colon **5.** . . . doomed: . . . Marx, I believe, made . . . **6.** Two dimes, a comb, and a book of matches: my pockets contain nothing more. **7.** Ripley, Warren. *Battleground*. Charleston, S.C.: News & Courier & Evening Post, 1983. **8.** Colons: Eight Miscellaneous Uses **10.** MODELS: A. 6:27 a.m. B. Isaiah 13:2 C. Dear Dr. Lamb: D. Note: Some authorities dispute the claim. **11.** MODEL: A dictionary, a thesaurus, and a one-volume encyclopedia: these I use almost every time I write.

80

Apostrophes in Contractions: To Keep he'll from Looking Like hell

After writing your answer(s) in the right-hand column, check this column to see whether you have responded correctly. If you have made a mistake, or if you need more practice, do whatever is asked below the dotted line in each answer frame.

Answers to questions for added practice can be found at the end of each lesson.

Understanding and Applying the Principles

1

An apostrophe can make a difference in meaning and in pronunciation. Say these pairs of words to yourself:

shell	shed	well	were	hell
she'll	she'd	we'll	we're	he'll

Are the words in the bottom row the same in meaning and in pronunciation as those in the top row? _____

Answers and Added Practice

1

    No

. . . .

If the apostrophe is omitted from *can't* and *won't*, two rather uncommon words result. What are they?

_____ _____

2

Expressions like *I'm*, *he's*, and *weren't* and those in the bottom row in Frame 1 are called *contractions* because they contract words—squeeze them together.

    A. In *I'm*, ___ [What letter?] has been squeezed out.

    B. In *he's*, ___ or ___ ___ has been squeezed out.

    C. In *weren't*, ___ has been squeezed out.

2

    A. *a* B. *i, ha* C. *o*

. . . .

    A. In *she's*, ___ ___ or ___ has been squeezed out.

    B. In *you'll* the apostrophe replaces ___ ___.

3

In writing a contraction, we put an apostrophe in the place where one or more letters have been squeezed out. Knowing this fact gives help in spelling.

    For instance, in the contraction of *does not*, the *o* in *not* is squeezed out. This shows that the correct spelling of the contraction is _____.

3

> doesn't

....

Spell the contractions:

they are _____

we are _____

have not _____

were not _____

4

Two odd contractions are *won't* and *shan't*. *Woll* is an old spelling of *will*. *Won't* is contracted from *woll not*, with letters squeezed out in two places, but only _____ [How many?] apostrophe(s) is (are) used.

Shan't is contracted from *shall not*, with letters again squeezed out in two places. It also is written with _____ [How many?] apostrophe(s).

4

> one, one

....

Shan't, along with *shall*, is used less and less frequently, but still exists, perhaps more commonly in England than in the United States.

5

> o'clock   ass'n   the Class of '91

The expressions above also show the use of apostrophes to indicate omission.

A. Since *o'clock* is short for *of the clock*, the apostrophe represents omission of __ [What letter?] and _____ [What word?]

B. In lists and the like, business people may write *ass'n* for *association*, omitting _____. [What letters?]

C. In '91, the apostrophe probably represents what number? _____

5

> A. *f, the*   B. *ociatio*   C. 19

....

Contractions such as *e'er* for *ever*, *e'en* for *even*, and *'tis* for *it is*, all once popular in poetry, are now seldom seen. *Halloween* was once *All Hallow E'en*, in which *E'en* meant "Evening." (*Hallow* is an old word for "Saint.")

6

An important point to remember is that possessives of pronouns are not contractions and should *not* be written with apostrophes. Probably nobody would write *hi's*, but it is just as undesirable to write *hers*, *yours*, *ours*, or *theirs* with an apostrophe.

It's is correct (with an apostrophe) when it is a contraction of ____ ____ [What two words?], but in *The cat drank its milk*, there is no contraction and therefore no apostrophe. [See also Lesson 63, Frame 6.]

6

> *it is*

....

Spell correctly the *s-* possessive form of each:

their _____   her _____

your _____   our _____

it   _____

7

In summary, we should insert an _____ in a contraction in the place where two or more letters have been

_____.

7

apostrophe, omitted

·····································

How do you know that *did'nt* is an incorrect spelling?

8

In Frames 8–14, spell correctly the contraction of the words listed.

I have   you have   she has   they have

8

I've, you've, she's, they've

·····································

In Answer Frames 8–14, choose one of the contractions at the top of the frame and write a short sentence using it.

9

I am   you are   he is   they are

9

I'm, you're, he's, they're

·····································

10

I had   we had   you had   she had

10

I'd, we'd, you'd, she'd

·····································

11

I would   we would   you would   she would

Note that these spellings are exactly the same as those for *I had*, etc.

11

   I'd, we'd, you'd, she'd

. . . .

12

   we shall   I shall   I will   you will
   he will   they will

12

   we'll, I'll, I'll, you'll, he'll, they'll

. . . .

13

   is not   are not   was not   were not
   will not   shall not   could not
   would not

13

   isn't, aren't, wasn't, weren't,
   won't, shan't, couldn't,
   wouldn't

. . . .

14

   does not   do not   did not   has not
   have not   can not   let us

14

   doesn't, don't, didn't, hasn't,
   haven't, can't, let's

15

Finish honestly: One thing I hope to remember from this lesson
is that . . .

(In this frame, any answer that you consider honest and accurate is acceptable.)

Lesson 80: Answers to Questions for Added Practice

1. cant, wont **2.** A. *ha, i* B. *wi* (or possibly *sha*) **3.** they're, we're, haven't, weren't **6.** theirs, hers, yours, ours, its **7.** MODEL: The apostrophe belongs where the letter *o* has been omitted. **8–14.** (Answers will vary according to the words chosen. Check to be sure that each apostrophe is properly placed.)

═══81═══

Apostrophes to Show Possession: Did You Ever Hear of the Cat's Pajamas?

After writing your answer(s) in the right-hand column, check this column to see whether you have responded correctly. If you have made a mistake, or if you need more practice, do whatever is asked below the dotted line in each answer frame.

Answers to questions for added practice can be found at the end of each lesson.

Understanding and Applying the Principles

1

Your great-grandparents in their youth may have described something they liked very much as "the cat's pajamas" or "the cat's meow." (The ways of slang are remarkable and inexplicable.)

The fact that the cat had pajamas (or a meow) is shown by the use of the _____ [What mark?] in *cat's*.

Answers and Added Practice

1

apostrophe

. . . .

Let's dress some other animals in unlikely attire. Write the possessive form of each italicized word.

a *dog* undershirt _____

a *mule* tuxedo _____

a *turtle* trousers _____

a *tiger* slippers _____

a *cow* brassiere _____

2

A. Does the word *cat* end in *s*? _____

B. To form the possessive of a noun that does not end in *s*, we add an apostrophe and *s*. So, to indicate pajamas belonging to a cat, we write *the _____ pajamas.*

C. To indicate the feet belonging to a man, we write *the _____ feet.*

D. To indicate the feet belonging to several men, we write *the _____ feet.*

2

    A. No B. *cat's* C. *man's*
    D. *men's*

....

Answer as in Answer Frame 1.

    a *woman* clothing _____

    two *women* dresses _____

3

Another cat joins the first. So now we have *cats*.

    A. Does the word *cats* end in *s*? _____

    B. To form the possessive of a noun that ends in *s*, all that we do is add an apostrophe. So, to show that both cats have pajamas, we write *the* _____ *pajamas.*

    C. To indicate the feet belonging to several ladies, we write *the* _____ *feet.*

3

    A. Yes B. *cats'* C. *ladies'*

....

Answer as in Frame 1. Regard each italicized word as a plural.

    horses collars _____

    dogs pants _____

    raccoons neckties _____

4

    Keats' poetry or **Keats's poetry**
    Burns' poem or **Burns's poem**
    Mr. Collins' house or **Mr. Collins's house**

Keats, Burns, and *Collins* are examples of names ending in *s*.

    A. The first example in each pair shows that it is proper to write the possessive of such a name with only an _____ _____ at the end.

    B. The second example in each pair shows that it is also proper to use both an _____ and the letter _____.

Note: Increasingly, editors are recommending the second forms because those reflect the usual pronunciations. However, when the following word starts with *s* or *z*, forms such as *Keats' sonnet* or *Burns' zeal* are usual.

4

    A. apostrophe
    B. apostrophe, *s*

....

To show that Jones has a car, we may write either _____ car or _____ car (but never, *never* Jone's car).

    To show that the Joneses have a car, we of course write the _____ _____ car.

5

    This is my uncle's house.
    The roof of the house is steep.

    A. Is an uncle a creature that has or had life? _____

    B. Is a house something that has or had life? _____

Things that can possess no life, such as a house (bridge, store, rock) are said to be *inanimate*.

5

A. Yes B. No

. . . .

Write *A* for Animate (living), *I* for Inanimate.

_____ stove

_____ shirt

_____ cousin

_____ poet

_____ hill

_____ donkey

6

Generally we form the possessive of an inanimate noun by using an *of*-phrase. It is not really wrong to say *the house's roof*, but many persons argue that a house, or anything else inanimate, cannot really possess anything. So, instead of *the house's roof*, they write _____ .

Note: A possessive that appears in frequently used expressions, such as *today's paper* or *a day's work*, is accepted without question.

6

the roof of the house

. . . .

Choose one of the three inanimate nouns in Answer Frame 5. Write a sentence with it, comparable to *The roof of the house is steep.*

7

The United States Postal Service does not approve apostrophes in names of most post office towns. So if you write to anyone in Devils Elbow, MO; Devils Lake, ND; Devils Tower, WY; or even Angels Camp, CA, use no apostrophes in the address.

In names not those of towns, though, everyone must simply remember whether or not an apostrophe is conventional in each—or look up the name in an atlas. Devil's Kitchen, California (some boiling springs), has an apostrophe, but Devils Desk, Alaska (a peak), does not.

A few common nouns that look like possessives have no apostrophes: a *teachers* college, for example. (The teachers do not own the college.)

If you address a letter to someone in Kings Creek, SC, do you need an apostrophe? _____

7

No

. . . .

General Zebulon Pike failed to climb *Pikes Peak*, which bears his name (no apostrophe).

In New Zealand, a bay is named *Hawke Bay*, but the land area next to it is *Hawke's Bay*.

8

A. We have seen that to form the possessive of a word like *duck*, which does not end in *s*, we add an apostrophe and an _____.

B. To form the possessive of a word like *ducks*, which ends in *s*, we add only an _____ .

C. To form the possessive of a name like *Watkins*, we may add either an _____ only or both an _____ and an _____.

8

    A. *s* B. apostrophe

    C. apostrophe, apostrophe, *s*

....

Write two other words that fit under each of the three principles summarized in Frame 8.

    A. _____ _____

    B. _____ _____

    C. _____ _____

9

Write the possessive form of each word in parentheses.

    A. a (mule) temperament _____

    B. a (student) books _____

    C. a (fly) wings _____

    D. a (brother) sarcasm _____

9

    A. mule's B. student's

    C. fly's   D. brother's

....

Proceed as in Frame 9.

    a (dog) life   _____

    a (canary) song _____

    a (king) crown _____

10

Each word in parentheses is a plural and ends in *s*. Write the possessive form.

    A. (mules) temperaments _____

    B. (students) books _____

    C. (flies) wings _____

    D. (brothers) sarcasm _____

10

    A. mules' B. students'

    C. flies'   D. brothers'

....

Proceed in the same way.

    (dogs) lives   _____

    (canaries) songs _____

    (kings) crowns _____

11

Decide first whether the thing mentioned in italics is animate or inanimate, and then choose the more appropriate form.

    A. _____ [*The fox's fur* or *The fur of the fox?*] was singed.

    B. _____

    [*This oil's viscosity* or *The viscosity of this oil?*] is high.

11

    A. The fox's fur

    B. The viscosity of this oil

....

Neither *The fur of the fox* nor *This oil's viscosity* would be wrong, but the answers reflect the preferred usage.

12

The principles in this lesson refer only to nouns, not to pronouns. That is, the possessive pronouns *mine, yours, his, hers, its, ours,* and *theirs* _____ [*should* or *should not?*] be written with apostrophes.

12

should not

. . . .

For practice in using apostrophes with pronouns only when a contraction is involved, copy these sentences exactly.

The glory is hers. It's yours. It is ours. It is theirs.

13

Write a sentence in which you use a possessive form in referring to a bicycle belonging to your cousin.

13

Model Answer

My cousin's bicycle is blue.

. . . .

Follow the instructions in Frame 13, but substitute some grain and a farmer.

14

Rewrite the sentence you wrote in Frame 13. This time the bicycle belongs to your cousins.

14

Model Answer

My cousins' bicycle is blue.

. . . .

Rewrite the sentence you wrote for Answer Frame 13. This time the grain belongs to several farmers.

15

Write a sentence in which you use the possessive form of *sister* and the *s* possessive of *you*.

15

Model Answer

My sister's dress is green, but yours is yellow.

16

Finish honestly: One thing I hope to remember from this lesson is that . . .

(In this frame, any answer that you consider honest and accurate is acceptable.)

Lesson 81: Answers to Questions for Added Practice

1. dog's, mule's, turtle's, tiger's, cow's **2.** woman's, women's **3.** horses', dogs', raccoons' **4.** Jones', Jones's, Joneses' **5.** I, I, A, A, I, A **6.** MODEL: The top of the stove was hot. **8.** MODELS: A. raven's, child's B. chickens', gorillas' C. Dickens' or Dickens's novels, Morris' or Morris's chair **9.** dog's, canary's, king's **10.** dogs', canaries', kings' **12.** The glory is hers. It's yours. It is ours. It is theirs. **13.** MODEL: The farmer's grain was destroyed. **14.** MODEL: The farmers' grain was destroyed.

═══82═══

Apostrophes in Unusual Plurals:
2's, m's, &'s, +'s, #'s, !'s

After writing your answer(s) in the right-hand column, check this column to see whether you have responded correctly. If you have made a mistake, or if you need more practice, do whatever is asked below the dotted line in each answer frame.

Answers to questions for added practice can be found at the end of each lesson.

Understanding and Applying the Principles

1

Singular	**Plural**	**Singular**	**Plural**
a tree	two trees	a box	several boxes

As the examples above remind you, almost all plurals in English are formed by adding ___ [What letter?] or ___ ___ [What letters?] to the basic word.

With a small number of items, however, an apostrophe and *s* form the plurals.

Answers and Added Practice

1

s, es

....

Write the plural of each word. (No apostrophes here, please!)

pigeon   _____

bush   _____

avenue   _____

catastrophe   _____

beach   _____

alumnus   _____

2

The first four vowels of *indivisible* are all *i*'s.

On a few occasions we may need to refer to the plural of a letter. We underline (italicize in print) the letter and then add an _____ [What mark?] and an ____. [What letter?]

2

apostrophe, *s*

....

In Answer Frames 2–5, write the plural of each item that is in parentheses.

   A. He wrote two odd-shaped (g) _____.

   B. There are three (n) _____ in *drunkenness*.

3

Do not use too many *and*'s and *so*'s.

Sometimes, as in the sentence above, we refer to words as words. Again we underline (italicize) and then add an _____ _____ and an ____.

Note: *and*s, *so*s, *moreover*s and the like are also permissible, but may be confusing, as *is*s certainly would be.

3

apostrophe, *s*

....

   A. I included several (therefore) _____ in my sentence.

   B. He used too many (but) ____ _____.

4

Many typewriters have &'s but no +'s.

The example above shows that a sign or a symbol is also pluralized _____. [Tell how]

4

by adding an apostrophe and an *s*

....

Write the symbols in parentheses as plurals:

   A. (#) _____

   B. (*) _____

5

The 1's, 2's, and 3's are always easier than the problems with the higher numbers.

As is true of other signs and symbols, _____ are usually pluralized by adding an apostrophe and *s*.

Note: Both *the 1980's* and *the 1980s* are permissible, as are *the 80's*, *the 80s*, and *the eighties*.

5

numbers (or figures)

....

Write the numerals in parentheses as plurals:

A. His (7) _____ look like (1) _____.

B. There are three (8) _____ in the zip code.

6

Wrong: **WELCOME TO OUR CHURCH'S**

In some places the roadsides bristle with unneeded apostrophes. Signboards urge us—all erroneously—to buy FRESH PEACH'S, GOOD EAT'S, and USED TIRE'S, to rent CHOICE ROOM'S, to stop for EXPERT REPAIR'S, or to go fishing with WORM'S.

If you ever become a sign painter, don't add to the clutter. Advertise FRESH _____, substitute GOOD FOOD for the peculiar noun-verb EATS and announce the availability of USED _____, CHOICE _____, EXPERT ____ _____, and, for the fisherman, _____. [Fill in the missing words, with *no* apostrophes.]

6

PEACHES, TIRES, ROOMS, REPAIRS, WORMS, (Of course, people are welcome to our CHURCHES)

....

Try to recall two or more words you have seen, on signs or elsewhere, in which unnecessary apostrophes have been used.

7

A. We have seen in Frames 2–5 that _____ referred to as letters, _____ referred to as words, _____ or signs such as # or &, and _____ _____ referred to as numbers may be pluralized with an apostrophe and _____.

B. In Frames 1 and 6 we were reminded that ordinary plurals _____ [*should* or *should not*?] be written with apostrophes.

7

A. letters, words, symbols, numbers, *s*

B. should not

8

Write a sentence in which you use a plural to tell what the first and last letters of *temperament* are.

8

Model Answer

The first and last letters of *temperament* are *t*'s.

....

Using a plural, tell how many times the letter *b* occurs in *hubbub*.

9

Write a sentence in which you use a plural form to tell a good friend that he or she uses the word *fantastic* too often in writing.

9

Model Answer

    Diana, darling, all those *fantastic*'s seem—too fantastic.

. . . .

Write the plural of *or* in a sentence.

10

On many typewriters and word processors is the symbol @, used commercially to mean "at" or "each." Write a sentence using the plural of that sign.

10

Model Answer

    The @'s on both machines were inoperative.

. . . .

Write the plural of * in a sentence.

11

Write a sentence containing the plural of 7.

11

Model Answer

    I remember the two 7's at the beginning.

. . . .

Write the plural of 18 in a sentence.

12

Finish honestly: One thing I hope to remember from this lesson is that . . .

(In this frame, any answer that you consider honest and accurate is acceptable.)

Lesson 82: Answers to Questions for Added Practice

1. pigeons, bushes, avenues, catastrophes, beaches, alumni **2.** A. *g*'s B. *n*'s **3.** A. *therefore*'s B. *but*'s **4.** A. #'s B. *'s **5.** A. 7's, 1's B. 8's **6.** (Personal recollection) **8.** MODEL: The word *hubbub* has three *b*'s. **9.** MODEL: Do you really need two *or*'s in that sentence? **10.** MODEL: She typed a line of *'s. **11.** No 18's are left on the rack.

≡83≡

Hyphens in Dividing Words: Avoiding Breakdowns in the Process

After writing your answer(s) in the right-hand column, check this column to see whether you have responded correctly. If you have made a mistake, or if you need more practice, do whatever is asked below the dotted line in each answer frame.

Answers to questions for added practice can be found at the end of each lesson.

Understanding and Applying the Principles

1

Look at the subtitle of this lesson. What do you notice that seems odd?

Answers and Added Practice

1

Model Answer

The word *breakdowns* seems to be divided oddly, and for a moment is difficult to read.

....

Other odd and incorrect divisions: thro-ugh, friends-hip, knickkn-acks

2

A. The word *breakdowns* consists of _____ [How many?] syllables. [If you pronounce a word rather slowly, you can usually recognize the individual syllables into which it may be divided.]

B. When a word must be divided at the end of a line, the division should be made only between syllables. So *breakdowns* should be divided between _____ and _____ .

2

    A. two
    B. break, downs

································

The words *friendship* and *knickknacks* should be divided after _____ and after _____ .

3

Pronounce the word *occasionally*. You will hear that the syllables are ___ ___, ___ ___, ___ ___ ___, ___ ___, and ___ ___. The word may be divided at any one of _____ [How many?] places.

3

    oc, ca, sion, al, ly; four

································

The syllables of *avalanche* are _____, _____, and _____ .

4

Typists and word-processor operators are taught not to divide a word in such a way that only one letter is on either line. (Some teachers say that no fewer than three letters should be on either line.)

    May *via* be divided? _____ *omit?* _____ *amend?* _____

4

    No No No

································

Which of these words may be divided?

    evoke, amuse, appeal, touchy, really, grimy

_____

5

    A. Divisions may be made only between syllables. May a one-syllable word be divided? _____
    B. May any of these words be divided? *smiles, right, wrong, bright, strong, though, through, steady* _____

5

    A. No B. No

································

Which of these words may be divided?

    length, signet, brooch, thought, defy

_____

6

As a rule, if a word has a prefix, such as *ante-, anti-, contra-,* or *hyper-,* the prefix should not be divided. Neither should most suffixes, such as *-ible, -eous,* or *-tion.*

    A. The word *anticlimax*, then, may be divided in one of ___ _____ [How many?] places?
    B. *Repetition* may be divided after ___ ___ ___, ___, or ___ ___ but not after the *t* or the *ti* in the suffix.

Note: Because dictionaries indicate how words are divided into syllables, they necessarily show a division in *an-ti* and other prefixes and suffixes. In your writing, however, it is not wise to divide them.

6

    A. two (after *anti* or *cli*)

    B. *rep, e, ti*

· ·

    A. May *interrupt* be divided after *in*? _____ May *intrude*? _____

    B. May *debatable* be divided after the *t*? _____ After the second *a*? _____

    C. May *climatic* be divided after the *t*? _____ May *explanation*? _____

7

The suffix *-ed* on a verb or the suffix *-es* on a verb or a noun should not be separated from the basic word. Neither should a contracted part (such as *n't*) or any part of a word that may cause misreading.

    A. Should *climbed* be divided? _____

    B. Should *thrushes* be divided? _____

    C. Should *unions*? _____ *didn't*? _____ *sources*? _____

7

    A. No B. No

    C. No, No, No

· ·

Write *Yes* before each word that may be divided.

_____ *haven't*   _____ *ditches*

_____ *swelled*   _____ *motto*

_____ *pitched*   _____ *pitcher*

8

A few other hints:

1. *sixty-one* (not *six-ty-one*; divide hyphenated words only at the hyphen.)
2. *tell-ing* (the basic word is *tell*), but *run-ning* (the basic word is not *runn*.)
3. *com-mand, for-give* (many divisions occur between consonants.)
4. Do not divide figures or abbreviations.

Rewrite with hyphens to show permissible places of division:

seventy-two _____

sitting _____ *falling* _____

combatting _____

8

    seventy-two, sit-ting, fall-ing, com-batting *or* combat-ting

· ·

Rewrite to show where each word may be divided:

calling _____

fifty-four _____

jamming _____

cutting _____

recalled _____

jabbing _____

9

Sometimes you may still be in doubt about where a word may be divided. If so, look at the divisions indicated by the pronunciations in your dictionary.

Write the following words with hyphens to show the place(s) where division is permitted:

posture   *hesitancy*   *pottery*   *identify*

9

    pos-ture
    hes-i-tan-cy
    pot-tery
    iden-ti-fy

In *pottery* and *identify -tery* and *iden-* are not divided, to avoid leaving a single letter on a line

---

10

Which of these words *may not* be divided?

    opaque   perform   straight   strength
    lucid   grainy   twenty-six

10

    opaque, straight, strength, grainy, twenty-six (except before *six*)

....

Copy the words that *should not* be divided.

    opine, opium, thorough, tacky, weight, weighty

11

Copy the letters that show at which places each of these words *may not* be divided.

    A B   C   D E   F G
con tra dict   hy per a cid i ty

    H   I   J K   L M N O
in sup port a ble   cou ra ge ous ness

11

    A, C, K, N

....

Follow the instructions in Frame 11.

    A   B C D
su per cil i ous

    E   F   G
in fra struc ture

12

Which of these *may not* be divided?

    foxes   wispy   spelled   tendon
    around   walked   1,000,000   U.S.A.F.

12

    foxes; wispy; spelled; around;
walked; 1,000,000; U.S.A.F.

· ·

Which of these *may not* be divided?

    *boxy, boxer, among, amount,
animal, 6,478*

13

Hyphenate to show correct places of division.

    swimming ――――――――――― yelling ―――――――――

    sagging ――――――――――― rebelling ―――――――――

13

    swim-ming, yell-ing,
sag-ging, re-bel-ling

· ·

Hyphenate at points of division.

    asking   ――――――――――

    stalling ――――――――――

    knitting ――――――――――

    slapping ――――――――――

14

Write a sentence of your own about a friendly raccoon, arranging it so that you need to divide at least one word at the end of a line.

14

Model Answer

    The friendly raccoon deliberately observed me as I approached.

15

Finish honestly: One thing I hope to remember from this lesson is that . . .

(In this frame, any answer that you consider honest and accurate is acceptable.)

Lesson 83: Answers to Questions for Added Practice

2. *friend, knick* **3.** av-a-lanche **4.** *appeal, really* **5.** *signet, defy* **6.** A. No (because the prefix *inter* should not be divided). Yes B. Yes. No C. Yes. No **7.** Yes before *motto* and *pitcher.* **8.** call-ing fifty-four jam-ming cut-ting re-called jab-bing **10.** *opine, tacky, weight, weighty* **11.** A, D, E **12.** *boxy, among, amount, 6,478* **13.** *ask-ing, stall-ing, knit-ting, slap-ping*

═══84═══

Miscellaneous Uses of Hyphens: Twenty-five Dollar Bills or Twenty Five-dollar Bills?

After writing your answer(s) in the right-hand column, check this column to see whether you have responded correctly. If you have made a mistake, or if you need more practice, do whatever is asked below the dotted line in each answer frame.

Answers to questions for added practice can be found at the end of each lesson.

Understanding and Applying the Principles

1

Look at the subtitle of this lesson.

   A. Would you prefer having 1) twenty-five dollar bills or 2) twenty five-dollar bills? _____ [1 or 2?]

   B. Why?

Answers and Added Practice

1

   A. 2 B. **Model Answer:** The first is $25; the second, $100.

. . . .

Sometimes a hyphen can prevent momentary misreading:

   The war destroyed statues can never be replaced.

(Put a hyphen after *war.*)

2

Twenty-five illustrates the use of a hyphen in a compound number. Compound numbers are those made of two words, such as the ones in the twenties, the thirties, and so on. The hyphen makes them look like a single word, but they are easier to read than *twentyone, eightyeight,* and so on would be.

Note: Ordinal numbers, such as *twenty-first* are also hyphenated.

   Should *forty-six* and *forty-sixth* both be hyphenated? _____

2

Yes

. . . .

Place hyphens where needed:

    A. Sixty third Street
    B. forty nine cents
    C. one hundred thirty two

3

two hundred crates   one thousand soldiers

Numbers such as *one hundred* and *four million* are not regarded as compound numbers and so _____ [*should* or *should not?*] be hyphenated.

Note: Lesson 83 mentioned that figures should not be divided and hyphenated. A figure such as *45,000,000* would be confusing if you placed *45,000,-* on one line and *000* on the next. Even more confusing would be *45,42-* followed by *6,489* on the next line.

3

should not

. . . .

In Answer Frame 2, is your answer to C correct? _____

4

One-fourth of two hundred is fifty.
Workers wasted one fourth of the cement.

    A. When a fraction refers to an exact amount, as in the first example, it _____ [*should* or *should not?*] be hyphenated.
    B. When it refers to an approximate amount, as in the second example, it _____ [*should* or *should not?*] be hyphenated.

4

    A. should   B. should not

. . . .

    A. **Count out one third of the pencils.**
    B. **About one third of the people are below age twelve.**

_____ [A or B] needs a hyphen in *one third*.

5

not **reemerge**, but **re-emerge**
not **skillless**, but **skill-less**

State in your own words what you think is the reason for recommending a hyphen in words like those above.

Note: Not all dictionaries show hyphens in such words, but it seems desirable to hyphenate when readers might otherwise be briefly confused. Such common words as *cooperate* are usually not hyphenated.

5

Model Answer
    The double *e* in *reemerge* and the triple *l* in *skillless* would make those words hard to read.

. . . .

Other examples: *bell-like, troll-like, anti-imperialistic, re-edit*

6

Because of a large stain, it was necessary to re-cover the sofa.

The hyphen in *re-cover* is needed to prevent confusion with the different word _____ .

6

recover

....

Do you see the difference between *recollect* and *re-collect*? _____ *recreation* and *re-creation*? _____

7

a fun-loving boy   a sinister-looking
weapon

In *fun-loving*, a noun (*fun*) and an *-ing* form of a verb (the present participle *loving*) are combined to serve as a modifier. In *sinister-looking*, an adjective and an *-ing* form are combined.

Hyphenate as necessary:

A. He pulled out an old stem winding watch.
B. I do not like bitter tasting coffee.

7

A. stem-winding   B. bitter-tasting

....

Place hyphens where needed.

A. a strange looking couple
B. an odd looking glass (meaning "strange")
C. an odd looking glass (meaning "mirror")

8

a well-read senior   a quiet-spoken man
a one-year guarantee

In those examples, the modifiers *well*, *quiet*, and *one* are combined with the past participles *read* and *spoken* or with the noun *year*.

Should *well played* (as in *a well played concerto*) and *below par* (as in *a below par round of golf*) both be hyphenated? _____

Note: When an expression like *well read* or *fun loving* comes after the word modified, it customarily is not hyphenated: **The senior was well read.** Also, no hyphen should be used after an adverb ending in *-ly* in phrases such as *an easily read thermometer* or *carefully made plans*.

8

Yes

....

Place hyphens where needed.

Trying to reenter the gas filled room, the twenty three guards were driven back by the vile smelling fumes.

9

ex-wife   self-indulgence
all-encompassing   pro-American
senator-elect

A. The first three examples above show that it is customary to hyphenate words that use the prefix _____ , _____ , or _____ .
B. The fourth example shows the use of a hyphen when a prefix comes before a word written with a _____ letter.
C. When *elect* is used as a suffix, it customarily is preceded by a _____ . [What mark?]

9

A. ex-, self-, all-
B. capital   C. hyphen

. . . .

Write five different words similar to the five examples in Frame 9.

10

The money was in five- and ten-dollar bills.

The hyphen after *five* is called a *suspension hyphen*. It remains "in suspension" (just hangs there) until it joins the word *dollar* later in the sentence.

Where should a hyphen be placed in the following sentence? **Several six and seven-year-old children were in the group.** _____

10

six-

. . . .

Place hyphens where needed.

The eight by sixteen foot bed-room seemed too narrow.

11

In Frames 11–13, insert a hyphen at a place marked by a caret if you think one is needed. Do not add unnecessary hyphens.

Twenty‸three of the seldom‸seen bats darted out of the suddenly‸well‸lighted cavern.

11

Twenty-three, seldom-seen, well-lighted

. . . .

In Answer Frames 11–13, follow the instructions in Frame 11.

Forty‸four of the still‸loved professor's former students were there.

12

When well‸dressed paraders began to re‸form to resume their slow‸moving and frequently‸ interrupted march, the Twenty‸first Brigade led the way down the avenue, which was unusually well‸lighted.

12

well-dressed, re-form, slow-moving, Twenty-first

. . . .

For the benefit of a late‸ arriving television camera-man, the medals were repre-sented to the pro‸American officers.

13

The new co‸owner of the semi‸independent newspaper granted eight‸ to ten‸dollar‸raises to the ex‸employees who had returned.

13

co-owner, semi-independent, eight-, ten-, ex-employees

. . . .

The Bible‸quoting gover-nor‸elect re̦encountered the suddenly‸hostile crowd.

14

Write the following, hyphenating where necessary.

  A. A short sentence that includes a compound number.

  B. A two-word expression that means "a bellow like the bellow of a bull."

  C. A sentence in which you use a hyphenated word to describe an insect that carries disease.

14

Model Answers

  A. I've never heard seventy-six trombones.

  B. bull-like bellow

  C. The *Anopheles* mosquito is a disease-carrying insect.

. . . .

Write a hyphenated word that means "like the shape of a hill."

15

Write the following, hyphenating when necessary.

  A. A sentence including *a two to four year* prison term.

  B. A sentence in which you use a hyphenated word that means "to educate again."

  C. A sentence in which you use *one hundred* and also a compound ordinal number, such as *forty-second*.

15

Model Answers

  A. John is serving a two- to four-year prison term.

  B. My father says that he would like to re-educate himself.

  C. Almost one hundred of such businesses are on Forty-second Street.

16

Finish honestly: One thing I hope to remember from this lesson is that . . .

(In this frame, any answer that you consider honest and accurate is acceptable.)

Lesson 84: Answers to Questions for Added Practice

1. war-destroyed **2. A.** Sixty-third **B.** forty-nine **C.** thirty-two (not between *one* and *hundred* or between *hundred* and *thirty*) **3.** (Personal answer) **4. A. 6.** (Personal answer) **7. A.** strange-looking **B.** odd-looking glass **C.** odd looking-glass **8.** re-enter, gas-filled, twenty-three, vile-smelling **9.** MODELS: ex-governor, self-rule, all-Canadian, anti-British, mayor-elect **10.** eight- by sixteen-foot **11.** Forty-four, still-loved **12.** late-arriving, re-presented, pro-American **13.** Bible-quoting, governor-elect, re-encountered **14.** hill-shaped

85

Dashes and Slashes: Useful in Moderation

After writing your answer(s) in the right-hand column, check this column to see whether you have responded correctly. If you have made a mistake, or if you need more practice, do whatever is asked below the dotted line in each answer frame.

Answers to questions for added practice can be found at the end of each lesson.

Answers and Added Practice

1

    No

. . . .

Someone once suggested that dashes be used for *all* punctuation marks. Doing so would make punctuating easier for writers. What would be one of the effects on readers?

Understanding and Applying the Principles

1

> **We drove through South Dakota—it was very hot—especially in the Badlands—and finally got to the Black Hills—near Rapid City—and saw the huge faces of the presidents—carved by Gutzon Borglum.**

Does that sentence seem smooth and easy to read? _____

2

People who use dashes excessively may be called "dashomaniacs." The dash is not an all-purpose mark. It is occasionally useful in informal writing, and less occasionally in formal writing, but it should not be employed to excess.

    In other words, we should use dashes _____ _____ . [How?]

2

in moderation (*or any term similar in meaning*)

....

An inscription in the Temple of Apollo at Delphi, in Greece:
  NOTHING TO EXCESS

What does that mean?

3

The dash should not be confused with the hyphen. (See Lessons 83 and 84.) In writing, use two hyphen-length lines for a dash, or a single line about twice as long as a hyphen. In typing, unless your typewriter or word processor has a dash, use two hyphens instead.

Look at a typewriter or word processor to which you have access. Does it have a dash? _____

3

(Personal answer)

....

A hyphen usually joins words (*twenty-one*, for example) to show that they are to be treated as one. A dash does not join, but separates rather forcefully.

4

"The sycamore trees are—but those trees aren't sycamores, are they?" Jane asked.

Perhaps the most frequent use of the dash is illustrated above. It is especially useful in reporting conversation. The speaker began her sentence in one way and then _____

_____ . [Did what?]

4

Model Answer
  changed abruptly to a different construction

....

Write another sentence in which a speaker turns suddenly to a different subject.

5

In addition to signaling an abrupt change in the structure of a sentence, a dash may indicate an unfinished sentence. This use, too, is important in reporting conversation, as in this example:

**Helen said, "After this year in college, I'll—"
She paused, wondering how to continue.**

Which is true, according to that example?

  A. The dash alone indicates the breaking-off of the sentence.

  B. A period should accompany the dash.

   _____ [A or B?]

5

A
....

Write another sentence which a speaker leaves unfinished for some reason.

6

1) **James Russell Lowell—poet, professor, editor, and diplomat—was one of the great figures of the nineteenth century.**

2) **The Prohibitionists had one major plank in their platform—outlawing the sale of intoxicants.**

A. In those two examples, would commas make the meanings as clear as the dashes do? _____

B. In 2, what other mark (usually more formal) could be used instead of the dash? _____

6

A. No   B. Colon
....

Finish with a dash and any words that fit:

I am going to college for one chief reason . . .

7

As we noted in Frame 6, dashes often help to make clear the parts of sentences containing appositives or other explanatory material. Commas are more usual for that purpose, but dashes may be used for clarity or when a stronger effect is needed.

Note the marks used with an appositive introduced by *that is, for example,* or *for instance*:

Several breeds of cattle—for instance, Aberdeen Angus, Hereford, Ayrshire, and Devon—are named for places in the British Isles.

The marks used to set off the appositive above are _____ .

7

dashes
....

Write a sentence similar to the example in Frame 7. The topic may be automobiles, college courses, or whatever you wish.

8

The Huns, Avars, Magyars, and Mongols—these expert riders showed the importance of cavalry in war.

Sometimes, as in the sentence above, we may wish to change the structure of a sentence by bringing in a summarizing expression such as *these, these groups,* or *those beliefs.* A _____ [What mark?] is useful for that purpose.

Note: For greater formality, a colon is preferable in such a sentence. (See Lesson 78.)

8

dash

....

Rewrite your sentence in Answer Frame 7 to make it similar to the example in Frame 8.

9

The league-leading hitter dug in, swung from the heels at a chest-high pitch—and struck out!

Once in a while, as in that example, a dash may be placed before a(n) _____ [What kind of?] sentence ending.

9

surprise, *or* unexpected (*or a word similar in meaning*)

....

Write your own sentence with a surprise ending. One possibility: getting an unexpectedly high or low grade.

10

**1979–1987   pages 4–14
Chapters 8–11   the April–June quarter**

A dash that is a little longer than a hyphen but a little shorter than a "regular" dash is used, especially by printers, in expressions like those above. Since few typewriters or word processors have this intermediate mark, a hyphen may be substituted.

  The shorter dash, as in the examples, is a substitute for _____ . [What word?]

10

through

....

Write a sentence using this pattern:

  Name of a famous dead person
  Date of birth—dash—date of death
  Statement about the person.

11

and/or   the pass/fail system   "I knew that I had never seen / Such a lively jumping bean."

The slash, more formally called a *virgule*, is one of the least-used marks.

  A. In the first two examples above, _____ and _____ show the use of the slash to mean that either possibility exists.

  B. The other example shows the slash that separates lines of quoted _____ .

11

    A. *and/or, pass/fail*

    B. verse (*or* poetry)

. . . .

The word *virgule* comes from a Latin word for "small rod." Why is that name appropriate?

12

Write a sentence in which someone begins a remark about children's toys and then switches abruptly to something else. Punctuate correctly.

12

Model Answer

    The children's toys are getting—oh, Mabel, what a lovely dress!

. . . .

Write another sentence using a similar pattern.

13

Write a sentence beginning with *Harry said.* Begin Harry's sentence, but show that he is interrupted before the end. Punctuate correctly.

13

Model Answer

    Harry said, "The ridge road is safer, and—"

    Gladys interrupted, "The valley road is faster."

. . . .

Write two other sentences, using the patterns illustrated above.

14

Write a sentence starting with *The students on the left.* Then say *that is,* and name the students. Finish the sentence. Punctuate correctly.

14

Model Answer

The students on the left—that is, Mary and Tom—finished first.

· ·

Write another sentence using a similar pattern.

15

Write a sentence that ends by naming a surprising (or terrifying, etc.) thing that you saw when you turned on a light.

15

Model Answer

Once, sleepy-eyed, I turned on the light in my brother's room and found myself confronting—a skeleton!

· ·

Write another surprise-ending sentence.

16

Use *and/or* or *pass/fail* in a sentence.

16

Model Answer

I dislike the pass/fail system of grading.

17

Finish honestly: One thing I hope to remember from this lesson is that . . .

(In this frame, any answer that you consider honest and accurate is acceptable.)

Lesson 85: Answers to Questions for Added Practice

1. MODEL: Readers would have more difficulty in understanding. (*Or* Readers would not be shown some of the differences in tone or emphasis that punctuation marks can reveal.) **2.** MODEL: Don't do anything excessively. **4.** MODEL: "I'll tell you about—the meat is burning!" **5.** MODEL: "Where did I put—" "It's in your pocket, Mother." **6.** MODEL:—to become a chemist. **7.** MODEL: Experienced race drivers—for example, Foyt, the Andrettis, and the Unsers—apparently have learned to avoid excessive risks. **8.** MODEL: Foyt, the Andrettis, and the Unsers—such experienced race drivers . . . **9.** MODEL: I opened the envelope and found—an A! **10.** MODEL: Louis Pasteur (1822–1895) is the man from whom pasteurized milk gets its name. **11.** MODEL: A virgule looks like a small rod. **12.** I haven't seen— why, George, I was just commenting that I haven't seen you! **13.** MODEL: Ella said, "The bananas are rotting, and—" Clyde stopped her by shouting, "Quit whining!" **14.** MODEL: The children in the back seat—Martha, Betty, and Paul—were fussing again. **15.** MODEL: The boxer in the black trunks glowered menacingly, dashed toward his opponent—and fell down at the first blow.

▬▬86▬

Parentheses:
To Show a Slight Relationship

After writing your answer(s) in the right-hand column, check this column to see whether you have responded correctly. If you have made a mistake, or if you need more practice, do whatever is asked below the dotted line in each answer frame.

Answers to questions for added practice can be found at the end of each lesson.

Understanding and Applying the Principles

1

Allan Pinkerton (1819–1884) founded a famed detective agency.

Does the material in parentheses have a very close connection with the rest of the sentence? _____

Answers and Added Practice

1

No

....

Obviously Pinkerton's dates of birth and death have *some* relevance to the sentence, or they should not be there at all. But the sentence says essentially the same thing without them.

2

A. uncertainty   B. No

C. Yes (It is in apposition to *Cervantes*.)

....

William Shakespeare was born in 1564, but the date may or may not have been April 23. Write a sentence about him, including that fact in the way illustrated in Frame 2.

3

No

....

In writing about a book concerning crickets, you want to call attention unobtrusively to Plate VII. Write the sentence.

2

Cervantes, the author of *Don Quixote*, was born on September 29 (?), 1547.

A. The question mark in the example shows _____ _____ [*certainty* or *uncertainty*?] about the exact date of Cervantes' birth.

B. Has the question mark any grammatical connection with the rest of the sentence? _____

C. Has the appositive any grammatical connection with the rest of the sentence? _____

3

A Solomon's seal (see the illustration on page 842) was a mystic symbol that was supposed to guard against disease.

Does the material in parentheses have any very close connection with the rest of the sentence? _____

4

Victor Hugo (he gained his first fame as a playwright) is still remembered as a novelist.

A. Is the sentence in parentheses closely related in meaning and grammar to the rest of the sentence? _____

B. Reread the example above and the one in Frame 3. When a parenthetical sentence is included in another sentence, does it start with a capital letter and end with a period? _____

4

> A. No B. No

....

The book on crickets also provides information about grasshoppers. Say so in a parenthetical sentence within another sentence.

5

> **Victor Hugo is still remembered as a novelist. (He gained his first fame as a playwright.) His *Les Miserables* is one of the world's greatest novels.**

A. When a parenthetical sentence is not included in another sentence, does it start with a capital letter and end with a period? _____

B. The period is _____ [*inside* or *outside*?] the closing parenthesis.

5

> A. Yes B. inside

....

Alter what you wrote for Answer Frame 4; write the parenthetical part as a separate sentence.

6

> **Hugo's greatest novel, *Les Miserables* (1862), narrates the most renowned manhunt in literature.**

In sentences like that example, a comma is placed _____ [*inside* or *outside*?] the closing parenthesis.

(Observe that the comma has nothing to do with the parenthetical material. In the example, commas are required before and after *Les Miserables*. The parenthetical material just happens to get in the way.)

6

> outside

....

This book about crickets, published in England (London, 1983) tells more about the cheerful little chirpers than I want to know.

Insert a needed comma in the proper place.

7

Sometimes a writer may be uncertain about whether to put parentheses, commas, or dashes around nonessential material in a sentence. Study of the following examples may help in the decision. (See also Lessons #72, 73, and 85.)

1) **Victor Hugo (he gained his first fame as a playwright) is still remembered as a novelist.**

2) **Victor Hugo, even though he gained his first fame as a playwright, is best remembered as a novelist.**

3) **Victor Hugo—he was first a playwright— is remembered as a novelist.**

A. The parentheses in 1) enclose a statement that seems _____ [*close* or *not close*?] to the rest of the sentence in meaning and grammatical construction.

B. The commas in 2) enclose a statement that seems _____ [*closer* or *less close*?] to the rest of the sentence than does the similar element in 1).

C. The dashes in 3) seem to call _____ [*greater* or *less*] attention to the enclosed statement.

7

    A. not close   B. closer
    C. greater

....

Insert the most appropriate marks (parentheses, commas, or dashes):

    A. The field cricket which sometimes enters houses may eat holes in clothing.

    B. The field cricket it doesn't always stay in the fields may hop into your house when you open the door.

    C. The field cricket cheerful sounding indoors but hungry for rugs and clothing is an import from Europe.

8

A minor use of parentheses:

> **The amount due is one thousand and sixty dollars ($1,060.00).**

Especially in legal and business documents, _____

_____ [What marks?] may be used to enclose figures that repeat words representing numbers.

8

    parentheses

....

Write your own example similar to that in Frame 8.

9

Parentheses are not often used, and should not be, for they break rather strongly into the flow of one's writing. However, when a desirable insertion _____ [*is* or *is not?*] closely related in meaning and grammar to the rest of the sentence or the passage, it may be enclosed in parentheses.

9

    is not

....

Overused parentheses, like overused dashes, result in an unsmooth, even jerky, style.

10

In Frames 10–12, put parentheses around whatever can justifiably be punctuated in that way.

    A. Alexander Graham Bell 1847–1922 was born in Edinburgh, Scotland.

    B. Cola di Rienzi was born in 1313? and died in 1354.

10

    A. (1847–1922) B. 1313(?)

....

Napoleon Bonaparte was born in 1769 and died in 1821. Using parentheses, write a sentence that includes his dates.

11

A. Boron see the chart on page 84 is a semimetallic element.

B. Babylonian clay tablets they are sometimes called the earliest books were made of clay inscribed with a stylus while still wet.

11

    A. (see the chart on page 84)
    B. (they . . . books)

....

Write a sentence including in parentheses part of this information:

    A *dhole* is a wild dog. It lives in Asia. It weighs about thirty-five pounds. It hunts in packs. It kills deer and wild sheep.

12

A. Goldfish have been bred in the Orient for many centuries. Their popularity in America is largely a twentieth-century development. The Chinese have produced many strange variations of them.

B. We hereby acknowledge receipt of your payment of three thousand dollars $3,000.00.

12

    A. (Their . . . development.)
    B. ($3,000.00).

....

Look again at Frame 12. Explain why the period in A belongs inside the added parentheses, but the one in B belongs outside.

13

Write a sentence, perhaps about someone in your family, in which you use justifiable parentheses to enclose one part.

13

Model Answer

    Mercedes (she's my youngest sister) slid down the banister.

. . . .

Write another sentence, perhaps about a game or pastime with which you are quite familiar. Again, use justifiable parentheses to enclose one part.

14

Rewrite your sentence in Frame 13, slightly changing the wording of the part you enclosed so that commas are preferable to parentheses.

14

Model Answer

    Mercedes, who is my youngest sister, slid down the banister.

. . . .

Rewrite your sentence in Answer Frame 13, slightly changing the wording of the part you enclosed so that commas are preferable to parentheses.

15

Finish honestly: One thing I hope to remember from this lesson is that . . .

(In this frame, any answer that you consider honest and accurate is acceptable.)

Lesson 86: Answers to Questions for Added Practice

2. MODEL: William Shakespeare, who was born April 23(?), 1564, was a successful dramatist by 1590. **3.** The field cricket (Plate VII) is black. **4.** This book about crickets (it deals with grasshoppers, too) is the work of a renowned naturalist. **5.** MODEL: This book about crickets is the work of a renowned naturalist. (He writes not only about crickets but also about grasshoppers.) **6.** . . . 1983), **7.** A. cricket, . . . houses, B. —it . . . fields— C. (cheerful . . . clothing) (Note: parentheses are also justifiable in B. and dashes in C.) **8.** MODEL: The amount assessed is two thousand six hundred dollars ($2,600.00). **10.** MODEL: Napoleon Bonaparte (1769–1821) ruled France for a while after the Revolution. **11.** MODEL: Dholes (the wild dogs of Asia) hunt in packs for deer and wild sheep. **12.** MODEL: In A the parenthetical element is not part of another sentence, but in B it is. **13.** MODEL: Soccer (much more popular in the rest of the world than in the United States) is a fast-moving game. **14.** MODEL: Soccer, which is much more popular in the rest of the world than in the United States, is a fast-moving game.

87

Brackets: Mainly for Comments Within Quotations

After writing your answer(s) in the right-hand column, check this column to see whether you have responded correctly. If you have made a mistake, or if you need more practice, do whatever is asked below the dotted line in each answer frame.

Answers to questions for added practice can be found at the end of each lesson.

Understanding and Applying the Principles

1

> **"How far that little candle throws his beam!**
> **So shines a good deed in a naughty [wicked]**
> **world."**—Shakespeare

Shakespeare did not write the word *wicked* in that passage. An editor has added it to explain the changed meaning of *naughty*, which in Shakespeare's day was a stronger word than it is today.

To show that *wicked* was not in the original, the editor has placed that word in _____ . [What marks?]

Answers and Added Practice

1

    brackets

. . . .

> **As Joel Chandler Harris**
> **wrote, "Licker [Liquor] talks**
> **mighty loud w'en it gits loose**
> **from de jug."**

Why is *Liquor* in brackets?

2

> **"Horace Greeley founded *The New York***
> ***Times* [actually the *Tribune*] to provide a good**
> **newspaper for the masses."**

Brackets are used in that sentence to show that a mistake appeared in the original quote, and the writer is making a _____ _____ in the quoted material.

2

correction (*or any word similar in meaning*)

....

"When Winston Churchill became Prime Minister in 1939 [actually 1940], he . . ."

Why are the words in brackets?

3

reaction of the stockholders (*or something similar*)

....

"I know some people who are glad to hear that the Senator will retire. They're all Republicans! [Laughter]"

Why is *Laughter* in brackets?

4

A. The word *sight* should be *site*.

B. [*sic*]

....

You are quoting from a book. What do you insert after one word in the following sentence? _____

"This experiement was conducted in a tiny laboratory at Syracuse University."

3

President Nelson said to the stockholders: "This year we expect to make a profit. [Applause] The days of dreary losses are past."

The bracketed comment in that quotation shows the _____

_____ .

4

"The University of Chicago was the sight [*sic*] of the most important research of this type," the journal states.

A. In quoting, we should quote exactly, including any mistakes that may be in the original. What is the mistake in the example above? _____

_____

B. To indicate that a mistake appears in original and that we didn't miscopy, we may insert a word in brackets. The word comes from Latin and now means, "That's the way it's really printed."
Copy, underline, and place brackets around the word.

_____

5

The professor discussed several books about women in Colonial times (for instance, Paul Engle's *Women in the American Revolution* [Chicago: Follett Publishing Company], 1976).

The use of brackets illustrated above is very rare and generally avoidable. It shows that brackets are used to enclose a parenthetical, or interrupting, element within _____ .
[What marks?]

5

parentheses

....

Another example: **One variety of Zoysia grass (*Zoysia tenuifolio* [also known as Mascarene grass]) grows best in the tropics.**

6

The chief use of brackets, as we have seen in Frames 1–4, is to enclose a comment or correction of one's own when one is

_____ .

[Doing what?]

6

Model Answer

quoting from someone else

....

Remember that brackets are not the equivalent of parentheses. They have much more limited uses and indeed are seldom seen.

7

Write the bracketed comment that might be appropriate to show crowd reaction to this sentence spoken at a political convention of one party:

"He is a man who carried New York two years ago by one hundred thousand votes! He . . ."

7

[Cheers] *or* [Applause] *or any other appropriate comment after* ". . . votes!"

....

Write a sentence that someone might have spoken at a labor union meeting. Show that the audience either jeered or booed.

8

Suppose that you use the following quotation in a composition of your own. What bracketed comment should you place after the erroneous word?

"Following the assassination of President Kennedy, a quite different sort of man, Lyndon B. Jackson, became President."

_____

8

[*sic*] or [Johnson]

....

Write in quotation marks a sentence in which a name or a figure is the wrong one. In brackets, insert your correction.

9

Quote a sentence from any source. Within the quotation, enclose a word or a few words of comment of your own. Punctuate correctly.

9

Model Answer

"As round as appel [an apple] was his face." (Your own comment within the quotation should be enclosed in brackets.)

10

Finish honestly: One thing I hope to remember from this lesson is that . . .

(In this frame, any answer that you consider honest and accurate is acceptable.)

Lesson 87: Answers to Questions for Added Practice

1. MODEL: It is used as an explanation and is not in the original sentence. **2.** MODEL: They are a correction of a mistake in the original. **3.** MODEL: It shows the reaction of the audience and is not in the original. **4.** [*sic*] (after the misspelled word) **7.** MODEL: "How do we workers react to this latest proposal from the owners? [Boos]" **8.** MODEL: "Lincoln's first term began in 1961 [1861]."

═══88═══

Quotation Marks: Is That Quotation Direct or Indirect?

After writing your answer(s) in the right-hand column, check this column to see whether you have responded correctly. If you have made a mistake, or if you need more practice, do whatever is asked below the dotted line in each answer frame.

Answers to questions for added practice can be found at the end of each lesson.

Understanding and Applying the Principles

1

Miss Lewis explained, "I have read that wallpaper originated as a cheap substitute for tapestry."

In that sentence, are Miss Lewis's exact (or presumably exact) words given? _____

Answers and Added Practice

1

Yes

....

"Malaria is not caused by mosquitoes, but it is transmitted by them," Mr. Clay said.

Are the quoted words presumably what Mr. Clay spoke? _____

2

Miss Lewis explained that she had read that wallpaper originated as a cheap substitute for tapestry.

In that sentence, are Miss Lewis's exact words given? _____

2

No

.... [*directly*

Mr. Clay said that mosquitoes transmit malaria but do not cause it.

Explain how that sentence differs from the one in Answer Frame 1.

3

A *direct* quotation gives a speaker's or writer's exact words (sometimes the supposed or imagined exact words).

An *indirect* quotation summarizes, or reports indirectly, what the speaker or writer says. It often omits unimportant parts. It is especially useful when no good reason exists for quoting the exact words.

    A. The quotation in Frame 1 is _____ . [*direct* or *indirect?*]
    B. The quotation in Frame 2 is _____ . [*direct* or *indirect?*]

3

A. direct   B. indirect

....

Look again at the sentences in Answer Frames 1 and 2. Answer Frame _____ [*1* or *2?*] contains a direct quotation.

4

    A. As the example in Frame 1 shows, a direct quotation _____ [*is* or *is not?*] enclosed in quotation marks.
    B. As the example in Frame 2 shows, an indirect quotation _____ [*is* or *is not?*] enclosed in quotation marks.

4

A. is   B. is not

....

The sentence in Answer Frame 2 does not have any quotation marks because Mr. Clay's words are quoted _____ . [*directly* or *indirectly?*]

5

Generally, an indirect quotation may be recognized by the words before it. Usually they are similar to *he said that, she remarked that, Mr. Calvin asked whether.*

In Frame 2, the words that help to identify the quotation as indirect are _____ .

Note: Sometimes verb tenses are changed in indirect quotations. Notice that *have* in Frame 1 becomes *had* in Frame 2.

5

explained that

. . . .

In Answer Frame 2, the words which show us that the quotation is indirect are _____

_____ .

6

are not

. . . .

Rewrite the sentence in Answer Frame 1 so that *Mr. Clay said* is near the middle. Punctuate correctly.

7

single-spacing, extra indentions

. . . .

Although no precise rule exists, normally a quotation treated in this way is at least forty or fifty words long.

8

a direct

. . . .

My older brother declared that Andrew Jackson was the nation's greatest President.

Rewrite that sentence, using a direct quotation. Punctuate correctly.

6

"I have read," Miss Lewis explained, "that wallpaper originated as a cheap substitute for tapestry."

Often, as in the sentence above, words like *he said* are inserted within a direct quotation.

When that happens, the words like *he said* _____ [*are* or *are not*?] enclosed in the quotation marks.

7

One special kind of quoting should be mentioned as a sort of footnote. If you were typing a term paper or a thesis, you would double-space it. If you used a short quotation, you would incorporate it as part of a sentence or paragraph, as described in this lesson. But if you used a long quotation, you would single-space it, indent it extra on both sides, and use no quotation marks.

The two things that would show it was a quotation would be the _____ and the

_____ .

8

We have seen that a direct quotation gives a speaker's or writer's exact words, but that an indirect quotation summarizes those words or reports them indirectly.

Quotation marks should be used around only _____

_____ [*a direct* or *an indirect*?] quotation.

9

In Frames 9–11, insert quotation marks around the direct quotations, but do nothing with the sentences containing indirect quotations.

    A. Mr. Cox explained that iridium looks like platinum.

    B. Mr. Cox explained, Iridium looks like platinum.

9

   B. . . . "Iridium looks like platinum."

. . . .

In Answer Frames 9–11, follow the instructions in Frame 9.

   Blenheim, the teacher told us, is a palace you should visit.

10

   A. "Greyhounds," Jan said, "have . . . hour."

   B. "Rogers Hornsby . . . times," the coach declared.

. . . .

   He told us that Blenheim was given to the Duke of Marlborough in gratitude for his military victories.

11

   B. "Marcus Livius Drusus," the history teacher said, "openly . . . allegiance."

. . . .

   The grounds around the palace are magnificently landscaped, the teacher asserted, as these pictures will show you.

12

Model Answer

   Your mother said that the appointment was changed to three o'clock.

. . . .

Write a sentence starting with *The mayor said in a speech that.* Punctuate correctly.

10

   A. Greyhounds, Jan said, have been clocked at thirty-five miles an hour.

   B. Rogers Hornsby was National League batting champion seven times, the coach declared.

11

   A. The history teacher told us that the taking of hostages was common in the Middle Ages.

   B. Marcus Livius Drusus, the history teacher said, openly used bribes to gain allegiance.

12

Write a sentence starting with *Your mother said that.* Use quotation marks only if necessary.

13

Rewrite the sentence you wrote for Frame 13. Change the mother's words to a direct quotation. Punctuate correctly.

13

Model Answer

Your mother said, "The appointment has been changed to three o'clock."

. . . .

Rewrite your sentence in Answer Frame 12. Change the mayor's words to a direct quotation and punctuate correctly.

14

Write a sentence in which you include this quotation from Queen Elizabeth I: *"A good face is the best letter of recommendation."* Punctuate correctly.

14

Model Answer

I almost agree with what Queen Elizabeth I said: "A good face is the best letter of recommendation."

. . . .

Write a sentence in which you include this verse from the Bible (Acts 26:24): "Much learning doth make thee mad."

15

Finish honestly: One thing I hope to remember from this lesson is that . . .

(In this frame, any answer that you consider honest and accurate is acceptable.)

Lesson 88: Answers to Questions for Added Practice

1. Yes **2.** MODEL: In this indirect quotation, the writer has merely summarized in his own words what Mr. Clay said. **3.** 1 **4.** indirectly **5.** *said that* **6.** "Malaria is not caused by mosquitoes," Mr. Clay said," but it is transmitted by them." **8.** My older brother declared, "Andrew Jackson was the nation's greatest President." **9.** "Blenheim," the teacher told us, "is a palace you should visit." **11.** "The grounds around the palace are magnificently landscaped," the teacher asserted, "as these pictures will show you." **12.** MODEL: The mayor said in a speech that the city needed to replace many sewers. **13.** MODEL: The mayor said in a speech, "The city needs to replace many sewers." **14.** MODEL: I doubt that the Biblical verse that says "Much learning doth make thee mad" is always true.

══89══

Quotation Marks:
Which Mark Comes First?

After writing your answer(s) in the right-hand column, check this column to see whether you have responded correctly. If you have made a mistake, or if you need more practice, do whatever is asked below the dotted line in each answer frame.

Answers to questions for added practice can be found at the end of each lesson.

Understanding and Applying the Principles

1

> **"When I went to school," said the author, "I never knew where to put a comma or a period with quotation marks, so I always put the quotation marks on top and the comma or period just below them."**

By looking carefully at the quotation above, you can tell the author that a comma or a period belongs _____ [*inside* or *outside*?] closing quotation marks.

Answers and Added Practice

1

inside

· ·

Insert in the proper places the missing comma and period.

> "On the other hand" the author said, "I placed question marks wherever I pleased"

2

> **The obnoxious child recited "The Boy Stood on the Burning Deck"; then she began what she called singing.**

The sentence above shows that a semicolon, unlike a period or a comma, belongs _____ [*inside* or *outside*?] closing quotation marks.

2

outside

· ·

Insert the missing semicolon in the proper place.

> We have just read Arnold's "The Forsaken Merman" it left me very sad.

3

> **I have only one reaction to the song "Sam-Sam-Sammy": it makes me ill.**

Not often does a colon appear with closing quotation marks, but when it does, as the example illustrates, it goes _____ _____ . [*inside* or *outside*?]

3

outside

································

Insert the missing colon in the proper place.

Frankly, this is what I think about his "great invention" he'll never be another Edison.

4

Does A or B summarize what we have seen so far about the proper order of four marks with closing quotation marks?

A.   ."   B.   ".
     ,"   ",
     ";   ;"
     ":   :"

_____ [A or B?]

4

A

································

Here's another way to visualize what we have noticed so far.

     "   ."
     "   ,"
     "   ";
     "   ":

5

1) **Tom asked, "Where is Tipperary?"**
2) **Did Tom say, "I was in Tipperary"?**

A. In 1, is the quotation a question? _____
B. In 2, is the quotation a question? _____
C. The first example shows that when a quotation is a question, the question mark belongs _____ [*inside* or *outside*?] the closing quotation marks.
D. The second example shows that when the whole sentence is a question but the embedded quotation is not, the question mark belongs _____ [*inside* or *outside*?] the closing quotation marks.

5

A. Yes B. No C. inside
D. outside

································

In the rare cases in which a sentence asks a question that ends with a quoted question, the question mark goes inside: *Did Tom ask, "Where is Tipperary?"*

6

1) **"What an inning!" Fred groaned.**
2) **What a time for the band to play "Happy Days"!**

A. In 1, is the quotation an exclamation? _____
B. In 2, is the quotation an exclamation? _____
C. The first example shows that when a quotation is an exclamation, the exclamation mark belongs _____ _____ [*inside* or *outside*?] the closing quotation marks.
D. The second example shows that when the whole sentence is an exclamation but the embedded quotation is not, the exclamation mark belongs _____ [*inside* or *outside*?] the closing quotation marks.

6

A. Yes   B. No
C. inside D. outside

. . . .

An exclamation within an exclamation: *What a time to shout "Hurrah!"*

7

"I bought a muskmelon."
"I bought a muskmelon," he said.

Explain in your own words what happens to the period at the end of a quotation when something is added to the sentence, as in the second example.

7

Model Answer

The period is changed to a comma, which remains inside the closing quotation marks.

. . . .

Punctuate properly:

These apples are too green Betty told us

8

Sue said, "I'll bring the peaches."

That example shows that after an introductory statement such as *Sue said, Greg asked,* or *Melanie answered quickly,* a _____ [What mark?] is generally used.

Note: Although the comma is customary, sometimes it is intentionally omitted when the following quotation is very short: *She said "OK." Alexander Pope said "To err is human."* Also, the comma should be omitted when what follows is a title: *Pope wrote "An Essay on Man."*

8

comma

. . . .

Punctuate in the customary way:

Helen remarked "I suppose that Lennie has reached Denver by now"

9

In Frames 9–13, fill in the blanks with anything that makes at least a little sense, and put in the necessary quotation marks and other marks in the proper order.

A. "An ostrich _____

_____ she said calmly.

B. She said calmly An ostrich _____

_____

9

Model Answers

   A. "An ostrich just strolled past," she said calmly.

   B. She said calmly, "An ostrich just strolled past."

. . . .

In Answer Frames 9–13, follow the instructions in Frame 9.

   The pilot announced "We are

_____

_____ .

There was a brief pause. Soon we'll _____

_____

he added happily.

10

We finished reading " _____
[Name a poem or a short story.] then we started analyzing it.

10

Model Answer

   We finished reading "My Last Duchess"; then we started analyzing it.

. . . .

They sang " _____

_____

however, no one sounded very cheerful.

11

"Did you find _____

_____ Patsy asked naively.

11

Model Answer

   "Did you find any barnacles on the binnacle?" Patsy asked naively.

. . . .

"Where is _____

_____

I inquired.

12

Has Harold finished reciting " _____

_____

12

Model Answer

   Has Harold finished reciting "The Ballad of Dan McGraw"?

. . . .

Have you read " _____

_____

[Name a short story or a short poem.]

13

"How _____ " she exclaimed

13

Model Answer

"How quaint!" she exclaimed.

. . . .

"I won't _____

_____

_____ the angry child yelled.

14

Copy the following sentence, putting in the necessary quotation marks and other needed marks in the proper order.

Your putting   the golf instructor told me
needs much improvement

14

"Your putting," the golf instructor told me, "needs much improvement."

. . . .

Follow the instructions in Frame 14:

I said Jane you are being unreasonable

Oh am I she retorted   Well do you think that *you* are reasonable

15

Finish honestly: One thing I hope to remember from this lesson is that . . .

(In this frame, any answer that you consider honest and accurate is acceptable.)

Lesson 89: Answers to Questions for Added Practice

(In these answers, note especially the placement of other marks in relation to quotation marks.) **1.** . . . hand,"   . . . pleased." **2.** Merman"; **3.** invention": **7.** "These apples are too green," Betty told us. **8.** . . . remarked,   . . . now." **9.** MODEL: The pilot announced, "We are passing south of Pittsburgh." There was a brief pause. "Soon we'll be descending into Washington's Dulles Airport," he added happily. **10.** MODEL: They sang "Yours Almost Forever"; however, no one sounded very cheerful. **11.** MODEL: "Where is the Delta baggage claim?" I inquired. **12.** MODEL: Have you read "Paul's Case"? **13.** MODEL: "I won't do it!" the angry child yelled. **14.** I said, "Jane, you are being unreasonable." "Oh, am I?" she retorted. "Well, do you think that *you* are reasonable?" (Note: "Oh, am I!" is also possible.)

═══90═══

Quotations Within Quotations: Boxes Within Boxes

After writing your answer(s) in the right-hand column, check this column to see whether you have responded correctly. If you have made a mistake, or if you need more practice, do whatever is asked below the dotted line in each answer frame.

Answers to questions for added practice can be found at the end of each lesson.

Understanding and Applying the Principles

1

> **Sally asked, "Was the song 'Some Enchanted Evening' originally part of a musical comedy?"**

One kind of diagram to represent the quoted part of the sentence above is this:

Sally asked,

Try to tell in your own words what each box stands for.

Answers and Added Practice

1

Model Answer

The larger box represents the quotation enclosed by " "; the smaller represents the quotation enclosed by ' '.

2

As Frame 1 illustrates, a quotation within a quotation requires single quotation marks, not double.

Copy, with the marks, the quotation within a quotation in Frame 1.

2

    'Some Enchanted Evening'

· ·

    "Did Martin say, 'Rupert *is* lying' or 'Rupert *was* lying'?" Helen asked.

A box representing that sentence would contain _____ [*one* or *two*?] smaller box(es).

3

You remember the old saying, Where there's smoke, there's fire, Penny remarked.

Make a diagram like that in Frame 1 for the sentence above. Write *Penny remarked* outside the boxes.

3

Penny remarked

· ·

Draw boxes representing the sentence in Answer Frame 2.

4

Copy the example from Frame 3, putting in the needed double and single quotation marks.

4

    "You remember the old saying 'Where there's smoke, there's fire,'" Penny remarked.

· ·

Copy the sentence above, but start with *Penny remarked.*

5

Notice the arrangement of the marks after *fire* in the answer to Frame 4. First comes the comma, then the _____ [*single* or *double*?] mark, and then the _____ [*single* or *double*?] mark.

5

single, double

....

In the sentence you wrote in Answer Frame 4, the correct order of marks after *fire* is ___ ___ ___ .

6

Whether a question mark precedes or follows a closing single quotation mark depends on whether the part inside the single marks is a question.

1) **Melvin continued, "Next the professor asked, 'How can Mendel's law explain those blue eyes?'"**

2) **"How should we know that unless we had read the professor's article 'Mendel on Eye Coloration'?" Pete asked.**

A. In 1, the part in single quotes _____ [*is* or *is not?*] a question. If it is a question, the question mark belongs _____ [*inside* or *outside?*] the closing quotation marks.

B. In 2, the part in single quotes _____ [*is* or *is not?*] a question. If it is not, the question mark belongs _____ _____ [*inside* or *outside?*] the closing single mark, as shown.

6

A. is, inside   B. is not, outside

....

A. "Has George read 'Sparks of Rebellion ___ ___ ___ I asked.

B. "George hasn't read 'Who Started the Rebellion ___ ___ ___ I said.

Add, in proper order, the missing marks.

7

A. We have seen that when a quotation appears within a quotation, it is enclosed in _____ [What kind of?] quotation marks.

B. We have also seen that when other marks appear with closing single quotation marks the order is _____ _____ [*the same as* or *different from?*] the order with double quotation marks. (See Lesson 89 for more about that order.)

7

A. single   B. the same as

....

Proceed as in Answer Frame 6.

A. "George has read 'The Rebellious Years ___ ___ ___ I said.

B. I exclaimed, "George has read 'The Rebellious Years ___ ___ ___

8

In Frames 8–11, copy each sentence, adding in proper order the five missing marks of punctuation. (Titles of short stories are enclosed in quotation marks.)

The teacher asked, Who wrote the short story Rip Van Winkle

8

The teacher asked, "Who wrote the short story 'Rip Van Winkle'?" [Marks must be in the right order.]

· ·

In Answer Frames 8–11, follow the instructions in Frame 8.

The teacher asked, Who has read the article called On Dining Well

---

9

The speaker began, The topic announced for my talk is Origins of the Alphabet

(Titles of lectures are enclosed in quotation marks.)

9

The speaker began, "The topic announced for my talk is 'Origins of the Alphabet.'" [Marks must be in the right order.]

· ·

He continued, A more accurate title is Early Alphabets

10

Finally Helen said, I like the blue one better   Roberta continued.

[Assume that Roberta spoke the first nine words.]

10

"Finally Helen said, 'I like the blue one better,'" Roberta continued. [Marks must be in the right order.]

· ·

Then I said, I like the blue one, too

[Assume that Roberta is still speaking.]

11

The clerk exclaimed, Blue   Roberta said.

[Roberta spoke the first four words.]

11

"The clerk exclaimed, 'Blue!'" Roberta said.

. . . .

Why did you say that   Helen asked her

[Six marks need to be added; assume that Roberta speaks all eight words.]

12

Write a sentence of your own in which someone who is being quoted refers to the title of a song. Punctuate carefully.

12

Model Answer

Betsy said, "While we were singing old songs like 'Blue Hawaii,' the boys began clowning."

. . . .

Write a similar sentence containing a title of a short literary work.

13

Write a sentence of your own in which someone who is being quoted includes someone else's words. Punctuate carefully.

13

Model Answer

Julius chimed in, "Just today my father said, 'The stock market has me worried.'"

. . . .

Write a similar sentence, but this time the quotation within a quotation should be a question.

14

Finish honestly: One thing I hope to remember from this lesson is that . . .

(In this frame, any answer that you consider honest and accurate is acceptable.)

Lesson 90: Answers to Questions for Added Practice

2. two

3. [boxed figure] , Helen asked. **4.** Penny remarked, "You remember the old saying 'Where there's smoke, there's fire.'" **5.** .'" **6.** A. '?" B. ?'" **7.** A. ,'" B. '!" **8.** The teacher asked, "Who has read the article called 'On Dining Well'?" **9.** He continued, "A more accurate title is 'Early Alphabets.'" **10.** "Then I said, 'I like the blue one, too.'" **11.** "'Why did you say that?' Helen asked her." **12.** MODEL: Jerry told us, "My favorite Robert Frost poem is 'Mending Wall,' but my brother likes 'Birches' better." **13.** MODEL: Julius said, "My father asked, 'What did Ford stock do today?'"

91

Quotation Marks: In Paragraphs of Conversation

After writing your answer(s) in the right-hand column, check this column to see whether you have responded correctly. If you have made a mistake, or if you need more practice, do whatever is asked below the dotted line in each answer frame.

Answers to questions for added practice can be found at the end of each lesson.

Understanding and Applying the Principles

1

> **Jim asked, "What courses do most of the college freshmen take?"**
> **"That depends largely on the curriculum they're in," Ken answered.**

How many persons spoke in the conversation reported above?

_____

Answers and Added Practice

1

Two

. . . .

Note the punctuation after *Jim asked* and before and after *Ken answered*.

2

Judging from the example in Frame 1, when the conversation of two or more persons is reported, we _____ [*start* or *do not start*?] a new paragraph with each change of speaker.

2

start

. . . .

"Are you in engineering?" Jim asked.

"No."

That example shows that a separate paragraph _____ [*is* or *is not?*] used when a speech is very short.

3

In addition to starting a new paragraph to indicate the change of speaker in Frame 1, we enclose the words of each speaker in _____ [What kind of?] marks.

3

quotation

. . . .

What is your curriculum   Jim persisted

Liberal arts

Add the punctuation needed in that example.

4

Jim asked, " _____ **."**

" _____ **," Ken answered.**

That diagram shows the start of a new paragraph with the change of speaker, as well as the use of quotation marks around the words of each _____ . [What?]

4

speaker (*or* person, etc.)

. . . .

For the example in Answer Frame 3, draw a diagram comparable to the one in Frame 4.

5

Now let us assume that the same person speaks two (or more) paragraphs without interruption—that is, without words of another speaker or without an expression like *he said*.

Tell in your own words why the quotation marks represented in the following diagram would be misleading to a reader:

WRONG: **Ken went on, "** _____

_____ **."**

" _____ **" he concluded.**

5

Model Answer

The quotation marks at the end of the first paragraph suggest that Ken stopped speaking at that point.

....

6

RIGHT: **Ken went on, "Some freshmen take much science, or mathematics, or music, or something else.**

"Most typically, though, a college freshman program includes English, social science, foreign language, physical or biological science, and physical education," he concluded.

Those two paragraphs of Ken's remarks are correctly punctuated. Draw a simple diagram to show the paragraphing and the quotation marks.

6

Ken went on, " _____

_____ .

" _____ ,"

he concluded.

7

A. We have observed that a _____ [What?] is started with each change of speaker in reporting a conversation.

B. We have also noted that _____ [What marks?] enclose the words of each speaker.

C. We have seen that when the same person speaks without interruption for two or more paragraphs, quotation marks are used at the beginning of each of the paragraphs he speaks and at the end of only the _____ [Which?] one.

7

A. paragraph
B. quotation marks
C. last (*or* final)

....

Ken said, " _____

_____ .

" _____ ."

That diagram shows two paragraphs spoken by _____ [*one or two?*] speaker(s).

8

We should notice one small exception to the principle of changing paragraphs for each speaker. Sometimes, in reporting a hubbub of conversation, it may not be important or even possible to indicate who said what. It is then permissible to include a number of conversational snatches in one paragraph, like this:

The soldiers were complaining. "Gonna stay here all day?" "This sun is hot." "Can't they make up their minds?" "Let's get goin'!" ____

_____

[Add another suitable quotation.]

8

Model Answer

"Are they trying to roast us alive?"

9

Draw a simple diagram to show the paragraphing and punctuation of a conversation in which Alice, Millie, and Fran speak in turn.

9

Model Answer

Alice said, " _____
_____."
  " _____ " Millie in-
terrupted. " _____
_____ ."
    " _____
_____," Fran added.

10

You are quoting, without interruption, three short paragraphs spoken by the same person.

Begin with *Mr. Harris explained*, and draw a simple diagram to show the paragraphing and use of quotation marks.

10

Mr. Harris explained, " ____

_____ .

" _____ .

" _____ ."

11

Pat asks a question, and Karen answers it. Write the conversation (not just a diagram this time). Punctuate and paragraph properly.

11

Model Answer

Pat asked teasingly, "When was the War of 1812?"

"That's supposed to be a trick question," said Karen. "The answer is really 1812 to 1815."

12

Melvin speaks without interruption, telling about two things that he believes your college needs. Write and punctuate correctly two brief paragraphs (a sentence or two for each) giving his remarks.

12

Model Answer

"First, we need better laboratory equipment.

"Second, our library needs an enlarged reference collection."

13

Write a paragraph to show a hubbub of conversation, perhaps at a girls' "slumber" party or in a locker room following a victory.

13

Model Answer

The boys were shouting. "Great game, Dick!" "Where's Coach?" "Didja see their biggest guy?" "I thought they'd make it close."

14

Finish honestly: One thing I hope to remember from this lesson is that . . .

(In this frame, any answer that you consider honest and accurate is acceptable.)

Lesson 91: Answers to Questions for Added Practice

2. is **3.** "What is your curriculum?" Jim persisted. "Liberal arts." **4.** " _____ "
Jim persisted. (New paragraph) " _____ " **7.** one

═══92═══

Quotation Marks with Certain Titles: Who Wrote "Old Ironsides"?

After writing your answer(s) in the right-hand column, check this column to see whether you have responded correctly. If you have made a mistake, or if you need more practice, do whatever is asked below the dotted line in each answer frame.

Answers to questions for added practice can be found at the end of each lesson.

Understanding and Applying the Principles

1

Holmes's poem "Old Ironsides" was responsible for saving the ship *Constitution*.

The sentence above shows that the title of a short poem is enclosed in _____ . [What marks?]

Answers and Added Practice

1

quotation marks

. . . .

In Answer Frames 1–6, insert quotation marks as needed. If you are in doubt about the placement of quotation marks with another mark, see Lesson 89.

Chicago is the title of the poem that first attracted much attention to Carl Sandburg.

2

Our class was asked to study Emerson's essay "Self-Reliance."

The example above shows that the title of an _____ (or article) is also enclosed in quotation marks.

Caution: When you write the title of your own composition at the top of the page, do not enclose it in quotation marks unless it is a quotation.

2

essay

. . . .

I read in *Popular Mechanics* an article called   How to Build an Icehouse.

3

Bret Harte's short story "The Outcasts of Poker Flat" tells of noble actions by a professional gambler.

The sentence above illustrates the use of quotation marks around the title of a _____ _____ .

3

short story

· ·

The Great Stone Face, one of Hawthorne's best-known short stories, is in this anthology.

Note: Titles of short plays are also enclosed in quotation marks.

4

Chapter III of *A Tale of Two Cities* is entitled "The Night Shadows."

The title of a chapter or other section of a book is enclosed in

_____ .

Note: The title of a book is underlined (italicized in print). See Lesson 93.

4

quotation marks

· ·

Is the first chapter of *Dr. Zhivago* called   The Five O'clock Express?

5

One of the songs in that old yellow song book was "The Bulldog and the Bullfrog."

Titles of _____ , as the example shows, are also enclosed in _____ .

5

songs, quotation marks

· ·

Her favorite song was   The Eyes Have It.

6

Dr. Downs will speak on "Librarianship as a Profession."

Explain what that example shows about the use of quotation marks.

6

Model Answer

Titles of speeches, lectures, and so forth should be enclosed in quotation marks.

· ·

Can You Go Home Again? was a speech critical of Thomas Wolfe's book *You Can't Go Home Again.*

7

The first six frames have illustrated the fact that quotation marks are used to enclose titles of A) _____ , B) _____ , C) _____ , D) _____ , E) _____ , and F) _____ .

7

A. poems B. essays
C. short stories D. chapters
E. songs F. speeches

· ·

In writing or typing, titles of book-length works, including epic poems, long plays, and operas, are underlined to represent italics.

8

Model Answer
"Mary Had a Little Lamb."

· ·

In Answer Frames 8–13, follow the instructions in Frame 8.

_____ , a
poem that I learned as a child, is one that I still like.

9

Model Answer
Singer's, "In Old Krakow."

· ·

_____
_____ , another of _____
_____ 's short stories, concerns Jews in modern New York.

10

Model Answer
"The First Person on Mars,"

· ·

I went to a lecture, _____
_____ ,
in Kendrick Hall.

11

Model Answer
"The Wanderers,"
the Progressives

· ·

One of my favorite songs is _____
_____ .

8

In your answers to Frames 8–13, you will be asked to supply certain titles. Use actual titles if you can; otherwise, invent them. Use quotation marks as needed.

A poem that I learned as a child is called _____
_____ .

9

One of _____ 's [author] short stories that I liked is called _____ .

10

_____ the title of a lecture given recently on our campus, caught my attention.

11

A song that I like is _____ ,
as sung by _____ .

12

An informative article in the newest issue of the *Atlantic* is ____
_____ .

12

Model Answer

"The Smallest Subatomic Particles"

. . . .

Note that names of magazines (journals, newspapers) are underlined in writing or typing.

13

A chapter in the book _____
_____ [Name the book, and underline the title for italics] is _____ .

13

Model Answer

The Tree of Language, "How Did Language Begin?"

. . . .

The second chapter of the book has the title _____
_____ .

14

Finish honestly: One thing I hope to remember from this lesson is that . . .

(In this frame, any answer that you consider honest and accurate is acceptable.)

Lesson 92: Answers to Questions for Added Practice

1. "Chicago" **2.** "How to Build an Icehouse." **3.** "The Great Stone Face," **4.** "The Five O'Clock Express"?
5. "The Eyes Have It." **6.** "Can You Go Home Again?" **8.** MODEL: "The Breeze and I," **9.** MODEL:
"In Search of Paradise," Singer's . . . **10.** MODEL: . . . lecture, "The Future of Krakatoa," **11.** MODEL:
"The Star-gazer." **13.** "The Language of Prehistoric People."

93

Underlining: Your Substitute for Italics

After writing your answer(s) in the right-hand column, check this column to see whether you have responded correctly. If you have made a mistake, or if you need more practice, do whatever is asked below the dotted line in each answer frame.

Answers to questions for added practice can be found at the end of each lesson.

Understanding and Applying the Principles

1

In a recent book the foreign word *Weltschmerz*, the book title *Of Time and the River*, and a few other words were set in italic type.

    A. Can you write italics? _____

    B. Can you type italics? _____

Answers and Added Practice

1

    A. No (unless with considerable effort).

    B. No (except with certain typewriters and word processors).

2

In writing or typing, we ordinarily need to use a substitute for italics. The accepted substitute is underlining with one straight line.

    So, if you were to write *Weltschmerz* and *Of Time and the River*, you would _____ the words.

2

    underline

· ·

Weltschmerz is a German word meaning "sadness caused by the illness of the world." Use the word in a sentence, underlining it.

3

Garrison Keillor's *Lake Wobegon Days* was acclaimed as the funniest book of the 1980s.

William Morris edited the *American Heritage Dictionary of the English Language* (first edition, 1969).

Those examples show that we underline (italicize) titles of _____ _____ [How long?] writings or compilations.

Note: Titles of short works are placed in quotation marks. See Lesson 92.

3

book-length (*or an equivalent expression*)

....

Underline the title:

> In his book The State of the Language Philip Howard says, "Slang is a district bounded on the north by jargon, on the south by argot, on the east by dialect, and on the west by poetry."

4

My father's favorite magazine is the *Atlantic*; his favorite newspaper, the *New York Times*; his favorite play, *Man and Superman*; and his favorite opera, *Lohengrin*.

The example shows that names of _____ ,

_____ , _____ ,

and long musical _____ are all italicized.

Note: Although usage varies, usually *the* as the first word of a title is not capitalized or underlined when it is part of a reference. Sometimes in the name of a newspaper the name of the city is not italicized.

4

magazines, newspapers, (long) plays, and (long) musical works (*or* compositions, etc.)

....

Write a similar sentence in which you list titles of some of your own favorites.

5

On the Discovery Channel I watched a half-hour program called "The Smallest Living Things."
My parents try never to miss any of the PBS presentations of *Great Performances*.

Those examples show that titles of single, short television programs are usually enclosed in _____ [What marks?] but that titles of series of long programs are usually _____ . [indicated how?]

5

quotation marks, italicized (*or* underlined)

....

A. Write a sentence naming a short, one-episode television program.

B. In another sentence, name a television series that you have liked.

6

The word *cemetery* contains three *e*'s.

That example shows that we italicize words referred to as words, and _____ referred to as _____ .

Note that in *e*'s or *and*'s or the like, the *s* is not italicized.

6

letters, letters

. . . .

Underline as necessary:

Mississippi has four i's, four s's, two p's, and one m.

7

The old expression *from the sublime to the ridiculous* is appropriate to describe the first and third acts of the play.

A phrase or other group of words, when referred to as words, may be _____ , as the example shows.

However, quotation marks are often used instead, especially if the phrase is a familiar one.

7

italicized (*or* underlined)

. . . .

Underline as necessary:

The term red-winged maize thief was once employed to describe a red-winged blackbird.

8

She shows off her knowledge of French by often inserting *oui, comme il faut,* or *je ne sais pas* in her conversations.

The example illustrates the fact that _____ [What kind of?] expressions are usually italicized when they appear in English.

Note: When a foreign expression such as *prima donna* or *à la carte* becomes well established in English, it is no longer italicized.

8

foreign

. . . .

Underline as necessary:

After he had spent two weeks in Italy, every woman became a donna and every man a uomo.

9

You *must* accept the invitation. She'll be positively *insulted* if you don't.

Two words are italicized in the sentences above to show that they should be _____ . Be cautious about this use of underlining, though. If used too frequently, it loses its effectiveness.

Note: Avoid double or triple underlining. Once is enough. Why shout?

9

emphasized (*or a synonym*)

. . . .

Just as some annoying writers try to emphasize too many words, so some annoying speakers stress too many words or the wrong words.

10

Without looking back, list as many as possible of the ten uses of underlining (italics) that have been mentioned.

10

titles of books, magazines, newspapers, long plays, long musical compositions; words and letters referred to as words or letters; phrases referred to as words; foreign expressions; words to be emphasized

---

11

Write a sentence in which you include the title of a book and the names of a magazine and a newspaper.

11

Model Answer

Reviews of *Athens Today* appeared in *Harper's* and the *Wall Street Journal.*

. . . .

Write a sentence in which you include the title of an opera or other long musical work, and of a television series.

12

Write a sentence in which you use a foreign word or expression that you happen to know.

12

Model Answer

We dined *al fresco.*

. . . .

Write a sentence including *au gratin* or some other foreign term.

13

Write a sentence in which you tell how many times a certain letter appears in a certain word.

13

Model Answer

    The letter *o* appears three times in *monopoly.*

....

Write a sentence telling how you sometimes miswrite or mistype a certain word.

14

Write a sentence in which you want to emphasize one word.

14

Model Answer

    "Don't <u>yell</u> at me like that!" my mother shouted.

....

Again emphasizing one word, write a sentence that could follow the model answer above.

15

Finish honestly: One thing I hope to remember from this lesson is that . . .

(In this frame, any answer that you consider honest and accurate is acceptable.)

Lesson 93: Answers to Questions for Added Practice

2. MODEL: The feeling that the Germans call <u>Weltschmerz</u> is perhaps most likely to afflict well-educated people. **3.** <u>The State of the Language</u> 4. (Titles will vary. Each should be underlined and properly capitalized.) **5.** A. (Title should be in quotation marks.) B. (Title should be italicized *or* underlined.) **6.** <u>Mississippi</u> has four <u>i</u>'s, four <u>s</u>'s, two <u>p</u>'s, and one <u>m</u>. **7.** <u>red-winged maize-thief</u> 8. <u>donna, uomo</u> **11.** MODEL: Ed and Marjorie watched Verdi's <u>Aida</u>, which was presented as part of a new TV series called <u>Music in Your Life.</u> **12.** MODEL: He concocted an unpleasant dish called <u>escargots au gratin</u>. **13.** MODEL: For some unknown reason I often type an <u>r</u> instead of the second <u>e</u> in <u>sentrnce</u>—whoops! I just did it again. **14.** MODEL: I shouted back, "I'm <u>not</u> yelling!"

═══94═══

Abbreviations: Form and Use

After writing your answer(s) in the right-hand column, check this column to see whether you have responded correctly. If you have made a mistake, or if you need more practice, do whatever is asked below the dotted line in each answer frame.

Answers to questions for added practice can be found at the end of each lesson.

Understanding and Applying the Principles

1

Today abbreviations are not used frequently except in reference books and in some other printed materials where it is desirable to save space. For that reason, in your own writing you should use _____ [*few* or *many?*] abbreviations.

Answers and Added Practice

1

few

· ·

In bygone days letters often contained many abbreviations and contractions, like these:

   **"Yrs. of the 7th inst. rec'd . . .
   Yr. ob'd't serv't . . ."**

Do you like such a style of writing?

_____

2

               The bus arrived at 3:25 a.m.

You learned years ago that most abbreviations are followed by periods. The sentence above shows that when an abbreviation occurs at the end of a sentence, _____
[*only one period is* or *two periods are?*] necessary.

2

only one period is

· ,

Punctuate properly at the end:

   Look at the alternate numbers:
   1, 3, 5, etc

3

        CBS   TWA   FBI   AFL-CIO
   Station KQED

The examples above show that in certain abbreviations (usually those requiring only capital letters) _____
[*periods* or *no periods?*] are necessary. Some organizations prefer periods, but others do not.

3

no periods

. . . .

Write two other examples of abbreviations that are usually written in capital letters with no periods.

4

> **Dr. Graves   9:20 p.m.   Roy White, Jr.**
> **A.D. 1492**

Notice that the abbreviations *Dr.* and *Jr.* (and *Sr.*) are correct when used with names, and that *p.m.* and *a.m.* are correct when used with numbers. Be sure not to write something like *at nine in the a.m.* or *8:45 a.m. in the morning.*

Explain why the abbreviations in the following sentence are incorrect:

> **When I saw the dr. this a.m., he told me that Jr. is getting along well.**

4

Model Answer

The abbreviations are not accompanied by names and numbers.

. . . .

Write the correct version of the example in Frame 4.

5

> **R.S.V.P.   St. Paul   Washington, D.C.**
> **Mr. Jordan, Mrs. Jordan, Ms. Jordan**
> **Floyd Winkle, Ph.D. (and other degrees)**

R.S.V.P. (an abbreviation of the French for "Please respond") may be used in a formal invitation. The other listed abbreviations may be used only with names. *Miss* is not an abbreviation and takes no period. Technically, *Ms.* is not an abbreviation of anything, but it is written with a period to harmonize with *Mr.* and *Mrs.*

Explain why the abbreviations in this sentence are incorrect:

> **His Mrs. is an M.D. from D.C.**

5

Model Answer

Each of the abbreviations should be accompanied by a name.

. . . .

Write the correct version of the example in Frame 5. What word must be substituted for *Mrs.?*

6

Satisfactory: **He began counting 5, 10, 15, etc.**
Unsatisfactory: **Most of these soldiers are tall, neat, etc.**

The abbreviation *etc.* should be used sparingly. (Note the spelling, which is short for *et cetera.*) Too often it seems to mean "and other things that I can't think of right now." It is satisfactory when it prevents an unnecessary enumeration of what the readers can fill in for themselves, as in the first example.

Explain why the second example is unsatisfactory.

6

Model Answer

A reader cannot be sure about what adjectives should follow *tall* and *neat*.

· ·

Complete the example in Frame 6, replacing *etc.* with one or two adjectives.

7

Some companies, for their own reasons, use abbreviations in their names: *M. Lowenstein & Sons.* The *&* is called an *ampersand.* Except for such an officially recognized use, and also perhaps in your own note-taking, it is best to avoid *&* and +. Instead, write out the word _____ .

7

and

· ·

The word *ampersand* has a rather interesting background. The sign *&* was used by lawyers and others to mean "and." They called it *and per se and,* meaning "by itself it means 'and.'" The four words were gradually compressed to *ampersand.*

8

Poor: **Election day is Tues., Nov. 6.**

Permissible but not desirable in letter headings:

**1113 W. Clay St.
Creston, IA 50801
Jan. 12, 1988**

Comment on the acceptability of abbreviations in this sentence:

**On Wed., Dec. 4, we moved into a house at
901 W. Clover Ave., Billings, Mont. 59103.**

Note: The Postal Service two-letter abbreviations, such as IA, MT, and NY, are written without periods.

8

Model Answer

All these abbreviations should be replaced with words.

· ·

Write the correct version of the sentence in Frame 8 beginning, *On Wed . . .*

9

In Frames 9–11, write the letter of the *one* sentence in each group in which all the abbreviations are used properly.

A. Jr. answered the door for the Dr.
B. In history we are studying depressions, etc.
C. Mr. Atkins arrived at 7:30 a.m.

_____

9

    C

....

In Answer Frames 9–11, rewrite the two incorrect sentences in the corresponding frames.

A.

B.

10

A. On Thurs. they will expect you in the p.m.
B. My best subjects are math. and Span.
C. Gilbert Hart, Sr., gave a talk about NBC.

    ———

10

    C

....

A.

B.

11

A. Label the cards A, B, C, etc.
B. From St. Louis, Mo., we went to Washington, D. C.
C. Our yrs. in N.M. were especially happy.

    ———

11

A
....

B.

C.

12

Although in research papers parenthetical notes are gradually taking over from footnote references, some teachers and learned journals still prefer old-style footnotes. The following abbreviations are generally acceptable in footnotes and in some parenthetical references, but usually should be avoided in other writing.

> **e.g. (for example)**   **viz. (namely)**
> **i.e. (that is)**   **ibid. (in the same place)**
> **et al. (and others)**
>   **p. or pp. (page or pages)**

Such abbreviations are useful in footnotes because they save

_____ .

12

space
....

Some students confuse *e.g.* and *i.e.* It may help to remember that *e.g.* comes from Latin *exempli gratia*, meaning "example free."

13

Write a sentence in which you use correctly the abbreviations for "morning" and "American Broadcasting Company."

13

Model Answer
The broadcast was on ABC at 11 a.m.
....

Write a sentence using correctly the abbreviations for "Doctor of Philosophy" and "Saint."

14

Write a sentence in which you use correctly the abbreviations for "Doctor" and "Senior."

14

Model Answer

Dr. R. E. Bley, Sr., was a country doctor.

. . . .

Write a sentence using two of these correctly: *Mr., Mrs., Ms., Miss.*

15

Write a sentence in which you use correctly the abbreviations for "Federal Bureau of Investigation" and "District of Columbia."

15

Model Answer

Our visit to the FBI headquarters in Washington, D.C. was informative.

. . . .

Write a sentence in which you use correctly the abbreviation for "before Christ."

16

Write a sentence in which you use the abbreviation *etc.* in such a way that readers will be able to fill in easily the missing items.

16

Model Answer

The basket contained citrus fruits: oranges, lemons, etc.

17

Finish honestly: One thing I hope to remember from this lesson is that . . .

(In this frame, any answer that you consider honest and accurate is acceptable.)

Lesson 94: Answers to Questions for Added Practice

1. (Personal answer. Today it seems not only old-fashioned but also artificial and insincere.) **2.** etc. (Only one period) **3.** MODELS: SEC, PBS **4.** When I saw the doctor this morning, he told me that Junior (*or* Carl, Jr.,) is getting along well. **5.** His wife is a medical doctor from Washington, D.C. (*or* from the District of Columbia) **6.** MODEL: Most of the soldiers are tall, neat, and well trained. **8.** On Wednesday, December 4, we moved into a house at 901 West Clover Avenue, Billings, Montana 59103. **9.** A. Junior (*or* James, Jr.,) answered the doorbell for the doctor. (*or* for Dr. Kane.) B. MODEL: In history we are studying depressions and other economic disturbances. **10.** A. On Thursday, they will expect you in the afternoon. B. My best subjects are mathematics and Spanish. **11.** B. From St. Louis, Missouri, we went to Washington, D.C. C. Our years in New Mexico were especially happy. **13.** MODEL: Baird Sloan, Ph.D., wrote his thesis about St. Francis of Assisi. **14.** MODEL: Mr. and Mrs. Robert Bruce are both lawyers. **15.** MODEL: A great battle was fought at Thermopylae in 480 B.C.

≡95≡

Capitalization: In Sentences, Quotations, and Letters

After writing your answer(s) in the right-hand column, check this column to see whether you have responded correctly. If you have made a mistake, or if you need more practice, do whatever is asked below the dotted line in each answer frame.

Answers to questions for added practice can be found at the end of each lesson.

Understanding and Applying the Principles

1

The waiter said, "Today the clam chowder is unusually tasty."

A. The first capital letter in the example above is used because *The* is the _____ [Which?] word in the sentence.

B. The second capital letter is used because *Today* is the _____ [Which?] word of a sentence, even though that sentence is in _____ . [What marks?]

Answers and Added Practice

1

    A. first B. first, quotation marks

· ·

Capitalize properly:

    my friend asked impertinently, "what's wrong with the usual taste?"

2

    complete

· ·

In Answer Frames 2–7, capitalize properly:

    "what's wrong with the usual taste?" my friend asked impertinently.

3

    A. No B. No

· ·

the waiter answered that the "usual taste" was merely superb.

4

    (Personal choice)

· ·

my friend said, "I've learned one thing: it doesn't pay to get smart with *that* waiter."

2

Notice that in Frame 1 the waiter's exact words are quoted. Within the quotation marks is a complete sentence. The first word of a quoted _____ [What kind of?] sentence is capitalized.

3

We wondered whether the chowder really would be "unusually tasty."

A. Are the quoted words a complete sentence? _____

B. Judging from the example, should quoted words normally be capitalized when not a complete sentence?

_____

4

Satisfactory: **The waiter was right: the chowder was excellent.**

Also satisfactory: **The waiter was right: The chowder was excellent.**

After a colon, the first word of a complete sentence may or may not be capitalized, as you prefer. The capital letter does make the following sentence a little more emphatic.

    Do you prefer the capitalized or the uncapitalized version of the example? _____

5

      We are the music-makers,
        And we are the dreamers of dreams.
             —Arthur O'Shaughnessy

As the example illustrates, ordinarily the _____ [Which?] word of each line of verse is capitalized. (Not all modern poets follow this convention.)

5

first

....

a man's best things are nearest
him,
lie close about his feet.
　　　　　—Richard Milnes

6

A. salutations (*or* greetings)
B. the first word　C.　name

....

dear grandma,
dear miss doan:
dear aunt emma,
my dear mr. drew:

7

A. complimentary closes
B. first

....

very sincerely,
cordially,
as ever,
yours very sincerely,

8

A. sentence (*or* word)
B. may or may not
C. first, name
D. first

....

Which, if any, of the items listed in
Frame 8 was not known to you before starting this lesson? _____

_____

6

Dear Miss Green:　　**Dear Customer:**
Dear Uncle Ray,　　**My own Darling,**

A. The examples are _____ [What
parts?] of letters.
B. They show that _____ [*all
words* or *the first word*?] of each salutation is capitalized.
C. They also show that the word or words representing the
person's _____ [What?] are capitalized.

7

Very truly yours,　　**Sincerely yours,**
Yours truly,　　　　**Sincerely,**
Yours sincerely,　　**With love,**

A. The examples above are _____
_____ [What
parts?] of letters?
B. They show that only the _____ [Which?] word of
a complimentary close is capitalized.

8

We have seen that:

A. The first word of a complete sentence is capitalized even
when the _____ follows quotation
marks.
B. After a colon, the first word of a complete sentence ____
_____ [*must* or *may or may not*?] be
capitalized.
C. In the salutation of a letter, the _____ word is
capitalized, and also the word or words that represent
the person's _____ .
D. In the complimentary close, only the _____ word
is capitalized.

9

In Frames 9–11, copy the numbers of the letters that should be
capitalized.

A. [1]the coach said that he was "[2]completely unhappy"
about the officiating. _____
B. [3]he said, "[4]those officials should be barred by the conference." _____
C. [5]one point must be emphasized: [6]no players protested
any of the calls in question. _____

9

A. 1 B. 3, 4 C. 5 D. 5 (6 is optional.)

. . . .

A. my father glared at me and said, "such behavior is shameful."

B. he continued by saying that he was "astonished and disturbed" by my conduct.

10

¹if what shone afar so grand
²turn to nothing in thy hand,
³on again! ⁴the virtue lies
⁵in the struggle, not the prize.
—Richard Milnes

_____

10

1, 2, 3, 4, 5

. . . .

the guest then says, quite ill at ease,
"a piece of bread, sir, if you please."
the waiter roars it through the hall:
"we don't give bread with one fish-ball!"
—G. M. Lane

11

A. ¹dear ²mr. ³gzowsky: _____
B. ⁴my ⁵dear ⁶miss ⁷platt: _____
C. ⁸dear ⁹mother, _____
D. ¹⁰yours ¹¹very ¹²sincerely, _____

11

A. 1, 2, 3 B. 4, 6, 7
C. 8, 9 D. 10

. . . .

dear susie,
    this seashore is as "beauteous" as you said it would be! as you told me, "the sand at Panama City is dazzling white."
        yours sunburnedly,

12

Write a sentence containing a quoted sentence—possibly a remark by a friend. Capitalize and punctuate properly.

12

Model Answer
    After I told Sally it would be difficult to find another man like me, she asked, "Why should I want to?"

13

Write a sentence in which you quote two to four words from the sentence below. Capitalize and punctuate properly.

Genius is always impatient of its harness; its wild blood makes it hard to train.
—O. W. Holmes

13

Model Answer

    The "wild blood" of genius, as Holmes called it, may make geniuses unpopular.

. . . .

Choose only a few words from the following quotation and include them in a sentence.

    "My problem lies in reconciling my gross habits with my net income."
          —Errol Flynn

14

You are writing a business letter to Mr. Weston, a prospective employer. Write an appropriate salutation and complimentary close. Capitalize correctly, and put a colon after the salutation and a comma after the complimentary close.

14

Model Answers

    Dear Mr. Weston:

    Sincerely yours,

. . . .

For a business letter to Mrs. Blake, to whom you owe money, write an appropriate salutation and complimentary close.

15

This time suppose that you are writing a letter to a good friend. Write an appropriate salutation and complimentary close. Capitalize correctly, and put a comma after the salutation and another after the complimentary close.

15

Model Answer
    Dear Marge,
    As ever,

16

Finish honestly: One thing I hope to remember from this lesson is that . . .

(In this frame, any answer that you consider honest and accurate is acceptable.)

Lesson 95: Answers to Questions for Added Practice

1. My, What's **2.** What's **3.** The **4.** My (optional capital in *it*) **5.** A, Lie **6.** Dear Grandma, Dear Miss Doan, Dear Aunt Emma, My dear Mr. Drew: (That last salutation may seem supercilious, condescending.) **7.** Very sincerely, Cordially, As ever, Yours very sincerely, **8.** (Individual answer) **9.** A. My, Such B. He **10.** The, A, The, We **11.** Dear Susie, This seashore is as "beauteous" as you said it would be! As you told me, "The sand at Panama City is dazzlingly white." Yours sunburnedly, **13.** MODEL: What Errol Flynn called his "gross habits" were widely publicized. **14.** Dear Mrs. Blake: Yours sincerely,

96

Capitalization: In Proper Names

After writing your answer(s) in the right-hand column, check this column to see whether you have responded correctly. If you have made a mistake, or if you need more practice, do whatever is asked below the dotted line in each answer frame.

Answers to questions for added practice can be found at the end of each lesson.

Understanding and Applying the Principles

1

The word *proper* comes from Latin *proprius*, meaning "one's own" or "a particular." A proper name, then, is the name of a particular person or thing. In contrast, a common noun is one that many persons or things share, or possess, in common; it means a class rather than an individual.

A. *Chicago* and *Alice* are _____ [*proper* or *common*?] names.

B. The names *city* and *girl* are _____ . [*proper* or *common*?]

Answers and Added Practice

1

    A. proper B. common

. . . .

Write two other proper names and the corresponding common names.

2

One term in each of the following pairs is a proper name. Copy the proper names.

    day, Tuesday   month, July
    Christmas, holiday   ship, *Queen Elizabeth II*
    river, Amazon River
    historical period, Middle Ages

2

    Tuesday, July, Christmas, *Queen Elizabeth II*, Amazon River, Middle Ages

. . . .

Capitalize each proper name: pepsi-cola, eiffel tower, headed north, grinnell college, lived in the south

3

When you look at the answers to Frame 2, you see that all these proper nouns _____ [*are* or *are not*?] capitalized.

Note: The names of God are capitalized, but not gods as a class. Also, a name based on a proper name, such as *derrick* or *begonia*, is not capitalized if the association with the proper name is not ordinarily made: few people who write of derricks or begonias recall the seventeenth-century English hangman Thomas Derrick or the French botanical enthusiast Michel Bégon.

3

are

. . . .

Capitalize each proper noun:

the elks club, july 4 is independence day, in the lake, in lake erie

4

Once more, copy the proper name in each pair.

The Way of the Masks, book
a street, Main Street   a drink, Sanka
Beechcraft, airplane   the East, walked east
department, Department of Education

In writing a literary title, as the first example shows, we capitalize the first word, the last word, and all other important words. Within the title, a word like *the, and,* or *in* is not capitalized unless it is the first or last word.

4

The Way of the Masks, Main Street, Sanka, Beechcraft, the East, Department of Education

. . . .

Note: In *walked east* we are referring merely to a direction, not a place, and so do not capitalize. But in *the East* (*the South,* etc.) we are using a section of the country as a proper name and therefore do capitalize it.

Capitalize properly:

a tale of two cities, the mystery of edwin drood, a buick, a holiday, stayed at a holiday inn

5

In your own words, summarize what we have been observing about the capitalization of proper names.

Note: Most newspapers use fewer capitals than are recommended here. They usually print *Main street* and *Amazon river,* for instance, instead of *Main Street* and *Amazon River.* The recommendations made here are those most often followed by magazine and book editors, although usage does vary.

5

Model Answer

Proper names are (almost always) capitalized.

. . . .

Capitalize properly:

the allegheny mountains, a god, god almighty, sir winston churchill, lady gregory

6

One more time, copy the proper name in each pair.

train, the Orient Express
a university, Indiana University
Cabell High School, a high school
a company, General Motors
an organization, Rotary International
a cereal, Wheaties

6

the Orient Express, Indiana University, Cabell High School, General Motors, Rotary International, Wheaties

. . . .

Capitalize properly:

cape cod bay, a long island, new york's long island, the united states senate, the first amendment to the american constitution

7

We have seen that proper names are capitalized. So, usually, are adjectives derived from proper names. We refer, then, to a *Miltonic* poem (from *Milton*), the *Julian* calendar (from *Julius*), the Gregorian calendar (from *Pope Gregory*).

Explain why *Shakespearean* and *Viennese* are capitalized.

7

Model Answer

They are derived from the proper names *Shakespeare* and *Vienna.*

. . . .

Capitalize properly:

roman customs, parisian clothing, swedish meat balls, an emersonian style, dickensian characteristics

8

In Frames 8 and 9, write the appropriate capital letter above each letter that should be capitalized.

Last wednesday was the day before thanksgiving, which is one of my favorite holidays. I walked down tenth avenue to the river, and then turned west. The november air was brisk, and the water in the wabash showed signs that ice was forming. At the gerhart baking company I stopped to buy some pumpkin pies.

8

Wednesday, Thanksgiving, Tenth Avenue, November, Wabash, Gerhart Baking Company (Any other added capitals are wrong.)

. . . .

In Answer Frames 8 and 9, follow the instructions in Frame 8.

During the second week in July, on a monday, we started the long drive to the west. After we had crossed the mississippi river, we thought that we were very far west indeed.

9

If you had lived at the time of the revolutionary war, you could not have attended walton high school, because then there were no high schools. You might have gone to harvard college, but certainly colleges and universities were not numerous. For reading material you might have chosen something like thomas paine's *common sense* or benjamin franklin's *the way to wealth.*

9

Revolutionary War, Walton High School, Harvard College, Thomas Paine's *Common Sense*, Benjamin Franklin's *The Way to Wealth* (Any other added capitals are wrong.)

· ·

We skated on lake st. martin, hiked along the river, and went back to the cabin to listen to hungarian music and look at ancient issues of the *saturday evening post*.

10

Write a sentence in which you mention the name of a street, the title of a book, and the name of a soft drink. Capitalize correctly.

10

Model Answer

Sipping from a can of Slice, I walked along Clark Street carrying a book called *Out of Our Past*.

· ·

Write a sentence in which you name a hotel, the street on which it is, and the city and state in which it is located.

11

Write a sentence in which you include the names of a high school, a college or a university, and a company or an organization.

11

Model Answer

Many graduates of Dover High School enter the University of Delaware or go to work for the du Pont Company.

· ·

Write a sentence in which you name the author and title of a book that you know.

12

Write a sentence in which you name a section of the country (for instance, the West), a book or a newspaper or a magazine, and a specific historical period.

12

Model Answer

George Washington's World concerns the East during the Revolutionary War.

. . . .

Write a sentence in which you name a city located beside a large body of water. Name the body of water.

13

Finish honestly: One thing I hope to remember from this lesson is that . . .

(In this frame, any answer that you consider honest and accurate is acceptable.)

Lesson 96: Answers to Questions for Added Practice

1. MODEL: Colorado—a state or a river, Labor Day—a holiday **2.** Pepsi-Cola, Eiffel Tower, Grinnell College, the South **3.** the Elks Club, July, Independence Day, Lake Erie **4.** *A Tale of Two Cities, The Mystery of Edwin Drood,* a Buick, a Holiday Inn **5.** the Allegheny Mountains, God Almighty, Sir Winston Churchill, Lady Gregory **6.** Cape Cod Bay, New York's Long Island, the United States Senate, the First Amendment to the American Constitution **7.** Roman, Parisian, Swedish, Emersonian, Dickensian **8.** July, Monday, the West, Mississippi River **9.** Lake St. Martin, Hungarian, *Saturday Evening Post* **10.** MODEL: The Hilton Hotel is on South Michigan Avenue in Chicago, Illinois. **11.** MODEL: A useful little reference book is Alden Todd's *Finding Facts Fast.* **12.** MODEL: Milwaukee is on the shores of Lake Michigan.

══97══

Capitalization: School Subjects, Relatives, Personal Titles

After writing your answer(s) in the right-hand column, check this column to see whether you have responded correctly. If you have made a mistake, or if you need more practice, do whatever is asked below the dotted line in each answer frame.

Answers to questions for added practice can be found at the end of each lesson.

Understanding and Applying the Principles

1

Charles is taking Spanish, English, history, and biology.

A. Spanish and English are both names of _____ . The example shows that names of _____ are capitalized.

B. Because *history* and *biology* are not names of languages, they _____ [*are* or *are not?*] capitalized.

Answers and Added Practice

1

    A. languages, languages

    B. are not

· ·

List the names (not the numbers) of subjects you are now taking or have recently taken. Capitalize properly.

2

This term I am studying Music 4 and Biology 2.

This example shows that the name of a school subject, even if it is not a language, _____ [*is* or *is not?*] capitalized when it has a number (or letter) with it to designate a particular course.

2

is
....
Repeat the list you prepared for Answer Frame 1, but this time include the numbers of the courses.

3

Three of my aunts were there, including Aunt Lucy.

The example above shows that the title of a relative is capitalized when the relative's _____ [What?] accompanies the title.

3

name
....
In Answer Frames 3–10 write the appropriate capital letter over each letter that should be capitalized.

My favorite uncle is uncle harold.

4

Then Father talked about the way his own father had disciplined him.

A. If you substitute *George* for *Father* in the sentence above, does the sentence still make good sense? _____

B. When a word like *Father* or *Grandma* is used in the same way that a person's name could be used, it _____ _____ [*should* or *should not?*] be capitalized.

4

A. Yes   B. should
....
Sometimes mother reminisces about the childhood escapades of my aunts and uncles.

5

Later, Colonel Fleck sent for two lieutenants.

The example shows that a title like *Colonel, Commander,* or *Lieutenant* is capitalized when it is followed by the person's _____ . The same rule applies to other titles, as in *Congressman Jones* or *Professor Archibald.*

5

name
....
Then general mathews called in colonel girard and two captains.

6

"But you must have seen the smoke, Lieutenant," the captain interjected.

The example shows that a military title (or a non-military title such as *Governor* or *Doctor*) _____ [*is* or *is not?*] capitalized when used in writing or speaking to the person.

Note that we saw something similar in Frame 4: a person's name can be substituted for *Lieutenant* in the example, but not for *captain.*

6

is

. . . .

"Tell me, colonel," he said, "why you and captain ray-mond did not reprimand the lieutenant."

7

When Washington became President, the authority of the office had not yet been completely defined.

When *President, Governor, Major,* or a similar title is used alone, as in the example, some people consider it respectful to capitalize it, but the uncapitalized version is at least as frequent. Take your choice.

I _____ [*prefer* or *do not like*?] to capitalize titles to show respect.

7

(Personal answer)

. . . .

The mother of ensign watts did an unforgivable thing: she wrote to admiral joad and complained that captain frye and a commander were discriminating against her son.

8

Summary:

A. In writing about school subjects, we capitalize names of _____ such as *French*. We also capitalize names of other subjects when they are accompanied by

_____ .

B. In writing titles of relatives, military personnel, governmental officials, and others, we capitalize them when they are followed by the persons' _____ or when they are used alone in a way that proper names (*George, Nancy*) could be used.

8

A. languages, numbers (*or* letters) B. names

. . . .

Then mother went to the telephone to call her own mother and her aunt priscilla.

9

In Frames 9 and 10, write the appropriate capital letter above each letter that should be capitalized.

Whenever aunt lucinda saw me, she asked me questions about my schoolwork. "You're taking latin, aren't you? Are you a good history student? What is history 310? What do you do in english? What science are you taking? Do you enjoy chemistry? Maybe chemistry 200 will be better."

9

Aunt Lucinda, Latin, History 310, English, Chemistry 200 (Any other added capitals are wrong.)

. . . .

My french and english are easy for me, but mathematics and art are difficult.

10

My sister is much impressed by military uniforms. The other day I heard her talking to our mother. "I'll say no if a private asks me to dance. Nothing less than a corporal for me! 'Why, corporal,' I'll say, 'I'll be delighted to dance with you. Oh, is that sergeant O'Rourke? Will you introduce us, please, corporal. Hello, sergeant. Oh, is that really your lieutenant? Hi, lieutenant.'"

10

Corporal (second and third), Sergeant (both), Hi, Lieutenant. (Other added capitals are wrong.)

. . . .

The lieutenant's father hopes that his son will soon be promoted to the rank of captain.

11

Write a sentence listing the subjects (with their numbers if you know them) that you will probably take next term. Capitalize properly.

11

Model Answer

I plan to take Russian 103, Physics 101, and some mathematics and chemistry.

. . . .

Write a sentence in which you list the subjects that a friend of yours is taking. Capitalize properly.

12

Write a sentence in which you address your father and say something about a grandfather and an uncle. Capitalize properly.

12

Model Answer

Tell me, Dad, whether Granddad and Uncle Henry knew each other when they were young.

. . . .

Write a sentence in which you mention three or more of your relatives. Capitalize properly.

13

Write a sentence in which you say something to a lieutenant about a sergeant named Larson and about another sergeant whose name you do not know. Capitalize properly.

13

Model Answer

Well, Lieutenant, I saw Sergeant Larson in town with another sergeant.

. . . .

Write a sentence in which you include the titles of at least three military officers. Capitalize properly.

14

Write a sentence in which you say that the highest official of your state (name him) is meeting with several other (unnamed) officials of the same rank in their states. Capitalize properly.

14

Model Answer

Several other governors are meeting today with Governor Metcalf.

15

Finish honestly: One thing I hope to remember from this lesson is that . . .

(In this frame, any answer that you consider honest and accurate is acceptable.)

Lesson 97: Answers to Questions for Added Practice

1. (Personal answer. Check it in light of Frame 1.) **2.** (All these course names should be capitalized.) **3.** My favorite uncle is Uncle Harold. **4.** (Only *Mother* should be capitalized.) **5.** General Mathews, Colonel Girard (no others) **6.** Colonel, Captain Raymond (no others) **7.** Ensign Watts, Admiral Joad, Captain Frye (Also, *she* may permissibly be capitalized, but no others.) **8.** Mother, Aunt Priscilla (no others) **9.** French, English (no others) **10.** (No added capitals) **11.** MODEL: George is taking German, English, American history, and geology. **12.** MODEL: Aunt Grace, Uncle Stuart, and one of my cousins arrived in a new Cadillac. **13.** MODEL: Colonel Waters, Major Trotter, and a captain or two were on the list for promotion.

98

Capitalization: Miscellaneous Usages

After writing your answer(s) in the right-hand column, check this column to see whether you have responded correctly. If you have made a mistake, or if you need more practice, do whatever is asked below the dotted line in each answer frame.

Answers to questions for added practice can be found at the end of each lesson.

Understanding and Applying the Principles

1

Thou, O Summer,

. . . .

Beneath our oaks hast slept, while we beheld
With joy thy ruddy limbs and flourishing
hair.

—William Blake

Two one-letter words are always capitalized. One is the often-used pronoun *I.* the other, which appears in Blake's lines above, is the seldom-used _____ .

Answers and Added Practice

1

O

. . . .

O should not be confused with the more common *oh. O* is most likely to be encountered in older poetry, in passionately addressing someone or something, often imaginary.

2

I worked in my father's store last summer.

In Frame 1, *summer* is capitalized because it is personified. A personification is a statement implying that a thing has qualities of a person.

    A. Summer in Frame 1 is said to be able to _____ [Do what?] and to possess _____ and _____ .

    B. So in Frame 1, summer is personified. Is it also personified here in Frame 2? _____

Note: In expressions such as *the Fall term* or the *Spring semester,* the "season" word is generally capitalized even though not personified.

2

   A. sleep, limbs, hair
   B. No

....

   A. **The icy breath of Old Man Winter reddened our cheeks.**
   B. **In the winter of 1986 I got my first job.**

Winter is personified in _____ . [A or B?]

3

  O Love, when thou gettest dominion over us, we may bid goodbye to prudence.
                 —La Fontaine

   A. In Frames 1 and 2, we saw that the name of a season is capitalized when it _____ [*is* or *is not?*] personified.
   B. The example above shows that when an abstract word (such as *love, liberty, justice, kindness, strength*) is personified, it _____ [*is* or *is not?*] capitalized.

3

   A. is B. is

....

   A. People who have little freedom value it most.
   B. "Of old sat Freedom on the heights, / The thunders breaking at her feet,"—Alfred, Lord Tennyson

In _____ [A or B?] freedom is personified.

4

George Herman Ruth was nicknamed Babe or the Bambino.

Tell what the example above shows concerning the capitalization of nicknames.

4

Model Answer
   Nicknames are capitalized.

....

Write a sentence in which you use the nickname of a friend.

5

We bought the *Post-Dispatch* on Thirty-third Street.

In a hyphenated proper name such as *Post-Dispatch*, both parts are capitalized, but in a compound number such as *Thirty-third*,

_____ .

[Finish the sentence.]

5

Model Answer
   Thirty is capitalized but not *third*.

....

Capitalize properly:

   The office of the *journal-review* is on twenty-first avenue.

6

   I. **Types of dictionaries**
      A. **Unabridged**
      B. **Abridged**

This example shows that the first word of each individual point in an _____ is capitalized.

6

outline

······························

Frame 6 illustrates a *topic* outline. Obviously, in a *sentence* outline each point also begins with a _____ _____ letter.

7

In Frames 7 and 8, write *T* or *F* to indicate whether each statement is true or false.

_____ A. Names of seasons are never capitalized.

_____ B. When an abstract quality, such as justice, is given human characteristics, it is said to be personified.

_____ C. Personifications are usually not capitalized.

_____ D. Both *Oh* and *I* should always be capitalized.

7

A. F   B. T   C. F   D. F

······························

T or F?

_____ A. Names of seasons are always capitalized.

_____ B. A word like *justice* should always be capitalized.

8

_____ A. Nicknames should be capitalized.

_____ B. This capitalization is correct: Forty-Eighth Street.

_____ C. In an outline the first word of each point should be capitalized only if the point is a complete sentence.

8

A. T   B. F   C. F

······························

T or F?

_____ A. This capitalization is correct: East Sixty-first Street.

_____ B. So is this: Joe Di-Maggio was nicknamed Joltin' Joe.

9

Write a sentence in which you name two seasons of the year. Here and hereafter, capitalize correctly.

9

Model Answer

I like summer better than winter.

······························

Now write another sentence for the other two seasons.

10

Write a sentence in which you refer to the nickname of a well-known person.

10

Model Answer

Abraham Lincoln was called Honest Abe.

. . . .

What nickname have you most disliked? Answer in a sentence.

11

Arrange these points in outline form. (See Frame 6.) forwards, basketball players, centers, guards

---

11

    I. Basketball players
       A. Forwards
       B. Centers
       C. Guards

12

Finish honestly: One thing I hope to remember from this lesson is that . . .

(In this frame, any answer that you consider honest and accurate is acceptable.)

Lesson 98: Answers to Questions for Added Practice

2. A **3.** B **4.** MODEL: Tiger Mack led the team from the field. **5.** *Journal-Review*, Twenty-first Avenue **6.** capital **7.** A. F B. F **8.** A. T B. T **9.** MODEL: I think that spring brings hope but that fall suggests the coming gloom. **10.** (The nickname should be capitalized.)

══99══

Numbers: When to Spell Them Out

After writing your answer(s) in the right-hand column, check this column to see whether you have responded correctly. If you have made a mistake, or if you need more practice, do whatever is asked below the dotted line in each answer frame.

Answers to questions for added practice can be found at the end of each lesson.

Understanding and Applying the Principles

1

> **twelve boys**   **one hundred boys**
> **123 boys**

Most newspaper stylebooks recommend using words for numbers from one through nine or ten, and figures for larger numbers. Most book publishers, however, follow the style of the examples above.

That is, they spell out numbers that can be expressed in _____ or _____ [How many?] words, and use figures for the rest.

Answers and Added Practice

1

   one or two

. . . .

This textbook, like most others, recommends following book publishers' usage. However, your instructor may prefer newspaper style.

2

In mathematics problems and in tables of statistics, of course, _____ [*words* or *figures*?] are used almost exclusively.

2

   figures

. . . .

Why are words used instead of figures in the first two examples in Frame 1?

3

Explain why you think publishers prefer *123 boys* to *one hundred twenty-three boys.*

3

Model Answer

The figures save space. (Perhaps, too, a reader can grasp them more quickly.)

....

If a number such as 1,246,857 were expressed in words, a typist would need to press down about 65 keys.

4

> **July 8, 1962**   **807 Fourth Street**
> **telephone 555–4398**   **Room 112**
> **Chapter 8 (or VIII)**   **page 276**
> **Interstate 65**   **Channel 6**

The examples above show that figures are used for dates, house numbers, _____ ,

_____ , _____

_____ ,

and _____ .

Note: *Not* July 8th, 1962. But when the year is not given, we may choose from *July 8, 8th,* or *eighth*; or *the eighth of July, 1962,* as well as *8 July, 1962.*

In indicating a span of years, the following are acceptable: in 1986–87 *or* in 1986–1987; 1981–1987 *or* 1981–87 *or* from 1981 to 1987.

4

telephone numbers, room numbers, chapter numbers, page numbers, highway numbers, channel numbers

....

Write a sentence telling someone precisely when and where you will meet him or her.

5

> **1208 West Sixth Street**
> **110 Twenty-first Street**
> **110 21 Street**
> **110 21st Street**

If a street has a one-word number for a name (*Sixth Street*), a word is generally used. If it is a compound number, though, like *Twenty-first Street*, the example shows _____ [How many?] different acceptable forms.

5

three

....

Write the three possible ways of indicating a place on East Eighty-eighth Street that has the number 2421.

6

> **The farmer sold 126 sheep, 90 hogs, and 29 cattle.**

That sentence shows that figures and words _____ [*should* or *should not*?] ordinarily be mixed in the same sentence or paragraph.

6

should not

....

Note: Sometimes it is impossible, or at least awkward, to avoid mixing words and figures. Example: Marian spent one month in jail in 1985.

Write a sentence telling how many points a good basketball player scored in each of four consecutive games.

7

Poor:	**186 fouls were called in the 4 games.**
Better:	**Officials called 186 fouls in the 4 games.**
Poor:	**2001, not 2000, will mark the beginning of the twenty-first century.**
Better:	**The twenty-first century will begin in 2001, not 2000.**

The sentences above show that it is considered undesirable to begin a sentence with a _____ .

7

figure

....

Rewrite:

1985 was the year in which my father went bankrupt.

8

a 3.5 grade average   1.06 meters

Those examples show that figures are used to indicate a number that contains a _____ point.

8

decimal

....

Use figures to show the following:

A. two point four five grams
B. Pi is three point one four plus.

9

In Frames 9–13, write *Words* or *Figures* to show which you should ordinarily use for each of the following items, all of which are expressed here in figures. (Follow the practice of book publishers, not of newspapers.)

A. 227 ice cream cones _____
B. 8 pairs of shoes _____
C. 100 books _____

9

    A. Figures B. Words
    C. Words

. . . .

In Answer Frames 9–13, follow the instructions in Frame 9.

    A. 313 days _____
    B. 8 days _____

10

    A. $200 _____
    B. 18 months ago _____
    C. 32,179 _____

10

    A. Words B. Words
    C. Figures

. . . .

    A. 27,646 _____
    B. April 17, 1984 _____

11

    A. Room 814 _____
    B. page 217 _____
    C. June 17, 1932 _____

11

    A. Figures B. Figures
    C. Figures

. . . .

    A. 147 jars and 12 glasses
    _____

    B. 5 plates were broken.
    _____

12

    A. 1270 Marshall Street _____
    B. 16 seniors made the trip. _____
    C. 327 seniors and 11 juniors arrived. _____

12

    A. Figures B. Words
    C. Figures (*or* Rewrite)

. . . .

    A. 10 Street _____
    B. telephone 428–1092 _____
    _____

13

    A. 7 juniors and 2 sophomores _____
    B. 5 Avenue _____
    C. Chapter XI _____

13

    A. Words B. Words
    C. Figures

. . . .

    A. 19 years old _____
    B. 2 men and 5 women _____
    _____

14

Write your complete address.

14

Model Answer

My address is Apartment 17, 1407 North Twenty-second Street, Lincoln, Nebraska 68503.

. . . .

Write a sentence referring to a large, specific sum of money (in dollars and cents).

15

Write a sentence in which you tell how many football players make up one team and how many are on a baseball team.

15

Model Answer

A football team has eleven players, a baseball team only nine.

. . . .

Write a short sentence beginning with a number. Then rewrite it to change that beginning.

16

Here are the season's totals for one professional basketball player:

246 baskets, including 19 3-pointers

143 free throws, missed 67

60 fouls

130 rebounds

198 assists

Write a sentence containing all that information.

16

Model Answer

During the season John Childs scored 246 baskets, including 19 3-pointers; made 143 free throws while missing 67; committed 60 fouls; pulled in 130 rebounds; and made 198 assists.

17

Finish honestly: One thing I hope to remember from this lesson is that . . .

(In this frame, any answer that you consider honest and accurate is acceptable.)

Lesson 99: Answers to Questions for Added Practice

2. MODEL: Those numbers can be written in one or two words. **4.** MODEL: I'll meet you at 8:30 p.m., July 6, 1987, in the lobby of the Biltless Hotel, 1249 South Walker, in Springfield, Missouri. **5.** 2421 East Eighty-eighth Street, . . . 88 Street, . . . 88th Street **6.** MODEL: In the four games Jerry scored 27, 21, 31, and 39 points. **7.** The year in which my father went bankrupt was 1985. **8.** A. 2.45 grams B. 3.14 + **9.** A. Figures B. Words **10.** A. Figures B. Figures **11.** A. Figures B. Words **12.** A. Words B. Figures **13.** A. Words B. Words **14.** MODEL: The new car cost $17, 469.27. **15.** MODEL: 317 days passed without rain. No rain fell for 317 days.

═══100═══

Numbers: Miscellaneous Conventions

After writing your answer(s) in the right-hand column, check this column to see whether you have responded correctly. If you have made a mistake, or if you need more practice, do whatever is asked below the dotted line in each answer frame.

Answers to questions for added practice can be found at the end of each lesson.

Answers and Added Practice

1

　Roman, Roman, Arabic
. . . .

The famous "To be, or not be be" speech begins at line 56 in the first scene of the third act of *Hamlet.* Say that more briefly.

Understanding and Applying the Principles

1

Look at Act II, Scene ii, lines 34–41.

The example above shows a frequently used way of designating passages in plays. (It may be shortened to II, ii, 34–41.)

　The number of the act is given as a _____ [What kind of?] numeral; the number of the scene, as a small _____ _____ numeral; and the number of the lines, as an _____ numeral.

2

The interest rate was then 8.5 (*or* 8½) per cent (*or* percent) on one-year deposits.

A. The example shows that _____ [*words* or *figures*?] are customarily used to indicate percentages.

B. It also shows that the term *per cent* [or *percent*] _____ _____ [*has* or *has no*?] period after it (except at the end of a sentence).

2

A. figures   B. has no

....

Write a sentence in which you say something about a current rate of interest, or about the per cent of shots made by a basketball player.

3

She was ready by seven o'clock, although Gary was not coming until eight.

Judging from the example above, we use _____ [*words* or *figures*?] with *o'clock*.

Note: Do not use both *o'clock* and *a.m.* or *p.m.* in the same construction, because anything that is *a.m.* or *p.m.* is obviously a clock reading.

3

words

....

In a college all classes start on the hour. Write a sentence telling at what hours a certain student has English and Russian.

4

She was ready by 6:45 p.m., although she did not expect Gary until 7:30.

Judging from that example, we use _____ [*words* or *figures*?] with *a.m.* and *p.m.*, especially if the times given are not exact hours.

4

figures

....

Write as figures, including the colon.

    A. half past nine in the morning _____

    B. twelve minutes past eleven at night _____

5

4,897   3,846,000

The examples show that when we write long numbers, we ordinarily use commas to set off the figures in groups of three, counting from the _____ . [*left* or *right*?]

5

right

....

Why are those commas in Frame 5
desirable?

6

However, commas are not used in numbers such as these:

street numbers: **10117 West Division**

telephone numbers: **(318) 482–9701**

years: **1926**

serial numbers: **359–88–27–49**

social security numbers: **310–12–8172**

zip code numbers: **47981** (*or* **47981–2491**)

Write the number of this year and your social security number.
Group the figures in the latter as in the example.

6

Model Answers
    1987   408–76–4119

....

Write your telephone number and
your zip code number.

7

a 1″ × 8″ board (*or* **a 1″ by 8″ board**)
The final score was 4 to 0.

For dimensions or scores, as the examples show, _____
[*words* or *figures?*] are used.

7

figures

....

A. Write the dimensions of a
   table top.
B. Write the score of a recent
   game.

8

In Frames 8–11, write A or B after each item to show which is
preferable.

1. A. Act III   B. Act iii   _____
2. A. Scene I   B. Scene i   _____
3. A. lines 6–8   B. lines six–eight _____

8

     1.A   2.B   3.A

· ·

In Answer Frames 8–9, follow the instructions in Frame 8.

    A. Act 3, Scene 3, line 8

    B. III, iii, 8 _____

9

1. A. seven o'clock   B. 7 o'clock _____

2. A. 3:36 a.m.   B. three thirty-six a.m. _____

9

     1. A   2. A

· ·

    A. seven o'clock a.m.

    B. seven o'clock in the morning

       _____

10

1. A. 349847   B. 349,847 _____

2. A. three point seven per cent   B. 3.7 per cent _____

10

     1. B   2. B

· ·

Change 11/100 to a decimal and then to a percentage.

11

1. A. a 2″ by 6″ plank   B. a two- by six-inch plank _____

2. A. a fifty-four to three loss   B. a 54 to 3 loss _____

11

     1. A   2. B

· ·

Write the length, width, and height of an imaginary dollhouse.

12

In a sentence, tell what time it is now and what the date is, including the year.

12

Model Answer
     It is 9:21 p.m. CST, February 14, 1988.

. . . .

Write a sentence referring to a specific act and scene of a play.

13

Substitute figures where needed:

     The interest for a year on two million dollars at seven and one-half per cent is one hundred fifty thousand dollars.

13

     The interest for a year on $2,000,000 (*or* $2 million) at 7.5 per cent is $150,000.

14

Finish honestly: One thing I hope to remember from this lesson is that . . .

(In this frame, any answer that you consider honest and accurate is acceptable.)

Lesson 100: Answers to Questions for Added Practice

1. MODEL: Hamlet's famous "To be, or not to be" speech begins with line 56 of Act III, Scene iii. **2.** MODEL: At present a one-year deposit of $10,000 or more earns interest at 10.3 per cent. **3.** MODEL: Lillian has English at nine o'clock, Russian at eleven. **4.** A. 9:30 a.m. B. 11:12 p.m. **5.** MODEL: They make large numbers easier to read. **6.** MODEL: (212) 487–4308   10016 **7.** A. MODEL: The table top is 42″ by 70″. B. The Badgers won 87–76. **8.** B. **9.** B **10.** 0.11   11 per cent **11.** MODEL: The doll house was 48″ by 20″ by 19″ high. **12.** MODEL: My opportunity to star came in Act II, Scene i.

Mastery Test
Punctuation and Mechanics

For directions, see page 335.

67. a. My handwriting is terrible professors sometimes can't read it.   A   U

    b. Will you please see whether my handwriting in this theme is readable.   A   U

    c. Please try to imagine that you are a professor when you read it.   A   U

68. a. Do all instructors have regular office hours?   A   U

    b. I wonder whether they post their hours on their office doors?   A   U

    c. Will they see students even without appointments.   A   U

69. a. Your new motorcycle is a beautiful machine.   A   U

    b. Look out! That car is going to hit us!   A   U

    c. Wow! What a close call!   A   U

70. a. When the campus police officers ran over the demonstrators walked away.   A   U

    b. Before the Old Main clock struck three students returned and entered the administration building.   A   U

    c. Even though I had seen these students only once, I recognized them.   A   U

71. a. That blue Blazer with the big, Mud King tires is mine.   A   U

    b. That Jeep with the chrome-plated show bars and, the vertical dual exhaust system is John's.   A   U

    c. On weekends we drive aggressively, proudly up steep hills about ten miles from campus.   A   U

72. a. English 101, a required course, is more important than many entering freshmen realize.   A   U

    b. Many college courses, ranging from the sciences to the humanities, require writing skills.   A   U

    c. My roommate, however, isn't convinced that any writing course can help him.   A   U

73. a. A girl, who won first prize in short story writing last year, sits behind me in English 405.   A   U

    b. This prize, which is presented each spring during the Literary Awards Banquet, includes a cash award.   A   U

    c. Professor Austin, who has coordinated this event for ten years, teaches creative writing.   A   U

74. a. Bob Lester Alan and I met the campus tour guide at   A   U

the Memorial Fountain, and all four of us followed him for three hours.

b. We walked through the library, past the administration building, and through three residence halls.   A   U

c. Freshman Orientation Day was informative but both my head and my legs ached before it was over.   A   U

75. a. Some college administrators, still act as though undergraduate students are not responsible adults.   A   U

b. In some cases, administrators will not release to the press the names of undergraduates who have committed illegal acts.   A   U

c. In other cases, administrators still defend outdated rules, that regulate the social life of all students, who live on campus.   A   U

76. a. Professions have their own vocabularies to enable workers to communicate effectively; however, these vocabularies can cause problems when professionals address the general public.   A   U

b. Computer specialists, for example, seem to take their technical jargon for granted; they assume that everyone else knows the terms they use.   A   U

c. The real offenders are pompous experts who overwork technical language in speaking to the general public; but most people tend to ignore specialists who speak that way.   A   U

77. a. Our university library has a computer-based informa-   A   U

tion service, which can find references to current literature in minutes; an on-line serials catalog, which will allow students to go to any computer terminal on campus to find out if our library has a particular magazine or journal; and an inter-library loan service, which gives students and faculty members access to sources available only in other libraries.

b. John, who is starting a research paper, is using the computer-based information service, Mary, who doesn't have the time to look through the printed periodical index in the library, is using the on-line serials catalog, and Melba, who needs to read a book not in our library, is using the inter-library loan service.   A   U

c. Serious students, ones really eager to learn, will use these library services; although less serious students, sometimes because of laziness or lack of interest, will never use them.   A   U

78. a. Daniel Defoe, an eighteenth-century British author, wrote this statement: "I have often thought of it as one of the most barbarous customs in the world, considering us as a civilized and Christian country, that we deny the advantages of learning to women."   A   U

b. Defoe proposed an academy that would teach these subjects to women: music, dancing, foreign languages, speech, and history.   A   U

c. Today many people believe that the roles of women are: dishwasher, cook, nurse, wife, and mother.   A   U

79. (In this item, *a*, *b*, and *c* are parts of a letter.)
   a. Dear Mr. Adams: A   U
   b. I cannot understand why your library records still show that *Censors in the Classroom: The Mind Benders* is still checked out to me.   A   U
   c. In fact, I remember these things: checking the book to make sure it wasn't overdue, asking the librarian if I should put it into the return slot, and hearing it hit the bottom of the bin behind the slot.   A   U

80. a. I'm still convinced that he wasn't telling the truth.   A   U
   b. Either he does'nt know it or he would'nt tell it.   A   U
   c. At ten o'clock we still weren't able to get much information from him.   A   U

81. a. Mr. Smith's Dry Cleaning Emporium is advertising a special price for ladies' coats and jackets.   A   U
   b. Mary's coat is on the chair, and my other roommate's coat is on her bed.   A   U
   c. Both roommates' coats have store coupons pinned to them.   A   U

82. a. I usually have to copy my handwritten theme's.   A   U
   b. Some instructors tell me that my *a*'s look like *o*'s and that my *l*'s look like *e*'s.   A   U
   c. These problems are not as serious as using too many *and*'s and *that*'s in my sentences, but they do make reading my papers difficult at times.

83. a. After playing this record for nearly a month, I am ready for something different.   A   U
   b. You may borrow it during spring break, but return it to me.   A   U
   c. I want to keep it because the singers have autographed the jacket.   A   U

84. a. When we arrived to sell tickets, we found sixty-three students sitting or sleeping on the floor by the ticket window.   A   U
   b. First-day sales were astounding; we sold six hundred five- and ten-dollar tickets.   A   U
   c. A few money-hungry individuals wanted to buy as many as twenty-five tickets to sell for a profit later, but we told them that each purchase was limited to two tickets.   A   U

85. a. "Perhaps we should look again at—oh, here it is on pages two and three," Professor Beeber said.   A   U
   b. Those pages—which we read in class—emphasized one fact—that a company has to be especially innovative to survive in technical fields today.   A   U
   c. Professor Beeber—psychologist, economist, and author of our textbook—discussed several ways in which creativity and technology are quite compatible.   A   U

86. a. Once one of my instructors didn't know it (he usually   A   U

hurried into class just after the bell), but his pants were unzipped.

b. I wanted to tell him about the problem, it was causing smiles as he walked around the room, but I didn't have an opportunity to do it.   A U

c. After John whispered to him (I wish I could have seen the instructor's face), the instructor sat behind his desk for the rest of the period and tried to look busy.   A U

87. a. "Robert Burnes [Burns] was born in southeastern [actually southwestern] Scotland."   A U

b. Major influences in his lifetime [1759–1796] were his father, the local folksongs, and his reading.   A U

c. The first line of "To a Mouse" reads, "Wee, sleekit [sleek], cow'rin, tim'rous beastie [*sic*]."   A U

88. a. My advisor said, "History 102 is filled up, so you can't sign up for it."   A U

b. My roommate said that "It sometimes helps to ask the instructor if it is possible to get into a class."   A U

c. I went to the instructor, and he said that he would take me.   A U

89. a. Professor Harris asked, "Can any other English word have exactly the same meaning as this word"?   A U

b. Joe exclaimed, "Of course it can!"   A U

c. "Please come to the overhead projector, Joe", Pro- fessor Harris said, "and give us an example".   A U

90. a. Mr. Jones wrote this statement on the chalkboard: "Ambrose Bierce said, 'A prejudice is a vagrant opinion without visible means of support.'"   A U

b. Mr. Jones then turned to the class and asked, "Does anyone know what Mr. Bierce's phrase 'a vagrant opinion' means?"   A U

c. After no one responded, Mr. Jones wrote this statement: "William Hazlitt said, "Prejudice is the child of Ignorance."   A U

91. (In a, b, and c, note especially the indention and the quotation marks in these paragraphs describing an oral discussion in a science laboratory.)

a. At the beginning of the science experiment, Mr. Brown said, "The flame is heating the air inside this gallon can. Hot air, as you know, rises.   A U

b. "Now, can anyone tell me what will happen to this can if I screw the top on it and leave it to cool?"   A U

c. "The can will squeeze together," answered Jake, who always was smart in science.   A U

92. a. The poem *Auld Lang Syne* was put to music in the song "Auld Lang Syne."   A U

b. Holmes first published the poem "The Wonderful One-Hoss Shay" in the *Atlantic Monthly* magazine.   A U

c. The short story *The Monkey's Paw* was once made into a television play.   A U

93. a. To be *really* accepted by members of the inner social circles in my home city, a guest who walks into a room must be able to use more than the word *atmosphere* to describe it; to fit in, a guest at least has to use the word *ambience*.   A   U

   b. *The Penguin Pocket Thesaurus* could be a handy book for social climbers in my home city.   A   U

   c. To join *le beau monde*, a person should also try to insert a few foreign words in conversations.   A   U

94. a. My prof. told me to make an appt. Mon. in the a.m.   A   U

   b. I called his secy. in biology, but she said that his appointment calendar was full.   A   U

   c. Trying to make an appointment with Dr. Hale is like trying to get a seat on a TWA flight two days before Christmas.   A   U

95. (In this item, a, b, and c are parts of a letter.)

   a. Dear Professor Schwarz:
   Shakespeare wrote this line in *Hamlet*:
   "neither a borrower nor a lender be."   A   U

   b. Someone else said, "Honesty is the best policy."   A   U

   c. This culprit confesses. I have your book.
                    Yours truly,   A   U

96. a. A graduate of Northwestern University gave a lecture about her trip on the yacht *Yankee*.   A   U

   b. She compared her voyage to the legendary voyage of Odysseus during the Homeric period.   A   U

c. The lecture was given at the Chicago Academy of Sciences on Sunday, December 13.   A   U

97. a. I told Mother that Aunt Ruth has accepted an English teaching position in a junior college in California.   A   U

   b. She and Captain Brown are married, and they will live on an air base.   A   U

   c. My aunt taught composition, drama, and a course called Black Literature at another college last year.   A   U

98. a. With temperatures dropping daily, the *New York Times* is bursting forth with quotations such as "Hence, rude Winter!"   A   U

   b. This year Old Man Winter will not catch me by surprise.   A   U

   c. After earning the nickname Old Mishap when my car stalled on Forty-second Street last year, I have resolved to have the car checked early.   A   U

99. a. The new shopping center on College Avenue will include 2 grocery stores, 1 copy shop, and 2 fast-food restaurants.   A   U

   b. As late as nineteen hundred seventy-two this was farmland.   A   U

   c. Now six restaurants, ten apartment buildings, and at least twenty shops and stores are close to campus.   A   U

100. a. For my sociology project, I studied all annual college enrollment reports from 1970 to the present.   A   U

b. I was amazed to see that   A   U
   our enrollment has grown
   to 23,546, an increase of
   34 per cent since the 1970
   report.

c. By eight o'clock Monday   A   U
   morning, I hadn't finished

writing, so I dialed
363,2041 to ask my professor if he would accept the
project one day late.

Answers to this test can be found on page 512.

Answer Key to Diagnostic Test—PART I—Sentence Structure

1. UUA	6. UUU	11. UAU	16. UUU
2. UAU	7. AAU	12. AUA	17. AUU
3. UUA	8. AAU	13. AUU	18. UUA
4. AAU	9. AUA	14. AUU	19. UUU
5. UUA	10. UUA	15. UUA	20. UAA

Answer Key to Mastery Test—PART I—Sentence Structure

1. UUU	6. UAU	11. UUU	16. UUA
2. UAU	7. UUU	12. UAA	17. UUA
3. UAU	8. UAA	13. UAU	18. UAA
4. AAU	9. UUA	14. UAU	19. UAU
5. UUA	10. AUU	15. UUA	20. UAA

Answer Key to Diagnostic Test—PART II—Usage

21. UAA	26. AAA	31. UAU	36. AAU	41. AAA	46. UUU
22. UAA	27. UAA	32. UAA	37. AAA	42. UAA	47. UUA
23. AAA	28. UUA	33. UAA	38. UUU	43. UAA	
24. AAU	29. AUA	34. AAA	39. UUA	44. UUA	
25. AUU	30. AAA	35. AAA	40. UUA	45. UUU	

Answer Key to Mastery Test—PART II—Usage

21. AUA	26. UAA	31. UUU	36. AUA	41. UUA	46. UUA
22. AAA	27. UAU	32. AAA	37. AUA	42. UUU	47. UUA
23. UAA	28. UUA	33. AAA	38. UUU	43. UAA	
24. AAA	29. UAA	34. AAA	39. UUU	44. UAA	
25. UAU	30. AAA	35. AAA	40. UUU	45. UUU	

Answer Key to Diagnostic Test—PART III—Diction and Style

48. UUU	53. UAU	58. UUU	63. UAU
49. UUU	54. UUA	59. AUU	64. UUU
50. UUU	55. UAU	60. UUU	65. UUA
51. UUU	56. UUU	61. UAU	66. AAU
52. UUA	57. AUU	62. UUA	

Answer Key to Mastery Test—PART III—Diction and Style

48. UUU	53. UUA	58. UUU	63. UUU
49. UAU	54. UAU	59. UUU	64. AUA
50. UUU	55. UAU	60. UUU	65. UUA
51. UUU	56. UAU	61. AUA	66. UUA
52. UUU	57. UUU	62. AUU	

Answer Key for Diagnostic Test—PART IV—Punctuation and Mechanics

67. AAU	72. AUU	77. AAU	82. AAA	87. AAA	92. AUA	97. AAU
68. UUA	73. AUU	78. UAU	83. UAU	88. AAA	93. AAU	98. AAA
69. AUU	74. AUA	79. AAA	84. AUA	89. UAU	94. AAU	99. UAA
70. UUU	75. UUA	80. AAU	85. AAA	90. AUA	95. UAU	100. AUU
71. AUU	76. UUU	81. AAU	86. AUA	91. UAA	96. UAU	

Answer Key for Mastery Test—PART IV—Punctuation and Mechanics

67. UAA	72. AAA	77. AUU	82. UAA	87. AAA	92. UAU	97. AAA
68. AUU	73. UAA	78. AAU	83. UAU	88. AUA	93. AAA	98. AAA
69. AAA	74. UAU	79. AAA	84. AAA	89. UAU	94. UUA	99. UUA
70. UUA	75. UAU	80. AUA	85. AUA	90. AAU	95. UAA	100. AAU
71. UUA	76. AAU	81. AAA	86. AUA	91. AUU	96. AAA	

═INDEX═

The numbers refer to *lessons*, not to pages.